THE CLASSICS
OF **WESTERN
SPIRITUALITY**

THE CLASSICS OF WESTERN SPIRITUALITY
A Library of the Great Spiritual Masters

President and Publisher
Lawrence Boadt, C.S.P.

EDITORIAL BOARD

John Calvin
WRITINGS ON PASTORAL PIETY

EDITED AND WITH TRANSLATIONS BY
ELSIE ANNE MCKEE

PREFACE BY
B. A. GERRISH

PAULIST PRESS
NEW YORK • MAHWAH, NJ

Cover art: NICHOLAS T. MARKELL lives in Golden Valley, Minnesota, where he makes his profession as an artist. In 1992, he received a master of arts degree in theology and a master of divinity degree from the Washington Theological Union in Washington, D.C. Working in a variety of mediums, Nicholas conveys a deep understanding of religious thought and spirituality in his art. Applauded for his artistic excellence, his original art has won national awards and has been exhibited and installed across the United States. This cover image is an illustration of John Calvin's personal seal created with a special technique using multiple thin layers of color and texture. The result is a subtle yet rich presentation of this simple emblem.

Book design by Theresa M. Sparacio

Cover and caseside design by A. Michael Velthaus

Library of Congress Cataloging-in-Publication Data

Calvin, Jean, 1509–1564.
    [Selections. English. 2001]
    John Calvin : writings on pastoral piety / edited and with translations by Elsie Anne McKee ; preface by B. A. Gerrish.
        p.   cm.—(The classics of Western spirituality)
    Includes bibliographical references and indexes.
    ISBN 0-8091-4046-2 (pbk. : alk. paper)—ISBN 0-8091-0541-1 (alk. paper)
    1. Pastoral theology—Reformed Church. I. Title: Writings on pastoral piety.
II. McKee, Elsie Anne. III. Title. IV. Series.

BX9420.A32 M24 2001
284′.2—dc21

                                                                2001032855

Published by Paulist Press
997 Macarthur Boulevard
Mahwah, New Jersey 07430

www.paulistpress.com

Printed and bound in the
United States of America

TABLE OF CONTENTS

CONTENTS

CONTENTS

Translator of This Volume

ELSIE ANNE McKEE is the Archibald Alexander Professor of Reformation Studies and the History of Worship at Princeton Theological Seminary. Born and reared in the central African country of Congo, she earned her B.A. from Hendrix College, a diploma in theology from the University of Cambridge, and her Ph.D. from Princeton Theological Seminary (1982). She has taught church history, historical theology, and the history of worship at Andover Newton Theological School and Princeton Theological Seminary. Her writings include *John Calvin on the Diaconate and Liturgical Almsgiving* (Droz, 1984); *Elders and the Plural Ministry: The Role of Exegetical History in Illuminating John Calvin's Theology* (Droz, 1988); *Katharina Schütz Zell. Volume One: The Life and Thought of a Sixteenth-Century Reformer* and *Katharina Schütz Zell. Volume Two: The Writings. A Critical Edition* (Brill, 1999).

Author of the Preface

B. A. GERRISH taught at the University of Chicago for thirty-one years. At the time of his retirement in 1996, he was John Nuveen Professor and Professor of Historical Theology in the University of Chicago Divinity School, and since then he has been Distinguished Service Professor of Theology at Union Theological Seminary and Presbyterian School of Christian Education in Richmond, Virginia. His main interests are in Western religious thought from the time of the Protestant Reformation and contemporary systematic theology. He has written widely on the Reformation and on German religious thought in the nineteenth century.

FOREWORD

John Calvin is well known as one of the most important Protestant reformers of the sixteenth century and a gifted stylist in both Latin and French. His classic volume of theological instruction, *The Institutes of the Christian Religion,* and his extensive biblical commentaries have continued to be read and studied since they first appeared, and they have been spread in new translations in modern times. It is less commonly remembered that Calvin was also both a preacher and a pastor; his sermons and prayers and letters offer important insights into the piety that transformed the communities which came to be called Calvinist. In fact, many parts of the *Institutes* and commentaries express the same moving spiritual counsel, especially when read in conjunction with the explicitly pastoral writings. Together they form a dynamic, demanding, and enduring spiritual legacy.

The present volume seeks to trace the lines of Calvin's piety or spirituality by drawing together his account of his own religious experience, along with his preaching and teaching about the human relationship with God. His purpose was to lead and challenge all who heard him, or read what he wrote, to realize that their true happiness consists in devotion to God for God's glory; that their salvation is assured by Christ's grace; and so their lives will be transformed by the power of the Holy Spirit and should be given over to the service of God and their neighbor. These texts illustrate also how Calvin's pastoral responsibilities for leading the people of God toward a renewed and strengthened devotion to God shaped his spiritual legacy as a vital force. Included are some excerpts from the *Institutes,* with sermons and sacramental liturgies, psalms and prayers, pastoral instructions and letters of counsel and consolation.

PREFACE

A Calvin very different from the common image of him meets the reader in the pages of this engaging anthology. Calvin is widely supposed to have been an authoritarian reformer and a coldly logical theologian, whose thought, presented in his *Institutes of the Christian Religion,* turned wholly around the dogma of predestination. After his death, and especially after the Reformed Synod of Dort (1618–19), *Calvinism* became virtually synonymous with *predestinarianism.* Hence it is not surprising that a *predestinarian piety* has been imputed to him, in which the supreme object of veneration is the arbitrary and inflexible will of a sovereign deity—an enlarged reflection of Calvin's own autocratic self. The *Dictionnaire de spiritualité,* for example, refers us to just two works by Calvin, his treatise on predestination and his series of sermons on the election of Jacob and the rejection of Esau, and declares that Calvin's God thinks only of his own glory and creates in order to exalt his power.

Professor McKee's Calvin, by contrast, is above all a caring pastor and teacher of pastors, and his piety is *pastoral piety.* McKee does not replace one narrow perspective on Calvin's piety with another; rather, she suggests "pastoral piety" as an inclusive rubric under which to gather various activities of this many-sided man and author of many kinds of writing. Her case is a strong one. Calvin's appointment in Geneva was never more than that of a pastor, or minister of the word; if the civil authorities listened to him, and his fellow ministers deferred to him, that was thanks to his personal influence, not to any dictatorial powers conferred upon him. The context for all his thinking was his faithful activity in pursuit of a pastor's vocation. Even his theological treatises and the *Institutes*–his *summa pietatis*–were pastoral works, directed to the nurture of piety. "The theologian's task," as he put it, "is not to divert the ears with chatter, but to strengthen consciences by teaching things true, sure, *and profitable"* (*Inst.,* 1.14.4; my emphasis). Calvin spoke of God to evoke the right attitude to God, which is piety. He chose to do theology within the limits of piety alone, and the pastoral commitment to edification shaped both the content and the style of his writing.

Insofar, then, as all that Calvin did and said was directed— in intention, at least—to the advancement of piety, it is difficult to know what to leave out from such a collection of extracts as this. Professor McKee draws from a wide range of his writings: the *Institutes,* to be sure, and the winsome *Short Treatise on the Lord's Supper,* but also his letters, sermons, liturgical writings, and prayers for a variety of occasions. The extracts are arranged and introduced with an expert editorial hand, and the entire collection is preceded by a revealing section on Calvin's self-understanding, including the much-discussed autobiographical preface to his *Commentary on Psalms.* It is interesting that the very first part of the *Institutes* to be translated into English in the sixteenth century was the section on the life of the Christian; in the 1559 edition it became chapters 6–10 of Book Three, and it was sometimes published separately as Calvin's *Golden Book of the Christian Life.* Calvin liked to call prayer "the chief exercise of piety," and preaching was central to his understanding of the church, the pastoral ministry, and public worship. But perhaps it is the letters that best reveal him as spiritual guide and director, comforting and encouraging the sick, the bereaved, and prisoners awaiting execution for their faith in the gospel.

But what is *piety*? A key word in Calvin's own vocabulary, Professor McKee rightly prefers it to *spirituality*. In one of the introductory chapters to the 1559 *Institutes,* Calvin ventures a definition: "I call 'piety' that reverence joined with love of God which the knowledge of His benefits induces" (*Inst.,* 1.2.1). He adds by way of explanation: "For until people recognize that they owe everything to God, that they are nourished by His fatherly care, that He is the Author of their every good...they will never yield Him willing service." Piety, as Calvin understands it, is evidently the exact correlate of his favorite images of God as "father" and "fountain (or author) of good." (In his first book, the *Commentary on Seneca's De Clementia,* he had asked rhetorically, "What is piety but a grateful disposition to one's parents?") Though he grants that the pious mind will acknowledge God as also a righteous judge, that is not, in his view, what makes it pious. The right and pious attitude is to recognize God as father and fountain of good, and therefore to regard believers as God's adopted children.

Calvin held that since Adam's fall it is faith alone that can recognize God in the fatherly persona that evokes piety. For a fallen humanity, fearful that the taint of sin deserves no more than God's anger and judgment, the root of piety is faith, because faith rests its assurance of God's goodwill solely on the freely given promise in Christ. But faith is more than intellectual belief or assent. It is a matter of the heart rather than the brain—a matter, that is, of the whole person. And it brings about nothing less than union with Christ, by which Christians receive a twofold grace: justification (or reconciliation with God) and sanctification (or regeneration), which is the life of piety. The careful balancing of justification with sanctification was characteristic of Calvin and remained characteristic of later Calvinism. "Do we not see," he asks, "that the Lord freely justifies His own in order that He may at the same time restore them to true righteousness by sanctification of His Spirit?" (*Inst.,* 3.3.19). And sanctification is the restoration of fallen humanity to the life of piety: "The whole life of Christians ought to be a sort of practice of piety, for we have been called to sanctification" (*Inst.*, 3.19.2).

This, then, is the essence of Calvinist piety, to which Professor McKee provides ready access through judicious extracts from Calvin's own hand. There is of course much more. Of the many other aspects of Calvin's piety to which she draws attention, three strike me as especially important. First, the Christian life for Calvin was suffused with a profound awareness that Christians are not their own: they belong to God by right of creation and still more by right of redemption (an echo of Paul's words in 1 Corinthians 6:19–20). The "sum" of the Christian life is self-denial, a deliberate renunciation of self-love and a commitment to live for God. To his friend William Farel, Calvin wrote (October 1540): "When I remember that I am not my own, I offer up my heart, presented as a sacrifice to the Lord." The metaphor of self-sacrifice to God was visually represented in Calvin's seal with its outstretched hand offering a heart; in the martyrdom of evangelicals he saw it sealed in blood.

The renunciation of self-love frees Christians to seek first the glory of God; at the same time, it makes them available to others. Hence a second point of emphasis in Professor McKee's anthology is what she calls the ethical-activist strand in Calvin's piety. "[P]iety, the right reverence and love for God," she explains, "leads to full acknowledgment of God's claim; that includes conforming our lives to the way God wills for God's people to treat the rest of the creation." In particular, a commitment to justice and love for the neighbor "may at times be the best evidence for the believer's real devotion to God." No doubt, this is a common enough principle in Christian thinking. But it acquired a distinctive prominence in Calvinist piety, not least in the Calvinist stress on the third and principal use of the divine law as both a pattern of Christian behavior and a stimulus to it. And in Calvin's exposition of the Ten Commandments the second table of the law cannot be detached from the first.

A third emphasis, implicit in the first and the second, is the social—more particularly the ecclesial—interest that is always evident in Calvin's piety. Again and again he affirms his twofold goal to seek both the glory of God *and* the good of the church. Reverence for the church made him hesitate, at first, to throw in his lot with the evangelical reformers; when persuaded, it was in order to raise the fallen standard of the church. The individualism commonly presumed to lie at the heart of Protestant faith finds little or no support in Calvin's piety. To his mind, the new birth in Christ and incorporation into the church are but two sides of the same experience. In a striking use of an old metaphor, he writes of the visible church: "[L]et us learn even from the simple title 'mother' how useful, indeed how necessary, it is that we should know her. For there is no other way to enter into life unless this mother conceive us in her womb, give us birth, nourish us at her breast, and lastly, unless she keep us under her care and guidance until, putting off this mortal flesh, we become like the angels" (*Inst.*, 4.1.4).

Professor McKee's keen eye for what matters most in Calvin's piety makes this volume a splendid contribution not only to the history of Western spirituality, but also to our understanding of Calvin himself. Of course, some aspects of his piety will strike the present-day reader as alien or even offensive. His critics are perhaps not mistaken in their complaints about his candid determinism, but only in their obsession with it. Along with the divine determinism goes a quietism that commends acceptance of one's station in life as ordained by God. And with the quietism goes an otherworldliness—a *contemptus mundi*—that consoles the passive victims of suffering and want with a better prospect in the world to come.

This is not the place to assess these and other possible lines of criticism against Calvin's understanding of the Christian life. Readers of this volume can see for themselves how much more there was to his Christian piety. My expectation is that some of them will be unwilling to turn his *Golden Book of the Christian Life* wholly over to the historians—the fate that threatens so many other classics of Protestant spirituality, such as Henry Scougal's *The Life of God in the Soul of Man* and Philip Doddridge's *The Rise and Progress of Religion in the Soul*. They may even conclude that sometimes, at least, Calvin speaks most forcefully to them precisely when his voice sounds most strange.

B. A. Gerrish
John Nuveen Professor Emeritus
The University of Chicago

ACKNOWLEDGMENTS
AND PERMISSIONS

It is a pleasure to thank those who have contributed to this volume. First, special thanks to Professor Bernard McGinn for inviting me to prepare this exploration of Calvin's spirituality, for his great patience with the long delay before I could begin the work, and particularly for his generous encouragement along the way. It is also a pleasure to thank Ms. Kathleen Walsh, the Paulist Press editor for the Classics of Western Spirituality, for her cheerful and skilled helpfulness throughout the project.

Particular thanks are due to Professor B. A. Gerrish for graciously consenting to write the preface, and to Professor Edward A. Dowey, Jr., and Dr. John A. McGlaughlin, for reading and offering helpful comments on the general introduction.

Thanks are also owed to the Rev. Austra Reinis, for timely work in tracking down and photocopying articles; to Mr. David Stewart and his assistants, for willing assistance in scanning printed texts; and to Princeton Theological Seminary for financial support for the project. All the remaining faults are my own.

It is with gratitude that I acknowledge permissions granted by various authors and publishers for use of specific translations, whole or in part, in order of appearance:

J. K. S. Reid's translation of "The Reply to Sadoleto" and "A Short Treatise on the Lord's Supper," from *Calvin: Theological Treatises* (Philadelphia, 1954), pp. 143–55, 246–53; used by permission of Westminster John Knox Press (North American rights) and the SCM Press (world rights).

Ford Lewis Battles' translation of *The Institutes of the Christian Religion* (Philadelphia, 1960), various excerpts; used by permission of Westminster John Knox Press and the SCM Press.

Charles Garside's translation of Calvin's "Foreword to the Psalter," from *The Origins of Calvin's Theology of Music* (Philadelphia, 1979), pp. 31–33; used by permission of the American Philosophical Society.

Ford Lewis Battles' translation of Calvin's psalms translations, from *Six Psalms of John Calvin* (Grand Rapids, 1978), pp. 13–21; used by permission of the Ford Lewis Battles Estate.

Bard Thompson's translation of Calvin's Sunday morning liturgy, from *Liturgies of the Western Church,* copyright Bard Thompson 1962; used by permission of Augsburg Fortress Press.

Benjamin Farley's translation of a sermon on the Sabbath, from *Calvin's Sermons on the Ten Commandments* (Grand Rapids, 1980), pp. 115–32; used by permission of Baker Books.

It is also appropriate to acknowledge the use of some materials now in the public domain: Translations of a commentary preface and prayers by the Calvin Translation Society, taken from reprints by the Wm. B. Eerdmans Publishing Co. with its permission; and translations of letters collected by Jules Bonnet, translated by Marcus Robert Gilchrist.

This book is dedicated with deep gratitude and affection to my father, the Rev. Charles T. McKee, Ngulumingi wa Ntalasha, pastor and teacher of pastors in the Democratic Republic of Congo and the United States of America.

ABBREVIATIONS

OC = *Ioannis Calvini opera quae supersunt omnia,* edited by G. Baum, E. Cunitz, and E. Reuss. 59 vols. Brunsvigae: C. A. Schwetschke, 1863–1900. (= *Corpus Reformatorum,* vol. 29–87).

OS = *Ioannis Calvini opera selecta,* edited by P. Barth, W. Niesel, *et al.* 5 vols. München: Christian Kaiser. 1926–62.

SC = *Supplementa Calviniana,* edited by H. Rückert, E. Mülhaupt, G. Barrois, *et al.* Neukirchener-Vluyn: Neukirchener Verlag, 1936– .

GENERAL INTRODUCTION

John Calvin was a pastor and teacher of pastors. The great theological classic for which he is best known, *The Institutes of the Christian Religion,* began as Calvin's response to the needs of persecuted French Protestants who had virtually no pastors to teach or defend them. Even in its expanded form the book conveys a care for souls that welcomes the reader who comes to it expecting cold logic. Calvin was an exile for his faith, living as a resident alien in often uncongenial circumstances, and his pastoral call had come through William Farel and Martin Bucer against his own inclination. Yet those very experiences of exile, and God's compelling voice heard through human instruments, gave a depth of passion and sensitivity to Calvin the pastor: he knew the cost of giving up his earthly home to keep faith with the eternal one, and he knew the power of God's speaking through human voices.

Faith and confession, word and act, must go together. God redeems women and men, old and young, high and low, by claiming them as children of God, so giving them the greatest joy they can experience. Men and women, young and old, people of every station in life, in turn glorify and serve God by acknowledging that claim, and living out that gift and challenge, in every fibre of their beings and every aspect of their existence. The gift is God's, in Christ, made alive in the human heart by the Holy Spirit. But

God accommodates the proclamation of this message of salvation to the measure of human beings by making them the instruments of sharing it with each other. The piety of Calvin was that of a pastor passionately and wholly committed to living out God's claim on him, and calling others to hear and heed, to rejoice in and witness to God's claim on them as the purpose and joy of their lives.

CALVIN AND SPIRITUALITY

Definitions of spirituality or piety are not uniform. Most descriptions of spirituality explain it as the (conscious) relationship of human beings with the divine and the shape which that relationship gives to human life. One definition of Christian spirituality is "the lived experience of Christian belief,...the reaction that faith arouses in religious consciousness and practice."[1] In some traditions, where the ethical receives more emphasis, spirituality might be seen as the visible fruit that persons bear because they are known by and know God. In setting out a person's spirituality, therefore, some attention must be given to how he or she understands the relationship with God, and then the implications of this for the person's own life and practice. For one who is regarded as a spiritual guide, a third focus is naturally what effect that person has on those who follow his or her teaching and example: What direction does this teacher's spirituality give others in their search for God and their effort to live in God's presence?

The pastoral image of Calvin sketched above may seem rather unexpected, if not in fact incongruous; it has not been customary to name "Calvin" and "spirituality" in the same sentence. On the other hand, though "spirituality" may not often be associated with Calvin's name, "sanctification" and "vocation" frequently are, and with good reason.[2] Both friends and foes have long recognized the force and power of the Calvinist ethos or morality, Calvinist discipline and religious activism. If one evidence of a person's spirituality is the way his or her convictions lead others to shape and reshape their lives, then it should be

GENERAL INTRODUCTION

rather obvious that Calvin and his followers had a remarkably dynamic form of spirituality. Before sketching a positive definition of Calvin's spirituality, it may be helpful to begin by considering briefly why the Genevan reformer has been disregarded as a spiritual guide, and yet why this neglect may do less than justice both to Calvin and to the concept of Christian spirituality.

Part of the problem for interpreting Calvin as a spiritual leader is his reputation as one of the most gifted and intellectually rigorous theologians of the sixteenth century. This view is not false but, as is true of most figures who have played a significant role in history, Calvin's reputation has become somewhat caricatured and more narrow and syllogistic than the man himself. The reputation as an intellectual is also one that modern readers have inherited shorn of the vital pastoral context in which the theology was written, a context which made it clear that the doctrine was an expression of the faith, the mind following after the heart. Commonly a strong emphasis on systematic theology is not considered conducive to a very deep sensitivity to spirituality. Or, to put this another way, too much attention to *lex credendi,* the pattern of believing, is regarded as somewhat detrimental to *lex orandi,* the pattern of praying. For the reformers of early sixteenth-century Europe, however, as for those in many other times and places, faith and worship, prayer and doctrine, were inextricably interrelated. In fact, although Calvin's theology is regarded as primarily intellectual, he himself put the greater weight on the heart; heart and head must go together but the heart is more important. It was problems they perceived in the way people were being taught to worship God, to find assurance of their own salvation, and to live their lives as Christians (see Calvin's "The Reply to Sadoleto," p. 47) that led Protestants to demand a reform of theology. Their well-known insistence on teaching and preaching and catechizing was intended primarily to revivify the relationship of God's people with God.

Another difficulty in seeing Calvin as a spiritual leader is the common tendency to interpret spirituality in individualistic terms. This often leads to neglect for "the collective, social dimensions that have been so important to the lived experience

3

of Christian faith," especially the central importance of corporate worship, liturgy.[3] If one defines spirituality as a person's private relationship with God, which issues in individual holiness, then Calvin manifestly has less to say than some other guides. Even his own very personal conviction of his relationship with God was, in his understanding, predicated on his being engrafted into Christ's body, for he was convinced that no Christian is a Christian apart from the rest of the body. Spirituality for Calvin was therefore never individualistic. It was personal, without question, but it was personal in the context of the community of faith, whether that community was immediately visible or not. Thus, although there are clearly parts of his theological writing that address individuals, Calvin never sees any Christian apart from the church, the body of Christ, the community of believers. His spiritual counsel never fails to put individual concerns in the perspective of the whole, and so it can sometimes seem less than personal to modern ears. In fact, for Calvin, spiritual formation was at least as much the fruit of the corporate worship of God as of individual direction. Not that he ever spared himself when any individual sought his counsel or comfort: on the contrary. But he drove himself to teach and shape the whole community in the patterns of life that would nourish its relationship with God and reflect its confession, and he did this most prominently by public and corporate means. Faith and prayer are central to the relationship with God, and both must first be inward. Neither faith nor prayer, however, can remain hidden; both must of necessity become part of the life of the community. Faith and prayer must then transform the community and the world as they transform each praying believer.

How then might Calvin's spirituality be described? It is helpful to begin by substituting the word *piety* for *spirituality; pietas,* piety or godliness, is a word Calvin frequently uses, while the traditional medieval word *spiritualitas* is foreign to his language.[4] The connotation of "piety" intended here centers on Calvin's usual interpretation of *pietas,* the attitude and actions directed to the adoration and service of God. It also includes in subordinate place some related themes that he often associates with that word,

4

especially the filial piety of human relationships and, more loosely, respect and love for the image of God in all human beings. And so for a kind of descriptive definition: Calvin's piety is the ethos and action of people who recognize through faith that they have been accepted in Christ and engrafted into His body by the sheer grace of God. By this adoption, this "mystical union," the Lord claims them as belonging solely and wholly to God in life and in death, as God's people and members of Christ, by the power of the Holy Spirit. This relationship established by God with believers restores the joy of fellowship with God; it evokes and requires a response, and so re-creates their lives. Acknowledging God's claim carries the obligation to worship God publicly and privately, as they find in God's Lordship their true happiness. It also includes recognizing in all human beings the image of Christ, to make God known to them and to give their earthly lives all the help possible.[5]

The content of Calvin's piety is fundamentally biblical, but it is a Bible expounded and applied to the heart and will even more than the mind. It is a piety in which prayer and worship are central, but prayer normally in the plural ("we") form and worship normally in the context of the community ("public"). From the word of God regularly heard and sacramentally experienced in the body of Christ, the ethos of each heart, each member, is formed. The "visible words" of baptism and the Lord's supper play a much more essential role in Calvin's piety than is sometimes remembered, and that role is more existential than rational. And yet, in one sense, it is possible literally "to see" Calvin's piety most clearly in its "this worldly" dynamic: it encompasses every aspect of every day's life for every person and the whole community, and it is fundamentally ethical. The worship of God is always primary, the relationship to God takes precedence over all else. However, that worship may be most sincerely expressed in how believers live their vocation, how Christians treat their neighbors; that relationship with God is most concretely witnessed by the transformation of every human relationship, and even the structures of human society.[6]

Because this biblical piety is strongly corporate and shaped by the theological conviction that God has chosen to accommodate revelation to human capacity, there is an important role for pastoral leadership in edifying the church. One aspect of divine accommodation is God's use of human beings to teach human beings. Christians need human direction in prayer and human leadership in worship; they need human instruction and example in how to live their vocations and bear their trials. They need these from one another and owe them to one another. But especially they need them from those who have been gifted by God's Spirit and called by the church to be pastors and other leaders, people who are able by training and by experience to speak God's word and be God's instruments in a special way. The instruments are not themselves different from other believers, but their office and gifts are particularly fitted to teaching and stirring others up to pray and live according to God's will. Therefore there is a strong pastoral element in the expression of Calvin's piety. Readers will hear others speaking to Calvin himself, but more often they will hear the pastor drawing on his own experience of his relationship with God, shaped by scripture, to address God's people.

The present volume invites the reader to become—temporarily—a member of Calvin's parish, or one of his colleagues in the pastoral ministry in sixteenth-century Geneva. It is an invitation to experience something of the community's life, whether its members are gathered for worship or going about their daily tasks in the sight of God and their neighbors.

A Brief Biographical Sketch
of Calvin and His Ministry

Who was the man John Calvin, and what was the outwardly visible life story of this teacher of spirituality? Born on July 10, 1509, in Noyon, Picardy, a city in northern France that was the seat of a bishop, young John was the brightest son of Gérard Calvin (usually written Cauvin). Gérard's father had been a cooper or boatman in a nearby village, but the younger man moved to Noyon and worked his way up to become the bishop's notary. This meant that Gérard was able to launch his own children on paths of advancement, and so the three sons were destined for the priesthood. Because of young John's intelligence, he was given a good education with the sons of the Montmors family, relatives of the bishop; then he accompanied them to Paris for the next stage of his studies, where he (like other priests-to-be) was supported by the usual system of church benefices. After John completed the arts degree at the University of Paris, his father decided that he should become a lawyer instead of a priest, and so the young man moved to Orléans and then Bourges, the two great centers of legal training in France. While he was earning his law degree, however, Calvin was increasingly influenced by the new humanist learning that was spreading through Europe. He began to study Greek and perhaps Hebrew and to delve into classical sources, which led to the publication of his first book, a commentary on Seneca's treatise *De Clementia (On Mercy)*.

However, during these years of study Calvin was also beginning to deal with the new religious ideas circulating in France—some homegrown in the circles of reform sponsored by Princess Marguerite, others associated with Martin Luther's name. In 1533 Calvin was back in Paris, where one of his friends, Nicolas Cop, had been elected the rector of the University. Cop's inaugural address on November 1, which drew on the ideas of both Erasmus and Luther, greatly shocked the ecclesiastical authorities. Since Calvin was in some way implicated, he quickly left Paris. It is probably at this time that Calvin came to the conviction that he had to break with the Roman Church in which he had been reared. He spent some time with Louis du Tillet, another friend who was also attracted to the new religious teaching, studying theology and the church fathers in the library of the Tillet country home. Then, in May 1534, he returned to Noyon to resign his benefices, thus marking his final break with Rome. At first Calvin did not plan to leave France; however, the "affair of the placards" in October 1534 forced him to change his mind. The placards were handbills attacking the Mass, which were scattered through Paris and other French cities. This attack on the church and its teaching produced a sharp reaction in which a number of people, including one named Etienne de la Forge, with whom Calvin was acquainted, were burned at the stake. It also made France untenable for those who publicly rejected the doctrine of the Roman Church.

And so, late in 1534, Calvin and Tillet left France for Basel. That famous university city, with its scholars and printers, had adopted the Protestant Reformation in a Zwinglian style some years earlier under the leadership of Johannes Oecolampadius. Here Calvin could continue his theological reading and writing. By August of 1535 he had completed the first edition of *The Institutes of the Christian Religion,* a pocket-sized book of six chapters, which would appear in print in the following March. The book was intended as a kind of catechism or primer for French followers of the gospel (Protestants), to help them understand their new faith better and be able to defend it clearly, and to witness to German Protestants that these persecuted folk were in fact suffering for the same faith that Luther and Zwingli had purified. The long preface to the book was a letter to King Francis I of France, an apologia for this teaching as truly Christian and its followers as faithful and peaceful believers. Entrusting the manuscript of the *Institutes* to the publisher, Calvin left Basel to travel during the autumn and winter of 1535–36. First he visited the French Princess Renée, now Duchess of Ferrara in Italy and a sponsor of reform; later he made a secret trip back to France on family business. As it was now plain that he must go into exile, Calvin decided to move to Strasbourg, a German-speaking city-state near the French border where many French Protestants had already found religious refuge. Strasbourg had become predominantly Protestant in the early 1520s, under the leadership of Matthew and Katharina Schütz Zell, Martin Bucer, Wolfgang Capito, Caspar Hedio, and civil magistrates like Claus Kniebis, Daniel Mieg, and Mathis Pfarrer, and it welcomed refugees from many places. When Calvin and his brother Antoine and sister Marie prepared to leave for Strasbourg, however, their route was blocked by the opposing armies of King

Francis I of France and Emperor Charles V of the Holy Roman Empire. And so it was that Calvin detoured through the small independent city-state of Geneva in July 1536.

What was Geneva? When Calvin arrived Geneva was a small, newly and precariously independent city-state. (It was not a part of Switzerland until 1815.) It had been the seat of a bishop and politically linked with its powerful neighbor to the west, the Duchy of Savoy, until in 1528 it forced its bishop to leave. Two years before, in 1526, Geneva had made an alliance with the Swiss cantons of Bern and Fribourg; now it called on these allies to help establish its independence over against Savoy, while at the same time trying to avoid being swallowed up by the allies themselves. Amid the crosscurrents of war and diplomacy there were religious changes at work in Geneva, encouraged by one of its new allies, Bern. Fribourg remained faithful to Rome and eventually withdrew from the alliance; Bern, however, had accepted the Protestant teaching in a Zwinglian form in 1528 and was eager to spread its new faith, including in Geneva. So it happened that in 1532, under the auspices of Bern, the fiery Frenchman William Farel began preaching in Geneva. He quickly developed a local following, and soon religious arguments broke out between Farel and his supporters and the traditional clergy and theirs; gradually, more and more citizens came to share the new ideas. The Mass was temporarily banned in the summer of 1535, but on May 21, 1536, the citizens voted to make this ban permanent and "to follow the gospel," that is, to become Protestant. The decision was made, but exactly what the new religious stance meant was not yet entirely clear. Organization was not Farel's forte, so he began to look around for someone to help him put the new Genevan Church on a solid footing.

Happily for Farel, he had just read Calvin's little booklet, *The Institutes of the Christian Religion,* which had appeared in March. When he heard one day in July that the author was passing through Geneva, Farel promptly went to talk with him. Calvin was convinced that his calling was to study and write in support of the faith, not to be a pastor, but Farel had other ideas. Calvin's own account of how Farel compelled him to remain in

Geneva is found in his autobiographical preface to the commentary on psalms: "And after having learned that my heart was set upon devoting myself to private studies, for which I wished to keep myself free from other pursuits, and finding that he gained nothing by entreaties, [Farel] proceeded to utter an imprecation that God would curse my retirement, and the tranquility of the studies which I sought, if I should withdraw and refuse to give assistance, when the necessity was so urgent. By this imprecation I was so stricken with terror that I desisted from the journey which I had undertaken; but sensible of my natural bashfulness and timidity, I would not bring myself under obligation to discharge any particular office" (see pp. 61–62). Calvin first became a lecturer on the Bible, a work for which he did consider himself fitted and which he pursued all his life, and then he also began to preach. Along with Farel, he worked to give Geneva's Church a clear form. A confession of faith, a catechism, and a church order were prepared, and the preachers began trying to reform the people's life and teach them the new understanding of the faith.

Geneva was ready to be Protestant, but it was not ready to follow Calvin's understanding of church practice.[7] Bern, the city's patron, was Zwinglian in its church order; this meant that the civil government was charged with the practical oversight of church life, including discipline and liturgical ceremony. In Calvin's view, the church must be autonomous in its own life; it should not only be free to preach the gospel but also to control its own government and worship practices. Geneva had adopted Bern's Zwinglian ideas quite happily before Calvin arrived. Now the city government wished to please its patron by copying liturgical ceremonies used in Bern, such as unleavened bread for the Lord's supper, the use of baptistries for baptisms, and the observance of specific holy days. When the government insisted that the preachers follow these practices, Farel, Calvin, and their colleague Elie Coraud refused to accept the ultimatum. However, the ministers' position was not very strong; they were hired city preachers, not settled pastors of specific parishes, and Farel and Calvin were also foreigners. Matters came to a head at Easter, April 21, 1538, when Calvin declared that in the current state of uproar he could not administer the Lord's supper, because the whole community should be reconciled before its members shared in the sacrament. The city council promptly ordered the three preachers to leave immediately.

Besides the theological arguments, there were other issues involved. Calvin's name is so closely linked with Geneva that it is often forgotten that he was a resident alien, a hired hand, a Frenchman in a foreign land. From the Genevan viewpoint, he was a potential French agent. (In fact, until late in the century almost all the ministers came from outside Geneva, because before the Academy was established in 1559, the city did not have any institutions to provide the learned preachers that the new pastoral ministry needed.) When Calvin arrived Geneva had only just achieved its independence from episcopal rule. It was in danger of being invaded as a heretical state by the Duchy of Savoy. It was not allowed to become an actual part of Switzerland because the Confederation feared to add another Protestant canton to those already living in uneasy balance between Roman and Protestant confessions. Trying to maintain a common purpose amid all these forces was very difficult for the council, particularly since not all the citizens thought alike, either about politics or the foreign ministers. Essentially, the problem was a combination of theological disagreement with political divisions. For Calvin, issues of church control of ceremonies and discipline were theological matters, and the civil government's determination to exercise these powers manifested its desire to do as it pleased and reject the biblical understanding of church order. For the city government, its control of these aspects of the common Christian life was both biblical and right, according to the teaching of their Zwinglian neighbors, and the ministers' insistence on ecclesiastical autonomy demonstrated a desire for clerical rule and possibly disloyalty. This issue would continue to be a source of conflict for a generation, until in the mid-1550s the Genevan community eventually came to a common mind on the subject of both church order and political orientation toward France. In 1538, it was the foreign preachers who were the losers.

Although he felt very deeply the pain of this failure, Calvin also concluded (with some relief) that he was indeed not really well fitted for the work of a pastor, and he prepared to return to Basel to continue his writing. Other church leaders did not agree with him, however, and Martin Bucer soon repeated the same act by which Farel had compelled Calvin to stay in Geneva. Bucer was seeking a pastor for the large French-speaking refugee community in Strasbourg, and he thought Calvin was exactly the right person. Faced with Calvin's reluctance, Bucer invoked the example of Jonah, which convinced the young Frenchman that God was now again calling him to the pastoral ministry, this time in Strasbourg. In fact, the three years he spent in that city were probably the happiest part of Calvin's ministry. He had good colleagues, led by Bucer, who managed the relationship between ecclesiastical and civil authorities. He had a congregation of fellow exiles, who had counted the cost of their confession and made the same choice that he had, to give up the earthly homeland for a place where they could worship God as they believed God wanted. He lived in a cosmopolitan community with a new and soon famous Academy, where he lectured on the Bible. He became involved in the larger church world of Catholic-Protestant colloquies or religious conferences, where he served as a spokesman for his co-religionists and at the same time made many new acquaintances and friends, including Philip Melanchthon. He also married (something Bucer was always encouraging his colleagues to do), and the home he established with Idelette de Bure, a widow with two children, was an important source of comfort and strength to his ministry, as his letters after her death make very clear (see pp. 52–54).

Though materially poor, Calvin's years as a pastor in Strasbourg were both rich and happy. He learned from his older colleagues, especially Bucer, and contributed to their work, while also developing his own understanding and practice of pastoral ministry. Some of his activities were a continuation of his earlier work of teaching the new faith to ordinary people and now increasingly to future ministers. A second and much expanded edition of the *Institutes* was published in 1539, followed by a French translation in 1541, and his commentary on Romans, the

first of many volumes of biblical exegesis, in 1540. The regular
worship of the community greatly occupied his attention. He
probably published a first form of his Sunday liturgy around 1540
(although no copy is named or extant, and evidence for both
printing and contents is circumstantial). More important from the
congregation's viewpoint was the psalter that Calvin brought out
in 1539. This contained metrical versions of nineteen psalms and
the Apostles' Creed, the Decalogue, and the Song of Simeon in
French, with melodies. Now everyone could have the biblical texts
of prayer and praise, which all would sing together in public worship and each would use at home in personal devotion.[8] Calvin
was actively involved as a pastor, working to convert and edify, to
baptize and counsel and prepare anxious souls for communion, to
care for the sick and dying and bereaved. One of his letters from
this time, written to the father of a young student living in
Calvin's home when the plague struck Strasbourg, conveys both
his comfort to the family and his own grief over the boy's death
(see pp. 293–301). It was a demanding but good and busy life.

But Calvin's time in Strasbourg was short. The Genevans
had discovered that they needed him. In 1539, the year after they
exiled Calvin, the city received a cordial letter from Cardinal
Jacopo Sadoleto, a reforming bishop of the neighboring diocese
of Carpentras, which invited them with humanist learning and
grace to return to Rome, the true church. Having no minister
sufficiently educated to answer this letter, the Genevan government sent it to Calvin with a plea that he should respond, which,
in loyalty to his understanding of his pastoral call, he promptly
did. However, a reply to Sadoleto was not all that the city needed.
By the following year Geneva was asking Calvin to return. Various colleagues in the Swiss Reformed Churches urged that this
was his duty, although Calvin himself and some of his Strasbourg
friends felt that he was well occupied in serving his congregation
there. At length he and the rest agreed that it was God's call for
him to return to Geneva. In 1540 one of his letters to Farel (who
was not invited back) expresses something of Calvin's sense of
being claimed by God—not being his own—and thus obligated to
follow where he was led, even if that was manifestly not going to

be comfortable (see pp. 50–52). It took some time to disengage responsibly from his Strasbourg duties, but on September 13, 1541, he arrived back in Geneva.

Calvin's first acts on his return were significant. He immediately insisted that a proper church order be accepted. (This had been one of his conditions for agreeing to come back.) Quickly he drafted the *Ecclesiastical Ordinances,* which the government then modified in various ways before voting them into law in November. The parish system was organized, and Calvin and Pierre Viret were now established as pastors of parishes, not merely city preachers. This meant that, although they and all but one of their several other ministerial colleagues were still essentially hired foreigners, they now held (traditionally identifiable) places of authority. Third, Calvin took up his preaching again precisely where he had left off in 1538, to indicate that he had been interrupted in his pastoral ministry rather than laid it down.[9] The Reformed pattern of preaching, called *lectio continua* or continuous reading, was to preach all the way through an entire book of the Bible. It was a "sermon series" in the sense of being a series of expositions of a text, accompanied by application to the hearers' own lives as Christians. For example, Calvin might begin with Romans 1:1–3; he would read several verses, as much as he could explain in a sermon of about an hour (although some preachers spoke much longer, a trait Calvin criticized). In the next sermon he would continue with the same book, Romans 1:4–6. (Usually New Testament readings tended to be two to five verses, Old Testament ones about twice as long.) Most of Calvin's early sermons were not preserved. Beginning in 1549, however, French refugees in Geneva regularly paid a stenographer, Denis Raguenier, to take down and then transcribe Calvin's preaching. Of these sermons, some were published in the sixteenth century by demand of the hearers or their friends (over Calvin's own objections that these had been intended for a particular congregation and also were not polished for the public). Most of the sermons remained in manuscript, though they were borrowed from the Genevan library in that form. In 1806 all but one of these manuscripts were sold to clear space on the library shelves, and many were permanently lost, although some have been recovered and are being edited in a series called the *Supplementa Calviniana*. Thus there are no extant sermons on books such as the Gospel of John or the Epistle to the Romans, on which Calvin preached before 1549. Many sermons recorded in the later years are also missing, although there are records of which texts he expounded.

The years of Calvin's second Genevan ministry extended from September 1541 until his death on May 27, 1564. It was a turbulent time, for Calvin and for Geneva. One of the chief minister's first tasks was to build up a responsible corps of learned ministers, a duty Calvin undertook with vigor. He worked hard to find and to hire more and better educated pastors, and to increase the availability of preaching and pastoral care; gradually this goal was achieved. A stronger body of ministers of the word and sacraments had been formed by around 1546, and then continued to grow to meet the needs of the expanding population and fuller schedule of daily services and visitation of the sick and needy. Alongside the task of providing edifying preaching and good pastoral care was the work of establishing a church order which more fully approximated the patterns Calvin understood to follow biblical teaching, as that applied to the contemporary church. (He did not intend a biblical literalism without regard for historical circumstances, but he believed that scripture provides "general rules" for ecclesiastical organization and practice.) This church order included developing the Consistory, the body of elders and pastors who together exercised oversight of the church, and also overseeing and coordinating the church's ministry to the poor and its work of education, tasks led by deacons and teachers.

Calvin's understanding of church leadership, based on the work of Oecolampadius in Basel and Bucer in Strasbourg, but refined and developed in his own way, was distinct from the Zwinglian form. Since Geneva had begun with a Zwinglian plan, Calvin's difference on this subject was one of the main reasons for the difficulties he encountered in implementing his church order. Like other Protestants, Calvin gave great importance to lay leadership in the church alongside the pastors. Unlike Luther,

Zwingli, and others, though, he believed that these lay officers—elders and deacons—are ministers of the church, not the Christian state, and he invested much effort in persuading Genevans to share his convictions.[10] Despite some lack of clarity about ultimate control, the work of deacons in poor relief developed fairly smoothly in Geneva. However, one of the main issues of conflict was the work of the Consistory, which the city government viewed in the Zwinglian manner as an organ of its own rule, and which Calvin understood as having its own autonomy in those religious matters that were not also civil crimes. The struggle to define and oversee discipline continued for some fifteen years, between Calvin and his supporters on the one hand, and the opposing voices in the government and city on the other. Finally, in 1555, Geneva's civil and ecclesiastical leaders came to a common understanding of the autonomy of the Consistory and the ecclesiastical character of elders, as Geneva also came to terms with the Frenchness of the pastors and refugees.

The pastoral role of the Consistory in Geneva has often been obscured by the conflicts surrounding its work. Although usually discipline is considered a negative category of correction and punishment, Geneva's Consistory functioned as something like a "compulsory counseling service," in which guidance for many aspects of piety was provided under corporate communal leadership.[11] In the early years the pastors and elders who made up the Consistory were often busy with questions of religious practice and education. A key goal was to see that, at a minimum, everyone in Geneva could recite the Lord's Prayer and the Apostles' Creed in French, a language they could understand, and not the Latin that most had memorized as children. As Calvin and his colleagues knew, faith is not merely comprehension. However, conscious knowledge of the basic confession is certainly one important foundation for the relationship with God and for living out the implications of that adoption into God's family. In this regard the Consistory worked together with the regular preaching and catechetical services to edify the people of Geneva, to teach them the fundamentals about their relationship with God.

GENERAL INTRODUCTION

In addition to learning how to pray, piety requires living
one's convictions. One of the main occupations of the Consistory
was to guide Genevans in acting on their profession. This
included, of course, oversight of sexual and economic morality.
Perhaps the most time-consuming and important task, though,
was mediating interpersonal and communal problems and conflicts, from marital disputes or wife-beating to neighborhood quar-
rels or slander. The goal was repentance and reconciliation, and
the usual procedure was to hear all the parties and their witnesses
in order to determine the rights of the case. The normal chastisement was then a stern exhortation or admonition to repent and
forgive and live together in peace. The Consistory is often associated primarily with arguments over excommunication from the
Lord's supper, because Calvin was convinced that this final religious sanction belongs to the ecclesiastical and not the civil
authority. In fact, however, restoration was an equally important
and often the more difficult task facing the church leaders. Sus-
pension from participation in the sacraments was usually a tempo-
rary thing, readmission being dependent on the person's
manifesting repentance. Genevans, like most of their contempo-
raries, commonly agreed that one should not take communion
while holding bitterness in one's heart, and many were reluctant to
come to the Lord's supper if they were not prepared to forgive
wrongs done them. The Consistory probably devoted more time
to trying to restore people to a state of reconciliation, and thus to
fitness to participate in the sacrament, than it did to excommunication. In the week before the celebration of the Lord's supper
there were always extra Consistory meetings with the specific purpose of giving those who were suspended an opportunity to
express their repentance and be reconciled, and so to demonstrate
their worthiness for admission to the Lord's supper.[12]

Calvin's pastoral ministry extended beyond Geneva and the
Genevans. Always aware of his exile, Calvin continued to be particularly concerned for the state of the infant Protestant Church in
France, and he tried to support the growing number of worshiping
communities there with literature and ministers. He also welcomed
those who made the choice that he had, to leave their homes for

17

their faith. French refugees were the most numerous, but others came to Geneva from many different lands; Calvin helped them establish congregations for preaching in their own languages: Italian, English, Spanish. He also corresponded with others scattered across Europe: with royalty like the queens Marguerite de Valois and Jeanne d'Albret of Navarre and their cousin the Duchess of Ferrara, or Edward VI and Elizabeth of England; with women and men of all ranks imprisoned for their faith; with people troubled by personal struggles or issues of conscience; with church leaders perplexed by questions of teaching or practice. (A few of these letters are found below, pp. 305–32.)

Calvin's own life was so intertwined with his ministry, whether immediately in Geneva or indirectly much farther afield, that it is difficult to speak of his personal biography apart from his office. Through the years of continuing conflict, however, Calvin was growing older and ever more frail in body, though no less active in his vocation. His wife, who had been in poor health since the premature birth of their son in 1542, finally died in late March 1549, and Calvin did not remarry but lived with the household of his brother Antoine. His health had never been robust, and as time passed Calvin developed more and more illnesses. Fevers, kidney stones, gout, hemorrhoids, tuberculosis, intestinal problems, and migraine headaches often overlapped; the treatment for one in fact frequently aggravated the suffering from another. Contrary to the common legend, Calvin deeply appreciated the beautiful gifts of God's creation, including food and drink, music and flowers, and many other natural joys, which should be valued as God's good gifts and used with glad and serious stewardship. In view of his own experience, however, it is small wonder that he often thought of the body as a prison. In his pastoral visitation he could certainly sympathize with those who suffered. When their pastor exhorted and comforted the sick with the consolation that everything comes to believers from the hands of their loving God, they knew that he also applied this to his own life. The blessings of this life are evidences of God's love to be received with gratitude, but they should never distract us from God's service, and they pale before the joys of the heavenly life.[13]

Calvin not only spoke of trusting God, he also continued to work to the end—even from the sickbed where in the last years he spent an increasing amount of time. There were three more greatly expanded editions of the *Institutes,* more and more commentaries (on practically the entire New Testament and much of the Old), and treatises of various kinds. He supported and encouraged those adding to the psalter, until in 1562 all one hundred-fifty psalms were published for worship in public and private. Work was constant: preaching and teaching, weddings and baptisms, meetings of the Consistory or consultations with the city council, visits to the sick and endless correspondence, and more preaching, visits, letters. Even when he could no longer walk, the preacher was carried to the pulpit in a chair to continue the proclamation of the word to his flock.

Calvin the pastor and spiritual guide did not offer easy answers, but there was coherence between what he expected of others and what he expected of himself. While he lived, always his vocation drove him on. When friends urged the dying man to rest he answered: "What? Would you have the Lord come and find me idle?" The lifelong refrain accompanied him, expressing trust and confidence in the promises of the faithful God who had claimed him and would always love him in life and death and beyond. "We are not our own....We are God's" (*Inst.*, 3.7.1).[14]

An Introduction to the Writings in This Volume

Calvin's classic, *The Institutes of the Christian Religion,* ranks as one of the most important theological books of the Reformation, and it has continued to be valued down to the present, experiencing a new extension of its influence in the twentieth century. Usually regarded as a tome of rigid doctrine, the *Institutes* in fact has a strongly pastoral orientation and long passages of devotional language. Because of the sheer size of the final

1559 edition (the most commonly translated form), the *Institutes* can appear a little daunting. Thus, at the risk of reprinting material readily available elsewhere, it was decided to include here excerpts of the sections most significant for understanding Calvin's teaching on piety, especially some definitions and selections on the Lord's Prayer, the Decalogue, and the Christian life.

The part of Calvin's work that was probably even more vital in his own eyes than the *Institutes* was the direct exposition of scripture. The commentaries and sermons that were the fruit of his steady determination to explain the Bible faithfully and intelligently, and to apply it seriously to the human condition, continue to be among the most readable and useful biblical studies inherited from the sixteenth century. Portions from commentaries are not included here, except for one preface and the concluding prayers from a few of his Old Testament lectures, but five of Calvin's sermons provide a taste of the exegetical and homiletical gifts of this lifelong student of the Bible. Most of the sermons are set in the context of actual liturgies, to give a more accurate feeling for one of the most important ways that people experienced spiritual direction in Calvin's Geneva. As the reformer himself said, Christians attend worship and listen to sermons not only to be taught something new but also to be stirred up and encouraged to live what they already know, and to be reproved when they are at fault.[15] Preaching is essential, and usually Genevans referred to the service as a whole as the "sermon." However, it is significant that Calvin himself entitled his liturgy *La forme des prières, The Form of Prayers:* public worship is shaped by prayer, that "chief exercise of piety" (*Inst.,* 3.20 title). And in fact, although Calvin is not usually remembered for the beauty of his prayers, his liturgy and sacramental rites reveal a rich interplay of biblical imagery. Another often neglected source of Calvin's piety is his correspondence, the letters to friends and fellow travelers on the pilgrimage of faith, where some of his most personal words of religious feeling and counsel can be found.

The sources of this volume, therefore, include some of Calvin's best known works and some of his writings that deserve to be more widely known. The organization is not according to source, however, but follows an existential pattern, from Calvin's personal religious experience and his basic theological stance; through the praise, preaching, sacraments, and daily prayer that he led in Geneva day by day and year after year; to the lived piety of the Christian pilgrim in the world, as Calvin worked with and for, exhorted, and comforted fellow travelers. The following outline explains in more detail why the specific selections were made and how they fit together to provide a picture of Calvin's practice and teaching of piety.

Part One: John Calvin was very reticent about his personal life. Most of his inner religious experience, his own relationship to God, can only be extrapolated from his teaching about the life of a believer, the trials of faith, the similarities between contemporary "followers of the gospel" and their biblical predecessors. At times, however, Calvin's experience of God's call and understanding of God's purpose for his life, his own struggles and his confidence in God's mercy, were preserved in words. Part One of this volume draws together the most important and revealing comments Calvin made about himself. The first is a thinly veiled, probably autobiographical, first-person narrative of how he would defend his Genevan ministry and his own break with Rome if he stood before God's judgment seat. Written in 1539, this excerpt from "The Reply to Sadoleto" offers a glimpse of both the believer's struggle and the pastor's obligation, as the young reformer felt and argued them. Several letters to his close friends, Farel and Viret, follow. One was written in 1540, as he turned back to the task of being pastor of Geneva, despite his human reluctance to reenter the scene of conflict from which he had been exiled only a few years earlier. This allows the reader to overhear Calvin's own quiet and almost matter-of-fact acknowledgment of God's claim on him. Two more very private letters from April 1549 describe for his friends his wife's death, and the faith and anguish of that grief, along with his appreciation for the support of friends and his determination to continue his ministry as best possible.

JOHN CALVIN

The last selection of Part One comes from Calvin's one famous public autobiographical statement in the preface to his commentary on his beloved psalms. Dated 1557, probably some twenty-three or four years after he became a "follower of the gospel" and more than twenty years after his arrival in Geneva, this tells the story of his youth, conversion, pastoral call, and the trials of his ministry. It also opens a window on Calvin's intensely personal love for and appropriation of the psalms—those songs inspired by the Holy Spirit and belonging to the whole church, which give expression to all the feelings of the human heart and provide words to voice the soul's cries of praise and pain. (Further reading in the commentary and sermons on the psalms is suggested for those who would like to hear the reformer praying "with pen in hand.") However little Calvin wanted to parade his personal religious experience, these glimpses of his own relationship with God can prepare modern readers to hear the reformer's teaching with some appreciation for the pastor's own inner life.

Part Two: In fact, Calvin's pastoral soul and his theology were not two things apart, but different manifestations of his experience of the human relationship with God. The biblical faith must be put into words so that people can know and confess what they experience, so they can teach and minister to others. The preaching of the word is fundamental, but scripture is extensive and has often been misinterpreted; therefore providing a guide, a summary, an explanation of biblical teaching is one of the duties of the preacher-pastor. This summary never replaces the proclamation of scripture, but it is an important servant of the Bible, a means for understanding it. Therefore Part Two gives several brief "definitions of terms" from Calvin's *Institutes of the Christian Religion* (which was first a catechetical writing, and only later a handbook for ministers to read alongside the reformer's biblical commentaries), in order to orient the reader to central points of Calvin's pastoral theology.

The first selection is Calvin's definition of piety. This is set in the context of his introduction to the whole *Institutes,* where he discusses how human beings know God and so can be consciously related to God. "I call 'piety' that reverence joined with love of God which the knowledge of His benefits induces. For until people recognize that they owe everything to God, that they are nourished by His fatherly care, that He is the Author of their every good, that they should seek nothing beyond Him—they will never yield Him willing service. Nay, unless they establish their complete happiness in Him, they will never give themselves truly and sincerely to Him" (1.2.1). For Calvin, piety is the fundamental quality of the human relationship with God when sinners recognize who they are, and who the holy and merciful God is—when they know that all their good and happiness come from God and so they give themselves completely to God and God's service.

The connection between God and human beings is faith, which Calvin discusses in Book Three of the *Institutes*. This is the fulcrum of his theology: the sheer grace of God justifying and regenerating human beings. Faith gives to each one the personal certainty of God's good will, because of the truth of the promises in Christ, which the Holy Spirit impresses on the hearts and minds of believers (see 3.2.7). Calvin's great pastoral goal was to bring peace to troubled hearts, to preach God's acceptance of sinners. Book Three, the work of the Holy Spirit, is the devotional center of his thought, where he treats prayer ("the chief exercise of piety") in its public and private forms, as well as other aspects of faith, such as the Christian life. The certitude of faith is clear in each individual heart, but the believer receives faith only within the body of Christ, the church. If the heart of piety, "reverence and love of God," is clearly the work of the Holy Spirit, the ordained earthly instrument for building up that piety is the church. For an adequate orientation to Calvin's piety, his teaching on faith must be paired with his doctrine of the church, Book Three of the *Institutes* with Book Four.

Calvin discusses briefly the church as it is known only to God, the elect throughout space and time, but he gives the great majority of his attention to the church as it is visible on earth. He calls this "the external means or aids by which God invites us into the society of Christ and holds us therein" (the title of Book Four). The church is one manifestation of divine accommodation to the small measure of human capacity: God wills to have the gospel proclaimed to humans by humans. This implies also that, while God may choose to work in other ways, we are bound to the ordained means of preaching and sacraments. Calvin carefully distinguishes between the marks of the church and the marks of Christians. The marks of the church are the pure preaching and hearing of the word and the right administration of the sacraments (4.1.9). These marks indicate where the church becomes visible; they are the infallible signs of God's calling to human beings. Where they are found, one must never separate from that church, however marred it may be in other ways; where they are absent there is no true church. The marks of Christians are confession of the faith, appropriate behavior, and participation in the sacraments. These are the tokens that God has given to enable us to identify "by charitable judgment" the members of the visible church, for the practical purpose of building up God's household in a way which glorifies God (4.1.8). The marks of Christians must be taken with great seriousness; they are all we on earth have to guide our actions regarding the boundaries of the church, but they are also all we need. The church must work to see that its members honor God in their words and deeds, and so it must exercise earthly discipline, but it must not confuse its judgments with God's vision. How well Calvin could keep to this distinction in practice is evident in his letter to Duchess Renée of Ferrara about her son-in-law the Duke of Guise (see pp. 307–13). The duchess complained that her Protestant pastor had identified Guise as one of the reprobate. Calvin knew quite well that the late duke had been one of the greatest persecutors of Protestants in France, and he was deeply distressed by the man's destructive actions, yet he did not share his colleague's judgment; he refused to pronounce on the persecutor's eternal state.

Part Three: The marks of the church—preaching the word and administering the sacraments—are, for Calvin, both the proclamation of the gospel for God's honor and human salvation, and the chief means of building up the people of God in piety. Part Three therefore sets out some of the major features of the public worship of the faithful: their praise and prayer, the preaching and sacraments ministered through the pastors, the teaching and confession of the faith. The first section treats Calvin's use of the psalms, primarily in public worship but also as they rightly and necessarily sing through every aspect of the believer's life. Included here are both some of his own psalms translations and his foreword to the psalter.

The second section invites the reader to share aspects of two Sundays in the life of a devout Genevan, the week before and the day of the celebration of the Lord's supper. The first Sunday outlines the four regular services held in Geneva. It begins with a description of the usual dawn service, which was normally a Liturgy of the Word, although on supper Sundays it included that sacrament. This was one popular time for baptism, which in Calvin's theology was never a private liturgy but had to be celebrated in the presence of the gathered community at a Service of the Word. Baptisms were also frequently held at Sunday catechism and weekday preaching services, and less often at the other Sunday services. The second service of the day, the main Sunday morning weekly Liturgy of the Word, is then outlined, taking note of some of the features that were specific to a day when the Lord's supper was not celebrated. Then comes an introduction to the third service of the day, the regular Genevan catechism held at noon, which was usually a time of teaching. Four times a year, however, on the Sundays before the supper was to be celebrated, there was a public examination of those deemed ready to give their own account of the faith in which they had been baptized. Here is presented the series of short questions-and-answers that was used to test the children's knowledge before they were admitted to the Lord's supper for the first time. The fourth and last service of the day was the regular Sunday afternoon preaching service, which was usually a popular time for weddings.[16] However, often the sermon at this service on the week before the Lord's supper included a brief exhortation in preparation for the supper. Various considerations, including space constraints, prevent a presentation of this service. Therefore the outline of the Sunday before the supper is followed by a brief excerpt from Calvin's 1541 "Short Treatise on the Lord's Supper." This text supplements the children's catechetical examination with a fuller picture of the kind of religious counsel that Calvin considered appropriate to guide those who might have problems of conscience, or other pastoral or theological issues that needed to be resolved before they came to the sacrament. The final entry in this section is the presentation of the next week's main Sunday morning service with the Lord's supper, giving the texts for the full service, including a sermon preached at the supper service on Easter Day in 1560.

A new elevation of Sunday worship and considerable revision of the liturgical calendar were common to all Protestants. Reformed Churches carried this further than some others, dropping not only saints' days but also most of the traditional christological cycle, especially such seasons as Advent and Lent. Many Reformed, including Geneva under the influence of Zwinglian Bern, retained six holy days: Christmas (December 25), Circumcision (January 1), Annunciation (March 25), Easter, Ascension, and Pentecost. Calvin objected to the observance of these days in the old manner; by 1550 Geneva had dropped Circumcision and Annunciation, and it celebrated Christmas and Ascension, as well as Easter and Pentecost, on Sundays. This "drastic simplification...with regard to time"[17] has drawn considerable criticism, but it is important to note what Calvin put in the place of the old system. It is clear that his revision of the traditional calendar did not mean any lessening of his sense of the importance of salvation history. In 1544 Geneva reestablished one rather traditional feature of the old calendar, a special series of sermons on the passion each year during the week before Easter, and Calvin preached at these services. One of these sermons is translated below, in the fourth section of Part Three, although without the full context of the daily liturgy that surrounded it. However, the special sermons on the passion were only one, and possibly the less important evidence for Calvin's particular sensitivity to salvation history. More significant is the language of his daily prayers. A reading of these demonstrates that for Calvin the passion and death of Christ should be remembered every day, and the hope of eternal life born of Christ's resurrection should light each day's journey through this world.[18] And so, it may be said that while Calvin revised the traditional observance of the liturgical year in a more extreme fashion than most of his fellow Protestants, and thus elevated Sunday even more highly as *the* holy day, he clearly retained the central importance of Easter and gave constant attention to the primary events of salvation history. He also reestablished the real significance of daily worship and developed a new structure for giving shape to that new sense of liturgical time.

The third section of Part Three guides the reader through basic aspects of weekday worship in Geneva. Given the weight he accorded to Sunday, Calvin has sometimes been interpreted as being Sabbatarian, but in fact he did not regard the literal interpretation of the Sabbath law as binding on Christians. Instead, for Christians all time belongs to God; every day is holy and should in principle be spent in praise of the Lord. Nonetheless, by God's generous accommodation, one day out of seven is all that must be kept free of work for worship, while six days were given to creatures (animals as well as humans) for work.[19] Work is good, a way of honoring God, but even on workdays the faithful are called to begin the day with worship, and in Geneva every day was provided with at least one service of prayer and preaching. From the beginning these services were held in two parish churches and later, as the population expanded and more parishes were added, services were begun in several more places throughout the city. Thus the first service to be presented here is the regular daily preaching service. Since baptisms were frequently celebrated at this early morning Service of the Word, Calvin's baptismal liturgy is set in the context of a weekday liturgy, complete with a sermon.[20]

The second weekday service to be presented is the Day of Prayer, a distinctively Reformed creation characteristic of Strasbourg and Geneva in particular. The establishment of this Day of Prayer for repentance and intercession, and sometimes for thanksgiving, was based on the initiative of Martin Bucer in Strasbourg during Calvin's sojourn there. Various churches adapted this practice, but Calvin seems to have developed it in specific ways and integrated it consistently into his understanding of liturgical time. The Day of Prayer, which in Geneva was set on Wednesdays, was marked by a special liturgy and the congregational singing of psalms (otherwise reserved for Sundays). On this day services were held at two different times, so that, in an age when a household might need to attend worship in relays because of domestic responsibilities, no one would be excluded from the Day of Prayer for practical reasons. Under Calvin's influence, in honor of this liturgy Wednesday also came to be accorded the status of a half-holiday, the only weekday when work was delayed until after worship.

When the Day of Prayer service was introduced in Geneva, Calvin wrote an explanatory preface, based on scripture, that reveals something of how worship and theology are related for Calvin. Particularly prominent are the doctrines of providence and mutual love among Christians. The primary theme of the preface is repentance. The Bible teaches that God uses chastisements like war and pestilence to call stubborn and blind hearts back to God's way, and so Christians must learn to read the signs of their instruction. The Day of Prayer invites and exhorts believers to be alert, to look for God's acting every day and in "ordinary" history (current events). It is in the happenings of daily life that one also sees God's mercies, and the faithful are given new reasons to praise and thank the Lord. The other theme of the Day of Prayer, intercession, goes hand in hand with this sense of God's immediate presence in each day's story. Awareness of being linked with other members of the body of Christ, near or far, is deeply rooted in Calvin's corporate understanding of the faith; therefore, petition for those in need is always a central theme of prayer. His concern for intercession is evident in the prayers of his Sunday and regular weekday services, but it receives particular attention on the Day of Prayer. Christians are commanded to pray for one another, and they should always be offering concrete intercessions for all who are tried by any afflictions of spirit, mind, or body, for all who suffer in the here and now.

This brief summary cannot do justice to the Day of Prayer. It is important to note, however, that this liturgy contributes a significant dimension to the understanding of Calvin's sense of religious time and the practice of piety. It supports the hypothesis that his revision of the calendar does not mean that he lacked a sense of liturgical time, but rather suggests that he had a somewhat different and less traditional perspective on it than some of his fellow reformers. This is not the place for a full discussion of that theory,[21] but it is worth pointing out that the whole weekday worship program and especially the Day of Prayer liturgy fit very coherently with prominent aspects of Calvin's theology, and vice versa. Both prayers and teaching manifest the Reformed tradition's focus on God's immediate presence in history. For Calvin, God is acting for us now, in this time and place, and, if only they will open their eyes, God's children may see that unfailing presence for their salvation and their consolation. And God's care extends beyond the visible congregation. Christians know they are only one part of a greater company of the faithful, who are obligated at least to watch and pray for one another even when they cannot give more concrete assistance. Thus the Day of Prayer reminds them to keep alert to see God acting not only for themselves but also for other members of Christ's body, in order to intercede for their needs and to offer thanks for their deliverance.

Part Four: The themes of Calvin's theology and piety are perhaps most simply expressed in his prayers, of which a selection are gathered here in Part Four. Prayer is for Calvin "the chief exercise of piety." Prayer is, in a literal sense, fundamental to all religious life. Calvin gives an extended discussion of the character of prayer in chapter 20 of the *Institutes,* touching on private and public, spoken, sung, and silent prayers. The teaching is only the tip of the iceberg of the practice that permeated every day of the pastor's life. Calvin seems to have accompanied almost every public act with prayer, and many of those words of praise and petition were recorded. The Lord's Prayer is of course the model prayer for Christians; Calvin recited it and paraphrased it in his liturgy, explained it in his catechism, and taught about it in the *Institutes,* from which the present excerpt is drawn. Biblical texts are the pattern for all praying; Christians are to be guided by the form of the Lord's Prayer, and they say and sing the psalms. However, they are not bound only to these words, as long as they follow their sense; thus Calvin himself wrote other prayers and prayed extemporaneously on many occasions.

Although most of his formal prayers were written for public worship, Calvin also provided some model prayers for individual or domestic use. These were appended to his catechism or liturgy and offered words for the child or adult or family in its daily devotional life. Most of these prayers were related to events or moments in ordinary life. Christians should pray without ceasing, but they should also stop at intervals throughout the day to pray for specific reasons: a morning thanksgiving for rest and the new day, which they commit into God's hands, thanksgivings before and after meals, petitions for guidance in daily work or school, and evening prayers to close the day. Like others, Calvin also recognized that there were special situations some people might face, for which words of prayer would be needed. Responding to the increasing confessional struggles all around him, but especially in France, Calvin appended to his liturgy a prayer for captives that also identifies with them. Prayers for times of day were common, both to the tradition and among Protestants, but Calvin's prayer for captives was somewhat unusual in the liturgy of an established church. The combination of confession of sin and petition for deliverance picks up the themes of the Day of Prayer; and the sense of present history as the place where God's action can and will be seen, and where human actors are called to be God's instruments, comes through clearly. This prayer also echoes Calvin's own lifelong awareness of being part of a church that lives under the cross.

Calvin began and ended every exposition of scripture with a prayer. The opening prayer for his sermons was the same each day, and the long concluding prayer also had a regular form, either published in the liturgy for Sunday mornings and Day of Prayer services, or unpublished. These texts are found in the services printed in Part Three. However, between a fixed initial phrase and the long concluding prayer, Calvin inserted a paragraph that reflected the text of the sermon. A selection of those sermon-specific prayers is translated here and may give some sense of the preacher's consistency and the range of his concerns. The prayers include, along with the regular acknowledgment of sin and petition for forgiveness, varied other themes: the wonder and gift of being united with Christ, expressions of confidence in God's grace and longing to join in the angels' eternal song, reminders of the obligation to love the neighbor, and even petition that God's children might so witness that all people on earth would be drawn to the faith and share in God's praise. The sermon prayers were copied down along with the sermons. Sixteenth-century publications include these texts, but most later printings have dropped them, and finding the prayers that Genevans heard from the pulpit requires effort, so the collection here attempts to give a representative selection.

Calvin also began and concluded his biblical lectures with prayer. The opening brief words were the same each day, the final prayer echoed the day's text. These prayers were dropped when Calvin reworked the lectures as commentaries, so prayers exist only for most of the Old Testament prophets, the books that remained in lecture form. Most modern printings omit these prayers. However, English-language readers are fortunate to have them easily available in the appropriate commentaries, as translated by the Calvin Translation Society in the nineteenth century; therefore only a small selection of these prayers is presented here.

Part Five: Prayer underlies all of life, and the piety articulated in prayer should also be expressed in daily living. Part Five follows Calvin out of the sanctuary into the world, to see how the piety given voice in the psalter and liturgy and sermon and prayer becomes embodied in action. The first section explores some facets of the Christian life according to Calvin, beginning with his teaching about the law. For Calvin, the law in its third and principal use is the pattern for regenerate life. No longer condemning those justified by faith, the law—summarized in the Golden Rule, set out more fully in the Decalogue—offers to the faithful a help in discerning God's will, a guide to what it should

31

look like to live as a child of God and member of Christ's body. The first great commandment and the first table of the Decalogue express what the devout person owes to God; the second great commandment and the second table of the law add the corollary of what reverence for God implies for the conduct of human society. Calvin's second sermon on the Sabbath illustrates how this law serves as a bridge between the two tables. The commandment to keep the Sabbath (which is found in the first table of the law and therefore directed to God, but which also requires rest for the whole household) points to the consequences of the relationship with God for life in the human community. To give rest to servants and domestic animals is not intrinsic to the worship of God, but it is an addition that God has made for human benefit; thus it looks to the same ends as the second table of the law. Following this sermon on the Sabbath are excerpts from Calvin's discussion of several commandments from the second table of the law. These illustrate how he reads the negative strictures as positive and all-encompassing, and so interprets them—in a remarkably imaginative way—as guides to love in action. For example, not to kill means to give my neighbor's life all the help I can; not to bear false witness includes not passing on or even listening to gossip, or telling jokes that hurt other people. Here piety, the right reverence and love for God, leads to full acknowledgment of God's claim, which includes conforming our lives to the way God wills for God's people to treat the rest of the creation.

If the Decalogue provides Calvin's corporate ethics, his counsel on living the Christian life adds a sensitive and surprisingly appealing little treatise on spiritual direction. Although he does not make explicitly personal remarks, it is clear that Calvin's words do not come from a pastor who has never felt the doubts and trials of life, but from one who is passing on what he has himself experienced. An earlier form of these chapters of Book Three of the *Institutes* was the first part of that text to be published separately in English, as *The Life and Communicacion of a Christen Man* (1549). This little treatise lives up to its purpose as a guide to the spiritual life...so long as the reader is prepared to recognize that

Calvin would not consider "being comfortable" a spiritual goal worthy of Christians. Christ's life was not comfortable, and Christians are engrafted into Christ's body, so they must be prepared for the cross, as well as ready to learn right appreciation for the earthly blessings God continues to bestow amid the trials of this pilgrimage. Meaning and purpose ring through these pages, where Calvin's convictions about the human relationship with God are expressed like a clarion call: "We are not our own....We are God's!" (3.7.1) All else follows from that.

The second section of Part Five accompanies Christians, pastors and people, through some of the major crises of life, showing how the fact of belonging to God manifests itself in day-to-day living: piety in practice. Sickness and death are the most universal human crises. Calvin's liturgy gives instructions for pastors visiting the sick. Interestingly enough, his church order, the *Ecclesiastical Ordinances,* adds instructions to the sick and their families with regard to seeking pastoral care and doing it in a timely fashion; all must work together in the body of Christ. Although it is probably often forgotten, Calvin was present at many sickbeds and deathbeds. The record of some of those times is preserved in letters that he then wrote to the bereaved, in which the reader catches a glimpse of faith in the valley of the shadow, looking toward the light of the resurrection. Besides illness and death, pastors and people alike face other challenges in the Christian life. A few of Calvin's many letters of personal counsel suggest the way he offered sympathy—always linked with exhortation. He takes individual trials very seriously, but he also helps the afflicted persons to put their suffering in a larger perspective, reminding them of their power and their call to serve God even in the midst of earthly troubles. Here, too, one sees the pastor taking comfort from his correspondents, promising prayer but also requesting it, prayer being a mutual expression of love that no distance can hinder.

The last series of letters provides evidence both of Calvin's pastoral counsel and of his energetic efforts for practical relief for the suffering. Calvin believed it was his duty, the duty of Christians, to seek any earthly aid possible for those persecuted or exiled or suffering affliction. Consequently, he made journeys and wrote letters and exhorted governments and church leaders to intercede for those imprisoned or oppressed or homeless and destitute. Using all legitimate means at hand is part of a Christian's duty, but the failure of earthly means does not limit God. Calvin also wrote to Protestants in prison, seeking to share their suffering as well as to exhort them. He would offer counsel or answers to their questions, but he also encouraged those facing martyrdom, and did so with a rare humility. Even when the prisoners of Lyons requested that he polish up the accounts that they wrote of their trials, Calvin refused, because he believed their words as written were more powerful than anything he could add. He expressed his deep respect for the power of the women imprisoned in Paris to witness to their captors and the church by their steadfast faith. He reminds them how astonished their persecutors are when women as well as men, artisans as well as nobility, can answer for their faith: the power to witness is not limited by earthly condition.

These few selections cannot give voice to the full range of Calvin's pastoral piety, but they may offer an introduction to the varied expressions of his personal religious experience and his teaching. They can also perhaps suggest something of the intensity and practicality, the biblical and all-encompassing character, the active and social manifestations, of this piety—a piety that reshaped religious life in the city of Calvin's exile and made it a "school of Christ" for many people who never met the pastor of Geneva.[22] So what was Calvin's pastoral piety? Intensely personal but never individualistic. Woven through with the great doctrines of justification by faith and regeneration of life, the glory of God and providence. Undergirded with prayer, proclaimed in word and shared in sacraments, sung in psalms. Embodied in action and demanding respect for the neighbor and solidarity with those who suffer in spirit, mind, or body. Not an easy or comfortable piety; it asks for one's all. Sturdy and down to earth, lived in the mundane context of daily work, yet always conscious of the presence of the transcendent God and the high calling of living before God. An energizing, lifelong response to God's liberating claim, God's righteous mercy, God's compelling love, a belonging that is all our joy. "We are not our own....We are God's!"

A WORD ABOUT TRANSLATIONS

The translations used in this volume are drawn from a number of sources. Some have been printed before, others have been newly made for this book; the translator of each text is indicated in the note at the beginning of the individual section or work. All translations by other authors have been collated with the original Latin or French; they are used with permission or acknowledgment, including permission to make such minor alterations as seemed necessary. Most of these changes are stylistic, intended to give the texts a coherent appearance.

Several practices should be noted. First, all second person singular forms of address for God (the traditional "Thee/Thou") have been translated as or changed to the more common "You" forms, partly because this is more natural in contemporary speech, partly also to facilitate reading. Second, pronouns for God have been consistently capitalized, in order to distinguish them from references to creatures. Calvin commonly uses "he" for both, in the same sentence; in a number of cases only context indicates whether God or a human being is meant, and without "He" for God, on first reading it is sometimes not clear who is acting. Third, as much as possible the words for human beings have been translated as "person/people" or occasionally the adjective "human," when it is clear that Calvin intends to include all people. This was already the occasional practice of some translators, for example, J. K. S. Reid and Benjamin Farley. However, F. L. Battles sometimes introduces the words "man/men/mankind" where Calvin's French or Latin does not in fact require that (e.g., *"tous"/"l'inique"/"le pauvre"/"justis"/"humanum genus"*), thus weighting Calvin's words in translation with a greater gender-specific impression than his original. Calvin's language is, of course, male oriented, and there is no intention of hiding that; therefore the pronouns have been left in the masculine ("the person"—"he"), since Calvin would have intended that. In addition, *pietas* has been consistently translated as "piety," to give the English reader a sense of Calvin's usage.

The reader should also note that introductory material provided in the various sections and subsections is set differently than the translated texts themselves. This was done in order to make them distinct from one another and to ensure that the exact nature of the material was clear to the reader. In addition, readers may notice that the use of quotation marks for cited material from scripture and other sources is not consistent. Those passages translated into English from the original sources specifically for this volume conform to contemporary standard style, that is, quotation marks are used to set off cited material. However, in the case of translation extracts taken from other English-language sources and included in this volume, the style used in the English-language originals is simply replicated here, and thus the reader will find that in those extracts citations from scripture and other sources sometimes appear in italics. The translations made for this volume also use quotation marks around "imagined" dialogue, which Calvin includes in some sermons, in order to clarify the nature of the exchanges for the reader.

Finally, the reader will note, especially in the liturgy sections, several distinct stylistic strategies meant to clarify the sources of different pieces of information:

- Words implied in the translation or necessary to make it clear to whom a pronoun refers (in the sermons, for example) are set in brackets.

- Words that are underlined but not set within brackets are editorial additions that are expressed in Calvin's texts or implied by the context. Calvin used rubrics sparingly, and though some of this language is his, some parts are my editorial summaries or additions. For example, Calvin speaks of the "Confession" when he means the "confession of sin"; he says where the first psalm is located in the Sunday liturgy, but the later instructions about where

36

psalms are sung come from rubrics in the psalter. Other headings (e.g., "Invocation," "Prayer") are my additions, implied by the text but not explicit.

• Words set within brackets as well as underlined and italicized are editorial additions drawn from other sources (not Calvin's own writings) meant to clarify the texts, especially liturgical texts. In some cases the information augments Calvin's own directives, which have been left in roman type.

In summary, the purpose of shaping these translations is to provide a coherent and accessible volume of texts for the modern reader. This requires finding a balance which, on the one hand, does not make Calvin speak in twenty-first century idiom, but which also, on the other, avoids creating unnecessary stumbling blocks for modern readers. A final point: Calvin's text is full of biblical language, but here usually only explicit citations are identified, since to include all the allusions would expand the text beyond the acceptable limits for this volume.

PART ONE:

AN AUTOBIOGRAPHICAL INTRODUCTION TO JOHN CALVIN

*J*ohn Calvin was a very reticent person and rarely spoke publicly of his own feelings. On some occasions, however, his personal experience of faith and conversion and calling, the depths of his prayer life and his personal sorrows, were shared either with close friends or with the larger community of the church. Here are presented, in chronological order, some of the most revealing statements Calvin himself made about his faith and piety. Covering practically the whole of his life as a pastor, the texts include an early defense of his ministry and break with Rome, some personal letters written to close friends at particular times of special crisis in his life, and his one major public autobiographical statement, published late in his life.

Section I:
"The Reply to Sadoleto,"
1539

In March 1539, Cardinal Jacopo Sadoleto, the highest ranking Roman Catholic priest in the neighborhood of Geneva, wrote to the city which had exiled Farel and Calvin. His pastoral letter, which was intended to draw them back from heresy to allegiance to Rome, included a sketch of the kind of justification he thought Calvin and his colleagues would make before God's judgment seat for their acts in leaving Rome. The leaders of Geneva concluded that they had no one capable of answering Sadoleto's letter, so they sent it to Calvin in Strasbourg with a request that he reply. In the course of his answer, Calvin defended his calling and faith by sketching why he had felt compelled to do as he had, both as a minister and as a Christian believer, responding to what he regarded as Sadoleto's caricature with the same kind of first-person speech the cardinal had used. This is not strictly an autobiographical statement, but it is very illuminating for the kinds of experiences and convictions that led Calvin himself to break with Rome. The original from which this excerpt is taken is in OS 1, pp. 457–89; the translation is by J. K. S. Reid.

But since toward the end a person has been introduced to plead our cause, and you have cited us as defenders to the tribunal of God, I have no hesitation in calling upon you to meet me there. For such is our consciousness of the truth of our doctrine, that it has no dread of the heavenly Judge, from whom we do not doubt that it proceeded. But it dwells not on those frivolities with which it has pleased you to amuse yourself, but which are certainly very much out of place. For what could be more inopportune than to come into the presence of God, and to set about devising I know not what follies, and framing for us an absurd defense which must immediately fail? In pious minds, whenever that day is suggested,

41

the impression made is too solemn to leave them at leisure so to amuse themselves. Therefore, frivolity set aside, let us think of that day which human minds ought always to expect with suspense. And let us remember that, while desirable to the faithful, it may well be alarming to the ungodly and profane and those who despise God. Let us turn our ears to the sound of that trumpet which even the ashes of the dead will hear in their tombs. Let us direct our thoughts and minds to that Judge who, by the mere brightness of His countenance, will disclose whatever lurks in darkness, lay open all the secrets of the human heart, and crush all the wicked by the mere breath of His mouth. Consider now what serious answer you are to make for yourself and your party; our cause, supported as it is by the truth of God, will be at no loss for a complete defense. I speak not of our persons, whose safety will be found not in defense, but in humble confession and suppliant petition; but insofar as our ministry is concerned, there is none of us who will not be able to speak for himself as follows.

Defense of his ministry

"O Lord, I have indeed experienced how difficult and grievous it is to bear the invidious accusations with which I was harassed on the earth; but with the same confidence with which I then appealed to Your tribunal, I now appear before You, for I know that in Your judgment truth reigns. Supported by confidence in this truth, I first dared to attempt, and assisted by it I was able to accomplish, whatever was achieved by me in Your church. They charged me with two of the worst of crimes, heresy and schism. The heresy was that I dared to protest against dogmas received by them.

But what could I have done? I heard from Your mouth that there was no other light of truth which could direct our souls into the way of life, than that which was kindled by Your word. I heard that whatever human minds of themselves conceive concerning Your majesty, the worship of Your deity, and the mysteries of Your religion, was vanity. I heard that their introduction into the church of doctrines sprung from the human brain in place of Your word was sacrilegious presumption. But when I turned my eyes toward the people, I saw very different principles prevailing.

42

Those who were regarded as the leaders of faith neither understood Your word, nor greatly cared for it. They only drove unhappy people about with strange doctrines, and deluded them with I know not what follies. Among the people themselves, the highest veneration paid to Your word was to revere it at a distance as something inaccessible, and abstain from all investigation of it. Owing to the supine dullness of the pastors and the stupidity of the people, every place was filled with pernicious errors, falsehoods, and superstition. They indeed called You the only God, but they did so while transferring to others the glory which You claimed for Your majesty. They imagined for themselves and esteemed as many gods as they had saints to worship. Your Christ was indeed worshiped as God and retained the name of Savior; but where He ought to have been honored, He was left almost destitute of glory. For, spoiled of His own virtue, He passed unnoticed among the crowd of saints, like one of the meanest of them. There was no one who duly considered that one sacrifice which He offered to You on the cross, and by which He reconciled us to Yourself; no one who ever dreamed of thinking of His eternal priesthood, and the intercession depending on it; no one who trusted in His righteousness only. That confident hope of salvation, which is both enjoined by Your word and founded upon it, had almost vanished. Indeed it was received as a kind of oracle; it was foolish arrogance, and, as they said, presumption, for anyone to trust in Your goodness and the righteousness of Your Son, and entertain a sure and unfaltering hope of salvation. These were so many profane opinions which, though they were the first principles of that doctrine which You delivered to us in Your word, they plucked up by the roots.

The true meaning of baptism and the Lord's supper also was corrupted by numerous falsehoods. And then, when everybody, gravely affronting Your mercy, put confidence in good works, when by good works they strove to merit Your favor, to procure justification, to expiate their sins, and make satisfaction to You (each of these things obliterating and emptying the virtue of Christ's cross), they were yet quite ignorant in what good works consisted. For just as if they were not at all instructed in righteousness by Your law, they had fabricated for themselves many useless trivialities as a means of procuring Your favor, and on these they so prided themselves, that in comparison with them they almost scorned the standard of true righteousness which Your law commended: to such a degree had human desires usurped the ascendancy and derogated, if not from the belief, at least from the authority, of Your precepts contained in it.

"That I might perceive these things, You, O Lord, shone upon me with the brightness of Your Spirit; that I might comprehend how impious and harmful they were, You bore before me the torch of Your word; that I might abominate them as they deserved, You disturbed my soul. But in rendering an account of my doctrine, You see what my own conscience declares, that it was not my intention to stray beyond those limits which I saw had been fixed for all Your servants. Whatever I did not doubt I had learned from Your mouth, I desired to dispense faithfully to the church. Assuredly the thing at which I chiefly aimed, and for which I most diligently labored, was that the glory of Your goodness and justice should disperse the mists by which it was formerly obscured, and might shine forth conspicuously, that the virtue and blessings of Your Christ, all disguises being brushed aside, might be fully displayed. For I thought it impious to leave in obscurity things which we were born to ponder and meditate. Nor did I think that truths, whose magnitude no language can express, were to be maliciously or falsely declared. I hesitated not to dwell at greater length on topics on which the salvation of my hearers depended. For the oracle could never deceive which declares (John 17:3): 'This is eternal life, to know You the only true God, and Jesus Christ, whom You have sent.'

"As to the charge of forsaking the church, which they are accustomed to bring against me, there is nothing here of which my conscience accuses me, unless indeed he is to be considered a deserter who, seeing the soldiers routed and scattered and abandoning the ranks, raises the leader's standard, and recalls them to their posts. For thus, O Lord, were all Your servants dispersed, so that they could not by any possibility hear the command, but had almost forgotten their leader, their service, and their military vow. To bring them together when thus scattered, I raised, not a foreign standard, but that noble banner of Yours which we must follow, if we would be classed among Your people.

"Then I was assailed by those who, when they ought to have kept others in their ranks, had led them astray, and when I would not at all desist they opposed me with violence. On this grievous tumults arose, and the contest flared up into disruption. Who was to blame it is for You, O Lord, to decide. Always, both by word and deed, have I protested how eager I was for unity. Mine, however, was a unity of the church which should begin with You and end in You. For whenever You recommended to us peace and concord, at the same time You showed Yourself to be the only bond for preserving it. But if I desired to be at peace with those who boasted of being the heads of the church and the pillars of faith, I had to purchase it with the denial of Your truth. I thought that anything was to be endured rather than stoop to such an execrable accommodation. For Your Christ Himself declared that, though heaven and earth should be confounded, yet Your word must endure for ever (Matt 24:35). Nor did I think that I dissented from Your church, because I was at war with those leaders. For You forewarned us both by Your Son and by the apostles that into that place there would rise persons to whom I ought by no means to consent. Christ predicted not of strangers, but of those who should pass themselves off as pastors, that they would be ravenous wolves and false prophets, and at the same time warned us to beware of them (Matt 7:15). Where Christ ordered me to beware, was I to lend my aid? And the apostles declared that there would be no enemies of Your church more pestilential than those from within, who should conceal themselves under the title of pastors (Acts 20:29; 2 Pet 2:1; 1 John 2:18). Why should I have hesitated to separate myself from persons whom they forewarned me to hold as enemies? I had before my eyes the examples of Your prophets who, I saw, had a similar contest with the priests and prophets of their day, though these were undoubtedly the rulers of the church among the Israelite people. But Your prophets are not regarded as schismatics because, when they wished to revive religion which had fallen into decay, they did not desist although opposed with the utmost violence. They still remained in the unity of the church, though they were execrated with awful curses by wicked priests, and thought unworthy of a place among people, not to say saints. Confirmed by their example, I too persisted. Though denounced as a deserter of the church and threatened, I was in no respect deterred or induced to proceed less firmly and boldly in opposing those who, in the character of pastors, wasted Your church more than any impious tyranny. My conscience told me how strong the zeal was with which I burned for the unity of Your church, provided Your truth were made the bond of concord. As the tumults which followed were not excited by me, so there is no ground for imputing them to me.

"O Lord, You know, and the fact has testified itself to others, that the only thing I asked was that all controversies should be decided by Your word, that thus both parties might unite with one mind to establish Your kingdom; and I declined not to restore peace to the church at the expense of my head, if I were found to be the cause of needless disturbance. But what did our opponents do? Did they not forthwith furiously fly to fires, swords, and gibbets? Did they not decide that their only security was in arms and cruelty? Did they not instigate all ranks to the same fury? Did they not spurn all methods of pacification? Thus it happens that a matter, which might at one time have been settled amicably, has blazed up into such a conflict. But although amid the great confusion human judgments were various, I am freed from all fear now that we stand at Your tribunal, where equity combined with truth cannot but decide in favor of innocence."

This, Sadoleto, is our plea, not the fictitious one which you, in order to aggravate our case, were pleased to devise, but one whose perfect truth is known to the good even now; and will be made manifest to all creatures on that day. Nor will those who, instructed by our preaching, have come over to our cause, be at a loss what to say for themselves, since each will have ready a defense like this.

Defense of a (Protestant) believer for breaking with Rome

"I, O Lord, as I had been educated from childhood, always professed the Christian faith. But at first I had no other reason for my faith than that which at the time everywhere prevailed.

Your word, which ought to have shone on all Your people like a lamp, was for us taken away or at least suppressed. Lest anyone should long for greater light, an idea had been planted in the minds of all, that the investigation of that hidden celestial philosophy was better delegated to a few, whom the others might consult as oracles; for plebeian minds no higher knowledge was proper than to submit themselves to obedience to the church. Now the rudiments in which I had been instructed were of a kind which could neither properly train me to the right worship of Your divinity, nor pave my way to a sure hope of salvation, nor train me aright for the duties of a Christian life. I had learned, indeed, to worship You alone as my God, but, as the true method of worshiping was altogether unknown to me, I stumbled at the very threshold. I believed, as I had been taught, that I was redeemed by the death of Your Son from liability to eternal death, but the redemption I thought of was one whose virtue could never reach me. I expected a future day of resurrection, but hated to think of it, as a most dreadful event. This feeling not only had dominion over me in private, but was derived from the doctrine which was then uniformly delivered to Christian people by their teachers. They indeed preached of Your clemency, but only toward those people who should show themselves worthy. Moreover they put this value on the righteousness of works, that only he was received into Your favor who reconciled himself to You by works. At the same time they did not disguise the fact that we are miserable sinners, that we often fall through infirmity of the flesh, and that to all, therefore, Your mercy must be the common haven of salvation. But the method of obtaining it which they pointed out was by making satisfaction to You for offenses. Then satisfaction was enjoined upon us: first, that after confessing all our sins to a priest, we suppliantly ask pardon and absolution; and second, that by good deeds we efface from Your remembrance our bad [ones]; lastly, that in order to supply what was still wanting, we add sacrifices and solemn expiations. Then, because You are a stern judge and strict avenger of iniquity, they showed how dreadful Your presence must be. Hence they bade us flee first to the saints, that by their intercession You might be easily entreated and made propitious toward us.

"When, however, I had performed all these things, though I had some intervals of quiet, I was still far from true peace of conscience. For whenever I descended into myself or raised my mind to You, extreme terror seized me which no expiations or satisfactions could cure. The more closely I examined myself, the sharper the stings with which my conscience was pricked; so that the only solace which remained was to delude myself by obliviousness. Yet as nothing better offered, I was pursuing the course which I had begun, when a very different form of doctrine started up, not one which led us away from the Christian profession, but one which brought it back to its source and, as it were, clearing away the dregs, restored it to its original purity. Offended by the novelty, I lent an unwilling ear, and at first, I confess, strenuously and passionately resisted. Such is the firmness or effrontery with which people naturally persist in the course they have once undertaken, that it was with the greatest difficulty I was induced to confess that I had all my life long been in ignorance and error. One thing in particular made me averse to those new teachers, namely reverence for the church. But when once I opened my ears and allowed myself to be taught, I perceived that this fear of derogating from the majesty of the church was groundless. For they reminded me how great the difference is between schism from the church, and studying to correct the faults by which the church herself is contaminated. They spoke nobly of the church and showed the greatest desire to cultivate unity. Lest it should seem they quibbled on the term church, they showed it was no new thing for Antichrists to preside there in place of pastors. Of this they produced several examples, from which it appeared that they aimed at nothing but the edification of the church, and in that respect made common cause with many of Christ's servants whom we ourselves included in the catalogue of saints. For, attacking more freely the Roman pontiff, who was reverenced as the vicegerent of Christ, the successor of Peter; and the head of the church, they excused themselves thus: Such titles as these are empty bugbears, by which the eyes of the pious ought not to be so blinded as not to venture to investigate and sift out the reality. It was when the world was plunged in ignorance and weakness as in a deep sleep, that the pope had risen to such an eminence; certainly neither appointed head of the church by the word of God, nor ordained by a legitimate act of the church, but of his own accord and self-elected. Moreover the tyranny which he let loose against the people of God was not to be endured, if we wished to have the kingdom of Christ among us in safety.

"Nor did they lack very powerful arguments to confirm all their positions. First, they clearly disposed of everything that was then commonly adduced to establish the primacy of the pope. When they had taken away all these supports, they also by the word of God tumbled him from his lofty height. As far as the matter allowed, they made it clear and palpable to learned and unlearned that the true order of the church had then perished; that the power of the keys under which the discipline of the church is comprehended had been seriously perverted; that Christian liberty had collapsed; in short, that the kingdom of Christ was prostrated when this primacy was erected. They told me, moreover, as a means of pricking my conscience, that I could not safely connive at these things as if they were no concern of mine; that so far are You from patronizing any voluntary error, that even he who is led astray by mere ignorance does not err with impunity. This they proved by the testimony of Your Son (Matt 15:14): 'If the blind lead the blind, both shall fall into the ditch'. My mind was now prepared for serious attention, and I at length perceived, as if light had broken in upon me, in what a dunghill of error I had wallowed, and how much pollution and impurity I had thereby contracted. Being exceedingly alarmed at the misery into which I had fallen, and much more at that which threatened me in eternal death, as in duty bound I made it my first business to condemn my own past life, not without groans and tears, and to accept Your life. And now, O Lord, what is left for a wretch like me but, instead of defense, earnestly to supplicate You not to judge according to its deserts that fearful abandonment of Your word, from which in Your wondrous goodness You have at last delivered me."

A Letter to Farel Regarding His Call to Return to Geneva, 1540

This letter to William Farel, one of his closest friends, who had shared exile from Geneva with him in 1538, expresses some of Calvin's thoughts when he felt compelled to return to that city (cf. above, pp. 13–14). Central themes are voiced in his words "when I remember that I am not my own, I offer up my heart, presented as a sacrifice to the Lord" and his sense "that it is God with whom I have to do." Here he also indicates his conviction that God can and does direct believers through other human beings. This and all following letters come from Jules Bonnet's collection translated by Marcus Robert Gilchrist.

Bonnet LXXIII.–To FAREL, #248 in OC 11:99–100
  Strasbourg, OC dates as Oct. 1540 [vs. Bonnet Aug. 1541]
When your letter was brought to me, mine was already written; and although you will find that it does not agree in all points to what you require of me [i.e., to return to Geneva], I have thought it best to forward it to you, that you may be aware what my feelings were at the time when it arrived. Now, however, after I have seen you press the matter further, and that our former guests associate openly in the same cause, I have again had recourse to our magistracy. Having read over your letter and those of the Genevese, I asked what in their opinion was now to be done. They answered that there could be no doubt that, without calling any previous meeting, I ought immediately to set out thither; for the question was not now open or doubtful, although it had not been formally settled. Therefore we prepare to start on the journey. In order, however, that the present need of that church may be provided for,

which we are not willing should continue destitute [until I (Calvin) can come], they are of opinion that Viret should by all means be sent for thither, in the meantime, while I am for the present distracted by another charge [in Strasbourg and the colloquies]. When we come back, our friends here will not refuse their consent to my return to Geneva. Moreover, Bucer has pledged himself that he will accompany me. I have written to them to that effect; and in order to make the promise all the more certain, Bucer has accompanied my letter by one from himself.

As to my intended course of proceeding, this is my present feeling: had I the choice at my own disposal, nothing would be less agreeable to me than to follow your advice. But when I remember that I am not my own, I offer up my heart, presented as a sacrifice to the Lord. Therefore there is no ground for your apprehension that you will only get fine words. Our friends are in earnest, and promise sincerely. And for myself, I protest that I have no other desire than that, setting aside all consideration of me, they may look only to what is most for the glory of God and the advantage of the church. Although I am not very ingenious, I would not lack pretexts by which I might adroitly slip away, so that I should easily excuse myself in human sight. I am well aware, however, that it is God with whom I have to do, from whose sight such crafty imaginations cannot be withheld. Therefore I submit my will and my affections, subdued and held fast, to the obedience of God; and whenever I am at a loss for counsel of my own, I submit myself to those by whom I hope that the Lord Himself will speak to me.

When Capito wrote, he supposed, as I perceive, that I would, in a lengthy and tiresome narrative, relate to you the whole course of our deliberation; but it is enough that you have the sum of it; although I would have done that also had there been time. But the whole day was taken up in various avocations. Now, after supper, I am not much inclined by sitting up longer to trifle with my health, which is at best in a doubtful state. This messenger has promised to return here at Christmas with the carriage, in which he can bring along with him to Wendelin, of the books which belong to him, ten copies of the *Institution*, six of [Oecolampadius's] Commentaries on Jeremiah: these you will give to be brought away with him. [CALVIN]

Calvin's Letters About His Wife's Death, 1549

Calvin has often been pictured as a very cold man. The letters about the death of his wife, Idelette de Bure, written to two of his closest friends, reveal a man of deep feeling who was convinced that the highest praise he could give her was to honor their shared devotion to God; he regarded his wife as "the best companion of my life" and one who shared his work as "the faithful helper of my ministry."

Bonnet CCXXXIX.–To FAREL. #1171 in OC 13:228–29

Geneva, 2 April 1549. [dating from OC; vs. Bonnet 11 April] Intelligence of my wife's death has perhaps reached you before now. I do what I can to keep myself from being overwhelmed with grief. My friends also leave nothing undone that may administer relief to my mental suffering. When your brother left, her life was all but despaired of.

When the brethren were assembled on Tuesday they thought it best that we should join together in prayer. This was done. When Abel [Poupin] in the name of the rest exhorted her to faith and patience, she briefly (for she was now greatly worn) stated her frame of mind. I afterwards added an exhortation which seemed to me appropriate to the occasion. And then, as she had made no allusion to her children, I (fearing that restrained by modesty she might be feeling an anxiety concerning them which would cause her greater suffering than the disease itself) declared in the presence of the brethren that I should henceforth care for them as if they were my own. She replied, "I have already committed them to the Lord." When I replied, that that was not to hinder me from doing my part, she immediately answered, "If the Lord shall care for them, I know they will be commended to you." Her magnanimity was so great that she seemed to have already left the world.

About the sixth hour of the day on which she yielded up her soul to the Lord, our brother Bourgoing addressed some pious words to her, and while he was doing so she spoke aloud so that all saw that her heart was raised far above the world. For these were her words: "O glorious resurrection! O God of Abraham and of all our fathers, in You have the faithful trusted during so many past ages, and none of them have trusted in vain. I also will hope." These short sentences were rather ejaculated than distinctly spoken. This did not come from the suggestion of others but from her own reflections, so that she made it obvious in few words what were her own meditations. I had to go out at six o'clock. Having been removed to another apartment after seven, she immediately began to decline. When she felt her voice suddenly failing her she said: "Let us pray, let us pray. All pray for me." I had now returned. She was unable to speak, and her mind seemed to be troubled. I, having spoken a few words about the love of Christ, the hope of eternal life, concerning our married life, and her departure, engaged in prayer. In full possession of her mind, she both heard the prayer and attended to it. Before eight she expired, so calmly that those present could scarcely distinguish between her life and her death. I at present control my sorrow so that my duties may not be interfered with. But in the meanwhile the Lord has sent other trials upon me.

Adieu, brother, and very excellent friend. May the Lord Jesus strengthen you by His Spirit; and may He support me also under this heavy affliction, which would certainly have overcome me had not He who raises up the prostrate, strengthens the weak, and refreshes the weary, stretched forth His hand from heaven to me. Salute all the brethren and your whole family. Yours,

John CALVIN.

Bonnet CCXXXVIIL.–To VIRET. #1173 in CO 13:230–31
Geneva, 7 April 1549
Although the death of my wife has been exceedingly painful to me, yet I subdue my grief as well as I can. Friends also are earnest in their duty to me. I confess that they profit me and themselves less than could be wished, yet I can scarcely say how much I am supported by their attentions. But you know well enough how tender, or rather soft, my mind is. Had not a powerful self-control, therefore, been vouchsafed to me, I could not have borne up so long.

And truly mine is no common source of grief. I have been bereaved of the best companion of my life, of one who, if anything more difficult had befallen me, would not only have been the willing sharer of my exile and indigence, but even of my death. During her life she was the faithful helper of my ministry. From her I never experienced the slightest hindrance. She was never troublesome to me throughout the entire course of her illness; she was more anxious about her children than about herself. As I feared these private cares might annoy her to no purpose, I took occasion, on the third day before her death, to mention that I would not fail in discharging my duty to her children. Taking up the matter immediately, she said, "I have already committed them to God." When I said that that was not to prevent me from caring for them, she replied, "I know you will not neglect what you know has been committed to God." Lately, also, when a certain woman insisted that she [Idelette de Bure] should talk with me regarding these matters, I heard her [my wife] give the following brief answer: "Assuredly the principal thing is that they live a pious and holy life. My husband is not to be urged to instruct them in religious knowledge and in the fear of God. If they be pious, I am sure he will gladly be a father to them; but if not, they do not deserve that I should ask for aught in their behalf." This nobleness of mind will weigh more with me than a hundred recommendations.

Many thanks for your friendly consolation. Adieu, most excellent and honest brother. May the Lord Jesus watch over and direct yourself and your wife. Present my best wishes to her and to the brethren. Yours,

John CALVIN.

SECTION III:
A SELECTION FROM THE PREFACE
TO THE COMMENTARY ON PSALMS, 1557

Calvin was always very shy about revealing his personal life and feelings to any but the closest friends. However, in the preface to his commentary on psalms written relatively late in his life, the reformer sketched the fullest outline of his education and conversion, his ministry and his personal struggles, to be found anywhere in his writings. It is significant that he does this in the context of introducing the Book of Psalms, which he calls "an anatomy of all the parts of the soul," where he demonstrates clearly that emotion is an important element in human life. The psalms provide the believer with the best vocabulary of prayer. Strange as that may sound, Calvin felt a deep affinity with David; though he never claimed to reach David's heights, Calvin recognized that they shared a similar struggle in leading the church and he modeled his own prayer life on that of the Old Testament psalm-singer. The original is in OC 31:13–36; the translation is by James Anderson.

John Calvin to the Pious and Ingenuous Readers, Greeting.

If the reading of these my commentaries confer as much benefit on the church of God as I myself have reaped advantage from the composition of them, I shall have no reason to regret that I have undertaken this work....

The varied and resplendent riches which are contained in this treasury it is no easy matter to express in words; so much so, that I well know that whatever I shall be able to say will be far from approaching the excellence of the subject. But as it is better to give to my readers some taste, however small, of the wonderful advantages they will derive from the study of this book, than to be entirely silent on the point, I may be permitted briefly to advert to a matter, the greatness of which does not admit of being fully unfolded. I have been accustomed to call this book, I think not inappropriately, "An Anatomy of all the Parts of the Soul"; for there is not an emotion of which any one can be conscious that is not here represented as in a mirror. Or rather, the Holy Spirit has here drawn to the life all the griefs, sorrows, fears, doubts, hopes, cares, perplexities, in short, all the distracting emotions with which human minds are wont to be agitated. The other parts of scripture contain the commandments which God enjoined His servants to announce to us. But here the prophets themselves, seeing they are exhibited to us as speaking to God, and laying open all their inmost thoughts and affections, call, or rather draw, each of us to the examination of himself in particular, in order that none of the many infirmities to which we are subject, and of the many vices with which we abound, may remain concealed. It is certainly a rare and singular advantage, when all lurking places are discovered, and the heart is brought into the light, purged from that most baneful infection, hypocrisy.

In short, as calling upon God is one of the principal means of securing our safety, and as a better and more unerring rule for guiding us in this exercise cannot be found elsewhere than in the psalms, it follows, that in proportion to the proficiency which a person shall have attained in understanding them, will be his knowledge of the most important part of celestial doctrine. Genuine and earnest prayer proceeds first from a sense of our need, and next, from faith in the promises of God. It is by perusing these inspired compositions, that people will be most effectually awakened to a sense of their maladies, and, at the same time, instructed in seeking remedies for their cure. In a word, whatever may serve to encourage us when we are about to pray to God, is taught us in this book. And not only are the promises of God presented to us in it, but oftentimes there is exhibited to us one standing, as it were, amidst the invitations of God on the one hand, and the impediments of the flesh on the other, girding and preparing himself for prayer: thus teaching us, if at any time we are agitated with a variety of doubts, to resist and fight against them, until the soul, freed and disentangled from all these impediments, rise up to God: and not only so, but even when in the midst of doubts, fears, and apprehensions, let us put forth our efforts in prayer, until we experience some consolation which may calm and bring contentment to our minds. Although distrust may shut the gate against our prayers, yet we must not allow ourselves to give way, whenever our hearts waver or are agitated with inquietude, but must persevere until faith finally come forth victorious from these conflicts. In many places we may perceive the exercise of the servants of God in prayer so fluctuating, that they are almost overwhelmed by the alternate hope of success and apprehension of failure, and gain the prize only by strenuous exertions. We see on the one hand, the flesh manifesting its infirmity; and on the other, faith putting forth its power; and if it is not so valiant and courageous as might be desired, it is at least prepared to fight until by degrees it acquire perfect strength.

But as those things which serve to teach us the true method of praying aright will be found scattered through the whole of this Commentary, I will not now stop to treat of topics which it will be necessary afterward to repeat, nor detain my readers from proceeding to the work itself. Only it appeared to me to be requisite to show in passing that this book makes known to us this privilege which is desirable above all others—that not only is there opened up to us familiar access to God, but also that we have permission and freedom granted us to lay open before Him our infirmities which we would be ashamed to confess before other people.

Besides, there is also here prescribed to us an infallible rule for directing us with respect to the right manner of offering to God the sacrifice of praise, which He declares to be most precious in His sight, and of the sweetest odor. There is no other book in which there are to be found more express and magnificent commendations, both of the unparalleled liberality of God towards His church, and of all His works; there is no other book in which there are recorded so many deliverances, nor one in which the evidences and experiences of the fatherly providence and solicitude which God exercises towards us, are celebrated with such splendor of diction, and yet with the strictest adherence to truth; in short there is no other book in which we are more perfectly taught the right manner of praising God, or in which we are more powerfully stirred up to the performance of this exercise of piety. Moreover, although the psalms are replete with all the precepts which serve to frame our life to every part of holiness, piety, and righteousness, yet they will principally teach and train us to bear the cross; and the bearing of the cross is a genuine proof of our obedience, since by doing this, we renounce the guidance of our own affections, and submit ourselves entirely to God, leaving Him to govern us and to dispose of our life according to His will, so that the afflictions which are the bitterest and most severe to our nature become sweet to us because they proceed from Him. In one word, not only will we here find general commendations of the goodness of God which may teach people to repose themselves in Him alone and to seek all their happiness solely in Him; and which are intended to teach devout believers with their whole hearts confidently to look to Him for help in all their necessities; but we will also find that the free remission of sins, which alone reconciles God towards us and procures for us settled peace with Him, is so set forth and magnified, as that here there is nothing wanting which relates to the knowledge of eternal salvation.

Now, if my readers derive any fruit and advantage from the labor which I have bestowed in writing these Commentaries, I would have them to understand that the small measure of experience which I have had by the conflicts with which the Lord has exercised me, has in no ordinary degree assisted me, not only in applying to present use whatever instruction could be gathered from these divine compositions, but also in more easily comprehending the design of each of the writers. And as David holds the principal place among them, it has greatly aided me in understanding more fully the complaints made by him of the internal afflictions which the church had to sustain through those who gave themselves out to be her members, that I had suffered the same or similar things from the domestic enemies of the church. For although I follow David at a great distance, and come far short of equaling him; or rather, although in aspiring slowly, and with great difficulty, to attain to the many virtues in which he excelled, I still feel myself tarnished with the contrary vices; yet if I have any things in common with him, I have no hesitation in comparing myself with him. In reading the instances of his faith, patience, fervor, zeal, and integrity, it has (as it ought) drawn from me unnumbered groans and sighs that I am so far from approaching them; but it has notwithstanding been of very great advantage to me to behold in him as in a mirror both the commencement of my calling and the continued course of my function; so that I know the more assuredly, that whatever that most illustrious king and prophet suffered, was exhibited to me by God as an example for imitation. My condition no doubt is much inferior to his, and it is unnecessary for me to stay to show this. But as he was taken from the sheepfold and elevated to the rank of supreme authority; so God having taken me from my originally obscure and humble condition, has reckoned me worthy of being invested with the honorable office of a preacher and minister of the gospel.

When I was as yet a very little boy, my father [Gérard Cauvin] had destined me for the study of theology. But afterwards, when he considered that the legal profession commonly raised those who followed it to wealth, this prospect induced him suddenly to change his purpose. Thus it came to pass, that I was withdrawn from the study of philosophy, and was put to the study of law. To this pursuit I endeavored faithfully to apply myself, in obedience to the will of my father; but God, by the secret guidance of His providence, at length gave a different direction to my course. And first, since I was too obstinately devoted to the superstitions of Popery to be easily extricated from so profound an abyss of mire, God by a sudden conversion subdued and brought to a teachable frame my mind, which was more hardened in such matters than might have been expected from one at my early period of life. Having thus received some taste and knowledge of true piety, I was immediately inflamed with so intense a desire to make progress therein, that although I did not altogether leave off other studies, I yet pursued them with less ardor.

I was quite surprised to find that before a year had elapsed, all who had any desire after purer doctrine were continually coming to me to learn, although I myself was as yet but a mere novice

and tyro. Being of a disposition somewhat unpolished and bash-
ful, which led me always to love the shade and retirement, I then
began to seek some secluded corner where I might be withdrawn
from the public view; but so far from being able to accomplish the
object of my desire, all my retreats were like public schools. In
short, while my one great object was to live in seclusion without
being known, God so led me about through different turnings and
changes, that He never permitted me to rest in any place, until, in
spite of my natural disposition, He brought me forth to public
notice. Leaving my native county, France, I in fact retired into Ger-
many, expressly for the purpose of being able there to enjoy in
some obscure corner the repose which I had always desired, and
which had been so long denied me. But lo! while I lay hidden at
Basel, and known only to a few people, many faithful and holy persons were burnt alive in France; and the report of these burnings
having reached foreign nations, they excited the strongest disap-
probation among a great part of the Germans, whose indignation
was kindled against the authors of such tyranny. In order to allay
this indignation, certain wicked and lying pamphlets were circu-
lated, stating that none were treated with such cruelty but Anabaptists and seditious persons, who by their perverse ravings and false
opinions were overthrowing not only religion but also all civil
order. Observing that the object which these instruments of the
court aimed at by their disguises, was not only that the disgrace of
shedding so much innocent blood might remain buried under the
false charges and calumnies which they brought against the holy
martyrs after their death, but also, that afterwards they might be
able to proceed to the utmost extremity in murdering the poor
saints without exciting compassion towards them in the breasts of
any, it appeared to me, that unless I opposed them to the utmost
of my ability, my silence could not be vindicated from the charge
of cowardice and treachery.

This was the consideration which induced me to publish my
Institutes of the Christian Religion. My objects were, first, to prove
that these reports were false and calumnious, and thus to vindicate my brethren, whose death was precious in the sight of the
Lord; and next, that as the same cruelties might very soon after be

exercised against many unhappy individuals, foreign nations might be touched with at least some compassion toward them and solicitude about them. When it was then published, it was not that copious and labored work which it now is, but only a small treatise containing a summary of the principal truths of the Christian religion; and it was published with no other design than that the peoples might know what was the faith held by those whom I saw basely and wickedly defamed by those flagitious and perfidious flatterers. That my object was not to acquire fame, appeared from this, that immediately afterwards I left Basel, and particularly from the fact that nobody there knew that I was the author.

Wherever else I have gone, I have taken care to conceal that I was the author of that performance; and I had resolved to continue in the same privacy and obscurity, until at length William Farel detained me at Geneva, not so much by counsel and exhortation, as by a dreadful imprecation, which I felt to be as if God had from heaven laid His mighty hand upon me to arrest me. As the most direct road to Strasbourg, to which I then intended to retire, was shut up by the wars, I had resolved to pass quickly by Geneva, without staying longer than a single night in that city. A little before this, Popery had been driven from it by the exertions of the excellent person whom I have named, and Peter Viret; but matters were not yet brought to a settled state, and the city was divided into unholy and dangerous factions. Then an individual who has now basely apostatized and returned to the papists, discovered me and made me known to others. Upon this Farel, who burned with an extraordinary zeal to advance the gospel, immediately strained every nerve to detain me. And after having learned that my heart was set upon devoting myself to private studies, for which I wished to keep myself free from other pursuits, and finding that he gained nothing by entreaties, he proceeded to utter an imprecation that God would curse my retirement, and the tranquility of the studies which I sought, if I should withdraw and refuse to give assistance, when the necessity was so urgent. By this imprecation I was so stricken with terror, that I desisted from the journey which I had undertaken; but sensible of my natural bashfulness and timidity, I would not bring myself under obligation to discharge any particular office. After that, four months had scarcely elapsed, when, on the one hand, the Anabaptists began to assail us, and, on the other, a certain wicked apostate, who being secretly supported by the influence of some of the magistrates of the city, was thus enabled to give us a great deal of trouble. At the same time, a succession of dissensions fell out in the city which strangely afflicted us. Being, as I acknowledge, naturally of a timid, soft, and pusillanimous disposition, I was compelled to encounter these violent tempests as part of my early training; and although I did not sink under them, yet I was not sustained by such greatness of mind, as not to rejoice more than it became me when in consequence of certain commotions I was banished from Geneva.

By this means set at liberty and loosed from the tie of my vocation, I resolved to live in a private station, free from the burden and cares of any public charge, when that most excellent servant of Christ, Martin Bucer, employing a similar kind of remonstrance and protestation as that to which Farel had recourse before, drew me back to a new station. Alarmed by the example of Jonah which he set before me, I still continued in the work of teaching. And although I always continued like myself, studiously avoiding celebrity; yet I was carried, I know not how, as it were by force to the Imperial assemblies, where, willing or unwilling, I was under the necessity of appearing before the eyes of many. Afterwards, when the Lord having compassion on this city, had allayed the hurtful agitations and broils which prevailed in it, and by His wonderful power had defeated both the wicked counsels and the sanguinary attempts of the disturbers of the Republic, necessity was imposed upon me of returning to my former charge, contrary to my desire and inclination. The welfare of this church, it is true, lay so near my heart that for its sake I would not have hesitated to lay down my life; but my timidity nevertheless suggested to me many reasons for excusing myself from again willingly taking upon my shoulders so heavy a burden. At length, however, a solemn and conscientious regard to my duty prevailed with me to consent to return to the flock from which I had been torn; but with what grief, tears, great anxiety and distress I did this, the Lord is my best witness, and many godly persons who would have wished to see me delivered from this painful state, had it not been that that which I feared, and which made me give my consent, prevented them and shut their mouths.

Were I to narrate the various conflicts by which the Lord has exercised me since that time, and by what trials He has proved me, it would make a long history. But that I may not become tedious to my readers by a waste of words, I shall content myself with repeating briefly what I have I touched upon a little before, that in considering the whole course of the life of David, it seemed to me that by his own footsteps he showed me the way, and from this I have experienced no small consolation. As that holy king was harassed by the Philistines and other foreign enemies with continual wars, while he was much more grievously afflicted by the malice and wickedness of some perfidious ones among his own people, so I can say as to myself, that I have been assailed on all sides and have scarcely been able to enjoy repose for a single moment, but have always had to sustain some conflict either from enemies without or within the church....This knowledge and experience have been of much service in enabling me to understand the psalms, so that in my meditations upon them, I did not wander, as it were, in an unknown region.

My readers, too, if I mistake not, will observe, that in unfolding the internal affections both of David and of others, I discourse upon them as matters of which I have familiar experience. Moreover, since I have labored faithfully to open up this treasure for the use of all the people of God, although what I have done has not been equal to my wishes, yet the attempt which I have made deserves to be received with some measure of favor. Still I only ask that each may judge of my labors with justice and candor, according to the advantage and fruit which he shall derive from them....I have felt nothing to be of more importance than to have a regard to the edification of the church. May God, who has implanted this desire in my heart, grant by His grace that the success may correspond thereto!

Geneva, July 22, 1557.

PART TWO:

THEOLOGICAL ORIENTATION

The *Institutes of the Christian Religion,* usually read in the final version of 1559, is Calvin's comprehensive, coherent statement of biblical and creedal faith. Some particular aspects of it are essential for understanding the framework of his teaching on piety, the lived faith of a whole community.

Piety, the first section, comes from Book One, which outlines the human condition before God, the knowledge of God and ourselves, and thus delineates Calvin's first definition of piety.

The Holy Spirit and Faith: The Personal Relationship of the Triune God and the Believer, the second section, is drawn from Book Three, which explains the character of the individual human relationship with God, Father, Son, and Holy Spirit. This is made possible by the gift of faith, the assurance of God's acceptance because of the work of Christ, which is made known in the written word and then impressed on the human mind and heart, both actions being the work of the Spirit. The fruit of faith is both justification and regeneration, forgiveness of sins and newness of life, the sinner's acceptance as if he or she has Christ's righteousness and the sinner's lifelong transformation to be more and more like Christ's restored image, through dying to self and living in Christ.

JOHN CALVIN

External Means: The Church and the Corporate Life of the Body of Christ, the third section, is from Book Four, which outlines the external means by which this faith is communicated and nourished. Although not restricted to these means, God by accommodation chooses to work through the church, the body of Christ, and Christians are that body as they are engrafted into Christ. The engrafting is vital. Salvation is personal but not individualistic; Christians are redeemed as members of a body. Christians believe in the church known only to God, the elect, but their business is with the church visible on earth. Preaching and the visible words of the sacraments are God's gifts, delivered by humans, to draw human beings to God. They present God's "living image" to God's people. (Calvin is known for his objections to "graven images," but it is often forgotten that he speaks of baptism, the Lord's supper, and even patterns of worship as a "living image of God," 1.11.13; 4.1.5; Easter sermon, p. 122.) The marks of the church, word and sacraments, are sure evidence of where the true church becomes visible. Inwardly assured of their own engrafting into Christ, Christians use charitable judgment to observe the members of the church around them. The marks of a Christian—profession of faith, example of life, and partaking of the sacraments—are the criteria for determining who is to be reckoned as a member of the church. For the honor of God and human salvation, the church as a whole (acting through duly constituted leadership) keeps watch to see that these marks are maintained as well as possible. (For more on this final point, see "A Short Treatise on the Lord's Supper," below pp. 104–11.) The original texts are found in OS 3–5; the translation is by F. L. Battles.

66

BOOK ONE: THE KNOWLEDGE OF GOD THE CREATOR
Chapter 1: The Knowledge of God and That of Ourselves Are Connected. How They Are Interrelated

1. Nearly all the wisdom we possess, that is to say, true and sound wisdom, consists of two parts: the knowledge of God and of ourselves. But, while joined by many bonds, which one precedes and brings forth the other is not easy to discern. In the first place, no one can look upon himself without immediately turning his thoughts to the contemplation of God, in whom he "lives and moves." For, quite clearly, the mighty gifts with which we are endowed are hardly from ourselves; indeed, our very being is nothing but subsistence in the one God. Then, by these benefits shed like dew from heaven upon us, we are led as by rivulets to the spring itself. Indeed, our very poverty better discloses the infinitude of benefits reposing in God. The miserable ruin, into which the rebellion of the first human being cast us, especially compels us to look upward. Thus, not only may we in fasting and hungering seek thence what we lack; but, in being aroused by fear, we may learn humility. For, as a veritable world of miseries is to be found in the human race, and we are thereby despoiled of divine raiment, our shameful nakedness exposes a teeming horde of infamies. Each of us must, then, be so stung by the consciousness of his own unhappiness as to attain at least some knowledge of God. Thus, from the feeling of our own ignorance, vanity, poverty, infirmity, and—what is more—depravity

and corruption, we recognize that the true light of wisdom, sound virtue, full abundance of every good, and purity of righteousness rest in the Lord alone. To this extent we are prompted by our own ills to contemplate the good things of God; and we cannot seriously aspire to Him before we begin to become displeased with ourselves. For what person in all the world would not gladly remain as he is—what one does not remain as he is—so long as he does not know himself, that is, while content with his own gifts, and either ignorant or unmindful of his own misery? Accordingly, the knowledge of ourselves not only arouses us to seek God, but also, as it were, leads us by the hand to find Him.

2. Again, it is certain that a person never achieves a clear knowledge of himself unless he has first looked upon God's face, and then descends from contemplating God to scrutinize himself. For we always seem to ourselves righteous and upright and wise and holy—this pride is innate in all of us—unless by clear proofs we stand convinced of our own unrighteousness, foulness, folly, and impurity. Moreover, we are not thus convinced if we look merely to ourselves and not also to the Lord, who is the sole standard by which this judgment must be measured. For, because all of us are inclined by nature to hypocrisy, a kind of empty image of righteousness in place of righteousness itself abundantly satisfies us. And because nothing appears within or around us that has not been contaminated by great immorality, what is a little less vile pleases us as a thing most pure—so long as we confine our minds within the limits of human corruption. Just so an eye to which nothing is shown but black objects judges something dirty white or even rather darkly mottled to be whiteness itself. Indeed, we can discern still more clearly from the bodily senses how much we are deluded in estimating the powers of the soul. For if in broad daylight we either look down upon the ground or survey whatever meets our view round about, we seem to ourselves endowed with the strongest and keenest sight; yet when we look up to the sun and gaze straight at it, that power of sight which was particularly strong on earth is at once blunted and confused by a great brilliance, and thus we are compelled to admit that our keenness in looking upon things earthly is sheer dullness when it comes to the

sun. So it happens in estimating our spiritual goods. As long as we do not look beyond the earth, being quite content with our own righteousness, wisdom, and virtue, we flatter ourselves most sweetly, and fancy ourselves all but demigods. Suppose we but once begin to raise our thoughts to God, and to ponder His nature, and how completely perfect are His righteousness, wisdom, and power—the straightedge to which we must be shaped. Then, what masquerading earlier as righteousness was pleasing in us, will soon grow filthy in its consummate wickedness. What wonderfully impressed us under the name of wisdom will stink in its very foolishness. What wore the face of power will prove itself the most miserable weakness. That is, what in us seems perfection itself corresponds ill to the purity of God.

3. Hence that dread and wonder with which scripture commonly represents the saints as stricken and overcome whenever they felt the presence of God. Thus it comes about that we see people who in God's absence normally remained firm and constant, but who, when He manifests His glory, are so shaken and struck dumb as to be laid low by the dread of death—are in fact overwhelmed by it and almost annihilated. As a consequence, we must infer that no one is ever sufficiently touched and affected by the awareness of his lowly state until he has compared himself with God's majesty. Moreover, we have numerous examples of this consternation both in The Book of Judges and in the Prophets. So frequent was it that this expression was common among God's people: "We shall die, for the Lord has appeared to us" (Judg 13:22, Isa 6:5, Ezek 2:1). The story of Job, in its description of God's wisdom, power, and purity, always expresses a most powerful argument that overwhelms people with the realization of their own stupidity, impotence, and corruption. And not without cause: for we see how Abraham recognizes more clearly that he is earth and dust when once he has come nearer to beholding God's glory (Gen 18:27); and how Elijah, with uncovered face, cannot bear to await His approach, such is the awesomeness of His appearance (1 Kgs 19:13). And what can a human being do, who is rottenness itself and a worm, when even the very cherubim must veil their faces out of fear? It is this indeed of which the

prophet Isaiah speaks: "The sun will blush and the moon be confounded when the Lord of Hosts shall reign" (Isa 24:23); that is, when He shall bring forth His splendor and cause it to draw nearer, the brightest thing will become darkness before it.

Yet, however the knowledge of God and of ourselves may be mutually connected, the order of right teaching requires that we discuss the former first, then proceed afterward to treat the latter.

Chapter 2: What It Is to Know God, and to What Purpose the Knowledge of Him Tends

1. Now the knowledge of God, as I understand it, is that by which we not only conceive that there is a God but also grasp what befits us to know and is proper to His glory, in fine, what is to our advantage to know of Him. Indeed, we shall not say that, properly speaking, God is known where there is no religion or piety. Here I do not yet touch upon the sort of knowledge with which human beings, in themselves lost and accursed, apprehend God the Redeemer in Christ the Mediator; but I speak only of the primal and simple knowledge to which the very order of nature would have led us if Adam had remained upright. In this ruin of the human race no one now experiences God either as Father or as Author of salvation, or favorable in any way, until Christ the Mediator comes forward to reconcile us to Him. Nevertheless, it is one thing to feel that God as our Maker supports us by His power, governs us by His providence, nourishes us by His goodness, and attends us with all sorts of blessings—and another thing to embrace the grace of reconciliation offered to us in Christ. First, as much in the fashioning of the universe as in the general teaching of scripture the Lord shows Himself to be simply the Creator. Then in the face of Christ He shows Himself the Redeemer. Of the resulting twofold knowledge of God we shall now discuss the first aspect; the second will be dealt with in its proper place.

Moreover, although our mind cannot apprehend God without rendering some honor to Him, it will not suffice simply to hold that there is One whom all ought to honor and adore, unless we are also persuaded that He is the fountain of every good, and that we must seek nothing elsewhere than in Him. This I take to mean that not only does He sustain this universe (as He once founded it) by His boundless might, regulate it by His wisdom, preserve it by His goodness, and especially rule the human race by His righteousness and judgment, bear with it in His mercy, watch over it by His protection; but also that no drop will be found either of wisdom and light, or of righteousness or power or rectitude, or of genuine truth, which does not flow from Him, and of which He is not the cause. Thus we may learn to await and seek all these things from Him, and thankfully to ascribe them, once received, to Him. For this sense of the powers of God is for us a fit teacher of piety, from which religion is born. I call "piety" that reverence joined with love of God which the knowledge of His benefits induces. For until people recognize that they owe everything to God, that they are nourished by His fatherly care, that He is the Author of their every good, so that they should seek nothing beyond Him—they will never yield Him willing service. Nay, unless they establish their complete happiness in Him, they will never give themselves truly and sincerely to Him.

2. What is God? Those who pose this question are merely toying with idle speculations. It is more important for us to know of what sort He is and what is consistent with His nature. What good is it to profess with Epicurus some sort of God who has cast aside the care of the world only to amuse Himself in idleness? What help is it, in short, to know a God with whom we have nothing to do? Rather, our knowledge should serve first to teach us fear and reverence; secondly, with it as our guide and teacher, we should learn to seek every good from Him, and, having received it, to credit it to His account. For how can the thought of God penetrate your mind without your realizing immediately that, since you are His handiwork, you have been made over and bound to His command by right of creation, that you owe your life to Him?—that whatever you undertake, whatever you do, ought to be ascribed to Him? If this be so, it now assuredly follows that your life is wickedly corrupt unless it be disposed to His service, seeing that His will ought for us to be the law by which

71

JOHN CALVIN

we live. Again, you cannot behold Him clearly unless you
acknowledge Him to be the fountainhead and source of every
good. From this too would arise the desire to cleave to Him and
trust in Him, but for the fact that human depravity seduces a
person's mind from rightly seeking Him.

For, to begin with, the pious mind does not dream up for
itself any god it pleases, but contemplates the one and only true
God. And it does not attach to Him whatever it pleases, but is content to hold Him to be as He manifests Himself; furthermore, the
mind always exercises the utmost diligence and care not to wander
astray, or rashly and boldly to go beyond His will. It thus recognizes God because it knows that He governs all things; and trusts
that He is its guide and protector, therefore giving itself over completely to trust in Him. Because it understands Him to be the
Author of every good, if anything oppresses, if anything is lacking,
immediately it betakes itself to His protection, waiting for help
from Him. Because it is persuaded that He is good and merciful, it
reposes in Him with perfect trust, and doubts not that in His
loving-kindness a remedy will be provided for all its ills. Because it
acknowledges Him as Lord and Father, the pious mind also deems
it meet and right to observe His authority in all things, reverence
His majesty, take care to advance His glory, and obey His commandments. Because it sees Him to be a righteous judge, armed
with severity to punish wickedness, it ever holds His judgment seat
before its gaze, and through fear of Him restrains itself from provoking His anger. And yet it is not so terrified by the awareness of
His judgment as to wish to withdraw, even if some way of escape
were open. But it embraces Him no less as punisher of the wicked
than as benefactor of the pious. For the pious mind realizes that
the punishment of the impious and wicked and the reward of life
eternal for the righteous equally pertain to God's glory. Besides,
this mind restrains itself from sinning, not out of dread of punishment alone; but because it loves and reveres God as Father, it wor-
ships and adores Him as Lord. Even if there were no hell, it would
still shudder at only offending Him.

Here indeed is pure and real religion: faith so joined with an
earnest fear of God that this fear also embraces willing reverence,

72

and carries with it such legitimate worship as is prescribed in the law. And we ought to note this fact even more diligently: all people have a vague general veneration for God, but very few really reverence Him; and wherever there is great ostentation in ceremonies, sincerity of heart is rare indeed.

SECTION II:
FAITH

BOOK THREE: THE WAY WE RECEIVE THE GRACE OF CHRIST: WHAT
BENEFITS COME TO US FROM IT
Chapter 2: Faith: Its Definition Set Forth, and Its Properties Explained

6....Now, therefore, we hold faith to be a knowledge of God's will toward us, perceived from His word. But the foundation of this is a preconceived conviction of God's truth....

7. But since our hearts are not aroused to faith at every word of God, we must find out at this point what, strictly speaking, faith looks to in the word....

It is plain then that we do not yet have a full definition of faith, inasmuch as merely to know something of God's will is not to be accounted faith. But what if we were to substitute His benevolence or His mercy in place of His will, the tidings of which are often sad and the proclamation frightening? Thus, surely, we shall more closely approach the nature of faith: for it is after we have learned that our salvation rests with God that we are attracted to seek Him. This fact is confirmed for us when He declares that our salvation is His care and concern. Accordingly, we need the promise of grace, which can testify to us that the Father is merciful: since we can approach Him in no other way, and upon grace alone the human heart can rest....But we have already seen that the sole pledge of His love is Christ, without whom the signs of hatred and wrath are everywhere evident....

74

Now we shall possess a right definition of faith if we call it a firm and certain knowledge of God's good will toward us, founded upon the truth of the freely given promise in Christ, both revealed to our minds and sealed upon our hearts through the Holy Spirit.

14. Now let us examine anew the individual parts of the definition of faith. After we have diligently examined it no doubt, I believe, will remain. When we call faith "knowledge" we do not mean comprehension of the sort that is commonly concerned with those things which fall under human sense perception. Faith is so far above sense that the mind has to go beyond and rise above itself in order to attain it. Even where the mind has attained, it does not comprehend what it feels. But while it is persuaded of what it does not grasp, by the very certainty of its persuasion it understands more than if it perceived anything human by its own capacity....But [believers] are more strengthened by the persuasion of divine truth than instructed by rational proof....From this we conclude that the knowledge of faith consists in assurance rather than in comprehension.

16. Here, indeed, is the chief hinge on which faith turns: that we do not regard the promises of mercy that God offers as true only outside ourselves, but not at all in us; rather that we make them ours by inwardly embracing them. Hence, at last is born that confidence which Paul elsewhere calls "peace" (Rom 5:1)....

21....When one is stricken by the thought that God is Avenger of iniquities, faith sets over against this the fact that His pardon is ready for all iniquities whenever the sinner betakes himself to the Lord's mercy. Thus the devout mind, however strange the ways in which it is vexed and troubled, finally surmounts all difficulties, and never allows itself to be deprived of assurance of divine mercy....

23....For not only does piety beget reverence toward God, but the very sweetness and delightfulness of grace so fills one who is cast down in himself with fear, and at the same time with admiration, that he depends upon God and humbly submits himself to His power.

75

24....[I]f you contemplate yourself, that is sure damnation. But since Christ has been so imparted to you with all His benefits that all His things are made yours, that you are made a member of Him, indeed one with Him, His righteousness overwhelms your sins: His salvation wipes out your condemnation; with His worthiness He intercedes that your unworthiness may not come before God's sight. Surely this is so: We ought not to separate Christ from ourselves or ourselves from Him. Rather we ought to hold fast bravely with both hands to that fellowship by which He has bound Himself to us....Christ is not outside us but dwells within us. Not only does He cleave to us by an indivisible bond of fellowship, but with a wonderful communion, day by day, He grows more and more into one body with us, until He becomes completely one with us....

29. We make the freely given promise of God the foundation of faith because upon it faith properly rests. Faith is certain that God is true in all things whether He command or forbid, whether He promise or threaten; and it also obediently receives His commandments, observes His prohibitions, heeds His threats. Nevertheless, faith properly begins with the promise, rests in it, and ends in it....Therefore, when we say that faith must rest upon a freely given promise, we do not deny that believers embrace and grasp the word of God in every respect: but we point out the promise of mercy as the proper goal of faith....

33. And this bare and external proof of the word of God should have been amply sufficient to engender faith, did not our blindness and perversity prevent it. But our mind has such an inclination to vanity that it can never cleave fast to the truth of God; and it has such a dullness that it is always blind to the light of God's truth. Accordingly, without the illumination of the Holy Spirit, the word can do nothing. From this, also, it is clear that faith is much higher than human understanding. And it will not be enough for the mind to be illumined by the Spirit of God unless the heart is also strengthened and supported by His power....

34....Indeed, the word of God is like the sun, shining upon all those to whom it is proclaimed, but with no effect among the blind. Now, all of us are blind by nature in this respect. Accordingly, it cannot penetrate into our minds unless the Spirit, as the inner teacher, through His illumination makes entry for it.

36. It now remains to pour into the heart itself what the mind has absorbed. For the word of God is not received by faith if it flits about in the top of the brain, but when it takes root in the depth of the heart that it may be an invincible defense to withstand and drive off all the stratagems of temptation. But if it is true that the mind's real understanding is illumination by the Spirit of God, then in such confirmation of the heart His power is much more clearly manifested, to the extent that the heart's distrust is greater than the mind's blindness. It is harder for the heart to be furnished with assurance than for the mind to be endowed with thought. The Spirit accordingly serves as a seal, to seal up in our hearts those very promises the certainty of which it has previously impressed upon our minds; and takes the place of a guarantee to confirm and establish them....

Chapter 3: Our Regeneration by Faith: Repentance

1....With good reason, the sum of the gospel is held to consist in repentance and forgiveness of sins....For since pardon and forgiveness are offered through the preaching of the gospel in order that the sinner, freed from the tyranny of Satan, the yoke of sin, and the miserable bondage of vices, may cross over into the Kingdom of God, surely no one can embrace the grace of the gospel without betaking himself from the errors of his past life into the right way, and applying his whole effort to the practice of repentance....

2....[No one] can apply himself seriously to repentance without knowing himself to belong to God. But no one is truly persuaded that he belongs to God unless he has first recognized God's grace....here it is not a question of how variously Christ draws us to Himself, or prepares us for the pursuit of piety. I say only that no uprightness can be found except where that Spirit reigns that Christ received to communicate to His members....

Chapter 11: Justification by Faith: First the Definition of the Word and of the Matter

1....Christ was given to us by God's generosity, to be grasped and possessed by us in faith. By partaking of Him, we principally receive a double grace: namely, that being reconciled to God through Christ's blamelessness, we may have in heaven instead of a Judge a gracious Father; and secondly, that sanctified by Christ's Spirit we may cultivate blamelessness and purity of life....[Justification] is the main hinge on which religion turns, so that we devote the greater attention and care to it. For unless you first of all grasp what your relationship to God is, and the nature of His judgment concerning you, you have neither a foundation on which to establish your salvation nor one on which to build piety toward God....

2....[J]ustified by faith is he who, excluded from the righteousness of works, grasps the righteousness of Christ through faith, and clothed in it, appears in God's sight not as a sinner but as a righteous person. Therefore we explain justification simply as the acceptance with which God receives us into His favor as righteous. And we say that it consists in the remission of sins and the imputation of Christ's righteousness.

11....[T]he grace of justification is not separated from regeneration, although they are things distinct. But because it is very well known by experience that the traces of sin always remain in the righteous, their justification must be very different from reformation into newness of life. For God so begins this second point [regeneration] in His elect, and progresses in it gradually, and sometimes slowly, throughout life, that they are always liable to the judgment of death before His tribunal. But He does not justify in part but liberally, so that they may appear in heaven as if endowed with the purity of Christ....

Section III:
The Church

Book Four: The External Means or Aids by Which God Invites Us into the Society of Christ and Holds Us Therein
Chapter 1: The True Church with Which as Mother of All the Devout We Must Keep Unity

1. As explained in the previous book, it is by the faith in the gospel that Christ becomes ours and we are made partakers of the salvation and eternal blessedness brought by Him. Since, however, in our ignorance and sloth (to which I add fickleness of disposition) we need outward helps to beget and increase faith within us, and advance it to its goal, God has also added these aids that He may provide for our weakness. And in order that the preaching of the gospel might flourish, He deposited this treasure in the church. He instituted "pastors and teachers" (Eph 4:11) through whose lips He might teach His own; He furnished them with authority; finally, He omitted nothing that might make for holy agreement of faith and for right order. First of all, He instituted sacraments, which we who have experienced them feel to be highly useful aids to foster and strengthen faith. Shut up as we are in the prison house of our flesh, we have not yet attained angelic rank. God, therefore, in His wonderful providence accommodating Himself to our capacity, has prescribed a way for us, though still far off, to draw near to Him....

2. The article in the Creed in which we profess to "believe the church" refers not only to the visible church (our present topic) but also to all God's elect, in whose number are also

included the dead....It is not sufficient for us to comprehend in mind and thought the multitude of the elect, unless we consider the unity of the church as that into which we are convinced we have been engrafted. For no hope of future inheritance remains to us unless we have been united with all other members under Christ, our head....

3....The "communion of the saints" ...very well expresses what the church is. It is as if one said that the saints are gathered into the society of Christ on the principle that whatever benefits God confers upon them, they should in turn share with one another....For here we are not bidden to distinguish between reprobate and elect—that is for God alone, not for us, to do—but to establish with certainty in our hearts that all those who, by the kindness of God the Father, through the working of the Holy Spirit, have entered into fellowship with Christ, are set apart as God's property and personal possession; and that when we are of their number we share that great grace.

5....We see how God, who could in a moment perfect His own, nevertheless desires them to grow up into maturity solely under the education of the church. We see the way set for it: the preaching of the heavenly doctrine has been enjoined upon the pastors....By this plan He willed of old that holy assemblies be held at the sanctuary in order that the doctrine taught by the mouth of the priest might foster agreement in faith....On the one hand, He proves our obedience by a very good test when we hear His ministers speaking just as if He Himself spoke. On the other, He also provides for our weakness in that He prefers to address us in human fashion through interpreters in order to draw us to Himself, rather than to thunder at us and drive us away....For, among the many excellent gifts with which God has adorned the human race, it is a singular privilege that He deigns to consecrate to Himself human mouths and tongues in order that His voice may resound in them. Let us accordingly not in turn dislike to embrace obediently the doctrine of salvation put forth by His command and by His own mouth. For, although God's power is not bound to outward means, He has nevertheless bound us to this ordinary manner of teaching....Believers were bidden of old to seek the face of God in the sanctuary (Ps 105:1), as is oftentimes repeated in the law, for no other reason than that for them the teaching of the law and the exhortation of the prophets were a living image of God, just as Paul asserts that in his preaching the glory of God shines in the face of Christ (2 Cor 4:6)....

7....Sometimes by the term "church" it means that which is actually in God's presence, into which no persons are received but those who are children of God by grace of adoption and true members of Christ by sanctification of the Holy Spirit....Often, however, the name "church" designates the whole multitude of people spread over the earth who profess to worship one God and Christ. By baptism we are initiated into faith in Him; by partaking in the Lord's supper we attest our unity in true doctrine and love; in the word of the Lord we have agreement, and for the preaching of the word the ministry instituted by Christ is preserved. In this church are mingled many hypocrites who have nothing of Christ but the name and outward appearance. There are very many ambitious, greedy, envious persons, evil speakers, and some of quite unclean life. Such are tolerated for a time either because they cannot be convicted by a competent tribunal or because a vigorous discipline does not always flourish as it ought.

Just as we must believe, therefore, that the former church, invisible to us, is visible to the eyes of God alone, so we are commanded to revere and keep communion with the latter [visible one], which is called "church" in respect to earthly observers.

8. Accordingly, the Lord by certain marks and tokens has pointed out to us what we should know about the church. As we have cited above from Paul (1 Tim 2:19), to know who are His is a prerogative belonging solely to God....But on the other hand, because He foresaw it to be of some value for us to know who were to be counted as His children, He has in this regard accommodated Himself to our capacity. And, since assurance of faith was not necessary, He substituted for it a certain charitable judgment whereby we recognize as members of the church those who, by profession of faith, by example of life, and by partaking of the sacraments, profess the same God and Christ with us. He

has, moreover, set off by plainer marks the knowledge of His very body to us, knowing how necessary it is to our salvation.

9. From this the face of the church comes forth and becomes visible to our eyes. Wherever we see the word of God purely preached and heard, and the sacraments administered according to Christ's institution, there, it is not to be doubted, a church of God exists....

21. Not only does the Lord through forgiveness of sins receive and adopt us once for all into the church, but through the same means He preserves and protects us there....Consequently, we must firmly believe that by God's generosity, mediated by Christ's merit, through the sanctification of the Spirit, sins have been and are daily pardoned to us who have been received and engrafted into the body of the church.

PART THREE:

LITURGICAL AND SACRAMENTAL PRACTICES

One of the most important forms of spiritual formation for Calvin, as for many Protestants, was the regular corporate worship that the whole community shared day by day, week after week, through the years. Included in these worship services were both the preaching of the word and the celebration of the sacraments of baptism and the Lord's supper, along with the prayers and praises of the people, and their expressions of mutual concern, particularly through intercession for those in need.

The centrality of corporate worship in Calvin's piety is evident in the length of Part Three of this volume. The first section introduces the prayers of the people, which are primarily their common sung praises, the psalms. The second explores the liturgies of the Lord's Day, the central day of worship for Calvin and all Protestants. The third section leads the reader through the daily worship services in Geneva, both on ordinary weekdays and on the special Day of Prayer. A final part provides an example from the series of passion sermons that Genevans heard each year during the week before Easter.

SECTION I:
PSALMS AND THE PSALTER

Much of Calvin's feeling for the psalms is found in the revealing preface he
wrote for his commentary (above, pp. 55–63). However, the psalms were not
simply the texts of the most important biblical prayer book for Calvin personally; they were also the core of the worship and devotional life of the whole
people of God, gathered as a body or living out their vocations from day to day.

Calvin wanted to introduce the singing of psalms in Geneva during his first
years of ministry there, but at that time there was no printed French psalter available. Within a few years, during his Strasbourg sojourn, this lack began to be reme-
died when Calvin published his first psalter in 1539. The book included six of his
own translations, along with twelve other metrical psalms by the noted French lyri-
cal poet Clement Marot, and metrical versions of the Song of Simeon (Luke
2:29–32), the Decalogue, and the Apostles' Creed. In later years, as more of
Marot's translations became available, Calvin's were withdrawn from the psalter.
After Marot's death in 1544, Theodore Beza continued the work of translating the
psalms, until in 1562 the entire 150 were completed. These were presented with a
remarkable collection of diverse melodies, in many different meters: a total of 125
for the psalms and the two biblical canticles that remained in use, the Song of
Simeon and the Decalogue. Most of these tunes, with their distinctive, sober-yet-
singing quality, were written specifically for the psalms they were to accompany by
outstanding musicians, of whom Louis Bourgeois is the best known.

The singing of psalms, understood as a part of prayer, was the people's
most important vocal participation in public worship. Psalms were used in the
liturgies for Sunday morning, Sunday afternoon, and the Day of Prayer. Beginning in 1546, the psalms to be sung on each occasion were designated in a
printed table, which indicated a given number of metrical verses, usually a
whole psalm for the shorter ones and half for the longer ones (except Psalm
119, which was divided over a number of days). Psalms were assigned to each of
the three services according to which texts were most appropriate for specific
days, the more joyful psalms being listed for the two Sunday services, the more
penitential ones to be sung on Wednesdays. At first the congregation sang only

once at each service, but by 1562 there were three appointed times for singing at each service. The first extant table indicating the text to be sung each time comes from 1549, and this was revised in 1553 and 1562, as the number of metrical psalms increased over the years.[23] The sequence of the psalms to be sung on each day loosely follows their biblical order, although since they were spread over three services each week this "continuous reading" effect was less obvious.

Calvin also preached on the psalms, the only Old Testament book he chose for Sunday sermons. Most of the sermons on psalms were preached on Sunday afternoons, though two individual ones were preached on special occasions of intercession and thanksgiving at the Wednesday Day of Prayer. Calvin's extant sermons on psalms begin in 1545, but most were scattered through the 1550s up to 1560. For these texts Calvin followed a modified *lectio continua* pattern, working in order through the psalms that had not yet (at the time of the sermon) been versified for singing. An example of his earliest extant psalm sermon is found in the liturgy for the Day of Prayer (below, pp. 160–72).

In this section of Part Three are presented three of Calvin's six French translations of psalms, and the foreword to the psalter that he wrote in 1542 and to which he added some further words in 1543. It is notable that the first part of this foreword gives a rather full picture of the liturgy, evidence for the fact that Calvin understood the Book of Psalms as the prayer book of the gathered church, which every member should have in his or her own hands. The 1543 addition indicates that this communal prayer book also supplies the words for daily devotion. Because the psalter was central to the corporate piety of believers, the foreword to the psalter provides a good introduction to Calvin's understanding of liturgy, the public worship of the people of God.

Calvin's Translations of Selected Psalms

Ford Lewis Battles has made English versifications of Calvin's translations of the psalms in a fashion to keep the strophic form of the original French. The latter is found in OC 6:211–21.

Psalm 46

For us our God is firm support,
Stronghold and fortress, certain help,
Where in our plight we shall possess
A present refuge, haven safe.
Whence firm assurance we will have,
Even when we will see the earth
Trembling and quaking, now removed,
Mountains now hiding in the sea.

While seas are loudly thundering,
As if with anger fierce they swell:
And lofty crags reverberate,
Are battered, toppled by the waves.
The chosen city of our God,
House to which He has given rain:[24]
Gentle and clear her stream will be,
And ever gladden her abode.

While God the Lord is in her midst
Firm and unmoved she will remain:
To aid her in both time and place
From early morning He will watch.
All pagan nations storm with rage,
Kingdoms have been in trouble thrown:
But God, chastising with His voice,
Makes in a moment them all calm.

God of the armies, leader, chief
The God of Jacob is for us:
And our protector He will be
Against our adversaries all.
Come, raise your eyes then to behold,
Each one of you now strain to see
The marvels that your God has done
In overcoming all His foes.

Only our God by His decree
Can set at peace the whole wide earth,
And unopposed can in the world
Cause every conflict now to cease.
He it is who can break the bows,
Shatter the warrior's spear to bits,
To chariots He will put His torch
And let them fall consumed with fire.

Now be it known to every man
That God it is who must be feared;

JOHN CALVIN

Because of His tremendous power,
Throughout the world exalted be.
God, ruler over heaven's hosts,
For us will ever guardian be,
The God of Jacob will for us
Refuge provide, us e'er preserve.

Psalm 91
Who under guard of God Most High
His dwelling and retreat will have,
As in a sure and peaceful place,
Beneath His shadow even will lie.
Boldly will I say to my God:
"Thou art my fortress and my hope;
In Thee my confidence will lodge,
Most surely will I rest in Thee."

Pondering deep within these thoughts:
"God will," I say, "deliver thee,
From everything that blocks thy way,
And thee from snares will extricate:
Under His wings thou art at peace,
Beneath His pinions safety hast,
Thou always wilt have God's own truth
As shield and buckler strong and stout."

This is why thou wilt never fear
Evil encounter in the night,
Nor feel the force of arrow aimed,
Shot forth at thee when daylight shines.
Whether in light or in the dark
Ruin may stalk with harmful force:
Wreaking destruction here and there,
Thou wilt be in tranquility.

Thou seest a thousand at one hand,
Ten thousand at the other slain,

All this misery thou wilt escape,
For it could ne'er come near to thee.
Clearly indeed thine eye will see
That on the wicked man will fall
Deadly affliction to confound:
This is the price that he must pay.

Thy comfort thou wilt seek in God,
Then will He give His aid to thee;
As if upon a solid rock
On Him thy refuge thou dost found.
Thee no misfortune will come near.
No wound to cause thee injury,
Or to oppress thy family
Ever will come upon thy tent.

God, to maintain thee safe and sound,
His angels over thee has set,
That on the paths thou hast to walk
By them firm-guarded thou wilt be.
They in their hands will carry thee,
And unto thee such succor give
That thy feet may never trip upon
Mischance or hindrance in thy path.

Upon the asp, the poison snake,
Upon the lion thou wilt tread:
Whelp of the lion, dragon fierce,
Unhurt thy foot will trample them.
God says to thee: "Him will I aid,
Since in esteem he holds Me fast,
Since He has recognized My name
Him will I lift to every good.

"Calling on Me, he will be heard,
Near Me in all anxiety
He'll be, and in the end rejoice
And be in honor set by Me.

My grace will on his life bestow
A happy, long, and blessed course;
And through My power, him will I help;
To safety lead him by the hand."

Psalm 113

Come, praise the Lord, ye servants all,
Praise Him, for He deserves it,
Upon your lips and in your throat
Be His name's praise and honor.
Let His most holy majesty
Magnified and exalted be
From this day forth and forever.

As far as sun its course extends,
High over all things earthly,
The name of God shines everywhere,
Filled with His might and glory.
Above all people, every land,
Almighty God is lifted up,
Higher is He than all heavens.

Where does our Lord His equal have,
Resembling Him in glory?
Who has so highly lifted up
His throne and habitation?
God humbles thence Himself to look
Upon the creatures He maintains
On earth even as in heaven.

The lowly man cast down to earth,
He raises him and sets free;
Out of the dung hill He revives
Man stript and prostrate lying,
That there, released from misery,
In lofty station may converse
Among the princes of nations.

He blesses now with fruitfulness,
The women who are barren;
She then who cannot bear a child
He multiplies with offspring.
Come, therefore, praise the Lord our God;
Give honor to His holy name:
Such praise His deeds surely merit.

Calvin's Foreword to the Psalter

The foreword to the psalter, which Calvin first wrote in 1542, and then expanded in 1543, provides a vivid sense of his understanding both of public worship, and of the gift of music, especially in public worship but also in the daily devotional life of Christians. The songs of the psalmists are the praise that should shape the piety of Christians throughout their lives. The text appeared in *La forme des prières* in 1542 and 1543, but thereafter only in the psalters, and hence it is commonly known as the foreword to the psalter, although its character illustrates why that book was regarded as the people's liturgical book. In fact, the psalter became the central prayer book of every devout Calvinist—so much so that in France, where that faith was prohibited in many places, "heretics" were identified by the "Genevan tunes" and French-language psalms they sang in worship and at work, as lullabies, and even as battle hymns. The original is in OS 2, pp. 12–18; the translation is that of Charles Garside.

Epistle to the Reader

As it is a thing rightly required by Christianity, and one of the most necessary, that each of the faithful observe and maintain the communion of the church in his neighborhood, attending the assemblies which are held on Sunday as well as on other days to honor and serve God, so is it also expedient and reasonable that everyone know and understand what is said and done in the temple in order to receive benefit and edification from it. For our Lord did not institute the order which we are bound to observe when we gather together in His name merely to amuse the world by a spectacle, but rather desired that from it profit would come to all His people, as Saint Paul testifies, commanding that everything which is done in the church be directed to the common edification of all (Rom 15:2, 1 Cor 14:26, Eph

4:29), something which the servant would not have commanded had it not been the intention of the Master.

Now this cannot be done unless we are taught to understand everything which has been ordained for our use. For to say that we can have devotion, either at prayer or at ceremony, without understanding anything about them, is a gross delusion, no matter how much it is commonly said. A good affection toward God is a thing neither lifeless nor bestial, but is a quickening movement proceeding from the Holy Spirit when the heart is truly touched and the understanding enlightened. And in fact, if one could be edified by things which one sees without understanding what they mean, Saint Paul would not so vehemently forbid speaking in an unknown tongue (1 Cor 14:16), and would not use the argument that there is no edification unless there is doctrine. Nevertheless, if we wish truly to honor the holy ordinances of our Lord which we use in the church, the most important thing is to know what they contain, what they mean, and to what purpose they tend, in order that their observance may be useful and salutary, and in consequence rightly regulated.

Now there are in sum three things which our Lord has commanded us to observe in our spiritual assemblies, namely, the preaching of His word, the public and solemn prayers, and the administration of His sacraments (cf. Acts 2:42). I refrain from speaking of preaching at this time, inasmuch as it is not in question. Touching the two other parts which remain, we have the express commandment of the Holy Spirit that prayers be made in the common language and understood by the people. And the Apostle says that the people cannot respond, Amen, to the prayer which has been made in an unknown tongue (1 Cor 14:15–17). Now since prayer is made in the name of all and on behalf of all, everyone should be a participant. Wherefore this has been a very great affront of those who have introduced the Latin language into the churches where it is not commonly understood. And there is neither subtlety not sophistry which can excuse them from this custom which is perverse and displeasing to God. For one must not presume that He will consider agreeable what is done directly contrary to His will, and, as it were, in defiance of Him. Nor can one any longer defy Him, acting thus against His prohibition, and glorying in this rebellion as if it were a thing holy and very praiseworthy.

As for the sacraments, if we look truly at their nature, we recognize that it is a perverse custom to celebrate them in such a way that the people have nothing but the spectacle, without explanation of the mysteries which are contained in them. For if these are visible words, as Saint Augustine calls them, they must not be merely an exterior spectacle, but doctrine must be joined to them to give them understanding. And so our Lord, in instituting them, expressly demonstrated this, for He says that they are testimonies of the alliance which He made with us, and which He confirmed by His death (Matt 26:26–29). It is certainly necessary, then, in order to accord them their proper place, that we know and understand what is said in them. Otherwise it would be in vain that our Lord opened His mouth to speak if there were no ears to hear. And this is not a subject for lengthy disputation, for when the matter is judged with a sober disposition, there is no one who will not admit that it is pure trickery to amuse the people with signs whose meaning is not explained to them. Wherefore it is easy to see that one profanes the sacraments of Jesus Christ, administering them in such a manner that the people do not understand the words which are spoken in them. And in fact one sees the superstitions which issue from this. For it is commonly agreed that the consecration, as much of the water at baptism as of the bread and the wine in the supper of our Lord, are like a kind of magic; that is to say that when one has breathed on them and pronounced the words, insensible creatures feel the effect, yet people understand nothing.

Now the true consecration is that which is made by the word of faith when it is declared and received, as Saint Augustine says. This is expressly realized in the words of Jesus Christ, for He does not say to the bread that it should become His body, but He directs His word to the company of the faithful, saying: Take, eat, and so forth (Matt 26:26). If we wish, then, rightly to celebrate the sacrament, it is necessary for us to have the doctrine by which what is signified in it, is declared to us. I know perfectly well that that seems like an outrageous opinion to those who are unaccustomed to it, as is the case with all new things. But it is certainly right, if we are disciples of Jesus Christ, that we prefer His institution to our practice. And what He instituted from the beginning ought not to appear to us like novel opinion.

If that still cannot penetrate everyone's understanding, it will be necessary for us to pray to God that it please Him to enlighten the ignorant, to make them understand how much wiser He is than anyone on earth, so that they will learn to be satisfied no longer with their own judgment or with the foolish and maddened wisdom of their blind leaders. Meanwhile, for the use of our church, it seemed well advised to us to have a formulary of prayers and the sacraments published, in order that everyone might know what he should say and do in the Christian assembly. The book will be profitable not only for the people of this church, but also for all those who wish to know what form the faithful should maintain and follow when they gather together in the name of Jesus Christ. We have therefore collected as in a summary the manner of celebrating the sacraments and sanctifying marriage; likewise the prayers and praises which we use. We will speak a little later of the sacraments.

As for the public prayers, there are two kinds: the first are made with the word only, the others with song. And this not a thing invented a short time ago. For from the first origin of the church, this has been so, as appears from the histories. And even Saint Paul speaks not only of praying aloud, but also of singing (Col 3:16). And in truth we know from experience that song has great force and vigor to arouse and inflame people's hearts to invoke and praise God with a more vehement and ardent zeal. There must always be concern that the song be neither light nor frivolous, but have gravity and majesty, as Saint Augustine says. And thus there is a great difference between the music which one makes to entertain people at table and in their homes, and the psalms which are sung in the church in the presence of God and His angels. Now when anyone wishes to judge correctly of the form which is here presented, we hope that he will find it holy and pure, seeing that it is simply directed to the edification of which we have spoken.

And how much more widely the practice of singing may extend! It is even in the homes and in the fields an incentive for us, and, as it were, an organ for praising God and lifting up our hearts to Him, to console us by meditating on His virtue, goodness, wisdom, and justice, something which is more necessary than one can say. For in the first place it is not without cause that the Holy Spirit exhorts us so carefully through the Holy Scriptures to rejoice in God (Phil 3:1, 4:4), and that all our joy is there, as it were, brought back to its true end. For He knows how much we are inclined to rejoice in vanity. Thus then, as our nature draws us and induces us to look for all manner of demented and vicious rejoicing, so to the contrary our Lord, to distract us and withdraw us from the temptations of the flesh and the world, presents us all means possible to occupy us in that spiritual joy which He recommends to us so much.

Now among the other things which are appropriate for recreating people and giving them pleasure, music is either the first or one of the principal, and we must value it as a gift of God deputed to that use. Wherefore that much more ought we to take care not to abuse it, for fear of fouling and contaminating it, converting it to our condemnation, when it was dedicated to our profit and welfare. If there were no other consideration than this alone, it may indeed move us to moderate the use of music, to make it serve everything virtuous, and that it ought not to give occasion for our giving free rein to licentiousness, or for our making ourselves effeminate in disordered delights, and that it ought not to become an instrument of dissipation or of any obscenity. But there is still more. For there is scarcely anything in the world which is more capable of turning or moving morals this way and that, as Plato prudently considered it. And in fact we experience that it has a secret and almost incredible power to arouse hearts in one way or another.

Wherefore we ought to be the more diligent in regulating it in such a way that it be useful to us and not at all pernicious. For this reason the ancient doctors of the church complain frequently of the fact that the people of their times were addicted to unseemly and obscene songs which, not without reason, they judge and call mortal and Satanic poison for corruption of the world. Moreover, in speaking now of music, I understand two parts, that is to say the letter, or subject and matter; second, the song or the melody. It is true that every evil word (as Saint Paul says, 1 Cor 15:33) perverts good morals, but when the melody is with it, it pierces the heart that much more strongly and enters into it; just as through a funnel wine is poured into a container, so also venom and corruption are distilled to the depth of the heart by the melody. What is there then to do? It is to have songs not only seemly, but also holy, which will be like spurs to incite us to pray to and praise God, to meditate on His works in order to love, fear, honor, and glorify Him. Now what Saint Augustine says is true, that no one is able to sing things worthy of God unless he has received them from Him.

Wherefore, when we have looked thoroughly everywhere and searched high and low, we shall find no better songs nor more appropriate to the purpose than the psalms of David which the Holy Spirit made and spoke through him. And furthermore, when we sing them, we are certain that God puts the words in our mouths, as if He Himself were singing in us to exalt His glory. Wherefore Chrysostom exhorts men as well as women and little children to accustom themselves to sing them, in order that this may be, as it were, a meditation for associating themselves with the company of angels. As for the rest, it is necessary for us to remember what Saint Paul says, that spiritual songs can be sung truly only from the heart (Eph 5:19, Col 3:16). Now the heart requires intelligence, and in that (says Saint Augustine) lies the difference between human singing and that of the birds. For a linnet, a nightingale, a parrot may sing well, but it will be without understanding. Now the peculiar gift of a person is to sing knowing what he is saying. The heart and the affection must follow after the intelligence, which is impossible unless we have the hymn imprinted on our memory in order never to cease from singing.

For these reasons the present book, even for this cause, in addition to the rest which has been said, ought to be under exceptional consideration by everyone who desires to enjoy himself in seemly fashion and in accordance with God, to look to his salvation and to the profit of his neighbors. And so there is no necessity for it to be particularly recommended by me, seeing that it carries its own value and praise. Only let the world be so well advised that in place of songs in part empty and frivolous, in part stupid and dull, in part obscene and vile, and in consequence evil and harmful, which it has used up to now, it may accustom itself hereafter to singing these divine and celestial hymns with the good King David. Touching the melody, it has seemed best that it be moderated in the manner which we have adopted, to carry gravity and majesty appropriate to the subject, and even to be suitable for singing in the church, in accordance with what has been said.

Geneva, 10 June 1543

SECTION II:
SUNDAY WORSHIP IN CALVIN'S GENEVA

Sunday worship was the central and most important liturgy of the week. There were, however, various Sunday services, a total of four, in fact.

At dawn (4 A.M. in summer, 5 A.M. in winter) a regular preaching service was held for servants or others who might have domestic duties the rest of the day. This service had certain similarities to the main morning service; on the Sundays the Lord's supper was celebrated, the dawn service was also a supper service, because no one should be excluded from sharing that most special sacrament simply because he or she was not free to attend the main morning service. The dawn service was a favorite time for baptisms and marriages. The latter were prohibited on days the supper was celebrated, and baptisms also were usually not held if the supper was, although this was essentially a matter of convenience, not precept.[25]

The other three Sunday services are better known. The central one was the main mid-morning service (usually 8 A.M. by the early modern clock), at which all the important announcements were made, and at which Calvin always preached unless prevented by travel, illness, or other church business, such as installing a new minister. The third service was the weekly catechism at noon, to which all children and others who were not yet able to give an accounting of their faith were obliged to come, until they could demonstrate publicly a sufficient understanding of the faith to be admitted to the Lord's supper. The fourth service was the Sunday afternoon preaching service, usually mid-afternoon (3 P.M., though in deep winter it was moved to 2 P.M.). Calvin also usually preached at this service, and since this was the other time (besides dawn) when marriages were held on Sundays, this is when Calvin most often performed weddings.

The outline above explains the sequence of a regular Sunday with its four services. Below are presented the texts for parts of two Sundays: the main morning Service of the Word and catechism one week, and the main morning service with the Lord's supper the next week, with a passage specifically explaining the supper intercalated.

98

• First Sunday: The Service of the Word is presented in summary fashion, in order to indicate how the liturgy flowed when the supper was not celebrated. (The main differences, besides not having the supper itself, were that the Decalogue, the Apostles' Creed, and the Song of Simeon were not included.) The noon catechism is represented by the examination that children were expected to pass before admission to the Lord's supper.

• Pastoral Preparation for the Supper: An excerpt from Calvin's "Short Treatise on the Lord's Supper" is given next to provide a fuller introduction to what being prepared for the sacrament meant, beyond the basic catechetical knowledge.

• Second/Supper Sunday: The final entry is a full service of word and sacrament, complete with sermon.

The texts of *La forme des prières,* which contain the liturgies for Sunday morning, the sacraments, and the Day of Prayer, are found in OS 2, pp. 11–58, although some changes have been made to follow later slightly revised editions, especially 1552/53.

The Lord's Day Service of the Word

The order is that of 1562, including three times of song; before 1562 only one psalm was sung between the confession of sin and the minister's prayer. The translation introduced here and given fully below is that which Bard Thompson made of the 1542 edition of Calvin's liturgy, *La forme des prières*, but it has here been modified slightly to follow the text of the liturgy as it was given final form in 1552. The beginnings of the prayers are indicated in a way that allows the reader to fill in the rest of the text from the following Sunday's service under *The Lord's Day Service with the Lord's Supper.* The psalms were chosen from the 1562 table published in the psalter, with week 7 being arbitrarily selected as an illustration of the way the congregational singing was fitted into worship.

Calvin's printed *La forme des prières* was very sparely provided with rubrics or instructions for gestures and movements, and in Geneva even some of the prayers (such as the minister's petition for the Holy Spirit to illumine the minds and seal the hearts of the hearers) must be found in other places. As was explained in the General Introduction, words printed here both in italics and underlined are the interpolations of the editor of this volume, for which the sources are explained elsewhere. In addition to the acts noted in the liturgy given here, the main Sunday morning service included a number of announcements on ordinary Sundays. The most common and probably most time-consuming announcements would be marriage banns. Much more rarely there might also be the convocation of someone (man or woman) who had failed to appear to fulfill a promise of marriage or who had abandoned a spouse; occasionally there might be announcements of excommunication or rituals of reconciliation. Also infrequently, a new minister might be presented to the people (installed). It is not clear when these additional aspects of the life of the worshiping community would be done; probably most of these would be made at the end of the service, and certainly the rituals of reconciliation would follow the service.[26]

The Main Morning Lord's Day Service *[which begins with the second ringing of the largest bell of St. Pierre, called Clémence]*

1562: PSALM #55 "O My God, Hear My Prayer" *[people probably seated for this and other singing]*

INVOCATION Our help is in the name of God, who made heaven and earth. Amen. *[minister in pulpit, people may kneel from opening scripture sentence until after the confession of sin; they certainly kneel for the confession]*

CONFESSION OF SIN My brethren, let each of you present himself before the face of the Lord, and confess his faults and sins, following my words in his heart.
   O Lord God, eternal and almighty Father, we confess and acknowledge unfeignedly before Your holy majesty...

PSALM #27 "The Lord Is My Light" [1st part]

MINISTER'S EXTEMPORE PRAYER FOR ILLUMINATION-SEALING
   We call upon our heavenly Father, Father of all goodness and mercy,...

BIBLICAL TEXT AND SERMON-EXPOSITION

PRAYER We bow ourselves before the majesty of our good God in recognition of our faults,...and persevere in this spiritual battle until we shall attain full victory, to triumph at last in Your kingdom with our Captain and Protector, Jesus Christ our Lord.

1562: PSALM #27 "The Lord Is My Light" [2nd part]

BENEDICTION The Lord bless you and keep you....

An Aspect of the Noon Catechism

The catechism service at noon in each Genevan parish was a regular time of weekly instruction. The substance of the study was Calvin's 1542–45 catechism, with its fifty-five divisions of questions on faith and the Apostles' Creed, law and the Decalogue, prayer and the Lord's Prayer, and the sacraments. The chief purpose of the catechism services was to prepare children and others for admission to the Lord's supper, and so it became the custom on the four Sundays each year prior to the celebration of the supper to have a public examination of the candidates who were considered ready to give an accounting of their faith. Calvin's catechism was a summary of the doctrine Genevans were supposed to understand, but in the examination the children were asked a series of much simpler questions. The earliest printed form of this particular question-and-answer pattern was published in 1551; it did not include recitation of the Creed, Decalogue, and Lord's Prayer, but these were added in several later versions of the text. Here the additions made in the second edition of the text are indicated in italics; the original is found in OC 6:147–60,[27] the translation is by E. A. McKee.

"The Way of Questioning the Children Whom You Wish to Receive at the Supper of Our Lord Jesus Christ"

First the minister [M] asks: In whom do you believe? *And in whom do you put all trust for your salvation?*

The child [C]: *I believe* in God the Father and in Jesus Christ His Son, and in the Holy Spirit, *and I hope for salvation only from them.*

M: The Father, the Son, and the Holy Spirit, are they more than one God?
C: No.
M: *What confession of faith do you make?*
C: *That which the Christian Church has always made, which is called the Apostles' Creed, which is: I believe in God...*
M: *What is the sum of this confession?*
C: *That God is the Father of our Lord Jesus Christ, and therefore of all of us by means of Him; He is the beginning and principal cause of all things, which He so guides that nothing is done without His ordering and providence. Then that Jesus Christ His Son came down into this world, and He did all that was required for our salvation;*

101

and He will come again from heaven in judgment, from where He ascended to sit at the right hand of the Father; that is, He has all power in heaven and earth. Also, that the Holy Spirit is true God, because He is the strength and power of God, and He impresses on our hearts the promises that have been made to us in Jesus Christ. So we confess that we believe in the Holy Spirit, as in the Father and the Son, who is the eternal Wisdom of God. Finally, we believe that the church is sanctified and delivered from her sins by the grace of God, and she will rise again to eternal life.

M: Must we serve God according to His commandments, or according to human traditions?

C: We must serve Him according to His commandments and not according to human commandments.

M: *Where do you find the commandments of God?*

C: *In various places in the Holy Scriptures, and especially in the twentieth chapter of Exodus (Exod 20:2–17); where it is recounted that God Himself spoke them aloud, saying: I am the Lord Your God...*

M: Can you accomplish the commandments of God by yourself?

C: No.

M: Who is it then that accomplishes them in you?

C: The Holy Spirit.

M: When God gives you His Holy Spirit, can you fulfill them perfectly?

C: Not at all.

M: And yet God curses and rejects all those who do not entirely fulfill His commandments (Deut 27:26).

C: That is true.

M: By what means then are you saved and delivered from the condemnation of God?

C: By the death and passion of our Lord Jesus Christ.

M: How is that?

C: Because by His death He has brought us back to life and reconciled us to God His Father, *and as St. Paul says, He died for our sins and has been raised for our justification (Rom 4:25).*

M: To whom do you pray?

C: To God.

M: In whose name do you pray to Him?

C: In the name of our Lord Jesus Christ, who is our Advocate and Intercessor.

M: *And how do you pray to Him?*

C: *As our Lord Jesus taught us in the prayer which He gave to His apostles for all His church, in which is contained all that we need to ask of our good God and Father, and it begins (Matt 6:9–13): Our Father who art in heaven...*

M: *Is it not permitted to use other forms of prayer, or to pray to God differently from this?*

C: *Yes, certainly. But all the forms must be measured by this one.*

M: *Why?*

C: *Because in this prayer is contained all that God wants us to ask of Him.*

M: How many sacraments are there in the Christian Church?

C: Two.

M: What are they?

C: Baptism and the holy supper.

M: What is the meaning of baptism?

C: There are two parts: for there our Lord represents the remission of our sins, and then our regeneration or spiritual renewal.

M: What does the supper signify to us?

C: It signifies to us that, by the communication of the body and blood of our Lord Jesus Christ, our souls are nourished in the hope of eternal life.

M: What do the bread and wine, which are given to us in the supper, show to us?

C: They show to us that the body and blood of Jesus Christ have the same power for our souls as the bread and wine have for our bodies.

M: Do you understand the body of Jesus Christ to be enclosed in the bread, or His blood in the wine?

C: No.

M: Where then must we seek Jesus Christ to have the fruition of Him?

C: In heaven, in the glory of God, His Father.

M: What is the means to reach to heaven where Jesus Christ is?

C: Faith.

M: Then we must have true faith before we can rightly use this sacrament.

C: Yes.

M: How can we have true faith?

C: We have it by the Holy Spirit, who lives in our hearts and who makes us certain of God's promises, which are given to us in the gospel.

M: *Go in peace, and may this good God increase His graces more and more in you and in all of us, His children.*

C: *So be it, by our Lord Jesus Christ. Amen.*

Excerpt from "A Short Treatise on the Lord's Supper"

This little treatise of five brief headings, published in 1541, is one of Calvin's most accessible explanations of the Lord's supper. The original is found in OS 1, pp. 503–50; here portions of the first three sections are presented in the translation of J. K. S. Reid.

It should be noted that Calvin appeals for a greater frequency of celebration than the four times a year that the Genevan government allowed, because the Lord's supper is food and medicine that the faithful should want as often as possible. He insists that the real worthiness needed in order to partake is repentance and trust in Christ, not perfection, though people of scandalous life and especially those harboring bitterness against others must not come to the table. Each person is to examine himself or herself, not the neighbor; the discipline of the community is the responsibility of the corporate leadership of the church, not individuals, whether ministers or parishioners. Calvin accepts that someone might abstain from the supper for a time because of some great spiritual hindrance, but this should not become a habit; as much as possible, everyone should commune each time Christ's body and blood are offered to the gathered company of believers. Calvin emphasizes that, besides feeding the believer, the supper is the bond of love that should incite the members of Christ's body to all acts of love for their neighbors.

Thus far Calvin's theology; however, in order to understand the practical pastoral sensitivity that accompanied it, it is helpful to look at what happened in Geneva. Those who were obviously not ready to share in the supper because of scandal or bitterness were carefully examined by the Consistory and told not to partake; their participation would dishonor God and harm themselves and the church. However, the main work of the church's corporate leadership was diligently to seek out any who could be brought to a right spirit, so that they might share in the sacrament. Reconciling neighbors was one of the most important tasks of Calvin's Consistory; in the week before the supper was to be held, that "disciplinary" body met more frequently than usual, specifically in order to help the entire community prepare to participate rightly in the great celebration of the supper.[28]

[Introduction omitted]

I. Reason for the Institution of the Holy Supper

As to the first article: Since it pleased our loving God to receive us by baptism into His church, which is His house, and which He will maintain and govern, and since He has received us not only to keep us as servants, but as His own children, it remains that, to discharge the office of a loving father, He nourish us, and provide all that is necessary to life....But just as God has set all fullness of life in Jesus, in order to communicate it to us by means of Him, so He has ordained His word as instrument by which Jesus Christ, with all His benefits, is dispensed to us. Yet it always remains true that our souls have no other pasture than Jesus Christ....We have already seen how Jesus Christ is the only provision by which our souls are nourished. But because it is distributed by the word of the Lord, which He has appointed as instrument to this end, it is also called bread and water. Now what is said of the word fitly belongs also to the sacrament of the supper, by means of which our Lord leads us to communion with Jesus Christ. For seeing we are so foolish that we cannot receive Him with true confidence of heart when He is presented by simple teaching and preaching, the Father, of His mercy, not at all disdaining to condescend in this matter to our infirmity, has desired to attach to His word a visible sign, by which He represents the substance of His promises, to confirm and fortify us, and to deliver us from all doubt and uncertainty.

...For this reason, the Lord instituted for us His supper, in order to sign and seal in our consciences the promises contained in His gospel concerning our being made partakers of His body and blood; and to give us certainty and assurance that in this consists our true spiritual nourishment; so that, having such an earnest, we might entertain a right assurance about salvation. Second, for the purpose of inciting us to recognize His great goodness toward us, so that we praise and magnify it more fully. Third, to exhort us to all sanctity and innocence, seeing that we are members of Jesus Christ, and particularly to unity and brotherly charity, as is specially recommended to us in it. When we have noted well these three reasons, which our Lord imposed in ordaining His supper for us, we shall be in a position to understand both what benefits accrue to us from it, and what is our duty in its right use.

II. Benefits of the Holy Supper

It is now time to come to the second point, namely, to show how profitable the supper of our Lord is to us, on condition that we make profitable use of it....Or to explain the matter more simply, as we in ourselves are lacking in all good and have not a particle of what might help us to salvation, the supper is attestation that, being made partakers of the death and passion of Jesus Christ, we have everything that is useful and salutary for us. Therefore we can say that the Lord here displays to us all the treasures of His spiritual grace, seeing that He makes us associates of all the blessings and riches of our Lord Jesus Christ. Let us remember then, that the supper is given us as a mirror, in which we may contemplate Jesus Christ crucified to deliver us from damnation, and risen again to procure righteousness and eternal life for us. It is indeed true that this same grace is offered us by the gospel; yet as in the supper we have a more ample certainty and fuller enjoyment, it is with good reason that we recognize such a fruit as coming from it.

...Now, if it be asked nevertheless whether the bread is the body of Christ, and the wine His blood, we should reply that the bread and the wine are visible signs, which represent to us the body and the blood; but that the name and title of body and blood is attributed to them, because they are as instruments by which our Lord Jesus Christ distributes them to us....It is a spiritual mystery, which cannot be seen by the eye, nor comprehended by the human understanding. It is therefore symbolized by visible signs, as our infirmity requires, but in such a way that it is not a bare figure, but joined to its reality and substance. It is therefore with good reason that the bread is called body, since not only does it represent it to us, but also presents it to us....Thus, as a brief definition of this benefit of the supper, we may say that Jesus Christ is there offered to us that we may possess Him, and in Him all the fullness of His gifts which we can desire; and that in this we have great assistance in confirming our conscience in the faith which we ought to have in Him.

The second benefit which the supper yields us is that it urges and incites us the better to recognize the blessings which we have received, and daily receive, from the Lord Jesus Christ, so that we may render Him such offering of praise as is His due....

The third benefit consists in our having a vehement incitement to holy living, and above all to observe charity and brotherly love among us. For since we are there made members of Jesus Christ, being incorporated into Him and united to Him as to our Head, this is good reason, first, that we be conformed to His purity and innocence, and especially that we have to one another such charity and concord as members of the same body ought to have....

III. The Right Use of the Sacrament

Let us come to the third chief head which we proposed at the beginning of this treatise, that is to the right use, which consists in observing the institution of our Lord with reverence. For whoever approaches this holy sacrament with contempt or indifference, not caring much about following where our Lord calls him, perversely misuses it and thus contaminates it....

If we wish, then, to communicate worthily in the sacred Supper of our Lord, we must hold in firm and hearty confidence the Lord Jesus Christ as our sole righteousness, life and salvation, receiving and accepting the promises which are given us by Him as certain and assured; renouncing on the other hand all other confidence, in order that, distrusting ourselves and all other creatures, we may rest fully in Him and content ourselves with His grace alone....Here, then, is how we should come to Him in true repentance, in the remembrance that our life is to be conformed to the example of Jesus Christ. While this should be general in all parts of our life, yet it has a special application to charity, which is above all recommended to us in this sacrament; for which reason it is called the bond of charity. For as the bread, which is there sanctified for the common use of us all, is made of many grains so mixed together that one cannot be discerned from the other, so ought we to be united among ourselves in one indissoluble friendship....We must then not at all presume to approach, if we bear any hatred or rancor against any living person and especially any Christian who may be within the unity of the church....

But because no one will be found on earth who has so advanced in faith and sanctity of life, that he does not still have much infirmity in the one as in the other, there might be a danger that some good consciences be troubled by what has been said, if one did not obviate it by moderating the commands which we have imposed concerning both faith and repentance. It is a perilous method of teaching that some adopt, to demand a perfect confidence of heart and a perfect penitence, and to exclude all who do not have them. For in so doing, all are excluded without exception....When we feel within us a strong distaste and hatred of all vices, proceeding from the fear of God, and a desire to live well in order to please our Lord, we are fit to partake of the supper, notwithstanding the vestiges of infirmity which we carry in our flesh. If indeed we were not weak, subject to mistrust, and imperfect in life, the sacrament would be of no service to us, and it would have been superfluous to institute it. Since then it is a remedy which God has given us to assist our frailty, to fortify our faith, to augment our charity, and to further us in all sanctity of life, so far from this making us abstain, we ought the more to make use of it the more we feel oppressed by the disease. For if we allege as pretext for not coming to the supper that we are still weak in faith or in integrity of life, it is as if a person excuse himself from taking medicine because he is sick. This then is how the frailty of the faith which we feel in our heart and the imperfections which persist in our life ought to incite us to come to the supper, as to a remedy designed to correct them. Only let us not come without faith or repentance. Of these, the former is hidden in the heart, and therefore our conscience must testify concerning us before God. The second manifests itself by works, and therefore must be somehow apparent in our life.

As to the time of using it, there can be no certain rule for all. For there are certain particular impediments which excuse a person for absenting himself. And besides we have no express command, constraining Christians to make use of it every day it is offered to them. However, if we have careful regard to the end for which our Lord intended it, we should realize that the use of it ought to be more frequent than many make it. For the more infirmity oppresses us, the more frequently we need to have recourse to that which is able and ought to serve to confirm our faith and further us in purity of life. Therefore, the custom ought to be well established in all churches of celebrating the supper as frequently as the capacity of the people will allow. And each individual in his own place ought to prepare himself to receive it whenever it is administered in the congregation, unless there be some grave hindrance which compels him to abstain....

The excuses which some allege on the other hand, are very frivolous. Some say that they feel themselves unworthy, and under cover of this abstain from it for a whole year. Others, not content with wondering about their worthiness, pretend that they cannot communicate with persons whom they see coming without good preparation. Some again think it is superfluous to use it often, since, if we have once received Jesus Christ, there is no need to return so often afterward to receive Him. I ask the first, who make a cover of their unworthiness, how their conscience can allow them to remain more than a year in so poor a state that they dare not invoke God directly? For they will confess that it is audacity to invoke God as our Father if we are not members of Jesus Christ. This we cannot be, unless the substance and reality of the supper be fulfilled in us. Now if we have the reality, we are, a fortiori, capable of receiving the sign. It is evident, then, that he who would exempt himself from receiving the supper because of

unworthiness, bars himself from praying to God. For the rest, I
have no intention of forcing consciences that are tormented with
certain scruples, that they present themselves, they know not
how; I rather advise them to wait till the Lord deliver them. Simi-
larly, if there is a legitimate cause of hindrance, I do not deny that
it is lawful to defer coming. Only I would point out that no one
ought to remain content for long to abstain from the supper
because of his unworthiness, seeing that to do so deprives him of
the communion of the church in which all our good consists.
Rather let him strive to contend against all the impediments
which the devil puts before him, in order not to be excluded from
so great a benefit and consequently from all the gifts of which
absence would deprive him.

The second class [of those with objections] have some plausibility, for they employ the following argument. If it is not allowed
to eat the common bread with those who call themselves brothers
but lead a dissolute and wicked life, a fortiori, we ought to abstain
from communicating with them in the bread of our Lord, which is
sanctified to represent and dispense to us the body of Christ. But
the reply is not very difficult. It is not the office of each individual
to judge and discriminate, in order to admit or reject as seems to
him good; seeing that this prerogative belongs generally to the
church as a whole, or rather to the pastor with the elders whom he
ought to have for assisting him in the government of the church.
For Paul does not command us to examine others, but each is to
examine himself (1 Cor 11:28). It is very true that our duty is to
admonish those whom we see to live disorderly, and, if they will
not listen, to advise the pastor of them, in order that he take pro-
ceedings on the authority of the church. But the right way of withdrawing from the company of the wicked is not to quit the
communion of the church. Moreover, it will most frequently happen that sins are not so notorious as to justify going the length of
excommunication. For though the pastor in his heart judge someone unworthy, yet he has not the power of pronouncing him to be
so, or of interdicting him from the supper, unless he can prove it
by an ecclesiastical judgment. In this case, we have no other remedy than to pray to God, that He would deliver His church more

and more from all scandals, and to await the Last Day, when the chaff will be manifestly separated from the good grain.

The third class [of those with objections] have no semblance of plausibility. For this spiritual bread is not given us in order that on the first occasion we eat our fill of it; but rather that, having had some taste of its sweetness, we may long for it the more and use it when it is offered us. This is what we have expounded above, that while we remain in this mortal life Jesus Christ is never communicated to us in such a way that our souls are wholly satisfied with Him, but He desires to be our continual nourishment.

The Lord's Day Service with Lord's Supper

For notes on the order of service and translation of the liturgy, see above under *The Lord's Day Service of the Word*; a careful comparison of the two texts will indicate the portions of the liturgy that are specific to the supper service. The Decalogue and Song of Simeon were sung only at the supper service. Before 1562, when there was only one psalm (between the confession of sin and the minister's prayer), the Decalogue replaced the psalm on the supper Sunday. By 1562 the congregation sang three times in the liturgy on Sunday mornings, afternoons, and the Day of Prayer, so at the supper service the Decalogue replaced the third psalm in the supper part of the liturgy. Calvin preached the sermon presented here on Easter, April 14, 1560. The original is edited in the *Supplementa Calviniana* series, volume 7, pp. 91–99, translated here by E. A. McKee; ellipses indicate lacunae in the manuscript. The psalms are chosen from the 1562 table, week 8, to follow those presented above for the previous week.

Service of the Word and Sacrament [after the second ringing of the great bell of St. Pierre, called Clémence]

1562: PSALM #60 "O God, You Have Cast Us Out"

INVOCATION Our help is in the name of God, who made heaven and earth. Amen.

CONFESSION OF SIN My brethren, let each of you present himself before the face of the Lord and confess his faults and sins, following my words in his heart.

O Lord God, eternal and almighty Father, we confess and acknowledge unfeignedly before Your holy majesty that we are

111

poor sinners, conceived and born in iniquity and corruption, prone to do evil, incapable of any good, and that in our depravity we transgress Your holy commandments without end or ceasing: Wherefore we purchase for ourselves, through Your righteous judgment, our ruin and perdition. Nevertheless, O Lord, we are grieved that we have offended You; and we condemn ourselves and our sins with true repentance, beseeching Your grace to relieve our distress.

O God and Father most gracious and full of compassion, have mercy upon us in the name of Your Son, our Lord Jesus Christ. And as You blot out our sins and stains, magnify and increase in us day by day the grace of Your Holy Spirit so that as we acknowledge our unrighteousness with all our heart, we may be moved by that sorrow which shall bring forth true repentance in us, mortifying all our sins, and producing in us the fruits of righteousness and innocence that are pleasing unto You; through the same Jesus Christ Your Son our Lord. Amen.

1562: PSALM #28 "O God You Are My Fortress" *[approximately 1546–62: Decalogue]*

MINISTER'S EXTEMPORE PRAYER FOR ILLUMINATION-SEALING

We call upon our heavenly Father, Father of all goodness and mercy, asking Him to cast the eye of His mercy on us His poor servants, not imputing to us the many faults and offenses we have committed, by which we have provoked His wrath against us, but [instead] seeing us in the face of His Son, Jesus Christ our Lord, as He has established Him as Mediator between Him and us. Let us pray that, as the whole plenitude of wisdom and light is in Him, He may guide us by His Holy Spirit to the true understanding of His holy teaching, and may make it bear in us all the fruits of righteousness, to the glory and honor of His Name, and the instruction and edification of His church. And we will pray to Him in the name and the favor of His beloved Son Jesus Christ, as we have been taught by Him, saying:[29] Our Father who art in heaven,...

> On the eve of the Sabbath, as the day began to dawn for the first day of the week, Mary Magdalene and the other Mary came to see the sepulchre. And behold, there was a great shaking of the earth, for the angel of the Lord came down from heaven and came and rolled the stone away from the door and sat upon it. And his face was like lightning and his clothing white as snow. (Matt 28:1–10)

We will have no profit from the resurrection of our Lord Jesus Christ unless we seek Him by faith, to be united to Him, in order also by this means to be participants in all that is His. And the example for that is offered to us here, when it is said that Mary Magdalene and her companions came to the sepulcher. It is true that there is some fault and roughness, in that they wanted to anoint our Lord Jesus Christ and they never thought of what He had foretold and testified so many times, that He must be resurrected. But still we see a good and holy zeal in the fact that they did not abandon their master, even though He had been crucified with such calumny that He could have been despised. For in His death He had not only been condemned by the people, but also bore in our person the curse of God, which He had pronounced in the law (Deut 21:23). That might well have disgusted these poor women, unless they had always persevered in that foundation: that our Lord Jesus Christ was the Redeemer who had been sent by God His Father. They had then this beginning [to lead them] to come and seek Him. There is, however, weakness and ignorance mixed in, but that is not imputed to them.

For our part, as I have already mentioned, we must follow this affection that the women had to seek our Lord Jesus Christ. But we must look further, because it has been sufficiently testified to us that He was raised in order to acquire the victory over death for us and to make us share in heavenly life. Since then that is so, let us note what is said by St. Paul: that He was raised according to the scriptures (1 Cor 15:4). See the way we are supposed to seek Him, that is, if we consider the fruit and power, if we consider also the use and purpose and

113

effect of His resurrection according to the way the scriptures show it to us. The angel had to come before the women to tell them that Jesus Christ was no longer in the grave. So the angel corrected the fault in these poor women, as we have already said. But when we have the witness of the Holy Scripture, and we are established on it and join with it what is here recounted by St. Matthew and by the other evangelists, which is that Jesus Christ, truly resurrected, has perfected and accomplished all that God testified in His law and by His prophets (Luke 24:25–27), then we have no need to be corrected by an angel, because we will be following the right path. This then in sum is what we must note in the first place: that Jesus Christ, rising from the dead, truly raised the banner to gather us to Himself, so that we might be assured that He acquired for us heavenly life, and that our hope will not be confounded when we know that He has been declared and proved to be the Son of God in His resurrection. And that His power was there demonstrated not only for His own person but in order that we might know that He also wants to bring us to life; and (as St. Paul says in the eighth chapter of Romans [Rom 8:11]) that the Holy Spirit by whom Jesus Christ was raised lives in us, inasmuch as He has given Him to us. Thus, since this Spirit is life and He has the Spirit in Himself, even though we have received only a small portion, still it is sufficient to destroy all that is mortal and corruptible in us.

For the rest, let us note that the angel spoke not only for the instruction of the women but also for ours, because we must join to it what is recounted here; that is, that the women were sent to the disciples to announce to them the resurrection of our Lord Jesus Christ. It was necessary that the apostles, although they had been chosen to proclaim the gospel throughout the world and to be the teachers of great and small, nevertheless had to go to school to women. It was because they had profited so little during the three years that Jesus Christ had properly taught them what was required for their salvation—there was such an ignorance in them, that they were as if fainting when they saw their master crucified. There was good reason that they were so shamed, that they learned from the women what they had not remembered from the Son of God, who is the wisdom not only of all the world but of the angels in paradise. Now then we see that when the angel spoke it was to confirm the women, and in the first place to remove this error that they had; and then by this means God wanted the apostles to know that Jesus Christ had risen, that this teaching might be of general profit to everyone. So then this voice of the angel, which is recounted here, is addressed to all those today who want to seek our Lord Jesus Christ, to adhere to Him.

It is said that the angel appeared with signs and marks of celestial glory. That was in order the better to prove his testimony, so that it might be beyond doubt. It is true that by their nature angels are invisible, but God, when He has appeared through them, has always given them some visible form of human nature. Yet He wanted them to show infallible signs that He had sent them, because we know that creatures do not have this authority to be able to order our faith and give us assurance; God has to speak. When He sends angels, He shows Himself as we see here, because He impresses on them the marks of His majesty, so that it may be understood that these are not phantoms or dreams, but that God in truth wants to appear there and to be known, and He also wants to have homage offered to Him and to have His truth received and accepted without contradiction. See then how what St. Matthew recounts of the appearance of the angel ought to serve us.

It is particularly said "that you must not seek Jesus Christ in the grave, inasmuch as He is risen." See also why it is said in St. John that Jesus Christ restrained the women when they grasped Him by the feet (John 20:17). St. Matthew and the others recount indeed that they worshiped Jesus Christ when they took Him by the feet, but this correction is particularly expressed...that our Lord Jesus Christ did not want them to stop there. And why? Because we are so heavy and earthly that we would like to have our Lord Jesus Christ according to our own likeness and fancy. We must raise both our eyes and our senses above to be united to

115

Him, as also St. Paul exhorts us to do (Col 3:1). Jesus Christ therefore said that He did not at all want to be touched in this fashion: He did not want it to be imagined that He continues to live on the earth, as when He had dwelt in the midst of people as He had done for a time, but He was ascending to God His Father. See then what we are warned about; that is, in order to be united to our Lord Jesus Christ we must not cling to the earth and be enveloped in our fleshly senses, but let us rise above all that is of the world and let us know that it is by faith that we must come to Him. Faith does not have feet or legs to walk here below, nor does it have wings only to fly over the earth and over the clouds, but it must raise us up above all that we can conceive, it must introduce us into the kingdom of God, because there is where our anchor is fixed, as the apostle says (Heb 6:19). Let us learn then to come to our Lord Jesus Christ by faith. That is what I already mentioned, that we are exhorted by St. Paul to seek Him above, in accordance with His resurrection, that is, through the scriptures.

Now the scriptures not only say that Jesus Christ had to rise for Himself and for His apostles, but at the same time the experience is there set out according to our ability to receive it and our measure of time. We see what has been said by the prophet Isaiah (Isa 26:19) and then by Daniel (Dan 12:2), and what had been said before in Psalm 22 (Ps 22:26–30). Because there the power and the fruit of the resurrection of the Son of God are depicted for us, when He says that He will praise the name of God with His brothers; and then that there will be a holy banquet prepared, and great and small will be satisfied and filled there, and that even those who go down into the grave where there is nothing but weakness, who are like lost people: even those will receive the vitality to be completely restored. It is also said by Isaiah: Who will announce His age (Isa 53:8)? And then it is said in Daniel that He will acquire eternal righteousness (Dan 9:24). We see then that the prophets not only said in a word that the Son of God should rise, but they showed at the same time that this was in order to give lasting life to all the body of His church. They showed what St. Paul says in the other passage (Rom 4:25), that the resurrection of our Lord Jesus Christ is our righteousness.

They showed that that should be applied to us, and that we do not have simply the word, but that God wants us to be nourished and satisfied that our Lord Jesus Christ prepares a solemn banquet for us, not for the nourishment and feeding of our bodies but of our souls. And on that account we may learn to sing praise to God with Him. See then what we have to remember from this warning given us by the angel, that is, that Jesus Christ, being raised, calls us to Himself and wants us to rise above the whole world, and that by faith we may be joined and united to Him in order to be participants in all that is His.

He particularly wanted His resurrection to be announced to His disciples so that they might be witnesses of it to us, and He calls them His brothers, as in this passage from the psalm we cited (Ps 22:23): the faithful are called thus [His brothers]. See then how we know and can be persuaded and sure that Jesus Christ did not rise for Himself but for our profit and salvation: by the means of the brotherhood He has with us when He calls Himself our brother and gives us that very honorable title. Here we ought to be confounded in ourselves and transported with astonishment, recognizing how good the Son of God is. He who is chief over the angels, the Lord of glory, God manifest in the flesh, He who is life, who had a majesty equal to that of His Father before the creation of the world; that He might come to put Himself so low as to name Himself brother to us, who are only poor vermin and corruption (according to the body), and then full of stinking and every abomination (as regards our souls), inasmuch as we are contaminated with sin; He comes down from paradise to us, who are lost and damned. Because when He wants to raise us up to Himself, where does He find us? He finds us among the limbs of Satan and under the tyranny of sin and hell, and submerged in total condemnation. Now then, as I have already said, on the one hand this name ought indeed to confound us and cause us to glorify the goodness of God even more. Then it should transport us, in that we see that He does not disdain to attribute to us such a high and excellent title, as the apostle says in the second chapter of Hebrews (Heb 2:11).

117

For the rest, in order that we may know that this was not said only of the apostles but that it extends to everyone without exception, it is said in St. Mark that He commands the women to go and tell His brothers and Peter (Mark 16:7). Now Peter was named apart there, not because he had a greater status, but because he had denied his master three times and he deserved to be banished from the kingdom of heaven forever. For he had heard this horrible sentence from the mouth of our Lord Jesus Christ: Whoever denies Me before people, I will deny him before God My Father who is in heaven (Matt 10:33). Peter, having heard that, denies his master, not only once but three times, and indeed with a curse. So then he well deserved to be cut off from all hope of salvation. Now our Lord Jesus Christ especially invites him and says that He accepts him, that He still retains him and maintains him. And how? In what status? As My brother, He says. When, then, we see that St. Peter obtained grace and mercy after such a great and enormous fall, let us know that our Lord Jesus Christ does not consider our merits when He speaks of His brothers, but He wants us to be united to Him, that we may be members of His body, to be children of God, inasmuch as we accept Him for our salvation, after having recognized that in ourselves there is nothing but damnation. After we have despaired in ourselves, let us come to taste His grace, let us receive it and accept it by faith. That is also what we have to remember.

It is true that one might allege that women gave this testimony. And one might ask why our Lord Jesus Christ did not show Himself at first with more pomp in order to prove His resurrection, seeing that it is something so necessary and that without it the gospel is destroyed and there is no longer any hope of life? But since God wanted to use such a means, we should forget all pride and presumption and simply subject ourselves to the fashion He has found good to use to teach us. Then, although women have not authority to teach, and they are not in public office, nonetheless, since God once wanted to do it this way—that our Lord Jesus Christ sent them His angel and He especially commanded them to go and proclaim His resurrection to His disciples—let us humble ourselves, as I have said. Let us recognize that the first way we have access to the gospel is to renounce every foolish presumption and not to be possessed with the pride to want to make a rule, or impose a law, on God, concerning what He ought to do. On the contrary, He wants to test our obedience when He takes away from us what our natural sense regards as desirable. Since then it is said that the women spoke, let us not consider only them, but let us recognize that when the angel appeared the earth was shaken; and God wanted to testify to the resurrection of His Son in such a way that, if we doubt it, that [doubt] proceeds from unbelief and malice. And at the same time there is a despicable ingratitude when we do not apply ourselves to study the works of God. In this way the voice of the women is so well confirmed for us that we have no occasion to argue about their testimony.

And yet let us come to what is added: that they went toward the disciples, and then Jesus Christ met them and they worshiped Him, and finally they announced His resurrection as He had instructed them. We see here the simpleness of the women, because inasmuch as they knew that the angel had been sent by God and that there was nothing doubtful about it, they ought to have submitted completely, knowing well that it was the true sign that God requires above all others, that we submit to His word. For there is no obedience in us when faith is lacking. That is what we must remember in the first place.

And we see how the women profited from what is here recounted, because it was to them that the angel addressed his words: "You, do not fear at all." By his presence he frightened those who ought to have been hardened to great noises and troubles. For look, the soldiers who had been sent to guard the tomb fell down as if half dead when the angel came and the earth shook. The angel left them there. Also unbelievers must be completely flattened in the presence of God, and the glory of our Lord Jesus Christ has to be turned into death for them, as St. Paul says that the gospel is an odor so deadly that unbelievers must perish simply in smelling it from a distance (2 Cor 2:15–16). See then the soldiers at the grave who are enemies of Jesus Christ, and profane people who are prostrated. But the

JOHN CALVIN

angel gives a suitable remedy to the women: "You," he says. We
see how they apply this word to their own use and instruction; let
us learn then to do the same today.

Then, when God gives us this grace, to call us by the gospel
to receive the good that has been acquired for us by the resurrection of His only Son, let us have our ears open and attentive to
receive the testimony of this teaching. For the rest, let us know
that not only the angel spoke, but Jesus Christ came and met the
women. Thus, since we have the testimony of the angel (even two
of them, as St. John recounts [John 20:12]), and the Son of God
Himself, who is the infallible truth, confirms and ratifies this
message which had been brought by the angels, is there any further occasion to doubt? If the angels were not sufficient for us, at
least let us give this honor to the Son of God, to receive what He
said for our use, and let us know that He shows us that His resurrection gives us reason to rejoice, when it is said to the women:
"Fear not." It is true that the women had been seized and possessed with fear, which could have turned them away from profit-
ing well in the resurrection of our Lord Jesus Christ. But be that
as it may, we are shown here that the Son of God, in rising, delivered us from the fear of death, as also the apostle says in the second chapter of Hebrews (Heb 2:15): we must always be held in
captivity and anguish and torment until we are assured that righteousness has been acquired for us and that it has gained the victory over sin and death. If we do not have that [assurance of
victory over sin], what will become of us? Because in Adam we are
already dead. So it is that when we are born, do we bring anything
except the condemnation of God from our mother's womb?
What rest and tranquility can we have then, until our Lord Jesus
Christ shall have drawn us back from this pit of terror? So let us
note that we cannot rejoice, except in knowing that we are participants in the life immortal that has been acquired for us in the resurrection of the Son of God. It is true that here this joy will always
be mixed with trembling and fear, as also is particularly said about
the women: they were troubled in their rejoicing. But that fear
refers to the reverence they had, knowing that God had acted in a
wonderful fashion, He had thus resurrected His Son, because

120

that [act] rose above all human comprehension. See how the women feared. As it is quite reasonable also that we should always tremble in the presence of our God when He gives us some sign of His majesty—then we must indeed fear, because otherwise it would be a very despicable kind of contempt and excessive despising of the glory of God, if we did not tremble before Him. All creatures must be humbled when God appears before them. But that fear is not one of horror, nor does it cause us to flee from God and turn our backs to Him, but it is only to induce in us reverence and humility. And we are not prevented from rejoicing when God declares Himself to us this way, for since His majesty is terrifying to us, when He wants to put that before us it would make us recoil or flee from Him. But knowing our limits, He declares Himself to us in such a way that He gives us courage and boldness to come to Him and approach Him familiarly. That is why Jesus Christ came before the women.

It is true that today He does not show Himself visibly, as He did once to these women of whom it is told here, and then to Peter and to St. John, and then to His apostles, and finally to so many disciples, more than five hundred, as St. Paul tells (1 Cor 15:6). But however that may be, we have the gospel which is the true mirror where we can contemplate our Lord Jesus Christ face to face, as St. Paul says in the third chapter of the second epistle to the Corinthians (2 Cor 3:18). So then our Lord Jesus Christ meets us, as much as is useful for our salvation, providing that we hold to the direction and the path that we have already said, which is to seek Him by faith. What was once spoken by His holy mouth ought to be practiced by us and profitable, when He said: "Go, tell My brothers to go to Galilee, there they will see Me." He sent His disciples to Galilee once, because it was necessary for Him to ascend into heaven in their presence. But today we do not need to be traipsing from one place to another to be united to Him; it is only a question of hearing the testimony that is given us by the gospel. This word "brothers" ought to indeed satisfy us with regard to that, because God shows that we cannot be separated from Him when we are united by faith to the body of His church to be members of His only Son. So it is certain that our

121

Lord Jesus Christ recognizes and avows us by adoption and grace as children of God His Father, and He has nothing separate, all [that is His] is common to us, even His life, which leads us to His immortal glory. It is not without cause that the power of the Holy Spirit is mentioned, and that, as He was crucified in the weakness of His flesh, so God exercised the infinite power of His Spirit and raised Him from the dead. That was in order that we might know that His resurrection is ours today and belongs to us.

We also have a visible image of this in the holy supper. Even though our Lord Jesus Christ is in heaven and He does not show Himself to be seen by the eye, still with His word He gives us the bread and the wine that we receive here as a living image, in which we contemplate (if we do not will to close our eyes in malice) that the Son of God truly lives in us, in a fashion incomprehensible to our senses. We do not at all need to drag Him from heaven to have this union which is spoken of here. It is an inestimable privilege that He gives us, when He makes us know His incomprehensible power and the wonderful virtue of His Holy Spirit, who makes things that are separated by a great distance nevertheless to be united. So then when we receive a small piece of bread, we know that Jesus Christ is the food of our souls, when we drink a drop of wine, it is to testify to us that His blood is our spiritual drink to comfort us and make us rejoice; in short, we have in Him complete perfection of life.

Let us note that Jesus Christ lives in us not only in His power, but in order that all that is His may be common to us, and especially His resurrection, in which consists the accomplishment of our salvation. St. Paul says that if we do not believe that He is risen, it is as if (to the best of our ability) we dragged Him out of heaven (Rom 10:6ff.). On the contrary, when we believe seriously and without hypocrisy that He is risen, and at the same time we know that He is seated at the right hand of God His Father, we know that all power is given to Him so that we may be maintained and governed by Him, that He is our defense against sin and death, and that all the good things that have been given to Him, He received in order that He might give us His Spirit, and He distributes to each one of us according to the portion He knows is suitable. See then how in believing without hypocrisy that our Lord Jesus Christ is risen—because we know that He has the power to guard us against every thing that could hurt us—when we are in His protection we are so confident that we are able to despise the devil and all our enemies; even death will be happy and a passage to celestial life for us. Then we know that all He possesses has been given to Him in complete fullness so that He may give it to us as alms and according to the poverty He knows to be in us. It is true that we will not have such perfection of them as He, but it is enough that He knows what is good and proper for us, and that we may be nourished by Him daily until we are united with Him in His glory in another fashion than we are now.

For our life must be hidden in order to be resurrected with our Lord Jesus Christ, and this in two ways. For we are already actually resurrected with Him, inasmuch as He gives us the grace to walk in obedience to His righteousness. Because what would we be unless the resurrection of our Lord Jesus Christ worked in us and produced its power and its fruit? We are given to every evil; we are so much of this earth that the brute animals are not plunged into so many corruptions as we naturally are, until God offers us a hand to draw us out of them. See then how we are resurrected with our Lord Jesus Christ: it is by the newness of life that He gives us, as is said in chapter six of Romans (Rom 6:3ff.)....And St. Paul also exhorts us, in Colossians, second and third chapters (Col 3:1ff.), that we must seek the things that are above, and must lay aside everything which is earthly; because we are resurrected with Jesus Christ, we must die to the world, that is, destroy all our cupidity and evil affections and all the weaknesses that envelop us until our Lord draws us back and lifts us above with Him. See then how we are already actually resurrected.

Now we have another kind of resurrection, that is, in hope we are already sharers in our Lord Jesus Christ, but the possession is not yet evident. That is what is said in the first chapter of Ephesians, that already we are seated in the heavenly places, we are with the angels of paradise (Eph 1:20). Now it is indeed certain that this is not so in present enjoyment or actuality; we do not see it. What then is needed? We must come back to what he

[Paul] says in the other passage, in chapter eight of Romans, that what we hope for we do not see (Rom 8:24), and our life must be hidden in order that we may wait in patience for Jesus Christ, who is our true life, to declare and show Himself so that we may come before Him. However that may be, we are not frustrated, we are assured and convinced that already the door of paradise is open to us and we live in God with His angels. That is what we must remember.

From this we learn what profit is brought to us by the holy supper, which is like the seal of all the promises of the gospel. That is, in the first place we may be able to glory with heart and mouth that, even though we are poor sinners and there is only corruption in us, still we are assured of heavenly life and an immortal inheritance, which has been acquired for us by the Son of God. And why? We are resurrected with Him. Because (as we have already said) He has nothing privately, but He wants everything to be in common with us. And in effect, He already gives Himself to us. He does not only say: "I give you the bread as a pledge that My resurrection belongs to you." But He says: "I am the bread of life, I am the resurrection and the life indeed, and I give Myself to you so that you may be in Me and I in you" (John 6:35, 11:25, 17:21ff.). We see then how our Lord Jesus Christ is ours, when we receive the promise that He gives us in the holy supper, and we do Him the honor of believing that His promise cannot fail us. Jesus Christ—is He in us like that? Not only are we resurrected in Him, but in His person we have already come forth from death. And though we do not possess such a benefit yet, and we do not have the enjoyment of it in actuality, still we possess it by faith. Even though it is as if we are in the midst of death, still we do not cease to rejoice always, seeing the inestimable good that is brought to us by the resurrection of our Lord Jesus Christ. So then for this point.

As for what I said, that we must bear patiently all that seems to be contrary to our life; for the afflictions which we suffer in this world might make us angry and torment us, and especially since they go on, and when we escape from one we have to enter again into another. That could make us so afflicted that our faith might fail, if we were not upheld by what I have advanced, that the hope of those who are truly united to the Son of God will never be confounded. That is for the first point.

There is a second point, which is what we have already brought forward from the passage of St. Paul to the Colossians (Col 3:1ff.). Since we have died and been raised with Jesus Christ, we must lay aside all that is earthly in us, because He calls our earthly members fornication, drunkenness, all kinds of dissolute behavior, and such like things. It is true that this fashion of speaking might seem strange at first glance, but St. Paul wanted to show that we are composed of all those wicked passions, as if one amassed dirt, excrement, and all kinds of filth and stink and made a great mound. It is not only a single kind of filth but different sorts. Thus, when we have considered well what we are and of what we are made, until Jesus Christ purifies us there are only these earthly members, these passions that are in rebellion against God and contrary to all right and justice, such as drunkenness, fornications and other dissolute behavior, thefts, kidnaping, deceits, lies, cruelty, extortions, pride, ambition, hatreds, bitterness, discontents, enmities, dissensions, evil-speaking. Behold, I say, of what we are made. So then, let us learn in the power of the resurrection of our Lord Jesus Christ to leave off what is earthly in us, and so to rise with Him that we may wait for and seek what is heavenly—purity of life and holy living, and we may strive and take pains to dedicate ourselves to the service of our God. See what we must learn when we come to the holy supper of our Lord Jesus Christ.

We must also remember what is said in the other passage (Rom 6:10), that is, that Jesus Christ died once to sin, but now He has entered into the heavenly life that is of God, which will never fail. Since we must be companions of the glory of His resurrection, let us be so not for one day or one meal only, but let us persevere in that and continue the whole course of our lives to withdraw ourselves from the world and from ourselves. Because, as we have said, there is no greater evil all around us than we will find in ourselves, for that is what will give us the most trouble and affliction. Yet let us have perseverance, not one day or one month or one year, but let us know that the life of our Lord Jesus Christ must grow in us and never fail. Since He is resurrected in God and in accordance with God, who is eternal, we also must have everlasting life in Him so that it may not fail. Let us not have an impulsive devotion to give ourselves to Him, a devotion that immediately vanishes. But let there be a firm constancy and let us demonstrate why He has adopted and chosen us for Himself. It is in order for us not to throw off the bridle when He has called us, and not to stop in the middle of the road, but so that we may hold to our course until we have arrived at the point of which St. Paul speaks in the other passage, to the Philippians, when he says that he continues to strive. He, who had so strongly worked for the edification of the church of God and who had endured and suffered so much, "nevertheless," he says, "alas, I have not yet attained it but I strive on until I will come to the glory of our Lord Jesus Christ, to share in it fully" (Phil 3:12ff.). So then, following the example of St. Paul, let us forget all the past things and let us esteem that we have done nothing. Even if we were a hundred times more able than we are, and if we had more excellent virtues than we can have, nevertheless let us know that we have done nothing unless we continue until the end with such endeavors that we may be assured that after death itself we will share in the power and the resurrection of our Lord Jesus Christ. Of that we now have only a little taste and we sense it only in part, so that its fullness may be shown to us when we are withdrawn from this fleeting world to be gathered into the kingdom of heaven.

PRAYER We bow ourselves before the majesty of our good God, in recognition of our faults, praying that He may make us so to feel them that it may draw us to a true repentance, so that we may not seek anything except to serve and honor Him in His Son our Lord Jesus Christ. May He be pleased to bear with our weaknesses and pardon us for the many vices which still remain there, until He has completely purged us of them. May He continue this grace until at last He may receive us to Himself and bring us fully to that [heavenly] place.

So we all say: Almighty God, heavenly Father, You promised to grant our requests that we make unto You in the name of Your well-beloved Son, Jesus Christ our Lord (John 16:23). By whose teaching and that of His apostles we have also been taught to gather together in His name, with the promise that He will be in the midst of us, and will be our intercessor with You, to obtain all those things for which we agree to ask on earth (Matt 28:20, 18:19–20).

First we have Your commandment to pray for those whom You have established over us as rulers and governors, and then for all the needs of Your people, and indeed of all peoples (1 Tim 2:1–2). Wherefore, with trust in Your holy doctrine and promises, and now since we are gathered here before Your face and in the name of Your Son, our Lord Jesus, we do heartily beseech You, our gracious God and Father, in the name of our only Savior and Mediator, to grant us the free pardon of our faults and offenses through Your infinite mercy, and to draw and lift up our thoughts and desires to You in such wise that we may be able to call upon You with all our heart, yea agreeably to Your good pleasure and only reasonable will.

Wherefore we pray You, O heavenly Father, for all princes and lords, Your servants, to whom You have intrusted the administration of Your justice, and especially for the magistrates of this city. May it please You to impart to them Your Spirit, who alone is good and truly sovereign, and daily increase in them the same, that with true faith they may acknowledge Jesus Christ, Your Son, our Lord, to be the King of kings and Lord of lords, as You have given Him all power in heaven and earth (1 Tim 6:15, Rev 17:14, Matt 28:18). May they seek to serve Him and to exalt His kingdom in their government, ruling their subjects, who are the work of Your hands and the sheep of Your pasture (Ps 100:3), in accordance with Your good pleasure. So all of us both here and throughout the earth, being kept in perfect peace, may serve You in all holiness and virtue, and being delivered from the fear of our enemies (1 Tim 2:2, Luke 1:74) may give praise to You all the days of our life.

We pray You also, O faithful Father and Savior, for all those whom You have ordained pastors of Your faithful people, to whom You have intrusted the care of souls and the ministry of

Your holy gospel. Guide them by Your Holy Spirit, that they be found faithful and loyal ministers of Your glory, having but one goal: that all the poor, wandering sheep be gathered and restored to the Lord Jesus Christ, the chief Shepherd and Prince of bishops (1 Pet 2:25, 5:4), so that they may grow and increase in Him daily unto all righteousness and holiness. On the contrary, be pleased to deliver all the churches from the mouths of ravening wolves and from all mercenaries who seek their own ambition or profit (Matt 7:15, John 10:12), but never the exaltation of Your holy name alone, nor the salvation of Your flock.

We pray You, now, O most gracious God and merciful Father, for all people everywhere. As it is Your will to be acknowledged the Savior of the whole world, through the redemption wrought by Your Son Jesus Christ, grant that those who are still estranged from the knowledge of Him, being in the darkness and captivity of error and ignorance, may be brought by the illumination of Your Holy Spirit and the preaching of Your gospel to the straight way of salvation, which is to know You, the only true God, and Jesus Christ whom You have sent (John 17:3). Grant that those whom You have already visited with Your grace and enlightened with the knowledge of Your word may grow in goodness day by day, enriched by the spiritual blessings, so that all together we may worship You with one heart and one voice, giving honor and reverence to Your Christ, our Master, King, and Lawgiver.

Likewise, O God of all comfort, we commend to You all those whom You visit and chasten with cross and tribulation, whether by plague, or war, or famine; people beaten down by poverty, prison, sickness, or banishment, or any other misery of the body or affliction of the spirit. Enable them to perceive and understand Your fatherly affection, which chastens them for their correction, that they may turn to You with their whole heart, and having turned, may receive full consolation and deliverance from every ill.

Especially we commend to You all our poor brothers who are dispersed under the tyranny of the Antichrist, being destitute of the nourishment of life and deprived of all freedom to call upon Your name publicly. They are even held prisoner or persecuted by the enemies of Your gospel. May it please You, O gracious Father, to fortify them by the power of Your Spirit so that they may never give up but that they may persevere stead-fastly in Your holy calling. Aid them and help them as You know they need, console them in their afflictions, guard them against the rage of the wolves, increase in them the gifts of Your Spirit so that they may glorify You whether in life or in death.

Finally, O God and Father, grant also to those who are gath-ered here in the name of Your Son Jesus, to hear His word and share His holy supper,[30] that we may acknowledge truly, without hypocrisy, what perdition is ours by nature, what condemnation we deserve and heap upon ourselves from day to day by our unhappy and disordered life. Wherefore, seeing that there is nothing of good in us and that our flesh and blood cannot inherit Your kingdom, may we yield ourselves completely, with all our love and steadfast trust, to Your dear Son, our Lord, the only Savior and Redeemer:

To the end that He, dwelling in us, may mortify our old Adam, renewing us for a better life, by which Your name, according as it is holy and worthy, may be exalted and glorified everywhere and in all places.[31] In this manner may You have lordship and dominion over us all, and may we learn more and more each day to submit and subject ourselves to Your majesty, in such wise that You may be King and Ruler over all the earth, guiding Your people by the scepter of Your word and by the power of Your Spirit, confounding Your enemies by the force of Your truth and righteousness.

And thus may every power and principality that stands against Your glory be destroyed and abolished day by day (2 Cor 10:4ff.), till the fulfillment of Your kingdom be manifest, and its perfection may be completely established, when You will appear in judgment in the person of Your Son. May we with all creatures give You true and perfect obedience, even as Your angels and heavenly messengers have no desire but to fulfill Your command-ments. And thus may Your will be done without any contradic-tion, and may all apply themselves to serve and please You, renouncing their own will and all the desires of their flesh. Grant that we who walk in the love and fear of Your name may be nourished by Your goodness, and supply us with all things necessary and expedient to eat our bread in peace. Then, seeing that You care for us, we may better acknowledge You as our Father and await all good gifts from Your hand, withdrawing our trust from all creatures, to place it entirely in You and Your goodness.

And since in this mortal life we are poor sinners, so full of weakness that we fail continually and stray from the right way, may it please You to pardon our faults, by which we are beholden to Your judgment; and through that remission, deliver us from the obligation of eternal death in which we stand. Be pleased, therefore, not to impute to us the iniquity that is in us, even as we, by reason of Your commandment, forget the injuries done to us, and instead of seeking vengeance, solicit good for our enemies. Finally, may it please You to sustain us by Your power for the time to come, that we may not stumble because of the weakness of our flesh. And especially as we of ourselves are so frail that we are not able to stand fast for a single moment, while, on the other hand, we are continually beset and assailed by so many enemies—the devil, the world, sin, and our own flesh never ceasing to make war upon us—be pleased to strengthen us by Your Holy Spirit and arm us with Your grace, that we may be able to resist all temptations firmly and persevere in this spiritual battle until we shall attain full victory, to triumph at last in Your kingdom with our Captain and Protector, Jesus Christ our Lord.

And[32] as our Lord Jesus Christ has not only offered to You His body and blood once on the cross for the remission of our sins, but also desires to impart them to us as our nourishment unto everlasting life, we beseech You to grant us this grace: that we may receive at His hands such a great gift and benefit with true sincerity of heart and with ardent zeal. In steadfast faith may we receive His body and blood, yea Christ Himself entire, who, being true God and true man, is verily the holy bread of heaven that gives us life. So may we live no longer in ourselves, after our nature, which is entirely corrupt and vicious, but may He live in us to lead us to the life that is holy, blessed, and everlasting, whereby we may truly become partakers of the new and eternal testament, the covenant of grace, assured that it is Your good pleasure to be our gracious Father forever, never reckoning our faults against us, and to provide for us, as Your well-beloved children and heirs, all our needs both of soul and body. Thus may we render praise and thanks unto You without ceasing, and magnify Your name in word and deed.

Grant us, therefore, O heavenly Father, so to celebrate this day the blessed remembrance of Your dear Son, to exercise ourselves in the same, and to proclaim the benefit of His death, that, receiving new growth and strength in faith and in all things good, we may with so much greater confidence proclaim You our Father and glory in You.

CONFESSION OF FAITH[33] I believe in God the Father almighty,...

1562: Decalogue *[before 1562 no singing] [minister may come to the table here]*

SCRIPTURE AND EXHORTATION Let us hear how Jesus Christ instituted His holy supper for us, as St. Paul relates it in the eleventh chapter of First Corinthians.

> I have received of the Lord, he says, that which I have delivered unto you: That the Lord Jesus, on the night in which He was betrayed, took bread: And when He had given thanks, He broke it and said, Take, eat, this is my body which is broken for you: this do in remembrance of me. After the same manner, when He had supped, He took the cup saying: This cup is the new testament in my blood: this do, as often as you drink it, in remembrance of me. For as often as you eat this bread and drink this cup, you proclaim the Lord's death till He come. Therefore, whoever shall eat this bread and drink of this cup unworthily shall be guilty of the body and blood of the Lord. But let each one examine himself and so let him eat of this bread and drink of this cup. For whoever eats and drinks unworthily, takes his own condemnation, not discerning the Lord's body. (1 Cor 11:23–29)

We have heard, my brethren, how our Lord observed His supper with His disciples, from which we learn that strangers,

131

those who do not belong to the company of His faithful people, must not be admitted. Therefore, following that precept, in the name and by the authority of our Lord Jesus Christ I excommunicate all idolaters, blasphemers, and despisers of God, all heretics and those who create private sects in order to break the unity of the church, all perjurers, all who rebel against father or mother or superior, all who promote sedition or mutiny, brutal and disorderly persons, adulterers, fornicators, thieves, ravishers, greedy and graspy people, drunkards, gluttons, and all those who lead a scandalous life. I warn them to abstain from this holy table, lest they defile and contaminate the holy food that our Lord Jesus Christ gives to none except those who belong to His household of faith.

Moreover, in accordance with the exhortation of St. Paul (1 Cor 11:28), let each one examine and prove his own conscience to see whether he truly repents of his faults and grieves over them, desiring to live henceforth a holy life according to God. Above all, let him see whether he has his trust in the mercy of God and seeks his salvation wholly in Jesus Christ and, renouncing all hatred and rancor, has high resolve and courage to live in peace and brotherly love with his neighbors.

If we have this witness in our hearts before God, never doubt that He claims us as His children, and that the Lord Jesus addresses His word to us, to invite us to His table and to give us this holy sacrament that He imparted to His disciples.

And yet, we may be conscious of much frailty and misery in ourselves, such that we do not have perfect faith but are inclined toward defiance and unbelief, or that we do not devote ourselves wholly to the service of God and with such zeal as we ought but have to fight daily against the lusts of our flesh. Nevertheless, since our Lord has granted us the grace of having His gospel graven on our hearts, so that we may withstand all unbelief, and has given us the desire and longing to renounce our own wishes, that we may follow His righteousness and His holy commandments, let us be assured that the sins and imperfections that remain in us will not prevent Him from receiving us and making us worthy partakers of this spiritual table. For we do not come here to testify that we are perfect or righteous in ourselves; on the contrary, by seeking our life in Jesus Christ we confess that we are in death. Know, therefore, that this sacrament is a medicine for poor sick souls, and that the only worthiness our Lord requires of us is to know ourselves sufficiently to deplore our sins and to find all our pleasure, joy, and satisfaction in Him alone.

Above all, therefore, let us believe those promises which Jesus Christ, who is the unfailing truth, has spoken with His own lips: He is truly willing to make us partakers of His body and blood, in order that we may possess Him wholly and in such wise that He may live in us and we in Him (John 6:51, 17:21ff.). And though we see but bread and wine, let us not doubt that He accomplishes spiritually in our souls all that He shows us outwardly by these visible signs, namely, that He is the bread of heaven to feed and nourish us unto eternal life. So, let us never be unmindful of the infinite goodness of our Savior, who spreads out all His riches and blessings on this table to impart them to us. For in giving Himself to us, He makes a testimony to us that all that He has is ours. Therefore, let us receive this sacrament as a pledge that the virtue of His death and passion is imputed to us for righteousness, even as though we had suffered them in our own persons. May we never be so perverse as to draw away when Jesus Christ invites us so gently by His word. But accounting the worthiness of this precious gift which He gives, let us present ourselves to Him with ardent zeal, that He may make us capable of receiving it.

To do so, let us lift our spirits and hearts on high where Jesus Christ is in the glory of His Father, whence we expect Him at our redemption. Let us not be fascinated by these earthly and corruptible elements that we see with our eyes and touch with our hands, seeking Him there as though He were enclosed in the bread or wine. Then [only] shall our souls be disposed to be nourished and vivified by His substance, when they are lifted up above all earthly things, attaining even to heaven, and entering the kingdom of God, where He dwells. Therefore let us be content to have the bread and wine as signs and witnesses, seeking the truth spiritually where the word of God promises that we shall find it.

DISTRIBUTION That done, the ministers, having informed the people that they are to come to the holy table in reverence and good order, distribute the bread and the wine to the people. *[After some earlier efforts at individual words to the men and the women who filed up in order, Calvin no longer tried that because no one could hear a complete sentence. Meanwhile a lector read aloud from the Gospel of John, beginning at the thirteenth chapter.]*[34]

THANKSGIVING Heavenly Father, we offer You eternal praise and thanks that You have granted so great a benefit to us poor sinners, having drawn us into the communion of Your Son, Jesus Christ our Lord, whom You delivered to death for us, and whom You give us as the meat and drink of life eternal. Now grant us this other benefit: that You will never allow us to forget these things, but having them imprinted on our hearts may we grow and increase daily in our faith, which is at work in every good deed. Thus may we order and pursue all our life to the exaltation of Your glory and the edification of our neighbors; through the same Jesus Christ, Your Son, who in the unity of the Holy Spirit lives and reigns with You, O God, forever. Amen.

SONG OF SIMEON *[probably beginning at least by approximately 1546]*

BENEDICTION The Lord bless you and keep you. The Lord make His face to shine upon you and be merciful unto you. The Lord lift up His countenance upon you and keep you in virtuous prosperity. Amen.

[In Strasbourg a collection for the poor was probably taken on the day the Lord's supper was celebrated, most likely at the door as the congregation departed. Calvin's teaching on the supper included an alms offering but it was probably not practiced in Geneva until 1568.][35]

SECTION III:
WEEKDAY WORSHIP IN CALVIN'S GENEVA

Sundays were the chief days of worship but every weekday was also provided with preaching services. There were two patterns and two ranks of importance. From the beginning, daily services of preaching and prayer were held from Monday through Saturday. In addition, the regular Day of Prayer, a distinctively Calvinist Reformed addition to the liturgical calendar, was held on Wednesdays and accorded a special status, next in importance after Sunday, in both religious and civil laws.

Ordinary Weekdays with the Baptismal Liturgy

According to Calvin's teaching, the sacrament of baptism could not be a private ceremony but must be a part of a regular worship service that included preaching. Children of confessing members of the community of faith, the people adopted by God, must be baptized in the presence of that gathered church family. The worshiping church would witness that these babies were also God's beloved children who were receiving the sign of that promised adoption. Since baptism does not effect salvation, and a child who died without the actual sacrament was nonetheless reckoned as saved, there was no emergency that would necessitate private baptism. Usually, however, most Genevans brought their babies for baptism within a few days or a week of birth.

Baptisms might be celebrated at any service on Sundays or weekdays. In Geneva, usually Sunday dawn and weekday mornings were favorite times, although Sunday catechism was also very popular. In some parishes, such as St. Gervais, baptisms were fairly common at the main Sunday morning service, although Calvin himself almost never baptized at that time; most of his baptisms were celebrated on weekday mornings. The baptismal liturgy was held at the end of the regular service. The baby, the family, and the godfather were required to appear at the beginning of the service, so that they might hear the whole sermon, though the latter was one of the preacher's current *lectio continua* series and not specific to the baptismal intent. When the prayers of the

135

regular service were concluded, the baptismal party came to the front of the sanctuary, while all the rest of the church remained seated. The baptism itself was most often celebrated by the preacher who had led the service, but it was also possible for parents to ask another minister to perform the sacrament. Frequently more than one child was baptized at a time; in fact, it was not unusual to have three, four, or sometimes even five babies presented at single service.[36]

The baptismal liturgy was essentially the same from 1542 onward, with one difference, that in the later 1540s the Apostles' Creed and Lord's Prayer came to be recited by the father and godfather instead of the minister. The prayers of the daily liturgy were not printed as a part of *La forme des prières* but essentially left to the preacher of the day; Calvin's usual prayers were recorded by some of his hearers. The latter first published the prayers in 1561, along with three of the sermons on Abraham and Isaac that Calvin had preached the previous year, from which the sermon presented here was chosen. This exposition of God's command to Abraham to sacrifice Isaac allows one to overhear Calvin's own powerful feelings about Abraham's struggles as a stranger in a foreign land and especially his agony over what the sacrifice of Isaac represented. The prayers and sermon are published in OC 23:741–57 and the baptismal liturgy in OS 2:31–38; all were translated by E. A. McKee.

The Usual Weekday Service [begins after the ringing of the second largest bell of St. Pierre, Rabat, now called Accord. People are seated, the minister enters and goes to the pulpit.]

MINISTER'S EXTEMPORE PRAYER FOR ILLUMINATION-SEALING

We call upon our good God, praying that He may be pleased to regard us His poor servants with His fatherly mercy, not imputing to us our many faults and sins, by which we never cease daily to provoke His wrath against us. And since we are not worthy to appear before His holy majesty, may He please to receive us in the name of His beloved Son our Lord Jesus Christ, accepting the merit of His passion and death in recompense for all our faults, because in our own works we cannot stand before His face. May He please to enlighten us by His Holy Spirit in true understanding of His holy word, enabling us to handle it faithfully, and to receive it in true fear and humility. May we be taught by it to put our full confidence in Him, that we may serve and honor Him as is fitting, to glorify His holy name with our whole life and to edify our neighbors by our good example. We ask all these things, as our good Savior and Redeemer Jesus Christ taught us, saying: Our Father who art in heaven,...

BIBLICAL TEXT AND SERMON-EXPOSITION

> Abram planted trees there and called on the name of the Eternal, the everlasting God; and he lived as a stranger in the land of the Philistines for many days. And after these things, God "tempted" Abraham, and said to him: "Abraham." He answered: "Here I am." And He said to him: "Take your son, your only son whom you especially love, Isaac, and go to the land of Moriah and there offer him in sacrifice on a mountain which I will tell you." (Gen 21:33–22:2)

We saw yesterday how Abraham offered tribute to the king of Gerar to fulfill his obligation. Now Moses adds that, being at peace, he solemnly called on God's name. Therefore the sum of what we must remember is that Abraham subjected himself of his own will to the one who had ruling status in the land; he did not wait to be driven or to be compelled to do his duty as a good and loyal subject, but he did it without being asked.

However, we see that, on the other hand, this act did not hinder him from offering homage to God. Though it was a hateful thing (as we have seen above) to have a separate religion, apart from that of those among whom he lived, nevertheless Abraham did not want to fail to make confession of his faith as God had commanded him. So we see that he behaved toward God and toward other people in such a way that he can be an example of true humility to us, to show us how we ought to be subject to those to whom we owe subjection, in such a way that God retains His sovereign rule, and that if people have any rank or preeminence it may not detract at all from the heavenly majesty that ought to overshadow every human eminence. It is certain that if Abraham had wished to please his neighbors, he would have conformed to their customs and not have said that he had a God whom he wanted to worship, renouncing all the idolatries that were in fashion and all the superstitions that filled and polluted the earth. Nevertheless, he insists that he wants to serve and worship God purely. For this reason, as we have seen, he has an altar on which he offers solemn homage to God and by this means renounces all the vices and corruptions among his neighbors—as if he condemned them and showed that there is only one true worship that is acceptable to God, as there is also only one living God and all the rest are only false imaginings and deception.

Previously, although there was no law [about worship] and although he was tossed about from side to side, [Abraham] did not cease to call on God wherever he went, that is, to show that he did not agree with all the errors that were in fashion in the world at that time. But here he has a special reason to call on God again in this place, because he has more rest and ease than before. Never before had he dared to plant a tree; now he plants several, since he is allowed to live there. And since he had offered homage to the earthly king to whom the land belonged, he wants also to show that he has not forgotten God, his earlier zeal has not become cold, he always holds God to be his sovereign prince, bows himself before Him, and wants to live in His protection. See then why Moses recounts that Abraham called on the name of the Lord. The law about dedicating houses had not yet been written, but he still observed it; that is, he showed in effect that his dwelling was a temple of God, as each believer ought to think to keep his house pure and clean of all pollution.

It is true that today we no longer have this ceremony that God commanded to the Jews, which is that they should dedicate their houses before using them. However, the truth remains for us and the purpose which God intended, that where we lodge not be a closet to exclude God's presence and we should not give ourselves license to follow our own appetites; but inasmuch as God has given us the blessing of having a house, even if it is only a little corner off somewhere, [still] He should be honored there, and the place should be dedicated to His service. Now this is not said about the walls and the roof but about the family, that we may be completely His and may offer Him the sacrifice of our bodies and souls, and take pains that all the rest [of the household] appear and be conformed to that. The father of the family must be the one to begin it in his own person, but he must also instruct his wife. If God has given him children or servants, they must all be kept in obedience to God. See then the way to dedicate houses, and then to call upon the name of the Lord, as it is said about Abraham here.

This is something that is not well practiced; we see how each one wants to serve God as he pleases, but God is treated as practically nothing. If the masters and mistresses employ their servants for their profit and ease, they are content with that. If God is blasphemed in it, if He is despised, if the house is profaned, if there is no zeal or religion, that is overlooked and let slide. It is certain that God does not rescind His rights and acquit us. Therefore, let us learn so to use the houses where we lodge that God may live there as our ruler, that small and great may dedicate themselves to Him, and offer not only their souls but also their bodies. Even those who cannot honor God for fear of their lives are not therefore excused, because the honor we owe Him is something too precious. We should not allege that [worshiping Him] is not permitted and we do not have the freedom to do it, for however that may be, what is told us here about Abraham must instruct us, because we know that he is the patron of all the faithful inasmuch as he is their father. Since it is so, even while we may be scattered among the enemies of God and of His truth, and persecution at hand, let us make confession of our faith, because we must always give precedence to the principal thing over the lesser ones. See then what we must remember about this passage.

It is notable that it is said that he "called on the name of the Eternal, the God of the ages" (21:33), that is, the everlasting God. Here Moses makes a kind of comparison of the changes and revolutions in which Abraham found himself, and the decisiveness of his faith, its constancy and firmness not to be shaken, whatever might come. Look at Abraham, who had been tossed from side to side; he had changed places of residence, even being blown about like a piece of straw in the wind. In spite of all that, he knew that he must remain firm in God, and his faith was so well founded that nothing could shake it, and he did not personally waver. See how Abraham always followed the path into which

God led him; and so he worshiped the eternal God, the God of the ages, even though it appeared that God was playing with him as with a ball, chasing him here and there.

Now it is said that [Abraham] lived in the country of the Philistines for a long time (Gen 21:34), but the word Moses uses means "to live as a stranger." And it is important to note this, because although he had permission to live there, although he was at peace there and they did not make further extortions or do him more violence such as he had suffered before, yet still [Abraham] recognized that he did not own this land. It is true that it was given to him even before he entered it, and God ratified that benefice several times; still it was said to him: "For four hundred years your seed will be strangers in another land" (Gen 15:13). Therefore Abraham always had to practice this teaching, that is, to be at ease, even though he was there as a stranger, a borrower, and he always had to be ready to move. In short, he was like a bird on the branch, as the saying goes. Look why he paid homage to the king of Gerar; he did not quit the gift God had given him, but because the time had not yet come to enjoy and enter into possession of it, he was content to be a stranger. This is why we will later see that he will buy a burying place for his wife, because he was not yet the owner of a foot of land and yet by faith nevertheless he had received what had been given to him. Thus we see that his hope extended beyond the present life, and that it is not without reason that it is said in Psalm 90 (Ps 90:1) that God has been the refuge from age to age for those who trust in Him. For Abraham had been exposed to the wind and the rain and all storms when he lived among barbarian peoples full of cruelty, and yet still God gave him shade; but that is because he had preferred to leave the land and raise his heart on high rather than look for the means to acquire wealth and inheritance. So he passed through this world in such a way that he did not amuse himself [with its goods]. Also, finally, God showed the result and execution of this promise; not that he [Abraham] saw any of it during his lifetime, but as we have said, his hope extended further, and consequently we can say with the apostle (Heb 11:8ff.) that he did not make his nest in this world and he did not have his goal in it. He could have returned to the land from which he had come, the land of his birth, Chaldea, but he remained there where he had no ownership, where he had no relatives or friends. Thus indeed we see that he looked higher than the world.

Now if that was so in him, in a time when there was not a teaching nearly so clear as we have today, what excuse is there for us when our Lord Jesus Christ has once appeared, when He has lived actively in the world and then entered into the kingdom of heaven, and He has opened the door for us and through His gospel is ceaselessly inviting us to desire to go there above? If, I say, we are always wrapped up in these corruptible things, is that not an infamous ingratitude? So let us learn to live in this world in such a way that we enjoy the good things God gives us here, but yet still we affirm with St. Paul that our home is truly in heaven, and we are already citizens there, even though it is only in hope (Phil 3:20). In fact, we should remember what is said in the other passage, that while we are living in these mortal bodies we must be as if at a distance from God (2 Cor 5:6ff.). We also see clearly that we are not enjoying His presence, given that our spiritual life is hidden; otherwise we would be enjoying it in actuality, and no longer by faith, because (as St. Paul says) what one hopes for is not visible (Rom 8:24–25). Therefore, since God seeks by all means to draw us to Himself, let us learn not to be so lazy that each one buries himself in the earth, and we are as if buried in muck and mud, but let us always stride on, knowing that this life is a path to draw us higher.

Now it is quite something that all that this is recounted about Abraham. Look at the great and praiseworthy virtues, that when God gave him rest he did not go to sleep. And when he had permission and freedom from the king to be at peace in his tent, still he knew he was a stranger; even when they were friendly to him and everyone was ready to agree with him, he separated from them and preferred to arouse and inflame the rage of all his neighbors against him rather than conform to their superstitions and idolatry, for he wanted to worship the living God. In all that (as I said) there are very fine virtues, but Moses adds another sacrifice

141

that is much greater and more perfect: Abraham was compelled to kill his own son, indeed, his only son (Gen 22:2). That surpasses anything that one could possibly imagine of obedience that a faithful person would be ready to give God! We must be His to live and to die. But what Abraham is here commanded to do is much more, because it is not just a question of Abraham's putting himself wholly at God's disposal, renouncing himself, and having the son who had been given to him taken away, and bearing patiently losing his son when it pleased God to take him back to Himself. It is not [just] that, but he must himself kill his son! Behold a thing so difficult and foreign that we cannot hear about it without becoming [upset to the point of being] lost.

It is not without cause that, from the ninth chapter on, after he has recounted the life of Abraham, Moses highlights this act and says that after these things God tested him again (Gen 22:1). It was quite a big "temptation" [test] when God took him from his father's house; even the words show this, when He says: "Go out of your father's house and away from all your relatives and the place of your birth" (Gen 12:1). Then where will he find a better place to live? "Come," He says, "to an unknown land, as a poor blind person with eyes closed. See the land where I want to lead you." But it was not known to [Abraham]; he had to be there as if he threw his hat into the wind, not knowing in what direction to turn. See, I say, a severe temptation for Abraham, when he had to follow where God called him, not knowing where he was going. Still it was just his ABCs, for see where God begins when He wants to teach [someone] in His school. But did [Abraham] enter into the land? We see how the famine chased him out, and his wife was stolen from him (Gen 12:10ff.). Then for the second time we see he was cast about here and there, he had no rest, there was no one who did not oppose him; and he bore all these things. Yet in spite of this he did not murmur against God, he did not become downhearted over all the troubles that came on him or any of the afflictions which he endured—as do those who are so delicate that if God does not treat them as they wish they stop right there and do not want to know any more about obeying Him. Now, however Abraham was treated so roughly, yet he did not cease to continue along the same path.

But after all these things, how much can he bear? It was not for three or four years, but he was so much distressed that when he had spent twenty or thirty or forty years in this land, he would always have to start over again and it would be worse than before, until he was even compelled to give up love of his firstborn son and send him away, which was already a kind of death. After he had these great temptations: God had promised to give him the land, and yet he was chased out as if he were not worthy to set his foot anywhere. God had promised him seed, descendants, yes, but he had come to the age of eighty and his wife was barren, so that it appeared that all this promise was a mockery. He came to the age of one hundred years, and he had Isaac. Yes, but he had to chase out and banish Ishmael, as we have seen (Gen 15–18, 21). If we could indeed feel these temptations, it certainly would cast us into astonishment that Abraham had such virtue and such constancy of faith to struggle against such attacks and always overcome them.

And when it said "after all these things" (22:1), it is to show that in the person of Abraham God wanted to give us such a mirror that when we must struggle it is good for us to follow in his steps; we should not find it strange or new to be conformed to him who is the father of the whole church. But it is certain also that when each one [of us] looks well at all the temptations that he must suffer, these do not come to one one-hundredth of what we have seen in Abraham. So let us note that [in proportion as] God gave Abraham His Spirit, so also He wanted to try his faith, because the gifts of God should not be left idle or unused in us; He treats each one according to his measure. He prepares us to endure, otherwise we could not bear up; we do not know how to lift a finger to do good unless our Lord makes us will it and gives us the power. Therefore when He sends us into combat He deploys the graces of His Holy Spirit. Now inasmuch as Abram was more perfect than we are (as far as men can be), we see also why God tested him in such strange ways—ways we cannot begin to approach. But we have so much the less excuse for our laziness, coldness, and weakness if we do not at least follow our father Abraham. And if we cannot have a constancy and faith equal to his, if we do not [at least] strive to follow at a distance according to our ability and infirmity, we are certainly completely inexcusable.

So we must learn from this passage that all of his life Abraham was troubled in body and in spirit. And when it came to the end, God wanted to test him again, more intensely than ever before, so as to make him despair a hundred thousand times if he had not been strengthened in a wonderful fashion by the Holy Spirit. Now [why] is that told to us about Abraham? It is not done simply in order for us to admire his virtue, to value and praise it, but so that we may learn not to be too delicate. When it pleases God to exercise us in whatever way, may we be tractable, allowing ourselves to be led by Him, may we have our feelings so much conquered, our affections so much put to death, that God alone may have the mastery, He may rule and employ us as He pleases. See, I say, what we must remember. And so, when we must bear some temptation, when we have endured some battle, if afterward God tests us, let us not find that a surprise. We do not serve Him on condition that, after He has treated us roughly for a day or a year, we are quits and may ask for a vacation. But on the contrary, let us be toughened because God continues to send us such trials to test our faith; let that be to give us practice, as we see that an old soldier can bear much more than one who is just beginning. A novice does not yet know what it is all about. It angers him to watch at night, to bear cold and heat, to endure the battle, to be always on guard; but one who is long accustomed to all that will be much more hardy. So it is necessary when our Lord has exercised us in one way and another, we must be ready to continue so much the better. Though it appears to us that God is quite rough and sharp with us if He redoubles His blows (in a manner of speaking) and we are almost pressed to the end, to the last extremity, still we should not find that strange. And why? We see our example in our father Abraham, to whom we should be conformed.

As for this word: "to tempt/to test" (22:1), we know what it means when it is attributed to God: is it not that He "tempts" us to

144

lead us into evil, because we are only too much inclined that way, and as St. James (Jas 1:14) says, each is tempted by his own concupiscence. We must not seek the cause of all these vices elsewhere, because we have the root of it, the heritage, from our mothers' wombs. So God does not tempt us in such a way as to say He is guilty and that we could impute to Him the evil that we do, as if He were the author. For as I have said, we find the source in ourselves. But God tests His own in order to sound them out. This word means, then, "to examine, to test"; not that He needs to inquire in order to know what is in us, because we know that He is called the judge of hearts and that nothing is unknown to Him and all human thoughts are uncovered before Him. We make a good pretext, we disguise ourselves well and produce a false appearance with these fictions, but everything must be clear and plain before God. The books are not yet open, but God knows and judges what will be evident at the last day. He does not need to sound and test us, because He knows what is in us. But this is related to the testing of our faith, because (as we have said) God does not want His gifts to be idle; He wants them to be applied so that He may be glorified by them, and we may also have reason to strengthen ourselves so much the more, seeing how much He values us. And according as we are patient, as we battle valiantly against all the attacks of Satan and the world, let us experience by that, that God is with us and He loves us. Thus we have reason to call on Him with so much the more confidence and to have our refuge in Him, to be supported by His goodness and never to doubt He will help us till the end. See in summary why God tests us: because He wants the gifts He has put in us to be used and to serve, so that His strength may be known among people, His power, goodness, and wisdom; and that He may therefore be glorified, as He deserves. This is especially so that we may recognize His paternal goodness to us and be so much the more incited to honor Him and give ourselves entirely to Him. And at the same time we may also have cause to trust Him.

See how Abraham was tested, as God tests His faithful today. Because if we live at our ease and it costs us nothing to serve God, what testing of our faith is there? And furthermore, how can we discern the true children of God, and those who devote themselves to Him in simplicity of heart, from the hypocrites? We must go through testings as gold and silver go through the fire. And we see also why St. Peter says that it is right that our faith be tested (1 Pet 1:7). Inasmuch as gold and silver are precious, they must be tested by the fire; and they are corruptible metals. But shall our faith, which is much more valuable, become rusty and buried in the ground and the glory of God not be acknowledged in it? No, but it must be tested. And for that reason let us not find it strange if our Lord treats us in such a way that the devil has free rein to lead us into evil, the wicked also torment us, and we also have other internal temptations. In short, when we have been exercised in whatever fashion, let us recognize that we need for our Lord from His side to put before us what is hidden and unknown. See why temptations should not seem bitter to us but rather sweet, inasmuch as our Lord turns them to our salvation and He uses them so that His name is glorified, and we may also profit more and more, if we know how to see the outcome.

In this temptation, as we have noted, Abraham was mortally wounded, as if God wanted to cast him into the deepest pit of despair one can imagine. Nevertheless, God supported him, because according to human weakness Abraham would have failed a thousand times when God commanded him to kill his son. But still it was not all, that Abraham was compelled to take the sword to kill his own son. There was a much more serious temptation, which must well be noted, and about which more will be said, but still we must be advised of it now. Because it is not just that a beloved child, who is the only son, should die, and die a violent death before the eyes of the father, and that the father himself should cut his throat. That is not yet all of it; but it is a question of the salvation for which Abraham was waiting. When men kill their children, it is nothing by comparison, because no one knows his son as his savior. But although Isaac was not the savior of Abraham, yet he knew that from him would come the savior of the world. Now where then did Abraham seek all his righteousness, all his good and salvation, if not in the person of

Isaac, that is, in Him who would come from Isaac? Now if Isaac is dead, behold the world lost and damned, behold the devil ruling and in power everywhere! Behold God, the enemy of people and of all creatures! There is nothing left but the wrath and vengeance of God, which is inflamed like a fire to devour everything. So this Isaac must be killed by the hand of Abraham, indeed the Abraham who had received this promise from God: "I will give you a son who will be such a blessing that all people will have their salvation in the grace which I will give him" (cf. Gen 12:3, 17:19). Yet still that one [Isaac] must die. See then what I have already said: hell is opened and the devil must rule in such a way that all is ruined, there is nothing left of all the promises of salvation, because the one who ought to bring life to all creatures is going to die. Where does that lead?

Here it is not a question of wounding Abraham's heart with human afflictions and sorrows, but it is a question of killing his faith and all the hope he had of salvation. It seems that God wanted to make Abraham trample under foot all that He had led him to expect from His grace and goodness. In short, it seems He was mocking Abraham, as if He said: "Go [on], you were only a beast when you trusted in Me and followed Me, when you went to so much trouble to obey Me. I promised you a line [descendant] from which all the salvation of the world would come, I fulfilled My promise in giving you your son Isaac, but you must now go and cut his throat, so that you will understand that it was only your simpleness and stupidity to trust what I promised, that you hoped you would have a line and that that line would be more valuable than anything in the world and a thousand worlds. For it is a matter of the eternal salvation of your soul and of the souls of all people, and now you are going to wipe all that out." Now (as I have said) it is impossible for us adequately to understand these things, and for us to be sufficiently touched to the quick, yet nevertheless we must meditate on them, because it is not without purpose that they have been written. So much then for the foreword to this story.

Now let us come to treat in detail what Moses puts here. "Take your only son, your son Isaac, your son whom you love particularly" (22:2). See how God is not content merely to pierce

Abraham's heart, as if He gave him a sharp, stabbing wound, but He holds him to torture, a varied torture; as if after giving him hell, He gave him chains of torture and then still another kind of torture. Because if God had commanded Abraham thus to kill his own son, was not it enough to say, "Go and sacrifice your son to Me"? But He says to him, "Take your son, your only son, your son Isaac, whom you love particularly," to show that all hope was taken away from Abraham. When He says, "Your son whom you love particularly," it is not only a paternal love such as fathers have, a natural love for their children, but Abraham had to love Isaac as he valued the salvation of his soul and of all the world, [the way] to be a companion of the angels and of all the world and to be heir of the kingdom of God. Finally, see what this phrase "only son" means, and "beloved." And then the word "Isaac," which here, is put forward as a kind of reproach, because God had given Isaac his name; it had not been invented by human fancy, but God had named the child. And what [does it mean]? Laughter, substance of joy (Gen 17:19). It seems that He now is mocking all that: It is certainly fitting now, "substance of joy"! "You rejoiced in Isaac and you thought he was the substance of rejoicing only. Now you must have a sorrow that pierces your heart, that you are yourself the executioner of this child whom you love so much, that you hold the unsheathed sword and the raised hand to cut his throat." After that, would not Abraham be regarded as an executioner? And by this means stir up against himself the rage of all his neighbors, who would say, "What! This wicked man went and killed his own son! See the madman, see the demoniac; isn't that rage more than diabolic?" See then how he was confounded before God and hateful before the world.

But that was still not enough. "Take your son," He says. "And what shall I do?" "Take him and go sacrifice him." "And where shall I lead him?" "To some mountain that I will tell you." Abraham is all but languishing, and besides the fact that he must kill his son, he must make a long journey and go without knowing where or having any address. That God should hold him there, not only drunk but in a hell so horrible that we cannot well comprehend it as it deserves—are these not matters that go beyond any human understanding? For as had been said to Abraham before, that in leaving his birthplace he did not know where God wanted to lead him, so also now the place was not specified except: "You shall go into the land of Moriah." He had to leave the place where he lived to such an old age (as we have already seen, he was very old). "Go," He says, "and when you have arrived there, then I will tell you where I want you to sacrifice your son." Here we see how, in all kinds of ways, God so sounded the heart of His servant that all the temptations we could pile up would be nothing by comparison; if we made comparison, what we might endure would be nothing next to it, if we compare [ourselves] with what we see here. We see that God wonderfully spares our weakness when He does not lead us so far. If it is a question of an illness we must bear, we will have some discontent to make us defy God. If the husband dies, the wife will be so desolate that there will be nothing but murmuring and impatience. If God takes away someone's child, even if he has several, there will be only discontent and excessive tears to defy God. So what would happen if God brought us to the point that we had to kill our own children? As it is said here, there was nothing left to him, his home was completely wiped out. And even if it were so, it would not be anything in comparison with Abraham, because the children God gives us today are not the foundation of our salvation; we do not cease to have our Lord Jesus Christ, the only Son of God, even if all human science perishes. But we recognize that God sustains us, pitying our fragility when He does not bring us to such a rough test as Moses tells about here.

Pursuing that [thought] then, let us be warned that if God tests us, let us bend the neck and allow ourselves to be tested by Him. It is also the principal [purpose] of our whole life that we hold ourselves captive in such a fashion that God may dispose of us according to His pleasure, and that we may not rebel, as if to say: "Let Him treat us in such and such a way!" That, I say, is the principal [purpose] of our life. It is true that it would be a great thing if we could walk in integrity with our neighbors, that we should do no evil to anyone, that we should be chaste and modest, sober in our life, fleeing all drunkenness and intemperance, that no blasphemy should come out of our mouths, and such like. Behold, these are great virtues, and one does not always see them. But this is not the principal matter. The principal thing is, as I have already said, that in serving God, if we are assailed with many annoyances, if the devil directs combat against us and sets ambushes for us, if people are so malicious and perverse that one pricks us, another strikes us, another tries to ruin us, and [if] on the other hand we drag our wings, are hungry and thirsty, accused and despised, when all that happens, still we must bless God's name. And may all our distresses and sufferings be eased and may we always be able to say, "Lord, Your will be done, and may You treat us as You wish; and if things are much worse, nevertheless we are completely ready to accept everything." When therefore we are so patient as this, it is certain that this is the principal thing toward which we should aim.

Especially we ought to prize this story so much the more, and meditate on it, given that our Lord has wished to tell us what we ought to understand about our father Abraham, in order to follow his example. As I have already said, when God leads us to such a point, may we ourselves and all He has given us be dedicated to Him. Because if Abraham had not had this [as his] beginning, he certainly would not have taken one step, and he would even have drawn back rather than approach God. But he had this principal [conviction] that he did not belong to himself, and that what God had given to him he ought not to use as he pleased to hold onto it, but he had to render an account: "Here I am." As in fact he demonstrates, because when God calls him, Abraham says: "Here I am, Lord" (22:1), and that response shows that Abraham was ready to receive the commandments God would give him, just as a servant is watchful to do. For if his master goes somewhere, [the servant] will be there at hand to say, "Do you want anything?" If his master rests, he will be there waiting to hear what his master wants to order, "Do this, go there." And so Abraham shows that he was not at all devoted to himself and his own feelings, but he was so much dedicated to God that everything he had was also dedicated to God. And he does not say this hypocritically, as many could well say (the words only), "Here I am," and meanwhile they do not stop withdrawing far from God. But when Abraham said "Here I am," he affirms by that that he is here before God; or afterward he affirms that he has feet and hands, eyes and ears, all his senses, all the parts of his body and his soul, prepared to serve God and to bend beneath His yoke, to go wherever he is sent.

See, therefore, what we must remember about our father Abraham; and so let us recognize that without this goal we do nothing but wander all our life, as I have said. We could have the most praiseworthy virtues in the world, we could be regarded as angels, but that is all nothing unless we know that God sees us and wants us always to go toward Him. Meanwhile also when He makes us turn from side to side, and we must work and struggle to the end, let us never cease to keep ourselves in obedience and subjection to Him, to say, no matter what, "Lord, here I am." Let us defy all the obstacles that get in our way and might slow us down, all the difficulties, the sufferings, and battles that are raised up against us. Let us (I say) despise all that, so that we may always follow our path until we may come to the goal to which God calls us, that is, that we may be delivered from all our struggles to enjoy heavenly rest.

PRAYER We bow ourselves before the majesty of our good God, acknowledging our faults and asking Him so to make us feel them, that we may be grieved and may put them off more and more; and that we may be so reclothed in His righteousness that He may rule completely in us, and by this means we may declare that we are truly His own as He has so dearly bought us; and that Jesus Christ, having died and been raised, has also bought us for Himself, to make us participants of His glory and to lead us always in life and in death.

May He give this grace not only to us but also to all people and nations on earth, bringing back all poor ignorant people from the captivity of error and darkness to the right way of salvation. For that purpose may He raise up true and faithful ministers of His word who do not seek their own profit and ambition but only the exaltation of His holy name and the salvation of His poor flock. On the contrary, may He will to wipe out all sects, heresies, and errors, which are seeds of trouble and division among His people, so that we may all live in good brotherly agreement together. By His Holy Spirit may He guide all kings, princes, and authorities who have the rule of the sword, so that their governing may not be in avarice, cruelty, or tyranny, or any other disordered feelings, but in good justice and righteousness. May we also who live under them give them the honor and obedience due to them, and by real peace and tranquility may we serve God in all holiness and honor.

May He comfort all the poor afflicted people whom He visits with varied crosses and tribulations: those whom He afflicts with plague, war, famine, or by His other rods; individuals beaten down with poverty, prison, sickness, exile, or other calamities of body or sufferings of spirit. May He give to all of them good patience until He may send them full relief from their afflictions. [*Marginal note:* "Here explicit prayer (by name) is made for anyone who is sick, who commends himself to the prayers of the church."] In particular may He have compassion on all His poor believers who are scattered in the captivity of Babylon under the tyranny of the Antichrist, who suffer persecution for their witness to His truth. May He strengthen them in true constancy, comfort them, and never allow the wicked and ravaging wolves to carry out their rage against them, but may He give them a true constancy so that His holy name may be glorified by them both in life and in death. May He strengthen all His poor churches who today travail and are assailed for the sake of His name. May He overthrow and destroy the counsels, machinations, and plans of all His adversaries, so that His glory may shine forth everywhere and the kingdom of our Lord Jesus Christ may grow and spread more and more.

We pray all these things as our good master and Lord Jesus Christ has taught us, saying: Our Father who art in heaven,...

CONFESSION OF FAITH We ask this good God to give us true perseverance in His holy faith, daily increasing it in us; and that we now confess, saying: I believe in God the Father almighty,...

BENEDICTION The grace of God the Father, the peace of our Lord Jesus Christ, communicated by the Holy Spirit, dwell with you eternally. Amen.

Baptismal Liturgy

INVOCATION Our help is in the name of God, who made heaven and earth. Amen.

QUESTION OF INTENT AND BIBLICAL MEANING OF BAPTISM
> Do you present this child to be baptized?
> Yes.

Our Lord shows us in what poverty and misery we are all born, when He says that we must be reborn (John 3:3). For if our nature must be renewed in order for us to enter into the kingdom of God, that is a sign that it is completely perverse and cursed. By that He warns us to humble ourselves and be grieved with ourselves, and so prepares us to desire and seek His grace by which all perversity and every curse of our first nature is wiped out. We are not able to receive this unless we are first emptied of all trust in our own power, wisdom, and righteousness, to the point that we condemn everything that is in us.

When He has admonished us how miserable is our condition, He comforts us in a similar fashion by His mercy, promising to regenerate us by His Holy Spirit to new life, which is like an entrance into His kingdom. This regeneration consists in two parts: that we renounce ourselves, not following after our own reason, pleasure, and will, but holding our understanding and our heart captive to the wisdom and righteousness of God, and putting to death everything in us which is of us and of our flesh; and afterward that we follow God's light, to please Him and to obey His good pleasure, as He shows it to us by His word and leads us to it by His Spirit. The fulfillment of both of these is in our Lord Jesus, whose death and passion have such power that in participating in them it is as if we are buried to sin, so that our carnal desires may be put to death. In like fashion, by the power of His resurrection we are raised to the new life that is of God, inasmuch as His Spirit guides and governs us, to do in us works that are pleasing to Him. However, the first and principal point of our salvation is that by His mercy He forgives us all our offenses, not imputing them to us but effacing the memory of them so that they will not be brought against us at His judgment. All these graces are bestowed upon us when He is pleased to incorporate us into His church by baptism; for in this sacrament He testifies to us the remission of our sins. And for this reason He has ordained the sign of water, to be a figure for us that, as by this element the bodily filth is cleansed, so He wishes to wash and purify our souls so that no spot may appear there. Then afterward He presents to us there [in baptism] our renewal, which, as has been said, consists in the mortification of our flesh and the life of the spirit that it produces in us.

Thus, we receive a double grace and benefit from our God in baptism, provided that we do not annul the power of this sacrament by our ingratitude. Here we have a certain testimony that God wants to be a propitious Father to us, not imputing to us all our faults and sins. Second, that He will aid us by His Holy Spirit so that we may fight against the devil, sin, and the lusts of our flesh, until we have the victory over them, to live in the freedom of His kingdom, which is the kingdom of righteousness.

Since it is so, that these two things are accomplished in us by the grace of Jesus Christ, it follows that the power and substance of baptism are comprised in Him. And in fact, we do not have any other cleansing than His blood, we do not have any other renewal than in His death and resurrection. But as He communicates His riches and blessings by His word, so He distributes them to us by His sacraments.

For our good God is not content only to have adopted us for His children, and to have received us into the communion of His church, but He has also wished to extend His goodness toward us more widely in promising that He will be our God and the God of our descendants, to the thousandth generation (Gen 17:7; Exod 20:6). Therefore, although the children of believers are from the corrupt race of Adam, still He accepts them by the power of this covenant, to acknowledge them as members of His own people. For this reason from the beginning He wanted to have the children in His church receive the sign of circumcision (Gen 17:12), by which He then represented all that He shows us today in baptism. And as He commanded that they be circumcised, He also acknowledged them as His children and said that He would be their God, as He is the God of their fathers.

Now then, since the Lord Jesus came down to earth not to diminish the grace of God His Father but to spread to all the world the covenant of salvation, which was then restricted to the Jews, there is no doubt that our children are heirs of the life He has promised to us. Therefore, St. Paul says that God sanctifies them from their mother's womb (1 Cor 7:14), to make a distinction between them and the children of pagans and unbelievers. For this reason our Lord Jesus Christ received the children who were brought to Him, as it is written in the nineteenth chapter of St. Matthew (Matt 19:13–15):

> Then they brought Him the little children for Him to lay His hands on them and pray. But the disciples rebuked them. And Jesus said to them: Let the little children come to Me, and do not prevent them, for of such is the kingdom of heaven.

Since He announces that the kingdom of God belongs to them and lays His hands on them and commends them to God His Father, by that He instructs us sufficiently clearly that we should not exclude them from His church. Following this rule then, we receive this child into His church, so that he may be made a participant in the good that God has promised to those who believe in Him. And first let us present him to Him by our prayer, all saying with a humble heart:

PRAYER O Lord God, everlasting and almighty Father, since it has pleased You by Your infinite mercy to promise that You will be our God and the God of our children: we pray that You may be pleased to confirm this grace in this child before You, begotten of a father and mother whom You have called into Your church. And as this child is offered and consecrated to You by us, may You will to receive him under Your holy protection, declaring Yourself to be his God and Savior, forgiving in him the original sin of which all the descendants of Adam are guilty; and then sanctifying him by Your Spirit, so that when he comes to the age of understanding he may know and adore You as His only God, glorifying You in all his life, to obtain from You always the remission of his sins. And so that he may obtain these graces, may it please You to incorporate him into the communion of our Lord Jesus, to be a participant in all His blessings as a member of His body. Hear us, merciful Father, that the baptism which we communicate to him according to Your ordinance may produce in him its fruit and virtue, such as is declared to us by Your gospel.

[The father and the godfather recite]: Our Father who art in heaven,...For Yours is the kingdom and the power and the glory, forever. Amen.

Since the object is to receive this child into the company of the Christian Church, do you promise, when he has come to the age of discretion, to instruct him in the doctrine that is received by the people of God, as it is summarized in the confession of faith which we all have? That is:

[The father and the godfather recite]: I believe in God the Father almighty,...the life everlasting. Amen.

Do you promise, then, to take pains to instruct [this child] in all this teaching, and generally in all that is contained in the Holy Scriptures of the Old and New Testaments, that he may receive it as the certain word of God, come from heaven? Also, will you exhort him to live according to the rule our Lord gave us in the law, which is summed up in these two points (Deut 6:4–5, Lev 19:18, Matt 22:37–40): that we may love God with all our mind, our heart, and our power, and our neighbor as ourselves? Likewise, [to live] according to the admonitions He made by His prophets and apostles, that renouncing himself and his own desires, [this child] may dedicate and consecrate himself to glorifying the name of God and of Jesus Christ, and edifying his neighbors?

[They promise; the minister asks the baby's name and it is given by the godfather; a bowl of water is brought forward and the minister takes some in his hand and puts a little on the baby's forehead,[37] *saying:]*

N., I baptize you in the name of the Father, and of the Son, and of the Holy Spirit.

[BENEDICTION: Calvin's Strasbourg service gives a text; the Genevan does not provide words or rubrics, but it is very unlikely that the service ended without a blessing, probably the usual benediction.]

The Weekly Day of Prayer

One of the most distinctive forms of Calvinist Reformed worship was the regular weekly Day of Prayer. Begun in Strasbourg, this special pattern spread to other communities, especially Geneva, where it was given a clearly defined place in the Reformed calendar. In essence, Calvinist Reformed gave relatively little attention to the traditional liturgical year, but this did not mean they lacked a clear sense of liturgical time; the difference was that for Calvin and those who followed him, religious time was primarily oriented toward the present historical context of the church. Easter, Pentecost, Christmas, and Ascension were celebrated, but these celebrations were held on Sundays, the only day of the week that was a full holiday after the Calvinist pattern of worship was fully implemented in 1550. The weekly Day of Prayer was the one other day that was a partial holiday: shops and businesses did not open until after worship on Wednesdays. There were also services at two times on Wednesday mornings, as on Sundays, so that everyone might be able to attend worship on this special day.[38]

The Day of Prayer was the only weekday service for which Calvin published a liturgy, and this was patterned on the Sunday service. It was also the only weekday on which the congregational singing of psalms was a part of the liturgy. The Day of Prayer service was primarily focused on repentance and intercession, an awareness of human sinfulness and human affliction, although it also could express thanksgiving for special mercies. The first main theme is clearly expressed in Calvin's explanatory preface to the prayers for the day; the second, intercessory theme is found in the prayers themselves; while the occasional third theme of special thanksgiving might be given voice in the biblical exposition of the day. Parts of the service were fixed, others changed according to various rubrics. The prayers were specific to the Day of Prayer and did not change from week to week. The psalms appointed for this liturgy were those which spoke particularly of petition to God (the psalms of joy and praise being assigned for Sundays). When the tables of psalms began to be published in 1546, the psalms to be sung on Wednesdays changed from week to week, not according to the minister's choice but in a fixed pattern rotating through the appropriate psalms available. Usually the sermon on the Day of Prayer was simply a part of the regular *lectio continua* series that the minister was preaching, the text being different each time and not directly related to the theme of the day.

The Day of Prayer was established as a weekly observance, but Calvin (like Bucer and other church leaders) recognized that there were special times when God spoke through particular events to call Christians to repentance and intercession, or to thanksgiving for mercies and blessings. At these times, therefore, the particular focus of the Day of Prayer might be shaped by the historical current events that seemed to threaten God's wrath or express God's gracious consolation and deliverance.

The Day of Prayer service presented here is a kind of combination of the regular weekly Day of Prayer with the specific texts from one of the occasional Day of Prayer services. The prayer texts are the usual ones published first in 1542, but presented here according to the slightly revised form first printed in 1553. (The Lord's Prayer in the long post-sermon prayer is recited rather than paraphrased.) The order of psalm singing is that of 1562, the fully developed form that provided for three times of congregational song. However, both the sermon and some of the specific psalms are the ones used on November 4, 1545, when at Calvin's request Geneva interceded especially for the Protestants Philip of Hesse and John Frederick of Saxony, who were defending themselves against their German Catholic opponent, Henry of Brunswick. For this occasion Calvin interrupted his usual weekday *lectio continua* series of sermons and took a text from the series of psalms he was expounding on Sunday afternoons. The day after this service, November 5, 1545, Geneva received news of the Protestant victory. Thereupon Calvin asked that the next Wednesday the Day of Prayer might be a thanksgiving service for God's deliverance of their fellow Christians, and the city council agreed also to this second special focus for the Day of Prayer. On that occasion Calvin also preached on a psalm text.

When it was learned that the minister Jean Cousin had taken down Calvin's sermons on these two days, copies were in great demand. Thus, early in 1546, Cousin got the preacher's reluctant permission to publish his sermons for the benefit of all who had not been able to hear them, and these were in fact the first of Calvin's sermons to appear in print. Cousin's edition also noted which psalms were sung at the services, and those notes have been followed here. In the liturgy in use in 1545, the rubrics specified only one occasion of singing, set before the minister's prayer and sermon. However, Cousin indicates that on November 4 Psalm 79 was divided to be sung before and after the sermon, effectively making two occasions of singing on this particular day. By 1562 three times of song were practiced, one at the very beginning of the service, the others before and after the sermon and its related prayers, so the psalm marked for the opening of this liturgy is the one that the 1562 table paired with Psalm 79. The gestures—sitting, kneeling, etc.—are the same as for Sunday morning and are not repeated here. The sermon is found in OC 32:455–66, the prayers in OS 2:26–30 modified by the 1553 final version of the liturgy. The texts are translated by E. A. McKee.

[The following section is Calvin's Introduction to this liturgy in "La forme des prières"]

Inasmuch as scripture teaches us that plagues, wars, and other such adversities are visitations of God by which He punishes our sins, when we see these come, we must recognize that God is aroused against us. And then, if we are truly faithful, we must recognize our offenses, be grieved with ourselves, turning back to the Lord in repentance and amendment of life, and pray to Him in true humility in order to obtain pardon.

For this reason, if we sometimes see that God threatens us, in order not to try His patience but rather to submit before His judgment falls on us—judgment which otherwise we see ready to be manifest—it is good to have a set day each week in which there may be special exhortation about these things, and on which we may make prayers and supplications according to the needs of the time.

And so follows a form of prayer for that purpose.

Day of Prayer liturgy [begins after second ringing of the largest bell of St. Pierre, called Clémence]

1562: PSALM 104 "Hear, Hear, My Soul [Bless the Lord]" [strophes 1–9]

INVOCATION Our help is in the name of God, who made heaven and earth. Amen.

CONFESSION OF SIN My brethren, let each of you present yourself before the face of the Lord, and confess his faults and sins, following my words in his heart.

O Lord God, eternal and almighty Father, we confess and acknowledge without pretense before Your holy majesty that we are poor sinners, conceived and born in iniquity and corruption, inclined to do evil, useless for any good, and that in our depravity we constantly and unceasingly break Your holy commandments.

By so doing, through Your righteous judgment we bring ruin and perdition on ourselves. Nevertheless, O Lord, we are grieved with ourselves to have offended You; and we condemn ourselves and our sins with true repentance, asking that Your grace may relieve our distress.

O most gracious God and Father, full of compassion, have mercy on us in the name of Your Son Jesus Christ, our Lord. Blot out our sins and stains, and magnify and increase in us day by day the graces of Your Holy Spirit, so that, acknowledging our unrighteousness with all our heart, we may be moved by that sorrow which brings forth true repentance in us; and that repentance, by putting to death in us all our sins, may produce in us the fruits of righteousness and innocence that are pleasing to You, through that same Jesus Christ Your Son, our Lord. Amen.

PSALM: Psalm 79 "The Nations Have Come into Your Heritage" [strophes 1–4]

MINISTER'S EXTEMPORE PRAYER FOR ILLUMINATION-SEALING

We call upon our heavenly Father, Father of all goodness and mercy, asking Him to cast His merciful eye on us His poor servants, not imputing to us the many faults and offenses that we have committed, which are only too deserving of provoking His wrath against us, but [instead] seeing us in the face of His Son, Jesus Christ our Lord, as He has established Him as Mediator between Him and us. We pray that, as the whole plenitude of wisdom and light is in Him, He may guide us by His Holy Spirit to the true understanding of His holy teaching, and may make it bear in us all the fruits of righteousness, to the glory and honor of His Name. And so, acknowledging that we owe Him the obedience servants render to their master and children to their father, we will pray as our good Master has taught us:[39] Our Father, who art in heaven,...

BIBLICAL TEXT AND SERMON-EXPOSITION

Not to us, Lord, not to us, but to Your name give the glory, for the sake of Your gracious goodness and truth. Why should the nations say: "Where now is their God?" For our God is in the heavens, He does whatever He pleases. (Ps 115:1–3)

Although in afflicting His faithful our Lord always aims at this end, to glorify His name, nevertheless there are various reasons why He allows them to be afflicted. Sometimes there is nothing that moves Him to that, except that it pleases Him that His truth may be confirmed by the patience of His servants. Or indeed when He has put them in some danger and He delivers them, in that also He wishes to be glorified; or there may be some other outcome. Sometimes He chastises them for their offenses. It is true that all of this also redounds to the glory of His name. So it is that when the faithful have sinned against Him, He punishes them for it. Sometimes He allows them to be persecuted by the wicked, who are His scourges, or He uses other means, since He has plenty of them available. So we see what we should note in the first place, in order to understand this psalm, which is that the principal end of everything we endure in this world is that God's name may be glorified.

Nonetheless, our Lord does not permit us always to be persecuted equal to the degree to which we have offended Him. This is not because He does not always have good reason, but He sometimes wishes us to witness to His truth by our patience, and after He has delivered us, [He wishes] us to attest how we have experienced His mercy and render Him thanks. Sometimes He chastises us for our faults because we have not lived as befits His children, we have not obeyed Him as a father. He raises up the wicked against us as His scourges, but just the same we must always come back to this point, that His name may be glorified in us.

Look at the direction of the psalm's argument. God's people, being afflicted by unbelievers, pray that He may not allow them to be completely destroyed. It is as if the faithful said: "Lord, behold the wicked who are wounding us; we have indeed deserved to be destroyed, we are not worthy of Your saving us. Yet do not consider our worth, but consider, Lord, that Your name will be blasphemed, the wicked will think that they have conquered not us alone [but also You]. We bear Your [identifying] mark. Mocking You, they will say: 'Where is their God?' Lord, do You want to allow Your name thus to be blasphemed?" See how we should apply this prayer in this present psalm. When God gives free rein to the wicked, we must call upon Him. How? Confessing that we are not worthy to be delivered, not maintaining our merits but reminding Him of the honor of His name. For the rest, let us put our trust in this: we have our God who has taken us into His care. He will keep us, whatever may happen; no power can rise up against Him, except to its own confusion. All the glory of the wicked is evil and perverse, founded only on ungodliness and abomination; they trust in idols, but we have the living God, who arranges and orders creatures as He wills.

But we must also note the order which the prophet follows here. First he says: "Not to us, Lord, do not give us the glory, but to Your name" (115:1). For greater emphasis that is repeated: "Not to us, not to us." Now in this a prayer is included that when we ask God to aid us against the wicked we do not allege our worthiness, we do not bring any boasts as if we have deserved His help, but the contrary. "Lord, do not regard what we are, for we confess that we have indeed deserved that You expose us to the cruelty of the wicked, we have not used well the understanding You have given us. Nonetheless, do not consider our life, do not regard our works, but consider Your name, Lord, it is Your name that must be glorified." Now it is this way: His mark is impressed on us, so He must deliver us. "Give glory to Your name" (115:1). He might say: "I will do it, but what will it profit you?" "O Lord, this [Your] glory cannot be, unless You deliver us, because Your name is engraved on us. If we perish, what will become of the memory of Your name?" God could raise up another people. But it must be understood that when we pray this prayer, we must be truly repentant for the offenses we have committed, we must come before Him humbled in heart and feelings, seeking Him for our God; then there is an indivisible connection between Him and us. This must be the beginning; that is, to join together God's name with our salvation. St. Paul says: He has called us to be His children, He has given us the witness of our adoption so as to be glorified in us (Eph 1:5f.). Thus when we say "Glorify

Your name," it means, "Glorify it in us, inasmuch as You have elected us. You must save us, or Your name will be blasphemed."

What follows expresses this more clearly: "For the love of Your mercy and truth" (115:1). When it is said "for the love of Your mercy," that means that we do not pretend to bring anything of our own in order to persuade Him to come to our aid. "Your goodness, Lord." "See, all that we claim of You is not that You are obligated [to us], not that we have deserved something from You, not at all. May it never happen that we presume to allege our merits! You are not bound to us. But it is Your goodness, You are good, that is the reason that You acknowledge us as Your people." Truth is joined with goodness, and not without reason, that is the common usage in scripture. For just as the promises of God are founded on His pure gratuitous mercy, so also their support comes from His truth. Now among people we often see that someone promises easily, because he is human and nice; but often there is also inconstancy, he does not keep to it. It is not so with God. As He is quick to promise, so, has He said the word? It will be done. We see therefore why it is that these words "His goodness and His truth" are joined. He is moved by His gratuitous mercy to make us promises. And, just as He is good and acts on that goodness, so also He is faithful, He is constant; He does not change His mind. Since it is so, let us have the assurance to hope in God, a constancy that is sure because He continues. In sum, there is here a declaration of what went before: We ask God that He may not give the glory to us or to our name, we cannot allege anything that obligates Him to us. But we ask that He may glorify His name, that His goodness may be known, that we may render Him thanks, recognizing that every good comes only from His mercy. And also that we may magnify His truthfulness, that He has given us a promise for [times of] need.

Here is another statement that follows in the second verse: "Why do the nations say, where now is their God?" (115:2). "Why? Because Your name will be blasphemed if You do not save us. The unbelievers mock You: would You suffer Your name so to be slandered? Thus it is necessary for You to help us. The wicked will take occasion to blaspheme You when we do not receive help from You." In the third verse there is a kind of meditation, that is, an idea that is given to us to enable us to resist the temptations that might come to us from unbelievers and even from Satan, who is more subtle than all the people, to incite us to rebellion. When we are in some affliction, the devil tries only to break our necks; if [in these circumstances] it happens that we invoke God, we are troubled, we do not know what we ought to ask of Him. For this reason we are here given a shield; God arms us. When we are attacked by unbelievers and it looks as if we are done for, we must take this shield: "Our God is in heaven, He does whatever He pleases" (115:3).

It is notable that it is said: "our God." If there were a God in heaven with whom we had no acquaintance, what good would that do us? But instead it is said: "our God." This is reciprocal; He is our God and He acknowledges us for His children. "He is in heaven." Not that He is enclosed there, scripture does not mean that, but it is said that way for two reasons. [The first reason is] to avoid every carnal imagination. We imagine things that are not fitting for His majesty, so scripture sends us up to heaven so that we may not presume to imagine anything about Him, [but] that we may adore His majesty in fear and reverence. The second [reason] is that, when it is said that "He is in heaven," it means that He rules everything. The sun, the moon, the stars are certainly high up, but God is above all. If an earthly prince is elevated on his throne three or four degrees above his subjects, he is indeed high, but our God [is] in heaven, in heaven. He rules over all the world. He holds all creatures in rein to subject them to His will, and nevertheless He is not only our God and Savior, but He is not the God of those who persecute us. This is also the prayer of the faithful against the wicked. God fights for us, we have our defense in Him, according to the promise that He will bless those who bless us (Gen 12:3). And on the contrary, we must conclude that He will curse all those who curse us. If He is our God, He will be the mortal enemy of our enemies.

Afterward there is a lovely phrase. "He does whatever He wants" (115:3). When the wicked have blasphemed to make us lose courage, let us come to this point: "our God does what He wants." Nothing will turn Him from helping us; the devil can suggest many fancies to us, but by this reflection, "God does what He wants," we can repulse his attacks. Now what is the will of God? It is true that we have not entered into His secret counsel to know how He has disposed everything, but He reveals to us sufficient for us to know as much as we have business knowing. We know that He wants to aid us! He has said it. He is not a deceiver. He "does what He wants"—He wants to aid us, He does not want to abandon us in our need. Therefore He will do it. That is the conclusion we must draw. When something is said about the will of God, it is not about God's secret will, but we must come back to the will that He has revealed to us in His scripture. If He afflicts us, even if this is for our sins, if we come to Him in repentance He will always be ready to accept us. That is where we ought to come out.

Now, following this, we have to apply this prayer to our own use, and today is certainly the time, for we see in what state the poor church of God is. We see her there as if in uncertainty. "Lord, we see the ambushes laid against Your faithful ones, we see the wicked who rise up in their rage. It is no longer a question of persecuting [only] some poor folk, but all are up in arms, a deadly war is raised up against Your church." And nevertheless there is no doubt at all that we have well deserved to be confounded by our Lord. However, when we hear that persecution is happening, let us think what grace God has given us. His gospel must not remain impotent in us; it must bear fruit. Let us rather consider how we have led perverse lives, how we have given cause for the wicked to open their mouths. Today all the papacy is confused in virtue of the doctrine we preach; even though the teachers of the Antichrist never cease to bark like dogs from a distance, when it comes to speaking in person [face to face] they do nothing but show their impudence. But what occasion, what excuse do they have? The scandals they see in our lives? They have there ample enough material. It is true that it is to their own confusion that they speak evil of the name of God. If we were the most wicked people in the world, our faults ought not to bring disgrace on the name of God. He is not subject to our stains.

But still, inasmuch as lies in us, we have done that for which the prophet reproaches the Jewish people: we have caused the name of God to be blasphemed (Mal 1:12). He revealed His will to us, and we have rebelled against Him. He still speaks, and our hearts are hardened like an anvil. He could indeed chastise us justly even if He destroyed us; we have all well deserved it. I do not speak only of Geneva, but of the towns and cities where His gospel is announced. Our life today ought to shine in order to close the mouths of unbelievers, so that they would not dare look at us. What is left to us? On one hand we see the scandal of our life in abusing His graces, regarding which we should think that we are much more than guilty. On the other hand, look at the war, particularly against the gospel; the wicked only scheme to make a universal confusion so that everything is ruined. We certainly have occasion to think, "Alas, Lord, if You should wipe us out we could not accuse You of cruelty; we have deserved it." Must we remain there, confounded? Not at all. But let us turn ourselves around in true repentance to our God, let us think of our past life, that we may be truly sorrowful to have lived so wickedly, with a repentance such as may be demonstrated by its fruits, that each one may be moved to convert to God. "You chastise us, Lord. When we think of ourselves there is only reason to be distressed. But when we consider those who make war on us— not because of our vices (though You could punish us for them) but because they want to bring to ruin the kingdom of Your Son, which ought to be upheld by You—that consideration is the grounds of our confidence." However, it is necessary to begin with humility. "Be willing to forget our faults. Consider the honor of Your name, Lord; if they succeed in their enterprise Your name will be blasphemed with complete abandon. O Lord, may You set things in order there, may You provide a remedy."

Today is the time to make the prayer written here; although it is for any time, nevertheless when the need is urgent we should make use of it. We should well have greater zeal. We [act as if we] know nothing about the union our Lord wanted there to be among His members. Are we the church? We must have a spiritual connection with all the faithful. As there is only a single

God, a single Redeemer, a single true teaching, a single faith, one baptism, so we ought to be one body. So we should have a union each with the others. If one member suffers, we all ought to have compassion. Now we see that this [situation] is not a question of one member; all the church is scattered: here a handful, there another. We all have the same gospel, we are surrounded by enemies. Should we separate [from each other]? Should we say: "Those [people in Germany] are far from us?" Not at all. They are of the church, and we are its members; because we have the same Father in heaven, let us have a brotherhood together which is indeed more than fraternal! Let us reflect that what happens to one member of the church happens to us. Behold troubles everywhere! If we consider men, we know what war is, we ought to have a horror at bloodshed. The wicked are enraged, they are possessed by the devil, who delights in murder. What should we expect? We should not be thus nonchalant. This is the time to seek God. We should forget everything else; we cannot help them [the German Protestants] with our hands, but we ought to pray to God for them as for ourselves: the condition of the church is not the [concern of only] one member. Moreover, let us fear that in a short time the storm may roll over our heads. If we do not have compassion for others, we will cry out in vain, and it will be entirely fair that our Lord should return the same to us, that we should get back the same measure we have given to others. And so we must be warned to call on God differently than we have done till the present.

This day has been established to offer prayers. Therefore let us be more diligent than is customary, not only to come and present ourselves [here], but let us be moved to humble ourselves before our God, asking Him to convert our hearts and change our lives, that He may not allow His poor church to be exposed to the fury of the wicked—which could happen if He does not set matters in order! I come to this view, which is that we have deserved for God to destroy us. When a war has arisen, one does not know what the end will be; when a sword has been drawn, one does not know when it will be re-sheathed. It is the devil who drives our enemies; he asks only to devour our Lord's poor sheep. We would soon be lost if we were not under the protection of such a good Shepherd. Let us guard ourselves from trusting in the arm of flesh. If we had the prudence and favor of the whole world, we should guard ourselves from presuming on that. Let us always say what we have seen in Psalm 20:33: "The wicked, the unbelievers, trust in their chariots and horses, in their lances and swords, but we hope in the name of Lord our God." Although the faithful may use the sword when that is done by public decree, as when God has provided some Christian princes, [then] we will have the ammunition, the means, the prudence. But where will be our glory, our confidence? In the invocation of God's name. May that always be shown, that God fights for us and that we rest, as Moses says of the people (Exod 14:14). And how was that? The people were fighting, but He did not rest. This means that the people did not trust in their power. So we will rest (even though we are on sentry duty) when we attribute all to the hand of God. For if we have any confidence in ourselves, that will be only smoke and worthless things of no value. What is more, all that will only be for our confounding. It is necessary therefore that God fight for us. This present psalm is as if God came there to present Himself, saying to us: "You see the church, [whose members] are in affliction, these are My brothers, they are your members; I have only one church. When My cause is gravely offended, it is a question of the honor of My name. Also, the trouble can reach you, where others are is not more exposed to danger than is where you are. Therefore do not sleep, when you see the fire kindled, when you see that Satan has roused his supporters; think of calling on Me. Here is a prayer I have made for you, though it came out of the mouth of my prophets. I give it to you." When God pushes us, stirs us up, acts as if to put words in our mouth, saying: "Here is your lesson"—is that not an immeasurable consolation? But let us not be deaf when God speaks thus, let our heart be open, that we may be moved. When He exhorts us, may that touch us.

Now we have given the prophet's meaning. Let us come to the text to apply it to our use. See how we must express our prayer: "Not to us, not to us, O Lord, but to Your name give the glory and honor" (115:1). For what could we find that would cause Him to be obligated to us? Nothing at all. What is more, if He did not turn His face away from our life, He would have good reason to chastise us more roughly than He does. To present our persons to Him is not a way to move Him to save us, but let us say "'Lord, may You look to the honor of Your name.' Those who make war on us are brigands and firebrands. Is not one who cuts throats in time of peace a brigand? But even so, Lord, it is not a question of their [wicked] life—if they are not worth anything, we are worth scarcely anything either—but it is You they address, Lord. Is it because we have committed some offense? No; they would like it if we were [even] more wicked. Therefore we must speak thus: 'It is for You, Lord, it is a question of defending Your people; rise up to confound these madmen.'" However, we must say this and use these words truthfully. In order to do that two things are necessary. The first is that we should feel that we are not worthy that God should harken to us, but on the contrary that we well deserve that He should punish us.

For the second, this remonstrance must not be like cold rhetoric, such as we use with other people, as when we say, "I pointed out to him that it is his honor and his profit [which are in question]." That is a pretext; we must not do such a thing with God. We cannot deceive Him. Let us not say "Give glory to Your name" when we do not have this feeling, [as if we] wished to trick God as if He were a mortal person. No! Let us have a true zeal, that we may value that [God's glory] more than our life, indeed I say more than the salvation of our souls, that we would perish rather than [see] His name diminished in the least. Therefore if we want to use this prayer as it has been made for us, let us prize His name more than everything else. "It is true that we are human, we ought not to be without humanity, and for this reason we ask that it may please You to have pity on our poor brothers." But especially may we have regard for the honor of His name. Still, if we could be destroyed without there being any harm to His name, that would be more endurable and easy to bear. Therefore let us have this understanding in the first place: that we indeed deserve that He should punish us, and that He may use not only His hand but also that of unbelievers. Like a judge, He will not punish a wrongdoer with His own hand but He will hand him over to the executioner; the Lord could do that with us. "O Lord," says the prophet, "confusion be on our faces, a curse on us, on our kings, on our princes, on our fathers" (Dan 9:8). As if he said: "There is nothing so worthy or so excellent that does not deserve to be punished. But, Lord, we do not present our prayers before You [on the basis of] our just behavior but on [the basis of] Your mercies, on Your great, indeed Your infinite goodness, which You have demonstrated before now and which You have promised to continue." Let us all say, following the example of the prophet: "Lord, You could abandon all of us in the hands of the wicked. We do not petition You because of our just behavior, we do not claim that we have anything to induce You [to hear us], we have sinned against You. But for the sake of Your love harken to us; Your name is invoked on us." Let us remember what the Lord said by Ezekiel. "I will do it, I will do it," says the Lord, "not because of the love of you. When I scattered you among the nations, you blasphemed My name more. Nevertheless I want to deliver you, but do not think that that is for the love of you" (Ezek 39:7ff., 25ff.).

And so today, "Lord, give glory to Your name, not to us, not to us" (115:1). Let us all use this confession, all of us from the greatest to the smallest, let none hold himself excused. "When I have confessed the sins of my people," says Daniel; does he add nothing further? "This done, I also add my own," he says (Dan 9:20). We see what kind of life he led in captivity, that he was concerned only to walk in the fear of the Lord. What did he always do? When he said "Confusion, confusion on our princes and on our fathers," he adds, "Behold, Lord, I speak to You not only in the name of all the people but in my own name." He did not act the solitary [penitent], as do the papists, who say we must bow down. He speaks what he fully believes in his heart. "O our God," says Daniel, "hear the prayer of Your servant and make Your face shine upon Your ruined sanctuary. For the love of the Lord," that is, for the love of Jesus Christ—it is as explicit a passage [about Christ] as can be found in all the Old Testament. We must address our prayers to our God because of the Lord, who has been given to us from the Father. If heretofore we have been negligent in praying to Him, so that we may even have caused His name to be blasphemed, let us now say, "Must God be dishonored? May the dogs come to say: Behold the lovely gospel!" If the papists had overcome us, would they come to blaspheme this holy word? It is the doctrine of truth, worthy of admiration by the angels; it would be treated as the teaching of dogs. And as they weigh the value of everything by events, they would confirm their wicked doctrine and their abominations [because of their victory over us]. It is the habit of hypocrites to think [success] is the salary of their deeds, if God gives them some grace. Just like a prostitute, if she earns some money in a brothel she takes that as reason to remain there. The prophet Hosea makes this comparison of idolaters: "Do they have abundant goods? Do they come out better off than they expected? That hardens them [in their ways], as if they had received payment for their shameful behavior" (Hos 2:5). On the contrary, the wicked also, when they see God's people afflicted, are strengthened in their ungodliness. That would be so among the papists; they only want to mock the teaching that we hold.

Therefore we must make this plea to God—not that He needs it, but He wants us to have this ardent affection, that we may be more moved when we see His name blasphemed than if the heavens were mixed up with the earth. And however unworthy we may be to experience His help, nevertheless for love of His name He holds out His hand to us, He calls us to Himself. And when He allows the wicked thus to rise up against us, it is to warn us to have our refuge in Him, to withdraw from our vices. Since He wants to wake us up to call upon Him to help us, and He puts the words in our mouth, what more could we need? "O, we do not deserve this." "That is true, but here are the words I give you. I am ready to receive you, if you are zealous for the glory of My name. Only advance My name, put it before Me, I am ready to help you." The papists indeed bear a sign of God's name, that is, baptism. But they have renounced the covenant of the Lord, they have turned away to idols. We see their rage; the

Lord's name is profaned among them. Therefore we ought to invoke our God against them, that He may arm Himself against them to confound them in their malice. And inasmuch as we see His great goodness toward us, let us seek Him with so much better courage. We are here as poor creatures, He is pleased to comfort us, teaching us individually and familiarly what we ought to say to Him in order to have His help.

After the prayer, let us remember how this thought is given to us, that "our God is in heaven" (115:3), in order that it may be for us a shield to withstand every evil thought—thoughts such as wondering whether our God can aid us at need, something that troubles the wicked. This must be imprinted in our memory: our God will aid us. The reason: nothing can prevent Him. And He has declared to us that it is His good pleasure never to fail us at need. Let us conclude therefore that nothing can happen to us outside His will. (The prophet does not speak of the secret will of God but of that which He has revealed to us in scripture, which is contained in His open promises.) Let us take and hold to this will [to save]. Then let us think about the power of God, and let us put that power into effect. God does everything that He wants; let us therefore comfort ourselves in our adversities. And if God does not help us at first, let us wait on Him; we will not be disappointed. Our God will come, and when? He knows when it will be time. There we have the sum of this verse, and how we should apply it to our own use.

PRAYER In that let us bow ourselves before His majesty, acknowledging our faults, and let us be grieved with ourselves as we ought to be for having angered Him: because we have lived wickedly. Let us so join together His goodness with His glory that we may always prefer the principal thing, which is that His name may be hallowed; and then that He may have regard for His poor church and that He may strengthen us against all those who seek to destroy us because of the love of His name.

Almighty God, heavenly Father, we recognize in ourselves and confess that it is true, that we are not worthy to lift up our eyes to the heavens to present ourselves before Your face; that we should not presume that our prayers will be heard by You if You consider what is in us. For our consciences accuse us and our sins give witness against us, and we know that You are a just judge who does not justify sinners and the wicked, but You punish the offenses of those who have transgressed against Your commandments. So, Lord, when we look at our whole life we are confounded in our hearts, and we can only abase ourselves and despair as if we were already in the abyss of death. Nonetheless, Lord, because by Your infinite mercy it has pleased You to command us to call upon You, even from the depths of hell—and so much the more because we are helpless in ourselves—that we might find our refuge in Your sovereign goodness. As also You have promised to hear our prayers and supplications, not taking into account what we have deserved, but [to hear us] in the name and by the merit of Our Lord Jesus Christ, whom You have established as our Intercessor and Advocate. Therefore, renouncing trust in all things human, we take courage from Your goodness alone to address You and to invoke Your holy name, in order to obtain mercy.

First, Lord, besides the infinite blessings which You distribute in general to all who live on earth, You have given us so many special graces that it is impossible to name them all or even adequately to grasp them.

Especially You have been pleased to call us to the knowledge of Your holy gospel, withdrawing us from the miserable slavery of the devil where we were, delivering us from the accursed idolatry and superstitions in which we were plunged, to lead us to the light of Your truth. Nevertheless, through ingratitude and misunderstanding, having forgotten the good things we have received from Your hands, we have departed and turned away from You to our own desires; we have not given Your holy word the honor or obedience due to it; we have not exalted and magnified You as You deserve; and even though You have always faithfully admonished us by Your word, we have not listened to Your admonitions. Thus we have sinned, Lord; we have offended against You. Therefore we acknowledge this, our state of disorder and shame, recognizing that we are grievously at fault before Your judgment, and that if You wished to treat us as we have

173

deserved, we could anticipate nothing but death and damnation. For when we wish to excuse ourselves, our consciences accuse us and our iniquity is before You to condemn us. And in fact, Lord, we see by the chastisements that have already come upon us that You have with justice afflicted us. For since You are just and fair, it is not without cause that You afflict Your own. So having been beaten by Your rods, we acknowledge that we have provoked Your wrath against us. And now we see Your hand again uplifted to punish us, because the swords You are accustomed to use to execute Your vengeance are now deployed, and the threats You use against sinners and the wicked are fully ready.

If You punished us much more rigorously than You have done until this hour, and if in place of one plague we had yet to receive one hundred—even if the maledictions by which You once corrected the offenses of Your people Israel fell on us—we confess that this would be just, and we do not deny that we would have well deserved this.

And yet, Lord, You are our Father, and we are only earth and clay; You are our Creator, and we are the work of Your hands. You are our Shepherd, and we are Your flock; You are our Redeemer, and we are the people whom You have ransomed; You are our God, and we are Your heritage. Therefore, do not be angry against us, to correct us in Your wrath. May You not remember our iniquity to punish it, but may You chastise us gently according to Your loving kindness. Your wrath is inflamed by our wrongdoing, but may You remember that Your name has been invoked upon us and we bear Your mark and Your standard. May You, rather, uphold the work You have begun in us by Your grace, so that the whole earth may know You are our God and Savior. You know that the dead in hell and those whom You have undone and confounded will not praise You; but sorrowful and desolate souls, their hearts beaten down, their consciences oppressed with the sense of their own evil and starving with desire for Your grace, they will You give glory and praise. Your people Israel frequently provoked You to anger by their iniquity; You afflicted them by Your just judgment, but when they submitted to You, You always forgave them. And however serious their offenses were, for the love of Your covenant, which You made with Your servants Abraham, Isaac, and Jacob, You turned aside Your rods and condemnation that were prepared for them, such that their prayers were never rejected by You. By Your grace we can point to a new and much better covenant, which You made and established by the hand of Jesus Christ our Savior, which You willed to have written in His blood and sealed by His death and passion. So, Lord, denying ourselves and all human hope, we hasten back to this blessed covenant by which our Lord Jesus reconciled us to You by offering You His body in sacrifice. Look then, Lord, upon the face of Your Christ, and not upon us, so that by His intercession Your wrath may be appeased and Your face may shine upon us in joy and salvation; and henceforth may You receive us under Your holy guidance and govern us by Your Spirit, who renews us to a better life by which

> Your name be hallowed, Your kingdom come, Your will be done on the earth as in heaven. Give us today our daily bread, and pardon us our offenses as we pardon those who have offended us, and do not lead us into temptation but deliver us from evil. For Yours is the kingdom, the power, and the glory from age to age. Amen.

And although we are not worthy to speak for ourselves and petition You in our need, nevertheless because You have been pleased to command us to pray for each other, we pray to You for all our poor brothers and fellow members [of Christ] whom You visit with Your rods and chastisements, asking that You may turn away Your wrath from them. In particular we name _____ and _____. Lord, may You remember that they are Your children as we are, and though they have offended You, may You not cease to follow them with Your goodness and mercy, which You have promised should be everlasting to all Your faithful.

Be pleased then to look with pity on all Your churches, and all the peoples whom You have now afflicted, whether by plague or war or by Your other scourges: persons beaten down by Your rods, whether of sickness, prison, or poverty; console all of them according to what You know they need. Make Your chastisements profit them for their correction; confirm them in real patience, and soften Your rigor; and so at last, in delivering them, give them full cause to rejoice in Your goodness and bless Your holy name. In particular, may You please to have under Your eye those who labor for the cause of Your truth, both in public and in private, to confirm them in invincible constancy, to defend them and assist them everywhere and in everything; overturning all the machinations and plots of their enemies and Yours, bridling their [enemies'] rage, confounding them in their audacity of working against You and the members of Your Son. Do not allow Christianity to be completely laid waste, or the memory of Your name to be wiped out in the earth; do not allow those to perish upon whom You have willed to have Your name invoked, nor that the Turks, pagans, papists, and other unbelievers should glory in blaspheming You.

We pray also, O heavenly Father, for all princes and lords, Your servants, to whom You have entrusted the administration of Your justice, and especially for the magistrates of this city. May it please You to impart to them Your Spirit, who alone is good and truly sovereign, and daily increase that same Spirit in them, so that with true faith they may acknowledge Jesus Christ, Your Son our Lord, to be the King of kings and Lord of all lords, as You have given Him all power in heaven and earth. May they seek to serve Him and to exalt His kingdom in their government, ruling their subjects, who are the creatures of Your hands and the sheep of Your pasture, according to Your good pleasure. So that here as well as throughout the earth, being kept in good peace, we may serve You in all holiness and virtue, and being delivered from the fear of our enemies, we may praise You throughout our life.

We pray also, O faithful Father and Savior, for all those whom You have ordained pastors of Your faithful people, to whom You have entrusted the care of souls and the ministry of Your holy gospel. Guide them by Your Holy Spirit, so that they may be found faithful and loyal ministers of Your glory, always having this goal: that all the poor, wandering sheep may be gathered and led back to the Lord Jesus Christ, the chief Shepherd and Prince of bishops, so that day by day they may grow and increase in Him in all righteousness and holiness. On the contrary, may You deliver all the churches from the mouths of ravening wolves and from all mercenaries who seek their own ambition or profit, but not the exaltation of Your holy name alone and the salvation of Your flock.

And now we pray, most gracious God and merciful Father, for all people everywhere. Since You will to be acknowledged as the Savior of the whole world through the redemption wrought by Your Son Jesus Christ, grant that those who are still strangers to the knowledge of Him, being in the darkness and captivity of error and ignorance, may be brought by the illumination of Your Holy Spirit and the preaching of Your gospel to the right way of salvation, which is to know You, the only true God, and the one whom You have sent, Jesus Christ. May those whom You have already visited with Your grace and enlightened with the knowledge of Your word daily grow in goodness, enriched by Your spiritual blessings: so that all together we may worship You with one heart and one voice and may give honor and reverence to Your Christ, our Master, King, and Lawgiver. Amen.

[1562:] PSALM: Psalm 79 "The Nations Have Come into Your Heritage" [last 3 strophes]

BENEDICTION The Lord bless you and keep you. The Lord make His face to shine upon you and be merciful unto you. The Lord lift up His countenance upon you and keep you in virtuous prosperity. Amen.

SECTION IV:
PASSION WEEK

Although after 1550 Geneva did not observe liturgical feasts such as Christmas and Ascension on the traditional dates, and had also completely dropped such seasons as Advent and Lent, the city continued to have one more traditional liturgical occasion associated with the most important feast of the year, Easter. At least from 1544 onward, the week before Easter each year was set apart as a time for sermons on the passion of Christ. This meant an interruption in the *lectio continua* pattern of texts preached at the daily services, Mondays through Saturdays. (At least sometimes the passion sermons began on the Sunday before Easter, but because of the limited evidence it is not possible to say whether this was always the case.)

Although many of Calvin's sermons for these occasions have not survived, there are at least two full series extant, which come from late in his life. One was published in 1558, shortly after it was preached; the other dates from 1562 and has been printed only in the last generation in the *Supplementa Calviniana* (1981). Although records show that Calvin did preach on the passion according to the Gospel of John, both extant series cover the last three chapters of the Gospel of Matthew, which early modern scholars considered the oldest of the synoptics. Presented here is the sermon preached on Friday, March 27, 1562; it is found in SC VII, pp. 150–59, translated by E. A. McKee. (The minor lacunae in the manuscript are marked by ellipses.)

> From the sixth hour there was darkness over all the earth till the ninth hour. About the ninth hour Jesus cried in a loud voice, Eli, Eli, lama hazabthani, that is, My God, my God, why have you abandoned me? And some of those who were present there, having heard that, said: He is calling Elijah. And immediately one of them ran and took a sponge and having filled it with vinegar he put it on a reed and gave Him something to drink. The others said: Stop, let's see if Elijah will come to deliver Him. Then Jesus, crying again in

178

a loud voice, gave up His spirit. And behold, the veil of the temple was torn into two, from top to bottom, and the earth trembled and the rocks broke open. And the tombs opened and after He was resurrected some bodies of the saints who had been asleep were raised. And coming out of the tombs they went into the holy city and appeared to some people. (Matt 27:45–53) [Calvin read to the end of the chapter but preached only through verse 53.]

Yesterday we began to see how God allowed His only Son to be extremely humiliated in order to gather us to the eternal glory from which we had been banished. From that we must learn that from one angle, that is, in our sight, this death was very shameful. But Jesus Christ did not fail to triumph over the devil, sin, and the world. So, when St. Paul says (Col 2:14) that the charge which stood against our salvation was wiped out, he adds that our Lord Jesus Christ bound it to His death, and He triumphed over every power, as if He were there on a royal throne. In truth, though death in itself was cursed in its nature, yet when the Son of God was put to death, the angels worshiped Him there as their chief and sovereign prince. And if we consider the power of His death and the fruit that comes to us from it, we will find it not at all a curse but it will be the fountain of justice, life, and salvation. This then is what we must remember: When it is said that our Lord Jesus Christ was as if destroyed with shame, let us know that it was in our persons, and let us be horrified and confounded by our sins, seeing that our salvation cost Him so dearly. However, let us also know that [His shameful death] was not [endured] for His majesty or His divine glory, and even that it did not diminish the honor which belongs to Him as our mediator. On the contrary, since His inestimable goodness shines in His suffering so much for us, that ought to incite us to be caught up to glorify Him more.

In fact, what is told about one of the thieves is a part of this article that I have said. Because, after he has recognized and confessed that our Lord Jesus Christ is righteous and that it is not for His [own] misdeeds that He suffers, and after recognizing also his own poverty and condemning himself out of his own mouth, [the thief] prays and shows a faith as fine as can be found in any living creature. He says: "Lord, remember me, when You come into Your Kingdom" (Luke 23:42). We must note the circumstances of the time: in what situation does he see our Lord Jesus Christ? He sees Him hung there on a gibbet, which was cursed even by the sentence of God and not only by human opinion. For it is written in the law: "cursed be one who is hung on the wood" (Deut 21:23). See therefore our Lord Jesus Christ has been cursed. [The thief] sees Him near to death, being mocked on one side, blasphemed on the other. In short, if this poor man had been brought up from childhood on the law and prophets and had studied them day and night, this temptation would be likely to turn him away and upset all the instruction he had previously received. For we well see that for the least scandal some people are turned away from the gospel and Christianity—indeed, even those who seem to be the most advanced in it. If, therefore, this poor man had had so much teaching as one could wish, it would serve to swallow up all his faith and cast him into despair when he looked at such a spectacle. He was like someone torn away from his mind, without fear or honor, a poor murderer who had tasted scarcely a bit of God and religion.

And he here sees our Lord Jesus Christ in such a scandalous situation, and yet he calls Him king. How is that? Does he see Him in royal majesty? So we see that God gave him a wonderful faith. And that is why I said yesterday that we shall have greatly profited in our whole life when we have been students of this thief, since he teaches that our Lord Jesus Christ can save poor sinners and he applies this to himself. For since he had continued for a long time in murders and every cruelty and rebellion, and was guilty of all kinds of crimes, it is amazing that he could taste the mercy of God and then seek it in our Lord Jesus Christ—seeing Him in such a state. Yet nevertheless he affirms that our Lord Jesus Christ will have mercy on him, and behold he is content and satisfied, as if he had received the fulfillment of complete happiness and joy. However, he was not without feeling. Even his arms and legs were broken, and he had already suffered a great deal of torment. So in the midst of his sufferings, when he had no other concern except to obtain mercy for his sins, and that by means of our Lord Jesus Christ, nevertheless he sees Him crucified there, next to him as his companion. In that (as I have said) we must well remember a good teaching from such an example. And that, not only to value what is told us here in order to magnify the virtue of this poor man, but so that we may exercise a true constancy when we are surrounded by many temptations—so when heaven and earth have conspired against us to cast us into the deepest depths, that we may not on that account cease to take courage and address ourselves to our Lord Jesus Christ.

It is said that the sun gave witness to its Creator at the same time, because its light failed from the sixth hour to the ninth. We must note here that in that time the hours were counted differently from today. They began the hours at the dawn of day, and as the days lengthened so did the hours, for there were never but twelve hours; and as the night lengthened, the hours also lengthened in proportion as [they did] in the day. Therefore, when it speaks of the sixth hour, it was right at noon that the sun was darkened, till the ninth hour, which was the third hour before the night. Thus it was six hours before night when the sun began to lose its light. And so we see that this darkening and eclipse was a certain and notable sign that our Lord Jesus Christ was the Son of the living God. We must not think that the darkness was seen throughout the world; also it could not serve [as a sign] except to this nation and to the country of Judea.

There was also at the end an upheaval of nature, as if there were good reason to be frightened when our Lord Jesus Christ thus put out the light of the sun. Some think that this was a figure for the blindness that had come upon that Jewish people, others that it was necessary that all righteousness be extinguished and that there must be only dissipation among that people. But it ought to be enough for us that our Lord Jesus Christ wanted to show an uncommon power, so that everyone might be attentive and not cease to glorify Him in His death, however that was mixed up with humiliation, as we have seen. Be that as it may, behold the sun is a witness to the divine majesty of our Lord Jesus Christ, there where our natural reason would find it strange. As when Moses also calls the heaven and earth to witness (Deut 4:26) and the prophet Isaiah says: "Hear, earth, and you, heavens, give ear" (Isa 1:2). Though these are not sentient creatures, yet we see that even though there is no intelligence there, God does not cease to act when He pleases. For the sun and the earth must indeed be teachers of the Jews, and if they had been able to receive this warning that was given to them, it would convert them and be the means to draw them to salvation. How much more worthy of condemnation, then, is their hardness and diabolic stubbornness when they were not moved, even though the nature of all the elements changed! The earth shook, there where God had given it stability so that we could live on it; the sun lost its light, which by its proper nature lights up all the world. When, then, God spoke by such power and the Jews continued to be unheeding, we see that they were like animals. And that is an example for us, that ought to lead us to fear God when we see that those who are rebuked do not change at all, even though God makes such creatures [as the sun and earth] change. When it speaks of deaf and dumb creatures and that God imprints His power on these visible things and yet they [the Jews] remain blind—when we see that, let us learn to pray that He may make us profit from contemplating His works and that we may devote our study to that, as it is our true wisdom.

"It is said that at the ninth hour our Lord Jesus Christ cried: Eli, Eli, lama hazabathani" (Matt 27:46). But this word is a little corrupted. When one changes from one language to another one always changes some syllables. But be that as it may, it was not without cause that the evangelist wanted to recite the exact words of our Lord Jesus Christ, in order to alert us that here is one of the principal articles of our faith, in this cry of our Lord Jesus Christ. It is taken from Psalm 22 (Ps 22:2), where David (as we have recounted previously) figuratively represents the mediator; there he does not speak in his own name and does not so much put forth his private cause as he tells what had to be accomplished in the One who had been promised as savior.

There He is in extremity and He begins with these words: "My God, my God, why have You abandoned Me?" In this we see how our Lord Jesus Christ not only suffered in His body but also in His soul. In fact, it would be a great absurdity to say that He was the savior only of our bodies. To bring about our salvation He had to pay the debt of our sins, and the corruption of our offenses was upon Him in order to reconcile us to God, as Isaiah says (Isa 53:5). We know that our bodies are not culpable in themselves; they are muddied with the sins we commit, but still the root of all sin is in the soul. So it was necessary for our Lord Jesus Christ to bear a spiritual punishment in order to gain acquittal and absolution for us from God; that is why He was cast into such anguish, in addition to the suffering of death. If you said that this [phrase] is not suitable for the person of the Son of God, because it is words of despair that God had abandoned Him, the answer is easy. There is no great difficulty in refuting the audacity and malice of His detractors, who want to cut away the most important part of our salvation when they say that our Lord Jesus Christ did not speak according to His own feelings and never felt any fear of the judgment of God, since He was there in the person of evildoers.

For there is a great difference between the natural feelings and emotions that we have, and faith. Why? According to our feelings we do not see the life that is prepared for us. It is hidden, says St. Paul (Col 3:3); otherwise there would be no place for hope. Yet we see life, since faith is a sight of things that cannot be seen to appear (Heb 11:1). Thus, according to our natural feelings we only see death all around; as St. Paul says in the other passage: "We are dead, our life is hidden in God and in our Lord Jesus Christ." It is as if the apostle said: "We are earth and ashes, we feel a fear of death." As in truth we must always return to this point to humble ourselves, inasmuch as it is [part of] every affliction. Our natural feelings, I say, side with what they apprehend, in accordance with [our experience that] God sends us afflictions. That arouses bitterness, we are angry and sad. However, faith battles against all our human emotions. And so it happens that though we are still sad, we do not cease to taste the goodness of God; when we are terrified, we do not cease to hope in God; and when we are like those who are [very agitated and so] lost, we

183

do not cease to flee [to Him], having our refuge in God who calls us and brings us to Himself. See why St. Paul says in the Second Epistle to the Corinthians (2 Cor 4:9) that when we are oppressed, we are not completely crushed, and if we are dead, we will not remain there in a pit of hell but will be drawn back. In fact, that is clear enough in these words of our Lord Jesus Christ. For here there are two parts, which are contraries, but they fit together very well, when we understand how to distinguish between faith and natural human feelings.

Here it says: "My God, my God." It is certain that we ought to use these words without hypocrisy (I say); that is, not unless we are convinced and persuaded that God is our Father and that He acknowledges us as His children. For we must always come back to this point: "I shall call you My people and you will call Me your God" (Lev 26:12). If we do not have a sure witness that we are His people, our mouths will be closed and we will be unable to hope that He will be propitious to us. When, then, our Lord Jesus Christ uses that title, let us not petition Him lightly, but let us call upon Him truthfully, with certitude of faith that He is watching over our salvation. And our Lord Jesus Christ was not satisfied to have said "My God" once, but He repeats it. And though that might be in order to fight against the temptation of the flesh, still He affirms at the same time that without doubt He recognizes that God is favorable to Him and is His savior. See then the kind of integrity of faith we should desire.

However, He adds, "You have abandoned me," according to human feeling, but that does not prevent Him from always hoping in God. And see why it is also said that we must hope beyond all hope (Rom 4:18); that is, that even though the occasion does not present itself for us to entrust ourselves to God, still we must imitate [our Lord Jesus Christ] and have all our [natural] feelings overcome and beaten down and held captive, so that faith may rule over all. See then what we are shown in this cry of our Lord Jesus Christ. Now it was necessary that He come to that point, so that we might be assured that we will never be abandoned by God, whatever may happen, as if He had withdrawn from us and rejected us. Knowing that our Chief fought against such temptations, we must be reformed to be like Him. Let us never lose courage, or cease to pray to God when it appears that He is opposed to us and even armed to thunder against us; let us not cease to return to Him and to call Him our God, whatever may happen. See then how in the midst of our anguish, when it appears that we must be brought down to the depths of hell, we ought nevertheless to strengthen ourselves and renounce all our human emotions, so that God may be glorified. And so we may show that the faith we have in Him is not founded on what can be seen today, but that it rises above all struggles and grasps things invisible. And though we may not at all grasp that God wants to save us, let us nevertheless wait in patience for His help, inasmuch as He has promised it. Let us not measure His power according to our perceptions and what can be seen with the eye, but [rather let us measure it] by this image that is offered us here, in His promise by which He opens the heavens for us. So that, if we are afflicted in this life, nevertheless we do not cease to have what we seek in our Lord Jesus Christ, when we are patient and we do Him the honor of hoping for what we do not today see, as we have said. And that is it for this point, where our Lord Jesus Christ laments that He is abandoned by God His Father.

Look how the scribes and priests still mock Him. Because there is no intention of attributing to the soldiers the mockery described here, where our Lord Jesus Christ calls: "Eli, Eli, lama hazabathani." So then there is no doubt that it was in mockery that they [the scribes and priests] changed that word there, which means "My God," into "lama zabathani." And in fact the Jews could not have any doubt or ambiguity about those words. In short, they mocked with a certain malice, in corrupting the cry of our Lord Jesus Christ, such that when He called on God, they refer it to Elijah, as if He were a profane man and were calling on the dead as the pagans do. In short, it is as if He had no salvation in Himself, and, seeing that He got no more help from God and received no care from Him, He had departed from God and awaited help from Elijah. And so they said: "Let's see if Elijah will come to help Him" (Matt 27:49). Behold a rage still more monstrous! that these miserable people, ones who despise God, here mock the name of God and make it a laughing matter and calumny. What an intolerable blasphemy! But they had to show on their side that the devil completely possessed them. And yet our Lord Jesus Christ was subjected to such temptations, so that today we may not find anything strange when we must pass that way. And in accordance with how He shows us the path, let us not doubt that He will lead us to the right way and place of honor. As for the rest, let us know that God watches over us; and that today, even in the midst of our struggles, we can triumph fearlessly, knowing that the victory acquired for us by the Son of God belongs to us, and that it was for our profit and not for Himself that He thus powerfully fought and overcame all assaults directed against Him.

Then it is also added "that the veil of the temple was torn" (Matt 27:51). That was to break open their hearts, unless they were hardened to the last degree, because they ought to know why this veil had been put in the temple. It divided their sanctuary in such a way as to hinder the people from entering into the presence of God, because the only one who could enter was the priest who brought the incense and offered the solemn sacrifice—the people were excluded. It is true that the priests bore the names of the tribes of Israel, in order to give access to God to all, but still the people were kept at a distance. Nevertheless, this was not to prevent entrance to the sanctuary but to keep them humble, because the glory of God and His abiding place should not be open to their acquaintance. However, they ought to know well that all these figures were only for a time, so that they might always be maintained in anticipation of the mediator who was promised to them. They could well understand that the joy for which we should hope is to rejoice in God's presence, but the veil was interposed. So then by this they were warned that God would never come close to His own until the coming of the Redeemer. Therefore, when today they see the veil of the temple torn, it is as though He revealed Himself in His Son, as if to say: Here I am, receive Me as your King and Savior!

But however that ought to profit them, still they are even more hardened, because there was another veil that blinded them and covered their face, as St. Paul says (2 Cor 3:7–16), citing what is told of the former people: that they could not bear the rays from the face of Moses so he had to wear a cloth [over his face (Exod 34:29–35)]. St. Paul says what that veil was: it was of dark shadows, and that then there was no illumination such as we have today in the gospel. Because God has appeared in the person of His Son, so that we might not be held in figures with them. But St. Paul speaks of another veil, that is, the stubbornness of the Jews who are completely blind, because even though they have the law of Moses and they are practiced in it, still they do not see a bit. For what is the law without Jesus Christ? It is a body without a soul. And when the Jews do not look to Him, and they are excluded and alienated, behold their veil: they are completely blind, such that they cannot draw near to Him. When, then, the veil of the temple was torn, that did them no good. But let us apply all this to our instruction. When we see that this veil has been torn, let us know that the ceremonies of the law are ended, and now we have the truth and substance of everything in our Lord Jesus Christ; as St. Paul says that this is the body, while the patriarchs had only the shadow (Col 2:17). Then let us know that all the ceremonies which there were under the law have been broken and abolished by the coming of the Son of God, because in Him we have the perfection of what was then in figures.

For the rest, let us recognize the inestimable benefit God has given us: that we do enter not into a temporal and material sanctuary to draw near Him, but by faith and prayers and speech we can easily come to God with our heads up, because the law is fulfilled in us by the blood of our Lord Jesus Christ. Seeing then that there is now no veil as there was in the time of the law, let us recognize the privilege that God has given us, that we may call upon Him freely. For our Lord Jesus Christ did not enter there [the sanctuary] for Himself, but for us and in our name. By His means we have such access to God His Father that there is no doubt that He will receive our prayers as if we were spotless, even though we are only corruption and earthworms, sticking to the earth. See what we must remember.

In order to be more confirmed in this teaching, let us add what is recounted by St. John, where our Lord Jesus Christ says "that all is accomplished" (John 19:30). For it is in virtue of this word that the veil was torn, because if anything had been lacking of what was figured under the law, it is certain that that would have continued always. But when perfection has come, what was ordained to lead the people to anticipate the Redeemer would be useless and superfluous today. And not only that, but it would be an injury to us, since each would create his own helps according to his fancy. As the papists have turned everything upside down by their follies, devoting themselves to fables and what they have made up, the imitation of the saints, which does nothing except to turn us away from the coming of our Lord Jesus Christ and envelop us such that there is nothing but confusion. Let us note well then, and weigh this word where it is said "that all is accomplished," because by that our Lord Jesus Christ wishes to set underfoot all that had then been practiced. And when the sacrifices of the law are spoken about, we know that they pointed to this perfection of our Lord Jesus Christ, which is now accomplished. When, then, we have one perfect One, let us not do as the papists do, who want to have a thousand and an infinite number each day, as they say that this stinking Mass is a sacrifice for the living and the dead. On the contrary, since our Lord Jesus Christ has spoken this definitive sentence, "that all is accomplished," it would only be blasphemy and abomination before God if we wanted to have other sacrifices than that which was accomplished in the death of the Son of God. See then how this tearing of the veil was an authentic signature of this word of our Lord Jesus Christ, so that we might seek the perfection of all that is required for our salvation in what He has done and suffered.

Then it is said that "the tombs were opened and after the resurrection of our Lord Jesus Christ some of the saints were seen in the holy city" (Matt 27:52). In this we have confirmation of what I mentioned before, that in things both high and low God wished to give proof for His only Son, so that His death was shown everywhere. But it is particularly said of the tombs so that this word would be manifest. And so they would also know that our Lord Jesus Christ was not resurrected for Himself or His own profit, but He was the first[born] from among the sleeping

[dead], as St. Paul says in First Corinthians 15 (1 Cor 15:20ff.). This does not contradict the common teaching where it is said that our life is hidden and the time of our resurrection has not come until our Lord Jesus Christ will come [again]. Because these two things can go together quite well, that is, that God wished to show these dead among the living for a time so that it might be certified that our Lord Jesus Christ was not resurrected for Himself but for the whole body of His church. However that does not detract from the glory He had even if He had to be [...] , as when Enoch and Elijah were taken up into heaven (Gen 5:24, 2 Kgs 2:11). (It is not that they were glorified in all glory, as that is promised to all the children of God, but God took them as though in trust and reserved for that day.) Thus those here could have been held in reserve after they were seen in Jerusalem; God took them into His keeping and they will share in the same glory with us and they await us there. See then how there is no contradiction. There was a special resurrection, which was earthly—that is, [what happened] was not to renew completely those [resurrected ones]. But it was to give them such life that people might recognize that our Lord Jesus Christ should draw after Him [out of death into life] those who had been given to Him by God His Father. To argue about how they live and in what state they are [now, is not appropriate]; it would be better to go on soberly, because we ought always to keep to the purity and righteousness of God. Then we have said why they were raised, which is so that the teaching of St. Paul in the Second Epistle to Corinthians (chapter 5) might be confirmed to us: since our Lord Jesus Christ is raised, let us not doubt our resurrection, because we are as if united inseparably to Him. So much then for this point.

That the city of Jerusalem is called "holy city" is not to honor the inhabitants, because they were then worse than Sodom and Gomorrah. It is called "holy" by Isaiah (Isa 48:2), and then it came to such an extremity [that the people] renounced Him who had adopted [them] as His people—that is indeed to render them more abominable before Him. But we also see that the grace of God can never be wiped out by human malice, as St. Paul shows us that He will be magnified in the midst of perverse

189

people, the wicked and the dissolute (Rom 3:3, 11:28f.). And if there were not ministers or prophets or teachers, still the Holy Spirit will always witness to His glory and majesty, and His promises will always be in force, as we also see that our Lord Jesus Christ witnesses to Himself when He says: Come to Me and you will have abundance of life (John 10:10, Matt 11:28ff.). But that is not to say that all those who come there [to Him] will profit, because to all hypocrites it will serve as a curse to have so profaned such a good thing. But also such profane people cannot destroy this promise, which belongs to all true believers. So then, nevertheless, the holiness our Lord put in Jerusalem was to double the condemnation of the people, that instead of this place being an earthly paradise as it ought, it was only a stinking thing and contagion. This is [said] so we may learn always to magnify God in all His graces, and at the same time let us also seek to use them worthily and fear to abuse them, lest they come back as a worse curse on us. So much for this point.

It is said that our Lord Jesus Christ "cried out again with a loud voice and gave up His spirit" (Matt 27:50). St. Luke tells what this cry was and what its content was, that is, He said: I commend to You My soul, Lord (Luke 23:46). See then the second cry of the Son of God, which is very different from the first. Because there is [first] this cry [that He is abandoned]. And now He commends His soul into the hands of God His Father and gives it to Him, knowing that He will be a good and faithful guardian. Thus we see that in His first lament [our Lord Jesus Christ] struggled so well that the witness had already come, that He could peacefully say: "My God, I commend to You My soul, and it will be safe when You take it in Your charge and it is in Your protection." We see then how it has been shown previously that our Lord Jesus Christ, in making His cries, directed them to the end where we must follow after Him also. That is, that we not feed on what can draw us to defy God but we must set all that underfoot so as to resist all temptations and call on God freely, as is now done by His Son our Lord Jesus Christ. Now this is taken from Psalm 31, where we see that, in the midst of danger, David commended his soul into the hands of God (Ps 31:6), and this was to signify that God could well save him, were he attacked by a hundred thousand deaths. [David] does not speak of commending his soul into His hands as if he meant to depart from this world, but it was in order that He might preserve [David's soul] until the time of his death. It is certain that David could not speak so did he not pass through death and rise above the blows of this world, because this dwelling place ought not so to hold us that we do not have our regard lifted higher. As it is said in the psalm, that we must seek to be so peaceable on earth in order to have lasting peace there above in heaven. David then would have had a very slight hope if he had rested his confidence here below. So there is no doubt but that he committed himself into God's hands for life and for death.

Now our Lord Jesus Christ gives the second cry, that is, He commits His soul into the hands of God His Father, even though it appears that it must die. Because while we are sojourning on the earth, still we can hope in some way that God will have us in His keeping and we will be protected by His power. But in death all will fail, if we take the counsel of human feelings, and one cannot think that a person is different from a donkey or a dog, as Solomon says (Prov 3:18f.): his nature is like that of the beasts. So we must come to this stance, which is that God may receive our souls in trust and He may be their guardian to keep them in peace. And let us not doubt that in dying we will live forever, inasmuch as if we die in this world and to visible sight, God will not cease to be our Father, and thus our life will rest in His mercy, it will endure always. See in sum what we must remember.

Let us note that our Lord Jesus Christ did not speak thus for Himself. It is true that when He cried out in a loud voice, the zeal and ardor in Him incited Him to do so; nevertheless, He made this petition public in order to put in our mouths the same words, and for us to call upon God at the point of death and for us to commit ourselves into His hands. When (I say) our Lord Jesus Christ formed this petition, it was not for Himself alone but it is common to all the faithful. This voice ought always to resound in our ears, and we should so listen to the Son of God that the sufferings which assail us may not turn us away from

Him who is the author of our salvation, so that we may remit our souls into His hand and never doubt that we will be heard.

And our Lord Jesus Christ has not only given us such an example, but at the same time He acquired the privilege of being the guardian of our souls, as St. Stephen shows. Because just as our Lord Jesus Christ called upon God His Father, also St. Stephen called upon Him at his death: "Jesus Christ," he says, "I commend my soul into Your hands" (Acts 7:58). He does not speak at random. For what does it mean to commend our souls into the hand of a protector? There must be all divine power. Now, St. Stephen recognized that our Lord Jesus Christ was consecrated to God His Father, the protector of our souls—that is for our instruction, so that we may always be bold to commend ourselves to Him. As He exhorts us in the tenth chapter of St. John, when He says that we are in His care and that all who have been committed to Him will have such a good guardian that none will be lost till the last day, when He will give accounting to God His Father (John 10:28). See then what we also must remember, that in dying we may not think that we are only emptying a breath into the air, but let us know that the souls which God created will return into His hand and will be kept until all will be restored in glory eternal. It is said that our Lord Jesus Christ died, so that we may know that He was the firstborn of the dead. Because if He had only come up to [the point of] death and God had delivered Him from it, what would that be to us when we are dying? We would be like people gone astray and lost. But when our Lord Jesus Christ goes before us even when we are dying, in that lies our hope—see how we can persevere in calling upon Him! Let us note well then that our Lord Jesus Christ not only died, after He had been condemned under Pontius Pilate, but He was raised so that we might be completely and throughout united and joined with Him; and that we might willingly follow Him to death with a true hope that we will share in His death and in His resurrection, to experience their fruit, because by that [death-resurrection] the devil is overcome.

We bow ourselves before the majesty of our good God in recognition of so many faults of which we are guilty, praying that

He may be pleased to make us so much profit from what we have now heard that we may be more and more attentive to a true repentance, to condemn in ourselves our vices. And that we may also have our refuge in our Lord Jesus Christ, to cast ourselves completely on Him and there have our whole refuge and resting place; and never to doubt that, when God is pleased to receive us into His keeping, though there may be only misery in all our life, and death may be horrifying to our natural feeling and judgment, still we will never fail to have lasting life and to be companions of the angels when we are brought under His hands. And may He grant this not only to us but to all peoples and nations on earth....

PRAYER

Prayer is usually and naturally understood as one of the most important expressions of the human relationship with God. Calvin included consideration of the unspoken prayers of the innermost heart in his discussion in the *Institutes* (3.20.4, 33), but he also gave significant attention to teaching people to pray and to leading his own congregation in prayer on virtually every public occasion when they were gathered. Calvin's primary liturgical prayers are found in the services of Part Three, in their natural liturgical contexts.

Part Four brings together prayers and teaching on prayer from a wide variety of places. The first section provides Calvin's exposition of the Lord's Prayer, *the* model for all Christian praying. The following three sections present prayers collected from a variety of circumstances. Included are the individual and family prayers Calvin prepared as patterns for Genevan children, adults, and households; then a number of prayers from his Old and New Testament sermons; and finally some of the prayers with which he concluded his biblical lectures.

SECTION I:
CALVIN'S EXPOSITION OF THE LORD'S PRAYER

The fundamental Christian prayer is the Lord's Prayer, and Calvin, like most teachers before and after him, made the exposition of this prayer central to his instruction as well as to his liturgical practice (cf. pp. 112, 129–30, 152, 156, 160, 175). Here is presented an abbreviated form of his teaching in the *Institutes,* Book Three, chapter 20. The original is found in OS 4; the translation is by F. L. Battles. Since Calvin's name is usually associated primarily with the doctrine of predestination, it is worth noting that in explaining the Lord's Prayer the theologian-pastor insists that the Christian prays "not only for those whom he at present sees and recognizes as [his brothers in Christ], but [for] all people who dwell on earth" (3.20.38).

36. First, at the very threshold we meet what I previously mentioned: we ought to offer all prayer to God only in Christ's name, as it cannot be agreeable to Him in any other name. For in calling God "Father," we put forward the name "Christ." With what confidence would anyone address God as "Father"? Who would break forth into such rashness as to claim for himself the honor of a son of God unless we had been adopted as children of grace in Christ? He, while He is the true Son, has of Himself been given us as a brother that what He has of His own by nature may become ours by benefit of adoption if we embrace this great blessing with sure faith....Thus, if we are His sons, we cannot seek help anywhere else than from Him without reproaching Him with cruelty and excessive rigor.

37. And let us not pretend that we are justly rendered timid by the consciousness of sins, since sins daily make our Father, although kind and gentle, displeased with us....He depicts and

represents for us in a parable this abundance of fatherly compassion: a son had estranged himself from his father, had dissolutely wasted his substance, had grievously offended against him in every way; but the father embraces him with open arms, and does not wait for him to ask for pardon but anticipates him, recognizes him returning afar off, willingly runs to meet him, comforts him, receives him into favor (Luke 15:20). For in setting forth this example of great compassion to be seen in a person, He willed to teach us how much more abundantly we ought to expect it of Him....But because the narrowness of our hearts cannot comprehend God's boundless favor, not only is Christ the pledge and guarantee of our adoption, but He gives the Spirit as witness to us of the same adoption, through whom with free and full voice we may cry, "Abba, Father." Therefore, whenever any hesitation shall hinder us, let us remember to ask Him to correct our fearfulness, and to set before us that Spirit that He may guide us to pray boldly.

38. However, we are not so instructed that each one of us should individually call Him his Father, but rather that all of us in common should call Him our Father. From this fact we are warned how great a feeling of brotherly love ought to be among us, since by the same right of mercy and free liberality we are equally children of such a father (Matt 23:9). For if one father is common to us all, and every good thing that can fall to our lot comes from Him, there ought not to be anything separate among us that we are not prepared gladly and wholeheartedly to share with one another, as far as occasion requires.

Now if we so desire, as is fitting, to extend our hand to one another and to help one another, there is nothing in which we can benefit our brethren more than in commending them to the providential care of the best of fathers; for if He is kind and favorable, nothing at all else can be desired. Indeed, we owe even this very thing to our Father. Just as one who truly and deeply loves any father of a family at the same time embraces his whole household with love and goodwill, so it becomes us in like measure to show to His people, to His family, and lastly, to His inheritance, the same zeal and affection that we have toward this heavenly Father. For He so honored these as to call them the fullness of His only begotten

Son (Eph 1:23). Let the Christian, then, conform his prayers to this rule in order that they may be in common and embrace all who are his brothers in Christ, not only those whom he at present sees and recognizes as such but all people who dwell on earth. For what God has determined concerning them is beyond our knowing except that it is no less devout than humane to wish and hope the best for them. Yet we ought to be drawn with a special affection to those, above others, of the household of faith, whom the apostle has particularly commended to us in everything (Gal 6:10). To sum up, all prayers ought to be such as to look to that community our Lord has established in His kingdom and His household.

39. Nevertheless, this does not prevent us from praying especially for ourselves and for certain others, provided, however, that our minds do not withdraw their attention from this community or turn aside from it but refer all things to it. For although prayers are individually framed, since they are directed to this end, they do not cease to be common. All this can easily be understood by a comparison. There is a general command of God's to relieve the need of all the poor, and yet those obey it who to this end succor the indigence of those whom they know or see to be suffering, even though they overlook many who are pressed by no lighter need because either they cannot know all or cannot provide for all. In this way they who, viewing and pondering this common society of the church, frame particular prayers of this sort, do not resist the will of God when in their prayers, with God's people at heart, in particular terms, they commend to God themselves or others whose needs He has been pleased to make intimately known to them.

However, not all aspects of prayer and almsgiving are indeed alike. For liberality of giving can be practiced only toward those whose poverty is visible to us. But we are free to help by prayer even utterly foreign and unknown persons, however great the distance that separates them from us. This, too, is done through that general form of prayer wherein all children of God are included, among whom they also are. To this may be referred the fact that Paul urges the believers of his time to lift pure hands in every place without quarreling (1 Tim 2:8). In warning them that strife shuts the gate to prayers, his intention is that they offer their petitions in common with one accord.

40. That He is in heaven is added....By this He obviously means that He is not confined to any particular region but is diffused through all things....But while we hear this, our thought must be raised higher when God is spoken of, lest we dream up anything earthly or physical about Him, lest we measure Him by our small measure, or conform His will to our emotions. At the same time our confidence in Him must be aroused, since we understand that heaven and earth are ruled by His providence and power.

To sum up: Under the name "Father" is set before us that God who appeared to us in His own image that we should call upon Him with assured faith. And not only does the intimate name "Father" engender trust but it is effective also to keep our minds from being drawn away to doubtful and false gods, permitting them to rise up from the only begotten Son to the sole Father of angels and of the church. Second, because His throne is established in heaven, from His governing of the universe we are forcibly reminded that we do not come to Him in vain, for He willingly meets us with present help....Here Christ declares both of these things to His Father: that our faith rests in Himself, then that we should surely be persuaded that our salvation is not overlooked by Him. For He deigns to extend His providence even to us....

41. The first petition is that God's name be hallowed; the need for it is associated with our great shame. For what is more unworthy than for God's glory to be obscured partly by our ungratefulness, partly by our ill will, and so far as lies in our power, destroyed by our presumption and insane impudence? Though all the ungodly should break out with their sacrilegious license, the holiness of God's name still shines....Because, therefore, God's holiness is so unworthily snatched from Him on earth, if it is not in our power to assert it, at least we are bidden to be concerned for it in our prayers.

To summarize: We should wish God to have the honor He deserves; people should never speak or think of Him without the highest reverence....Here we are bidden to request not only that God vindicate His sacred name of all contempt and dishonor but also that He subdue the whole human race to reverence for it. Now since God reveals Himself to us partly in teaching, partly in works, we can hallow Him only if we render to Him what is His in both respects, and so embrace all that proceeds from Him. And His sternness no less than His leniency should lead us to praise Him, seeing that He has engraved marks of His glory upon a manifold diversity of works, and this rightly calls forth praises from every tongue. Thus it will come about that scripture will obtain a just authority among us, nor will anything happen to hinder us from blessing God, as in the whole course of His governance of the universe He deserves....

42. The second petition is that God's kingdom come. Even though it contains nothing new, it is with good reason kept separate from the first petition; for if we consider our languor in the greatest matters of all, it behooves us to extend our discussion in order to drive home something that ought to have been thoroughly known of itself....God reigns where people, both by denial of themselves and by contempt of the world and of earthly life, pledge themselves to His righteousness in order to aspire to a heavenly life. Thus there are two parts to this kingdom: first, that God by the power of His Spirit correct all the lusts of the flesh, which by squadrons war against Him; second, that He shape all our thoughts in obedience to His rule. Therefore, no others keep a lawful order in this petition but those who begin with themselves, that is, to be cleansed of all corruptions that disturb the peaceful state of God's kingdom and sully its purity. Now, because the word of God is like a royal scepter, we are bidden here to entreat Him to bring all people's minds and hearts into voluntary obedience to it. This happens when He manifests the working of His word through the secret inspiration of His Spirit in order that it may stand forth in the degree of honor that it deserves. Afterward we should descend to the impious, who stubbornly and with desperate madness resist His authority....We must daily desire that God gather churches unto Himself from all parts of the earth; that He spread and increase them in number; that He adorn them with gifts; that He establish a lawful order among them; on the other hand, that He cast down all enemies of

pure teaching and religion; that He scatter their counsels and crush their efforts....

Thus this prayer ought to draw us back from worldly corruptions, which so separate us from God that His kingdom does not thrive within us. At the same time it ought to kindle zeal for mortification of the flesh; finally, it ought to instruct us in bearing the cross. For it is in this way that God wills to spread His kingdom....For this is the condition of God's kingdom: that while we submit to His righteousness, He makes us sharers in His glory....Meanwhile, He protects His own, guides them by the help of His Spirit into uprightness, and strengthens them to perseverance. But He overthrows the wicked conspiracies of enemies, unravels their stratagems and deceits, opposes their malice, represses their obstinacy, until at last He slays Antichrist with the Spirit of His mouth, and destroys all impiety by the brightness of His coming (2 Thess 2:8).

43. The third petition is that God's will may be done on earth as in heaven. Even though it depends upon His kingdom and cannot be separated from it, still it is with reason added separately on account of our ignorance, which does not easily or immediately comprehend what it means that "God reigns in the world." It will therefore not be absurd to take it as an explanation that God will be King in the world when all submit to His will. Here it is not a question of His secret will, by which He controls all things and directs them to their end....But here God's other will is to be noted—namely, that to which voluntary obedience corresponds....We are therefore bidden to desire that, just as in heaven nothing is done apart from God's good pleasure, and the angels dwell together in all peace and uprightness, the earth be in like manner subject to such a rule, with all arrogance and wickedness brought to an end.

And in asking this we renounce the desires of our flesh; for whoever does not resign and submit his feelings to God opposes as much as he can God's will, since only what is corrupt comes forth from us. And again by this prayer we are formed to self-denial so God may rule us according to His decision. And not this alone but also so He may create new minds and hearts in us....In sum, so we may wish nothing from ourselves but His Spirit may govern our hearts; and while the Spirit is inwardly teaching us we may learn to love the things that please Him and to hate those which displease Him. In consequence, our wish is that He may render futile and of no account whatever feelings are incompatible with His will.

Here, then, are the first three sections of the prayer. In making these requests we are to keep God's glory alone before our eyes, while leaving ourselves out of consideration and not looking to any advantage for ourselves; for such advantage, even though it amply accrues from such a prayer, must not be sought by us here. But even though all these things must nonetheless come to pass in their time, without any thought or desire or petition of ours, still we ought to desire and request them. And it is of no slight value for us to do this. Thus, we may testify and profess ourselves servants and children of God, zealously, truly, and deeply committed, to the best of our ability, to the honor that is owed our Lord and Father. Therefore, those who do not, with this desire and zeal to further God's glory, pray that "God's name be hallowed," that "His kingdom come," that "His will be done," should not be reckoned among God's children and servants; and inasmuch as all these things will come to pass even against such people's consent, the result will be their confusion and destruction.

44. The second part of the prayer follows, in which we descend to our own affairs. We do not, indeed, bid farewell to God's glory, which as Paul testifies is to be seen even in food and drink, and we ask only what is expedient for us (1 Cor 10:31). But we have pointed out that there is this difference: God specifically claims the first three petitions and draws us wholly to Himself to prove our piety in this way. Then He allows us to look after our own interests, yet under this limitation: that we seek nothing for ourselves without the intention that whatever benefits He confers upon us may show forth His glory, for nothing is more fitting than that we live and die to Him.

But by this petition we ask of God all things in general that our bodies have need to use under the elements of this world, not only for food and clothing but also for everything God perceives to be beneficial to us, that we may eat our daily bread in peace. Briefly, by this we give ourselves over to His care, and entrust ourselves to His providence, that He may feed, nourish, and preserve us. For our most gracious Father does not disdain to take even our bodies under His safekeeping and guardianship in order to exercise our faith in these small matters, while we expect everything from Him, even to a crumb of bread and a drop of water. For since it has come about in some way or other through our wickedness that we are affected and tormented with greater concern for body than for soul, many who venture to entrust the soul to God are still troubled about the flesh, still worry about what they shall eat, what they shall wear, and unless they have on hand abundance of wine, grain, and oil, tremble with apprehension. So much more does the shadow of this fleeting life mean to us than that everlasting immortality. Those who, relying upon God, have once and for all cast out that anxiety about the care of the flesh, immediately expect from Him greater things, even salvation and eternal life. It is, then, no light exercise of faith for us to hope for those things from God which otherwise cause us such anxiety. And we benefit greatly when we put off this faithlessness, which clings to the very bones of almost all.

What certain writers say in philosophizing about "supersubstantial bread" seems to me to agree very little with Christ's meaning; indeed, if we did not even in this fleeting life accord to God the office of nourisher, this would be an imperfect prayer. The reason they give is too profane: that it is not fitting that children of God, who ought to be spiritual, not only give their attention to earthly cares but also involve God in these with themselves. As if His blessing and fatherly favor are not shown even in food, or it were written to no purpose that "piety holds promise not only for the life to come but also for the present life" (1 Tim 4:8)! Now even though forgiveness of sins is far more important than bodily nourishment, Christ placed the inferior thing first that He might bring us gradually to the two remaining petitions, which properly belong to the heavenly life. In this He has taken account of our slowness.

But we are bidden to ask our daily bread that we may be content with the measure that our heavenly Father has deigned to distribute to us, and not get gain by unlawful devices. Meanwhile, we must hold that it is made ours by title of gift; for, as is said in Moses, neither effort nor toil, nor our hands, acquire anything for us by themselves but by God's blessing (Lev 26:20)....The word "today,"...bridled the uncontrolled desire for fleeting things....[W]e are bidden to ask only as much as is sufficient for our need from day to day, with this assurance: that as our Heavenly Father nourishes us today, He will not fail us tomorrow. Thus, however abundantly goods may flow to us, even when our storehouses are stuffed and our cellars full, we ought always to ask for our daily bread, for we must surely count all possessions nothing except insofar as the Lord, having poured out His blessing, makes it fruitful with continuing increase. Also, what is in our hand is not even ours except insofar as He bestows each little portion upon us hour by hour, and allows us to use it....[H]e shows it is by His power alone that life and strength are sustained, even though He administers it to us by physical means....

Yet those who, not content with daily bread but panting after countless things with unbridled desire, or sated with their abundance, or carefree in their piled-up riches, supplicate God with this prayer, are but mocking Him. For the first ones ask Him what they do not wish to receive, indeed, what they utterly abominate— namely, mere daily bread—and as much as possible cover up before God their propensity to greed, while true prayer ought to pour out before Him the whole mind itself and whatever lies hidden within. The others ask of Him what they least expect, that is, what they think they have within themselves. In calling the bread "ours," God's generosity, as we have said, stands forth the more, for it makes ours what is by no right owed to us....[W]hat has been obtained by just and harmless toil is so designated, not what is got by frauds or robberies; for all that we acquire through harming another belongs to another. The fact that we ask that it be given us signifies that it is a simple and free gift of God, however it may come to us, even when it would seem to have been obtained from

205

our own skill and diligence, and supplied by our own hands. For it is by His blessing alone that our labors truly prosper.

45. Next follows: "Forgive us our debts." With this and the following petition, Christ briefly embraces all that makes for the heavenly life, as the spiritual covenant that God has made for the salvation of His church rests on these two members alone: "I shall write my laws upon their hearts," and, "I shall be merciful toward their iniquity" (Jer 31:33; 33:8). Here Christ begins with forgiveness of sins, then presently adds the second grace: that God protect us by the power of His Spirit and sustain us by His aid so we may stand unvanquished against all temptations. He calls sins "debts" because we owe penalty for them, and we could in no way satisfy it unless we were released by this forgiveness. This pardon comes of His free mercy, by which He Himself generously wipes out these debts, exacting no payment from us but making satisfaction to Himself by His own mercy in Christ, who once for all gave Himself as a ransom (Rom 3:24)....

Finally, we petition that forgiveness come to us, "as we forgive our debtors": namely, as we spare and pardon all who have in any way injured us, either treating us unjustly in deed or insulting us in word. Not that it is ours to forgive the guilt of transgression or offense, for this belongs to God alone (Isa 43:25)! This, rather, is our forgiveness: willingly to cast from the mind wrath, hatred, desire for revenge, and willingly to banish to oblivion the remembrance of injustice. For this reason, we ought not to seek forgiveness of sins from God unless we ourselves also forgive the offenses against us of all those who do or have done us ill. If we retain feelings of hatred in our hearts, if we plot revenge and ponder any occasion to cause harm, and even if we do not try to get back into our enemies' good graces, by every sort of good office deserve well of them, and commend ourselves to them, by this prayer we entreat God not to forgive our sins....

Finally, we must note that this condition—that He "forgive us as we forgive our debtors"—is not added because by the forgiveness we grant to others we deserve His forgiveness, as if this indicated the cause of it. Rather, by this word the Lord intended partly to comfort the weakness of our faith. For He has added this as a sign to assure us He has granted forgiveness of sins to us just as surely as we are aware of having forgiven others, provided our hearts have been emptied and purged of all hatred, envy, and vengeance. Also, it is partly by this mark that the Lord excludes from the number of His children those persons who, being eager for revenge and slow to forgive, practice persistent enmity and foment against others the very indignation that they pray to be averted from themselves. This the Lord does that such people dare not call upon Him as Father....

46. The sixth petition, as we have said, corresponds to the promise that the law is to be engraved upon our hearts, but because we obey God not without continual warfare and hard and trying struggles, here we seek to be equipped with such armor and defended with such protection that we may be able to win the victory. By this we are instructed that we need not only the grace of the Spirit, to soften our hearts within and to bend and direct them to obey God, but also His aid, to render us invincible against both all the stratagems and all the violent assaults of Satan....And these temptations are either from the right or from the left. From the right are, for example, riches, power, honors, which often dull people's keenness of sight by the glitter and seeming goodness they display, and allure with their blandishments, so that, captivated by such tricks and drunk with such sweetness, they forget their God. From the left are, for example, poverty, disgrace, contempt, afflictions, and the like. Thwarted by the hardship and difficulty of these, they become despondent in mind, cast away assurance and hope, and are at last completely estranged from God. We pray God, our Father, not to let us yield to the two sorts of temptations....that we may not be puffed up in prosperity or yet cast down in adversity.

Nevertheless, we do not here ask that we feel no temptations at all, for we need, rather, to be aroused, pricked, and urged by them, lest, with too much inactivity, we grow sluggish....But God tries in one way, Satan in another. Satan tempts that he may destroy, condemn, confound, cast down, but God, that by proving His own children He may make trial of their sincerity, and establish their strength by exercising it; that He may

207

mortify, purify, and cauterize their flesh, which unless it were forced under this restraint would play the wanton and vaunt itself beyond measure. Besides, Satan attacks those who are unarmed and unprepared that he may crush them unaware. God, along with the temptation, makes a way of escape, that His own may be able patiently to bear all that He imposes upon them (1 Cor 10:13, 2 Pet 2:9). It makes very little difference whether we understand by the word *evil* the devil or sin. Indeed, Satan himself is the enemy who lies in wait for our life (1 Pet 5:8)....Now we seek to be freed from his power, as from the jaws of a mad and raging lion; if the Lord did not snatch us from the midst of death, we could not help being immediately torn to pieces by his fangs and claws, and swallowed down his throat. Yet we know that if the Lord be with us, and fight for us while we keep still, "in His might we shall do mightily" (Ps 60:14). Let others trust as they will in their own capacities and powers of free choice, which they seem to themselves to possess. For us let it be enough that we stand and are strong in God's power alone....While we petition, then, to be freed from Satan and sin, we anticipate that new increases of God's grace will continually be showered upon us, until, completely filled therewith, we triumph over all evil.

47. These three petitions, in which we especially commend to God ourselves and all our possessions, clearly show what we have previously said: that the prayers of Christians ought to be public, and to look to the public edification of the church and the advancement of the believers' fellowship. For each one does not pray that something be given to him privately, but all of us in common ask our bread, forgiveness of sins, not to be led into temptation, and to be freed from evil....

Moreover, there is added the reason why we should be so bold to ask and so confident of receiving...that His "is the kingdom, and the power, and the glory, forever." This is firm and tranquil repose for our faith. For if our prayers were to be commended to God by our worth, who would dare even mutter in His presence? Now, however miserable we may be, though unworthiest of all, however devoid of all commendation, we will yet never lack a reason to pray, never be shorn of assurance, since His kingdom, power, and glory can never be snatched away from our Father. At the end is added, "Amen."...By this the saints not only express the end of their prayers but confess themselves unworthy to obtain it unless God seeks the reason from Himself, and that their confidence of being heard stems solely from God's nature.

SECTION II:
OCCASIONAL PRAYERS FROM THE CATECHISM AND LITURGY

Calvin prepared five prayers as a second, shorter part of his 1542/45 *Catechisme*. These corresponded to the times of day he named in the *Institutes* (3.20.50) as those occasions for personal prayer that all devout people should observe: "when we rise in the morning, before we begin daily work, when we sit down to a meal, when by God's blessing we have eaten, when we are getting ready to retire." Three of these prayers: #1 for the morning, #2 for the child before school, and #5 for evening before bed, were originally expressed in first person singular "I"; the other two, #3 and #4, the thanksgivings before and after meals, were written in the plural "we" form. In 1551 the printer Jean Crespin published a little *L'ABC françois*, a simpler catechism than Calvin's, containing along with various other prayers four of Calvin's first five prayers— all except the child's prayer before school. Instead of this last, he inserted a prayer (by Calvin) to be said before doing one's work, expressed in the plural, thus in a way revising the list of prayers to make the series appropriate for adults. In 1561 this prayer and a second alternative to be said before daily work (also expressed in the plural) were added to some editions of the liturgy and catechism. In 1552 Calvin appended to the liturgy *(La forme des prières)* a prayer to be said by someone suffering persecution, expressed in the singular, and this also was taken into the catechisms in the late 1550s.

In 1561 the printer Jean Rivery used a number of Calvin's prayers to create a family devotional liturgy to be used morning and evening, and added this to his publication of the catechism. He edited Calvin's original morning and evening prayers in a plural "we" form. For the morning he added both the Lord's Prayer and the Apostles' Creed, and prefaced this with the confession of sin from Calvin's regular Sunday morning liturgy, introduced by a very slightly expanded variant of Calvin's exhortation to pray. It is not clear how much Calvin had to do with developing this, but he certainly approved of parents and family heads leading their households in worship. Various other printings of the prayers in the catechism either followed Rivery in changing singular to plural, or made minor additions or rarely subtractions, usually involving only a few words (here given in italics).

Here Calvin's first five prayers are given in the original form, with italics to mark any important later addition. The other three prayers, two alternative ones to be said before work and one for one or more person(s) suffering persecution, are presented next. Only one of these, the second one for work, appears to have been altered within Calvin's lifetime, and the changes are mostly minor, although an important phrase (which had been accidentally dropped from Rivery's first printing in 1561) is restored from a 1562 version (cf. OC 6:137–38 n.3). Finally, it seems worthwhile to present Rivery's edited compilation of Calvin's prayers for a family devotional liturgy in order to illustrate how his parishioners understood their pastor's instructions were to be applied to the little community of the church that householders were to lead for their children and dependents.

The texts are found in OC 6:138–46, translated by E. A. McKee. The first five prayers are usually translated from the Latin, but except for schoolboys, their teachers, and the clergy, most people probably used these prayers in French. Therefore it was decided to translate these five as well as the others, which were virtually always used in French, from that language. Those who are interested in comparing the French with the Latin can consult the translations of prayers #1–#5 in Calvin's *Tracts*, vol. 2, pp. 95–99. Some of the altered nuances reflect the differences of the languages, but others suggest the more accessible character of Calvin's way of addressing nonacademic members of his congregation.

Calvin's Occasional Prayers

1542/45 "Catechisme"

"Prayer to say in the morning, when rising."

My God, my Father, and my Savior, since You have been pleased to give me the grace to come through the night to the present day; now grant also this favor, that I may employ it entirely in Your service, that I may not think, say, or do anything except to please You and obey Your good will; so that by this means all my works may be to the glory of Your name and the edification of my neighbors. And as You have been pleased to make Your sun shine upon the earth to give us bodily light, grant me also the light of Your Spirit to illumine my understanding and my heart, to direct me in the straight way of Your righteousness. Thus

211

whatever I apply myself to do, may my chief purpose and intent always be to walk in the fear of You, to serve and honor You, awaiting all my good and prosperity only from Your blessing, so as not to attempt anything except what may be pleasing to You.

Moreover, as I am working so much for my body and the present life, may I always keep my eyes fixed above, on the heavenly life You have promised to Your children. Nevertheless, be pleased to be my protector in body and in soul, strengthening me against all the temptations of the devil and delivering me from all the dangers that could befall me. And because it means nothing to begin well if one does not persevere, please receive me into Your holy guidance not only for this day but for all my life, daily continuing and increasing Your grace in me until You have led me to full union with Your Son Jesus Christ our Lord, who is the true Sun of our souls, shining day and night, eternally and without end. And so that I may obtain such graces from You, please forget *all* my past faults, forgiving me by Your infinite mercy, as You have promised to all those who seek You with a good heart. *Hear me, merciful Father, by our Lord Jesus Christ. Amen.*

"Prayer to say before studying his lesson at school."

O Lord, You who are the fountain of all wisdom and learning, because You have pleased to give me the means of instruction as a child, so I may know how to rule myself in holiness and honorable behavior throughout the course of my life: Please also illumine my understanding, which of itself is blind, so that it may grasp the teaching that will be given to me; please strengthen my memory to be able to remember well, dispose my heart to receive (what is taught) willingly and with due eagerness, so that the opportunity You present to me may not be lost because of my ingratitude. To do this, please pour out Your Holy Spirit on me, the Spirit of all intelligence, truth, judgment, prudence, and teaching, Who will make me able to profit well so that my teachers' efforts to teach me may not be lost. Whatever the studies to which I apply myself, grant that I may direct them to the true purpose, which is to know You in our Lord Jesus Christ, to have full confidence of salvation and life in Your grace alone, and to serve You rightly and purely, according to Your pleasure, so that everything I learn may be an instrument to aid me in that [serving Your pleasure].

And because You promise to give wisdom also to the small and humble, and to confound the proud in the vanity of their minds—and likewise to manifest Yourself to those of right heart, and on the contrary to blind the wicked and perverse—grant that I may be brought under the rule of true humility, by which I may be made teachable and obedient: first to You, secondly to those in authority over me, whom You have appointed to rule and teach me. Moreover, please dispose my heart to seek You without pretense, renouncing every carnal and evil affection. And in such a way I now am preparing myself to serve You one day in the estate and calling to which You may be pleased to appoint me when I have come of age. *Hear me, merciful Father, by our Lord Jesus Christ, Amen.*

"Prayer to say before the meal."

O Lord, from whom flows the fullness of all good things, please extend Your blessing upon us, Your poor servants, and sanctify for us the gifts that we receive from Your bounty, so that we may use them soberly and purely, according to Your good will. By this means we may acknowledge You as Father and Author of all loving kindness, seeking always chiefly the spiritual bread of Your word by which our souls are nourished forever, by Jesus Christ, Your Son, our Lord. Amen.

"Thanksgiving after the meal."

O Lord God, we give You thanks for all the benefits that we constantly receive from Your hand, that You are pleased to sustain us in this bodily life, giving us all the things we need. And especially we thank You that You have been pleased to regenerate us in the hope of a better life, which You have revealed to us by Your holy gospel. We ask You not to allow our affections to be tangled in these corruptible things, but that we may always raise our eyes above, anticipating our Lord Jesus Christ, until He will come (again) for our redemption. Amen.

"Prayer to say before going to sleep."

O Lord God, since You were pleased to create the night for us to rest, as You ordained the day for work, please grant me the grace so to rest in the body this night that my soul may always be watching for You and my heart may be lifted up in Your love, and I may so let go of all earthly cares as to be comforted and eased as my weakness requires. May I never forget You, but may the remembrance of Your goodness and grace remain always imprinted on my memory, so that by this means my conscience also may have its spiritual repose as my body takes its physical rest. Moreover, do not let my sleep be excessive, to gratify beyond measure the ease of my flesh, but only to satisfy the frailness of my nature, so that I may be disposed to Your service. Also, please preserve me unpolluted in my body as in my spirit, and protect me from all dangers so that even my sleep may be to the glory of Your name. And because no day passes that I do not offend You in many ways, since I am a poor sinner, as all is now hidden by the darkness that You send on the earth, please also bury all my offenses by Your mercy, so that I may not be driven back from Your face by them.[40] Hear me, my God, my Father, my Savior, by our Lord Jesus Christ. Amen.

ABC Book (1551) and/or "La forme des prières" (1561-)

"Prayer to be said before doing one's work."

May the Lord God and Father be present with us by His Holy Spirit, and so govern and guide us, that all that we do, say, or think may be to His honor and glory, in the name of His Son, Jesus Christ, our Lord. Amen.

"Another prayer for the same purpose."

Our good God, Father and Savior, since You have pleased to command us to work to meet our needs, by Your grace may You so bless our labor that Your benediction may extend to us: without it we cannot continue to live. And may (Your) favor serve us as a witness of Your goodness and presence, that by it we may recognize the fatherly care You have for us.

Moreover, O Lord, please grant us aid by Your Holy Spirit, so that we may faithfully work in our place and vocation, without any fraud or deception; may we pay attention to following Your ordinance rather than satisfying our own lust for gain. And if it please You to prosper our labor, may You also give us the heart to support those who are in need according to the ability You have given to us—but always without our wishing to set ourselves above those who have not received such generosity from You. And where You choose to give us greater poverty and lack than our flesh would like, You, O Lord, grant us the grace to acknowledge that You always feed us by Your goodness, so that we may not be tempted to defy You. But may we wait with patience for You to fill us not only with Your temporal graces but also with spiritual ones, so that we may always have greater reason and occasion to thank You and to repose entirely on Your goodness alone. Hear us, most merciful Father, by Jesus Christ, Your Son, our Lord. Amen.

"La forme des prières" *(1552–)*

"Prayer for the believer held in captivity under the Antichrist."
O Lord God, You who are a just judge to punish all those who continue to offend You, as You are a compassionate Father mercifully to receive all who submit to You: Grant me the grace to be truly touched by the knowledge of my sins, and instead of flattering myself or falling asleep, may my heart be confounded by my poverty, and may I also confess it with my mouth, to give You honor in humbling myself. And as You instruct us about this in Your Word, may it so illumine my conscience that in examining all my life I may learn to be grieved with myself. Also, may all the chastisements You send to me serve me to the same purpose, and by all means may I be brought to think more carefully about myself, so as to seek from You pardon for all my past faults. And may it please You for the future to direct me in the right path and reform me to a proper obedience to Your righteousness.

Especially may I recognize that the unhappy captivity in which I am bound under the tyranny of the Antichrist is a just punishment, because I have not served and adored You as I ought; and even now I am greatly lacking in my service toward Your majesty. And in fact, if it was not without cause that You permitted Your people to be transported to Babylon, to be subject in body to the yoke of unbelievers, with much more reason does this very hard and cruel servitude that we bear on our souls proceed from our sins, inasmuch as we have provoked Your wrath and do not deserve You to reign over us fully. Nevertheless, Lord, may You please to take pity on so many poor souls whom You have ransomed at such a price and not allow Satan to lead them into destruction. Among other [reasons], because You have already given me the gift of showing me how I should glorify You, grant me also a wholehearted affection to be employed in doing that, such that I may dedicate body and soul to exalting Your holy name. And since I do not do this well, fearing human menaces rather than Your voice, and allowing myself to be led by the infirmity of my flesh rather than by the power of Your Spirit, do not allow me to remain in such a great vice, nourishing Your wrath and vengeance against me by my hypocrisy; but rather touch me to the quick, so that, aspiring to a true repentance, I may long continually for You.

And also, O Lord, even though I am not at all as well disposed to seek You as I ought, do not cease to hold out to me Your mighty hand to draw me back from this dirt and filth and to deliver me from this abyss. And because according to my ignorance and sensuality I can see no means [for that], please find the means by Your wondrous counsel, since it is easy for You to do what seems impossible to us. And when You please to give me some opening, do not let me be slow and lazy to leave this accursed prison, to seek the liberty to serve Your glory. Grant me the grace to forget all my carnal comforts, indeed to forget myself, so that nothing may hinder me from following Your will. Deliver me from all defiance and every excessive anxiety, so that with full courage I may allow myself to be guided by Your Word. And so that I may obtain such mercy from You, please do not consider my weakness (which You know and which manifests itself only too much) unless it is to correct that weakness; and so, may the imperfection in me not hinder You from completing what You have begun. And because we are not worthy to present ourselves before Your majesty, hear me in name of our Lord Jesus, Your Son, as You have ordained Him as our Advocate; and may the merit of His intercession make up for the lack in us. Amen.

Jean Rivery's Family Devotional Compilation

"The practice of the father of the family, and all his household, to pray in the morning."

Exhortation

My brethren, let each of us bow ourselves most humbly before the face of the high and sovereign majesty of our good God and Father, acknowledging what we are, that is, poor and miserable sinners, all saying with a good heart as follows:

Confession of Sin

O Lord God, eternal and almighty Father, we confess and acknowledge unfeignedly before Your holy majesty that we are poor sinners, conceived and born in iniquity and corruption, inclined to do evil, useless for any good, and that in our depravity we constantly and endlessly transgress Your holy commandments. By so doing we purchase for ourselves, by Your righteous judgment, our ruin and perdition. Nevertheless, O Lord, we are grieved with ourselves to have offended You; and we condemn ourselves and our sins with true repentance, asking that Your grace may relieve our distress.

O God and most gracious Father, You who are full of compassion, have pity upon us in the name of Your Son, Jesus Christ, our Lord. By blotting out our sins and stains, magnify and increase in us day by day the graces of Your Holy Spirit, so that as we acknowledge our unrighteousness with all our heart, we may be touched by the sorrow that brings forth true repentance,

217

which, causing us to die to all our sins, may produce in us the fruits of righteousness and innocence pleasing to You; through that Jesus Christ, Your Son, our Lord. Amen.

Prayer

Our God, Father, and Savior, since You have been pleased to give us the grace to come through the night to the present day, now grant also this favor, that we may employ it entirely in Your service, that we may not think, say, or do anything except to please You and obey Your good will; so that by this means all our works may be to the glory of Your name and the edification of our neighbors. And as You have been pleased to make Your sun shine upon the earth to give us bodily light, grant us also the light of Your Spirit to illumine our understanding and our hearts, to direct us in the straight way of Your righteousness. Thus whatever we apply ourselves to do, may our chief purpose and intent always be to walk in the fear of You, to serve and honor You, awaiting all our good and prosperity only from Your blessing, so as not to attempt anything except what may be pleasing to You.

Moreover, as we work so much for our bodies and the present life, may we always keep our eyes fixed above, on the heavenly life You have promised to Your children. Nevertheless, be pleased to be our protector in body and in soul, strengthening us against all the temptations of the devil and delivering us from all the dangers that could befall us. And because it means nothing to begin well if one does not persevere, please receive us into Your holy guidance not only for this day but for all our lives, daily continuing and increasing Your grace in us until You have led us to full union with Your Son, Jesus Christ, our Lord, who is the true Sun of our souls, shining day and night, eternally and without end. And so that we may obtain such graces from You, please forget our past faults, forgiving us by Your infinite mercy, as You have promised to all those who seek You with a good heart.

Therefore we offer our supplications for all people, as for ourselves, in the name of Your Son, our Lord Jesus Christ, praying as He has taught us: "Our Father, who art in heaven,..."

Also, O Lord, grant us the grace to persevere in Your holy faith, which You have planted in our hearts by Your mercy; increase it and make it grow in us from day to day, until it reaches its true fullness. We confess our faith, saying: "I believe in God, the Father almighty,..."

SECTION III:
PRAYERS FROM CALVIN'S SERMONS

Calvin concluded his sermons with long prayers. These prayers had three parts: the first was an introductory phrase, which varied slightly over the years; the second was a paragraph reflecting the sermon just preached; and the third a fixed form that followed three different patterns. There was one pattern for Sunday mornings and another for the Wednesday Day of Prayer, both of which were published in *La forme des prières*. There was also a third one, not printed until some parishioners wrote it down, which Calvin used on the other weekdays (and, apparently, most Sunday afternoons). For examples of each full prayer, see the liturgies for those days in Part Three. In the period of his recorded sermons, Calvin preached on the Old Testament on weekdays, the New Testament on Sundays (always in the morning and often in the afternoon), and Psalms usually on Sunday afternoons, though also occasionally on Wednesdays.

The following is a selection of the prayers giving only the introductory phrase and the distinctive part of the prayer reflecting the day's sermon, concluding with the opening line of the fixed prayer appropriate for that day. It should be noted that Calvin's extempore prayers are usually one long run-on sentence, which editors and translators must divide in some fashion to make good English sense. In an effort to keep some sense of the flow, the punctuation used here loosely employs colons and semicolons where it is difficult to find suitable places for periods. Locations of texts of each prayer are given with the translations, which are by E. A. McKee.

Prayers Reflecting Old Testament Sermon Texts

All prayers come from regular *lectio continua* series; most are from "ordinary weekdays" (third part beginning with "May He give this grace..." or occasionally with the second sentence of that fixed form, "And for this may He please to raise up true and faithful ministers of His word..."); a few come from Wednesdays (third part beginning "And so we all say: almighty God, heavenly

Father...."). Wednesday sermon prayers were usually shorter than those on other weekdays. The order of the biblical texts does not follow the Bible but the chronology of the sermons, according to when Calvin preached on different books, and so begins with the earliest sermons. This allows the reader to observe the changes of the opening phrase.

Sermons sur Jérémie: [Late in 1548–5 Sept. 1550] SC VI

sermon 20 = Jer 17:24–27, 5 Aug. 1549, p. 140.

Following this holy teaching, we bow ourselves before the face of our good God in acknowledgment of our offenses, asking that He may give us a better sense of them than we have had; and that He not permit us to be brought down by hypocrisy, but that we may know that He justly punishes us. May we learn to recognize His graces so that we may praise Him not just one day of the week but throughout our life. May He give this grace not only to us but also to all peoples and nations on earth....

Sermons sur Michée: [12 Nov. 1550–10 Jan. 1551] SC V

sermon 5 = Mic 2:1–3, 24 Nov. 1550, p. 44.

Following this holy teaching, we bow ourselves before the face of our good God in acknowledgment of our offenses, asking that He may be pleased so to reform us that we may no longer be given over to the enticements and vanities of this world as we have previously been; but that being content with what He sends us, we may walk in justice and equity toward our neighbors. That we may no longer be subject to evil but rather, according to the opportunity that He gives us, we may take counsel to do good to everyone, and have that fraternal love that He commends to us: so that, each meeting the others' needs, we may be the more incited to glorify and magnify God's name, that we may all participate in His heavenly inheritance. May He give this grace not only to us but also to all peoples and nations on earth....

sermon 6 = Mic 2:4–6, 25 Nov. 1550, p. 52.

Following this holy teaching, we bow ourselves before the face of our good God in acknowledgment of our offenses, asking that He may be pleased so to open our eyes that, relying entirely on His goodness, we may not stop short with the things of this world. May He make us so profit in the teaching of His truth that we may be more and more confirmed in His will, that when we receive the benefit of having His word purely preached to us, we may at the same time learn to conform ourselves to His will: so that by this means the ignorant, seeing our good life and behavior, may be drawn to acquaintance with Him, so that His name may be glorified by all in common accord. May He give this grace not only to us but also to all peoples and nations on earth....

sermon 21 = Mic 6:1–4/5, 26 Dec. 1550, pp. 181–82.

Following this holy teaching, we bow ourselves before the face of our good God in acknowledgment of our offenses, asking that He may be pleased so to open our eyes that we may recognize better than heretofore the benefits we have received from His hand: that we may know for what purpose He has lavished on us His spiritual riches, and what He gives us daily for the body as well as for the soul; that as we seek Him as a gracious and favorable Father, He may treat us as His beloved children. That we may not provoke His wrath against us so that He must enter into judgment with us; but rather that He may give us the grace so to use all His gifts that we may apply them to the true purpose for which He ordained them: which is that we may glorify His name throughout our life. May He give this grace not only to us but also to all peoples and nations on earth....

sermon 22 = Mic 6:6–8, 27 Dec. 1550, p. 191.

Following this holy teaching, we bow ourselves before the face of our good God in acknowledgment of our offenses, asking that He may give us a vivid sense of them that we may know how we must depart from them to bring ourselves under Him. And because He is gracious to extend His hand to us and wants to keep us among His own, and witnesses to this by His word, may we not be so unhappy as to pull back when He draws us so gently, but may we do Him the honor to subject ourselves entirely to Him and His teaching. Moreover, when we see that there is such infirmity in us, let us seek the remedy from Him from whom we can have succor, our Lord, Jesus Christ; that as He has once united us in one body to God, His Father, so we may ask nothing else than to live with our neighbors in justice and equity and good peace; so that by Him we may come to the immortal glory in which we shall all be united in perfection as He has promised us. May He give this grace not only to us but also to all peoples and nations on earth....

Vingtdeux Sermons (on Psalm 119): [Sunday afternoons in 1553]
(Genève, François Estienne, 1562. [reprint of 1554])

sermon 15 = Ps 119:113–20, 30 April 1553, pp. 309–10.

Following this holy teaching, we bow ourselves before the face of our good God in acknowledgment of our offenses, praying that He may be pleased to make us feel the sweetness of His word, with which His servant David had his hunger satisfied: so that we might have such an ardent appetite for it that it would make us forget all the lusts of this world that too much envelop us. And that we may cut off all the excesses of our flesh, so as to dedicate ourselves in all holiness to our God, to confirm ourselves more and more in His service. And being once brought into the path of salvation by Him, while we must still walk in this world, and since we are surrounded by so many dangers, may He always have His hand extended over us to guard us and keep us under His protection until the end. May He give this grace not only to us but also to all peoples and nations on earth....

sermon 18 = Ps 119:137–44, 21 May 1553, pp. 370–71.

Following this holy teaching, we bow ourselves before the face of our good God in acknowledgment of our offenses, asking that He may make us feel them more than we have done. That, recognizing the poverty and unhappiness that are in us and how much we need His assistance, we may hasten back to Him; having all our refuge in His goodness and mercy, and relying on His promises, never doubting that He is faithful and loyal in everything He says and that He accomplishes all that He shows us in

His word; that is, that He will so unite us to Him, that after having separated us completely from all the pollutions of this world, He will make us participants in His righteousness and finally in His glory. May He give this grace not only to us but also to all peoples and nations on earth....

Sermons sur Job: [1554–1555, weekdays]
(Genève, Iean de Laon, 1563)

sermon 1 = Job 1:1, [26 Feb. 1554], f6.

We bow ourselves before the face of our good God in acknowledgment of our offenses, asking that He may make us so feel them, that in recognizing our poverty we may seek the remedy He gives us. That is, that in forgiving all our offenses, He may so govern us by His Holy Spirit. However much Satan may be named the prince of the world, and he may have such popularity that the greater part of the people are thus perverted (as we see); that nevertheless we may not live in debauchery with them, but that this good God may keep us in His obedience, and we may know to what we have been called in order to follow it. That we may keep that brotherhood He has ordained among us, and be so united each with the others that we may ask nothing but to procure the good of our neighbors: so that we may more and more be confirmed in His grace, which He acquired for us by our Lord Jesus Christ, until we receive the fruit of that grace in His heavenly glory. May He give this grace not only to us but also to all peoples and nations on earth....

sermon 15 = Job 4:7–11, [probably early April 1554], f81.

We bow ourselves before the face of our good God in acknowledgment of our offenses, asking that He may make us feel them more than we have done. And in considering His promises, by which He draws us so sweetly to Himself, may we know that when we walk in the fear of God He will never forget us, however we may have offended against Him in all kinds of ways, so that we are quite worthy of His rejecting us. And also when Satan seeks to make us believe that we may never be received into His mercy, that nevertheless He may make us know that He has forgiven us, indeed that He is ready to receive us each and every time that we want to return to Him. And to do this let us rely on His promises, that He may so guide us by them that we may arrive at the fulfillment of all His blessings, which He has promised to us and prepared for us in heaven. May He give this grace not only to us but also to all peoples and nations on earth....

sermon 72 = Job 19:26–29 [Wed., probably early Aug. 1554], f401.

We bow ourselves before the face of our good God in acknowledgment of our offenses, asking that He may make us so feel them that we may look to amend our ways. And at the same time may each of us look to humble ourselves beneath His mighty hand; and, instead of condemning others, may we learn to feel the evils in ourselves, in order to ask God to purge us and cleanse us of them, until He has fully reclothed us in His righteousness. And so we all say: almighty God, heavenly Father....

Sermons sur Esaïe, chap. 13–29: [22 Feb. 1557–31 July 1557] SC II

sermon 8/74 = Isa 14:24–27, 9 March 1557, pp. 75–76.

We bow ourselves before the majesty of our good God, in acknowledgment of our offenses, asking that He may make us feel them more and more. And at the same time that He may show us the love He has for us: when, before we were born, indeed before the creation of the world, already He had taken us for His heritage; and since then He has ratified His adoption when He pleased to call us to the knowledge of His gospel. And, recognizing His goodness to us, let us turn back to Him and, however much we may be assailed with many temptations, let us never cease to hope that He will continue to the end His goodness toward us, which we have already experienced. That has already been certified to us not only by words and even an oath, but by the grace of His only Son, whom He gave for the guarantee of all that He promised us, demonstrating that we can never be separated from Him. And, seeing that there is such a bond and union that by Him we are united to God His Father, to be guided to life eternal, may He please make us feel this by the power of His Holy Spirit, so that we may continue to serve Him, not being turned aside or corrupted by all the enticements and corruptions of this world. May He give this grace not only to us but also to all peoples and nations on earth....

sermon 23/89 = Isa 19:23–25, 19 April 1557, p. 217.

We bow ourselves before the majesty of our good God, in acknowledgment of our offenses, asking that He may make us so feel them that we may weep over them and be grieved. And may we be so abased in ourselves as to be drawn to magnify His graces toward us, that we may be more and more devoted to serving and honoring Him and may offer Him all praise. May we learn to walk in such a fashion that He may make use of us, and we may make His praises resound everywhere. At the same time, let such brotherhood and union be among us that, having set under foot all enmity and bitterness, we may ask nothing except to employ ourselves for each other, to range ourselves under that Chief ordained for us, our Lord, Jesus Christ. May He give this grace not only to us but also to all peoples and nations on earth....

sermon 28/94 = Isa 22:4–11, 24 April 1557, pp. 266–67.

We bow ourselves before the majesty of our good God, in acknowledgment of our offenses, asking that He may make us feel them more and more, so that we may return to Him with tears and weeping, and also with full assurance that we will always find Him propitious to us, and He will never cease to show Himself still our Savior, whatever unbelief there is in us. And even though we have provoked Him in so many ways, let us not cease still to have our eyes always fixed on our Lord Jesus Christ, inasmuch as it is in Him that we will find the means to reconcile ourselves with God, His Father and ours, when we have offended Him. And may this be not only for us, but may we have compassion on so many poor souls who are perishing today. May the good God please to have pity on all His poor world: to gather us all together and give us grace, that we who have already known His word may profit in it better than we have heretofore; and that we may bring back the poor straying and blind ones to His flock, so that, being all gathered under His obedience, we may seek only to glorify His holy name throughout our life. And for this may He please to raise up true and faithful ministers of His word....

sermon 31/97 = Isa 22:20–25, 7 May 1557, p. 297.

We bow ourselves before the majesty of our good God, in acknowledgment of our offenses, asking that He may make us so feel them that, being cast down in ourselves, we may be lifted up by the grace of our Lord, Jesus Christ; and that we may learn to keep ourselves there in such fashion that all the days of our life we may persevere [in leaning on that grace] with constancy. May we not stray away here and there, as we have been accustomed to wander after our foolish imaginings. But may His word be so impressed on our hearts that, when He has promised us His aid, we may not doubt that He will do it; and may this give us courage to practice all that is our office and duty, and to acquit ourselves so faithfully that each one, great or small, may give an accounting of what has been committed to us, so that all of us in common accord may learn to adore Him as our God and to give Him the honor and homage due to Him. And for this may He please to raise up true and faithful ministers of His word....

sermon 51/117 = Isa 27:6–9, [Wed.] 30 June 1557, p. 496.

We bow ourselves before the majesty of our good God, in acknowledgment of our offenses, asking that He may make us feel them more than we have done, so that we may grieve over them so much that we may find all our pleasure in Him. And that, having tasted and savored the mercy that He offers to us, we may be so ravished with desire for it that we may forget all the enticements of Satan; and may so renounce this world that we seek only to be new creatures, reformed by the Spirit of our Lord Jesus Christ. And thus we all say: Almighty God, heavenly Father,...

sermon 65/131 = Isa 29:19–22, 30 July 1557, p. 639.

We bow ourselves before the majesty of our good God, in acknowledgment of our offenses, asking that He may make us so feel them that He may not have to raise His hand to us to confound us. But that, inasmuch has He has shown Himself our Father and has called us to aim at the hope of the heavenly life, to be fellow heirs with His only Son, to whom belongs the plenitude of all good things, as He is the fountain of life, happiness, and glory; that He may keep us always united to Himself, and may gather us so that we never stray away, and may reform us by His Holy Spirit, so that we may follow our calling to the end. And in the midst of all our miseries and the afflictions we must endure in this world, that we may never fail, but may continue in faith and hope to rest in Him and entrust everything to Him, until He leads us to the full enjoyment of the good things we now anticipate through faith. May He give this grace not only to us but also to all peoples and nations on earth....

Sermons sur Esaïe, chap. 30–41: [4 Aug. 1557–30 Dec. 1557] SC III

sermon 13/145 = Isa 32:5–8, 28 Aug. 1557, pp. 126–27.

We bow ourselves before the majesty of our good God, in acknowledgment of our offenses, asking that He may make us feel them more and more, in order to lead us back truly to Him in such a way that His name may be glorified in us, and that nothing may come from our mouths except what may magnify His majesty, so that with one accord we may give Him such reverence as is due. May there be brotherhood and mutual concern among us, so that we may come to each other's help and employ ourselves in what He commands us, to make us so much the more sure we can truly claim Him as our Father, when we unite under the bond He has put among us, the bond of love and justice, and when we do not pollute ourselves with the evil doings we see in the world. But may this rather be to lead us to the recognition of our sins, so we may grieve over them, and that we may much rather be persecuted in this world than become somnolent and fall asleep. And may He please at the same time to make the corrections He sends us profitable to us, so that the poor world, which remains obstinate, may thus be brought back to Him; so that all together we may serve and adore Him as our only God. And for this may He please to raise up true and faithful ministers of His word....

sermon 28/160 = Isa 35:8–10, 5 Oct. 1557, p. 265.

We bow ourselves before the majesty of our good God, in acknowledgment of our offenses, asking that He may make us feel them more and more, to be grieved over them and so to renounce them, in order to be reclothed with His graces, and to be made participants of the good things we have heard that He promises to His faithful people. And when He presents Himself to be our guide, let us not doubt that He always has a mighty hand to keep us steady; and He will not allow us to fail, but in His power we will rise above all the difficulties that would hinder us from coming to Him. And however we may now have cause to be sorrowful about many things—and some are afflicted in body and others in spirit—that nevertheless this good God will always give us the grace to be led under His hand until, enjoying the fruit of the victory He has promised us, we may rejoice fully, singing His praises with the angels of paradise, when we have been brought forth out of all weeping. May He give this grace not only to us but also to all peoples and nations on earth....

sermon 32/164 = Isa 36:18–22, 9 Oct. 1557, pp. 305–6.

We bow ourselves before the majesty of our good God, in acknowledgment of our offenses, asking that He may make us feel them more and more; so that we may be brought under Him in such fashion that we ask nothing except to put off our own thoughts and affections, knowing that these are so many vices that turn us away from obedience to Him. And let us recognize how easy it is for us to become debauched, in order that we may [seek to] be restrained by His word; and being grounded upon His promises, may we call upon Him throughout our life and even at death; that we may be so assured of our salvation that we may be enabled to surmount all the temptations of this world and willingly to quit all that could hold us here below, even our own life. And let us not find it difficult to entrust ourselves into the hands of Him who justifies us, that in life and in death He will never fail all those who trust in Him. May He give this grace not only to us but also to all peoples and nations on earth....

sermon 37/169 = Isa 37:18–22, 21 Oct. 1557, p. 356.

We bow ourselves before the majesty of our good God, in acknowledgment of our offenses, asking that He may make us feel them more and more. As we now see His rods raised throughout the world, let us lower our eyes and, in recognition of the offenses we have committed, let us pray that He may bury them so that nothing may hinder us from being rescued by Him at need, and also to pray with true confidence that He may grant us the grace to have His promises so impressed on our hearts that nothing may turn us from them. And when it seems as if the whole world must be turned upside down, nevertheless may we always remain grounded upon this foundation; that is, the immutable and enduring truth of God, never doubting that as He was pleased to choose us for Himself and keep us in the faith of our Lord Jesus Christ, He will give us true perseverance and support us in all our weaknesses, until He has put off from us this mortal body and all our imperfections. May He give this grace not only to us but also to all peoples and nations on earth....

sermon 52/184 = Isa 40:2–5, 29 Nov. 1557, pp. 493–94.

We bow ourselves before the majesty of our good God, in acknowledgment of our offenses, asking that He may make us feel them more than we have; and then that He may bend down to call us to Himself, seeing that we draw back instead of approaching Him and cannot lift a foot to advance a single step unless He works in us by the power of His Holy Spirit. May He not allow the many exhortations that we hear daily to be vain and useless, exhortations by which He draws us and even pricks us to approach Him; but may He give power to His word to touch us to the quick in our hearts. And may He always increase such constancy in us that we may struggle against all the assaults Satan sends against us; and may we not cease always to pursue our course until we have completely fulfilled it and are come to taste in its entirety the love that He bears us and the goodness that He shows to us. And may that [love-goodness] be the means to make us renounce this world and to put off the corruptions that hold us back here, so that we may ravished with an ardent love for Him, and it may make us quit all the things that hold us here below, and even all the enticements Satan offers us to keep us enveloped as in a net. May He give this grace not only to us but also to all peoples and nations on earth....

Sermons sur la Genèse (1:1–20:7).
[4 Sept. 1559–15 May 1560]. SC XI

sermon 88 = Gen 18:24–33, 20 April 1560, p. 1003.

We bow ourselves before the majesty of our good God, in acknowledgment of our offenses, asking that He may be pleased to move us more and more to a true repentance; and that He may bear with us in our infirmities and vices, not to nourish them but to purge us of them by His Holy Spirit, until He has conformed us in everything to His holiness and has so withdrawn us from the corruptions of this world that we may be truly joined and united with His angels, because it has pleased Him to call us to the same salvation. May He give this grace not only to us but also to all peoples and nations on earth....

Predigten über Samuel: [23 May 1562–3 Feb. 1563] SC I

sermon 5 = 2 Sam 2:8–17, 4 June 1562, p. 44.

We bow ourselves before the majesty of our good God, in acknowledgment of the infinite offenses of which we are guilty, asking that He may make us feel them more and more: to lead us into true repentance, and to divest us entirely of our carnal affections, until we may be reclothed with His righteousness; that we may be patient in all our adversities, peaceable and modest toward each one; and at the same time that we may be magnanimous when it is a matter of fighting for Him, and especially that we may take up spiritual weapons to fight against Satan and all iniquity; that we may never doubt that He will undergird and strengthen us more and more when we seek that from Him with right affection, until He puts an end to all our struggles and calls us to His eternal rest. May He give this grace not only to us but also to all peoples and nations on earth....

sermon 6 = 2 Sam 2:18–32, 5 June 1562, p. 53.

We bow ourselves before the majesty of our good God, in acknowledgment of all our offenses, asking that He may make us so to feel them that we may be more and more grieved with ourselves. And that in our afflictions and in all our struggles He may give us an invincible constancy, so as to walk straight ahead according to His word, and to hold to Him completely, and not to make any agreement with the wicked when we have recognized their cruelty and stratagems. And yet may we have pity on them, without compromising what we have been taught by our Lord: indeed, in such way that we may always be kept back and dedicated wholly to glorifying Him, not to deviate or be turned aside from our vocation in any way. May He give this grace not only to us but also to all peoples and nations on earth....

sermon 13 = 2 Sam 5:6–12, 30 June 1562, p. 114.

We bow ourselves before the majesty of our good God, in acknowledgment of the many offenses of which we are guilty, asking that He may please to make us feel them more and more; that we may attribute to Him all the praise of our prosperity, doing homage to Him from all the good things that we have received from His hand; indeed dedicating ourselves completely to Him and glorifying Him, not only with our mouths but with all our works. May He give this grace not only to us but also to all peoples and nations on earth....

sermon 16 = 2 Sam 6:1–7, 3 July 1562, p. 141.

We bow ourselves before the majesty of our good God, in acknowledgment of our offenses, asking that He may make us so to feel them that we may be more and more drawn to Him and devote ourselves to His service. So that we may not follow the hypocrites, who have only the external figures and ceremonies, but that [we may act] with a heartfelt affection and may be so ardent in reciting His praises that this will be our principal concern. And that we may so well profit together, each one with the others, that with one accord we may affirm that truly all our good flows from Him and consists in Him; and this may incite us more and more to come to seek Him, there to find rest. May He give this grace not only to us but also to all peoples and nations on earth....

sermon 26 = 2 Sam 7:25–29, [Wed.] 29 July 1562, p. 234.

We bow ourselves before the majesty of our good God, in acknowledgment of the infinite offenses of which we are guilty, asking that He may more and more direct us; and at the same time that He may mercifully receive us, and grant us the grace that His name may be glorified in us; and by this means we may have a true mark that He accepts us and keeps us as His people. Thus we all say: Almighty God, heavenly Father,...

sermon 66 = 2 Sam 19:41–20:1, 24 Nov. 1562, p. 580.

We bow ourselves before the majesty of our good God, in acknowledgment of the many offenses of which we are guilty, asking that He may be pleased to make us so to feel them, that we may battle powerfully against all our vices; that we may so tread underfoot all that might hinder us from devoting ourselves to Him and to our profit, in pure simplicity, that we may not cease always to struggle. And that, instead of the way we see the children of this world killing each other, we may seek to maintain love and procure the good of our neighbors and relatives, knowing that God will also take care of our good. May He give this grace not only to us but also to all peoples and nations on earth....

Prayers Reflecting New Testament Sermon Texts

These prayers come from Sunday sermons: some are from regular *lectio continua* series, others from special feast days. Some are morning sermons concluding in the formal prayer published in *La forme des prières,* others are from Sunday afternoons, when Calvin appears to have used the weekday prayer. The order is, first, prayers from a collection of sermons preached on particular days of the liturgical year, a book published in the sixteenth century; and then, prayers from several *lectio continua* series, in the chronological order in which Calvin preached the sermons (which also happens to be the biblical order).

Plusieurs sermons touchant la divinité, humanité, et nativité de nostre Seigneur Iésus Christ (Genève: M. Blandier, 1563)

Sermon on the Nativity (Luke 2:1–14), p. 72.

We bow ourselves before the majesty of our good God in acknowledgment of our offenses, asking that He may make us feel them more; and by this means may we learn to submit ourselves to our Lord Jesus Christ, knowing that if we are separated from Him, our whole life and all the good things that we receive from God will be turned to our greater condemnation; and may we feel that the fruit of His death and passion is communicated to us, that He acknowledges us as members of His body, so that the afflictions we endure in this world may be so many aids to our salvation. Thus we all say: Almighty God, heavenly Father,...

Sermon 1 on the Passion (Matt 26:36–39), p. 96.

We bow ourselves before the majesty of our good God in acknowledgment of our offenses, asking that He may make us so to feel them: that we may not only grieve over them, but may also more and more be divested and purged of them; to fight against ourselves so that He alone may rule in us, and we may be in right accord with His holy will. And at the same time that He may also please to cast the eye of His mercy on His poor world; and as in general He has willed that His only Son should be Redeemer of all, and that the gospel should be published to all, may He not permit people today to be hardened and to turn away from such a gift; but that they may be attentive to it and we may draw each other to it, until He has led us to Himself in perfection. Thus we say all with one heart, humbly, Almighty God, heavenly Father,...

Sermon 7 on the Passion (Matt 27:45–54), p. 234.

We bow ourselves before the majesty of our good God in acknowledgment of our offenses, asking that He may make us feel them more than ever; and that we may be so moved by them as to grieve over them, that we may return again to our God with repentance, not only for one day but with continual sighs and tears. And at the same time, as we are held in this prison of servitude, may we not cease still to have our hearts lifted on high and to address our God in a familiar fashion, seeing that He is inclined to mercy and He even draws us of His own will, not waiting for us to seek Him. Seeing that our Lord Jesus not only drew near to us in order to tell us of such love, but He willed to be as if abased for a time, in order to raise us above, let us never fear to aspire there by faith, while we are all waiting to be gathered there. May He give this grace not only to us but also to all peoples and nations on earth....

Sermon 4 on Ascension (Acts 1:9–11), p. 527.

Following this holy teaching, we bow ourselves before the face of our good God in acknowledgment of our offenses, asking that He may not allow us to remain there forever asleep, but that He may gather and unite us to His Son. And because He has called us to the knowledge of Him, may He give us the grace to profit from that, until we have come to the perfection to which He calls us. Thus we all say: Almighty God, heavenly Father,...

Sermon 2 on Pentecost (Acts 2:13–17), p. 569.

And because it is so, that we do not know how to please God except by means of our Lord Jesus Christ, we bow ourselves before His face in the name of that One [Christ]; praying that He may be pleased to teach us in such a way, by His Holy Spirit, that we may know that it is by Him that the prophets spoke for our instruction, and we may know well how to make that profitable for us; that this may be done to the glory and exaltation of His holy name and the edification of our neighbors. Thus we all humbly say: Almighty God, heavenly Father,...

Sermon 3 on Pentecost (Acts 2:18–21), p. 585.

Following this holy teaching, we bow ourselves before the face of our good God in acknowledgment of our offenses, asking

235

that He may be pleased give us the grace to call upon Him in such confidence that our prayers may be pleasing to Him; and being delivered from all superstitions and idolatries, we may maintain His true service, so that we may have Him as Father and Savior, and He may acknowledge us at the last as His children. Thus we all say: Almighty God, heavenly Father,...

Sermons on Acts: [25 Aug. 1549–11 Jan. 1551 = chap. 1–7] SC VIII

sermon 2 = Acts 2:36–38, 22 Dec. 1549, p. 17.

Following this holy teaching, we bow ourselves before the face of our good God in acknowledgment of our offenses, asking that He may be pleased to give us the grace, that, being grieved by our vices, we may be able to seek all our pleasure and consolation in Him and His teaching; and by this means we may be able so to come to Jesus Christ that, after He has communicated His body and blood to us in this world, to nourish and maintain our souls while they are held in this mortal body, He may guide us to the heavenly kingdom. Thus we all say: Almighty God, heavenly Father,...

sermon 10 = Acts 4:5–12, 20 April 1550, p. 88.

Following this holy teaching, we bow ourselves before the face of our good God in acknowledgment of our offenses, praying that He may be pleased to move us to true repentance; and being so grieved by our vices, after we have asked His forgiveness for them may we walk in all purity of conscience. And being guided by His Holy Spirit, may we live in this world in such harmony and friendship each with the others, that even unbelievers who see our good way of living may be constrained to praise Him. And when that is done, His name will be magnified and exalted in everything and everywhere. Thus we all say: Almighty God, heavenly Father,...

sermon 27 = Acts 7:1–4a, 7 Sept. 1550, pp. 244–45.

Following this holy teaching, we bow ourselves before the face of our good God in acknowledgment of the countless offenses that we do not cease daily to commit against His holy majesty; praying that He may please so to touch us to the quick that, being grieved for having committed them, we may no longer be given to so many vices that have turned us away from Him in the past. And at the same time, that we may be so united by true love and brotherhood each with the others, that we may be equally well able to cling to Him, so that we may acknowledge Him as our Father and Savior and He may accept us as His children. And since we are not worthy to present ourselves before His face because of so many infirmities that envelop us, may He be pleased to receive us in the name and by the act of our Lord Jesus Christ. Thus we all say: Almighty God, heavenly Father,...

sermon 30 = Acts 7:9b–16a, 28 Sept. 1550, p. 271.

Following this holy teaching, we bow ourselves before the face of our good God in acknowledgment of the countless offenses by which we do not cease daily to rouse His wrath against us; asking that He may be pleased to open our eyes, so that, knowing the providence by which He governs this world here, we may be so much the more stirred up to entrust ourselves entirely to Him, resting on His goodness and grace. At the same time, may all our affections be oriented toward glorifying Him throughout our life, that we may never be turned away by the afflictions and tribulations that have come to us, so that we would not always persevere in serving and honoring Him, and giving Him the honor and homage that are due. Thus we all say: Almighty God, heavenly Father,...

Sermons sur 1 Corinthiens: [20 Oct. 1555–14 June 1556]
Ms. being prepared for SC by E. A. McKee

sermon 2 = 1 Cor 1:1–5, 20 Oct. 1555, f27a–f27b.

We bow ourselves before the face of our good God in acknowledgment of our offenses, asking that since we are such miserable sinners He may receive us mercifully; and after having reconciled us to Himself, that He may fill us with the gifts of His Holy Spirit, such that we may show that it is not in vain that we have been called to the knowledge of His gospel; and at the same time may He increase and confirm the faith of all His own people, so that they may ask nothing except to glorify and increase the kingdom of our Lord Jesus Christ, His Son; and that those who are now separated from us may be united [with us] in a true brotherhood; and that God may advance His word more and more, so that it may be a bond to reunite what is now separated throughout the world, and by this means we may all be able to call upon Him with one voice. And for this may He please to raise up true and faithful ministers of His word....

sermon 8 = 1 Cor 1:22–25, 10 Nov. 1555, f67b.

We bow ourselves before the majesty of our good God in acknowledgment of our offenses, asking that He may make us feel them more and more: until we have learned to subject ourselves to Him, until His majesty may so rule over us that we may not seek force or power or wisdom except in what He may be pleased to give us. And that we may hold all our goods (as coming) from Him, in such a way that we may use them for His service and the glory of our Lord Jesus Christ, to whom all authority has been given to rule over us, so that He may enjoy possession of both our bodies and our souls, and that everything may be presented to Him in true sacrifice. May He give this grace not only to us but also to all peoples and nations on earth....

Sermons sur Ephesiens [beginning 15 May 1558–]
(Genève, Iean Baptiste Pinereul, 1562.)

sermon 10, Eph 2:3–6, [probably sometime in June 1558], pp. 200–201.

We bow ourselves before the majesty of our good God in acknowledgment of our offenses, asking that He may make us so to feel them that we may not only confess three or four of them, but may look back to our birth to recognize that there is nothing but sin in us, and there is no means to be reconciled with our God except by the blood and death and passion of our Lord Jesus Christ. And so, each and every time that we feel the remorse which may turn us aside from the grace of God and summon us before His judgment seat, let us have no other refuge than this sacrifice by which our Lord Jesus Christ has brought about a reconciliation between God and us. And when we are weak, let us pray to Him to remedy that by His Holy Spirit, indeed by the means that He has ordained to make us participants in all His graces. And let us so persevere in doing that, that we may be an example to others; and let us endeavor to draw them with us into a like faith and unity of teaching. And by our life and good way of conducting ourselves, let us demonstrate that it is not in vain that we have been in such a good school as that of the Son of God. May He give this grace not only to us but also to all peoples and nations on earth....

Sermon 21, Eph 3:20—4:2, [perhaps early Aug. 1558], p. 419.

We bow ourselves before the majesty of our good God in acknowledgment of our offenses, asking that He may draw us to a true repentance, that we may be completely abased in ourselves in order to be raised up again in His service. And may this not be only for one day, but may we persevere until the end. And as His grace never fails, may we on our side never be weary in serving Him; but as He increases His gifts in us, let us be more and more ardent to approach Him and to be completely united to Him. Thus we all say: Almighty God, heavenly Father,...

SECTION IV:
PRAYERS FROM CALVIN'S LECTURES

Calvin lectured on the Bible regularly, three times a week, usually in alternate weeks. Normally, he followed a *lectio continua* fashion of working straight through each book, skipping nothing, though a few commentaries are presented as harmonies, again without omitting anything. Calvin took the Hebrew or Greek text to class, read a portion, and expounded it. The lectures were taken down by his hearers, including some of his colleagues, who often collated their versions and then checked these with Calvin. Later Calvin reworked all of the New Testament and a number of the Old Testament lectures in his study as commentaries, and these naturally lost the form of lectures.

Calvin began each lecture with the same one sentence prayer and closed each day with a fairly short prayer related to the theme of the biblical text he had been expounding. The prayers were recorded with the lectures, but they were omitted when the lectures were revised as commentaries. Thus Calvin's prayers on biblical lectures were preserved only for the expositions of Old Testament books that retained the lecture format in the sixteenth-century Latin editions, or in some seventeenth-century reprints. There are *Praelectiones* with prayers for all of the prophets except Isaiah, that is, for Jeremiah, Lamentations, Ezekiel (1–20), Daniel, and the Minor Prophets. These prayers were usually not included in later Latin printings; the editors of the nineteenth-century *Opera Quae Supersunt Omnia* dropped them. They were, however, retrieved by the editors of the Calvin Translation Society and included in their nineteenth-century English translations and the twentieth-century reprints. Here the Calvin Translation Society texts have been collated against the Latin found in the collected works published in the mid-seventeenth century in Amsterdam by Schipper. Because these prayers are available in the English commentaries, a very brief selection is given here. The first volume/folio reference is for Schipper, the second volume/page number is the translation.

Daily Opening Prayer

vol. 4, f*3v (unnumbered preface)

May the Lord grant that we may be engaged in the mysteries of His heavenly wisdom with a true increase of piety, for His glory and our edification. Amen.

Some Prayers Concluding Old Testament Lectures (Biblical Order)

Lecture 10, Jer 2:36–3:4, vol. 4, f33; vol. 1, p. 160.

Grant, Almighty God, that as You have once been pleased not only to adopt us as Your children, but also to unite us to Yourself by the bond of marriage, and to give us a pledge of this sacred union in Your only begotten Son: O grant that we may continue in the faith of Your gospel, and so sincerely cherish the pledge given to You that You may show Yourself to us as a husband and father; and that to the end we may experience in You that merciful kindness which may keep us in the holy fear of Your name, until we shall at length enjoy fellowship with You in Your celestial kingdom, through the same Christ our Lord. Amen.

Lecture 23, Ezek 8:15–9:4, vol. 4, f74; vol. 1, p. 305.

Grant, Almighty God, since You have deigned to approach us so familiarly, that in return we may also desire to approach You and remain in firm and holy union; so that while we persevere in that lawful worship which You prescribe for us in Your word, Your blessings may increase toward us, until You lead us to fullness, when You shall gather us into Your celestial kingdom, by Christ our Lord. Amen.

Lecture 4, Dan 1:17–2:2, vol. 5, f13–14; vol. 1, p. 121.

Grant, Almighty God, since every perfect gift comes from You, and since some excel others in intelligence and talents, yet as no one has anything of his own, but as You deign to distribute to each one a measure of Your gracious liberality: Grant that whatever intelligence You confer upon us, we may apply it to the glory of Your name. Grant also that we may acknowledge in

241

JOHN CALVIN

humility and modesty that what You have committed to our care is Your own; and may we study to be restrained by sobriety, to desire nothing superfluous, never to correct true and genuine knowledge, and to remain in that simplicity to which You call us. Finally, may we not rest in these earthly things, but learn rather to raise our minds to true wisdom, to acknowledge You to be the true God, and to devote ourselves to the obedience of Your righteousness; and may it be our sole object to devote and consecrate ourselves entirely to You, so that Your name may be glorified in our whole life, through Jesus Christ our Lord. Amen.

Lecture 11, Dan 2:44–46, vol. 5, f34–35; vol. 1, p. 192.

Grant, Almighty God, since You have shown us by so many, such clear and such solid testimonies, that we can hope for no other Redeemer than Him whom You have set forth: and as You have ratified His divine and eternal power by so many miracles, and sealed it by both the preaching of the gospel and the seal of Your Spirit in our hearts, and You confirm the same by daily experience: Grant that we may remain firm and stable in Him. May we never decline from Him; may our faith never waver, but withstand all the temptations of Satan; and may we so persevere in the course of Your holy calling, that we may be gathered at length into that eternal blessedness and perpetual rest which has been brought forth for us by the blood of the same, Your Son. Amen.

Lecture 29, Hos 10:14—11:5, vol. 5, f100; vol. 1, p. 396.

Grant, Almighty God, that as You deigned to choose us before the foundations of the world were laid, and included us in Your free adoption when we were the children of wrath and doomed to utter ruin, and afterward embraced us even from the womb, and at length favored us with a clearer proof of Your love in calling us by Your gospel into fellowship and communion with Your only begotten Son: O grant that we may not be unmindful of so many and so singular benefits but may respond to Your holy calling and labor to devote ourselves wholly to You. And labor, not for one day, but for the whole

242

time designed for us here, both to live and to die according to Your will, so that we may glorify You to the end, through our Lord Jesus Christ. Amen.

Lecture 4 (41), Joel 2:1–11, vol. 5, f143; vol. 2, p. 55.

Grant, Almighty God, that as You invite us daily so kindly and delightfully, and make known to us Your paternal goodwill, which You once showed to us in Christ Your Son, O grant that, being allured by Your sweetness, we may surrender ourselves wholly to You, and become so teachable and submissive that wherever You guide us by Your Spirit You may follow us with every blessing. Let us not in the meantime be deaf to Your warnings; and whenever we deviate from the right way, grant that we may immediately awake when You warn us and return to the right path; and deign also to embrace us and reconcile us to Yourself through Christ our Lord. Amen.

Lecture 7 (55), Amos 3:15—4:6, vol. 5, f191; vol. 2, p. 233.

Grant, Almighty God, that as You would have our life formed by the rule of Your law, and have revealed in it what pleases You, that we may not wander in uncertainty but render You obedience, O grant that we may wholly submit ourselves to You and not only devote our life and all our labors to You, but also offer to You as a sacrifice our understanding and whatever prudence and reason we may possess, so that by spiritually serving You we may really glorify Your name, through Christ our Lord. Amen.

Lecture 3 (83), Mic 1:15—2:6, vol. 5, f294; vol. 3, p. 196.

Grant, Almighty God, that as You are pleased to try our patience by requiring mutual justice and the offices of love and benevolence, O grant that we may not be wolves one to another but show ourselves really to be Your children by observing all those duties of justice and kindness that You command, and thus follow that justice through the whole course of our life, that we may at length enjoy that blessedness which is laid up for us in heaven, through Christ our Lord. Amen.

Lecture 8 (88), Mic 4:3–4, vol. 5, f311; vol. 3, p. 268.

Grant, Almighty God, that since at the coming of Christ Your Son, You really did perform what Your servants, the prophets, had previously so much foretold, and since You daily invite us to the unity of faith, that with united efforts we may truly serve You, O grant that we may not continue torn asunder, every one pursuing his own perverse inclinations at a time when Christ is gathering us to You; nor let us only profess with the mouth and in words that we are under Your government, but prove that we so feel in true piety. And may we then add to the true and lawful worship of Your name brotherly love toward one another, that with united efforts we may promote each other's good, and that our adoption may thus be proved and be more and more confirmed, that we may ever be able with full confidence to call on You as our Father, through Christ our Lord. Amen.

Lecture 8 (125), Zeph 3:6–9, vol. 5, f434; vol. 4, p. 286.

Grant, Almighty God, that since it is the principal part of our happiness that in our pilgrimage through this world there is open to us a familiar access to You by faith, O grant that we may be able to come with a pure heart into Your presence. And when our lips are polluted, O purify us by Your Spirit, so that we may not only pray to You with the mouth but also prove that we do this sincerely, without any dissimulation, and that we earnestly seek to spend our whole life in glorifying Your name; until being at length gathered into Your celestial kingdom, we may be truly and really united to You, and be made partakers of that glory, which has been brought forth for us by the blood of Your only begotten Son. Amen.

Lecture 14 (147), Zech 7:10–14, vol. 5, f503–4; vol. 5, p. 189.

Grant, Almighty God, that as You have adopted us as sons with this regulation, that we may cultivate brotherly kindness one toward another, and labor for our mutual benefit. O grant that we may prove [by the whole tenor] of our life that we have not been called by You in vain, but that we may so live in harmony with one another that integrity and innocency may prevail among us. And may we so strive to benefit one another that Your name may be thus glorified among us, until having at length finished our course, we reach the goal You have set before us, that having at last gone through all the evils of this life, we may come to that blessed rest which has been prepared for us in heaven by Christ our Lord. Amen.

Lecture 10 (178), Mal 3:4–8, vol. 5, f601; vol. 5, p. 586.

Grant, Almighty God, that since You have been pleased to choose us as priests to Yourself, not that we may offer beasts to You but consecrate to You ourselves with all that we have. Grant that we may with all readiness strive to depart from every kind of uncleanness to purify ourselves from all defilements, so that we may duly perform the sacred office of priesthood and thus conduct ourselves toward You with chasteness and purity. May we also abstain from every evil work, from all fraud and all cruelty toward our brethren, and so deal with one another that we may testify with our whole life that You are really our Father, ruling us by Your Spirit, and that true and holy brotherhood exists among us. May we live justly toward one another so as to render to each his own right, and thus show that we are members of Your only begotten Son, so that He may acknowledge us when He shall appear for the redemption of His people and shall gather us into His celestial kingdom. Amen.

PART FIVE:

PIETY IN THE CHRISTIAN LIFE, ETHICS, AND PASTORAL CARE

*P*rayer is the "chief exercise of piety" (*Institutes* 3.20 title) but it is not the only one. As most students of spirituality readily acknowledge, how Christians live their daily lives is a vital and necessary working out of their relationship with God. For Calvin, this earthly life of Christians, which is transformed because it is claimed by God and lived in God's presence, includes both individual and communal aspects. Indeed, the corporate effects of sanctification are particularly important because the Christian never lives alone or dies alone; even the personal counsel Calvin gives is shaped by the consciousness of being a member of the body of Christ, part of a community that lives before God.

JOHN CALVIN

The first section of Part Five explores Calvin's teaching on the corporate ethics that are the pattern for communal life, and then his most personal counsel about the heart of the Christian life. Here are presented a sermon and a number of excerpts from the *Institutes*. The second section offers a glimpse of Calvin's individual pastoral ministry to the sick and bereaved and troubled in heart, and those persecuted for their faith. Here the sources are primarily his letters, although some limited instructions come from the Genevan liturgy and church order.

SECTION I:
PIETY, ETHICS, AND THE CHRISTIAN LIFE

Calvin's piety can be characterized as intensely activist, a devotion to God lived out in the practical present daily world. The love and service of God, taught in the first table of the law and summarized in the first great commandment, are fundamental to all Calvinist life. One of Calvin's most frequent single-word captions for this joyous obligation to love God with all one's being is *pietas*, piety or godliness. However, Calvin was also intensely aware that there is a second table of the law, a second great commandment, which is subordinate to the first but which must never be separated from it. In fact, keeping the law of righteousness and justice, loving one's neighbors as oneself, may at times be the best evidence for the believer's real devotion to God. Liturgy may be hypocritical, but love for neighbors (summarized as *charitas*) cannot really be maintained apart from a real love for God. For Calvin, therefore, the larger pattern of Christian devotion to God can only be lived out fully when worship and justice, liturgy and love for the neighbor, go hand in hand.[41]

    This section examines various aspects of Calvin's instruction in lived piety, the Christian life and daily pilgrimage of the people of God. First is the second of his two sermons on the Sabbath commandment, which shows how the worship of God and justice for God's people are inextricably connected, how the Lord's Day and the weekdays together form a continuum of the "holy time" of faithful lives. Then, after an introduction on the usefulness of the law for believers (Book Two of the *Institutes*), a few brief excerpts from Calvin's treatment of several commandments from the second table of the law illustrate the supportive structure that the third use of the law offers for a spiritual life. This section concludes with excerpts from Calvin's sensitive guide to the Christian life, a portion of the *Institutes* added in 1539 (with minor editing later as part of Book Three). These chapters form a kind of little treatise of biblical counsel that is frank about the pain of life and yet offers a moving testimony to how the devout person can appreciate God's good gifts on earth, yet especially see through the veils of the present life and be sustained with joy in the hope of the resurrection. All of it is piety in daily practice.

JOHN CALVIN

The original texts of the sermon are found in OC 26:295–308, translated by Benjamin Farley, with the prayer translated by E. A. McKee from *Sermons sur les dix commandemens* (Genève: Conrad Badius, 1557), p. 91. The second and third parts of this section are found in OS 3 and 4; the translations are by F. L. Battles.

The Second Sermon on the Sabbath

Friday, June 21, 1555, Sermon Six, Deuteronomy 5:13–15.

> [You shall work six days, and you shall do all your labor; but the seventh day is the rest of the Eternal, Your God. You shall not do any work on that day; neither you, nor your son nor your daughter, nor your man servant nor your maid servant, nor your ox nor your ass nor any of your animals, nor the stranger who is within your gates; that your man servant and your maid servant may rest as you do. And you shall remember that you were a slave in the land of Egypt, and the Eternal, Your God brought you out with a strong hand and an outstretched arm; that is why the Eternal Your God has commanded you to keep the day of rest. Dt 5:13–15.]

Yesterday we discussed how and why the commandment to keep the Sabbath day was given to the Jews; (in brief) it was said that it stood as a symbol for spiritual rest, which the faithful had to observe in order to worship God. Now insofar as our Lord Jesus Christ has brought us the fulfillment of that, we are no longer obligated to be limited by this shadow of the law; rather let us be satisfied that our old man has been crucified in virtue of the passion and death of our Lord Jesus Christ in order that we might be renewed for the purpose of fully serving our God. But nevertheless we [still] have need of some order and guidance in our midst. Thus it is fitting that we should have a particular day for our assemblage in order that we might be confirmed in the doctrine of God and benefit from it every day, that is to say, for the rest of our life: that we might also be well-trained to call upon His name [and] to make a confession of our faith. And in the meantime the remainder of the day should be spent in considering the favors we receive all the time from God's hand in order that He might be glorified in them that much more.

But now we need to note what is said in Moses' text. *You shall work six days,* says the Lord (5:13). This must not be interpreted to mean that God commands us to work. Truly we are [already] born to that [end]. Moreover, we know that God does not intend for us to be lazy living in this world, for He has given people hands and feet; He has given them industry. And even before the fall, it is said that Adam was placed in a garden in order to tend it. But the work in which people are now engaged is a punishment for sin. For it is pointed out to them: "You will eat your bread by the sweat of your brow; it is a curse that has been placed on all human beings" (Gen 3:19). For we are unworthy of enjoying this condition that [supposedly] belonged to our father, that he could live a life of ease without harming himself. But still, before sin had come into the world and we were condemned by God to painful and forced work, people were already required to engage in some [type of] labor. And why? Because it is contrary to our nature to be like a block of useless wood. Therefore it is certain that we must apply ourselves to some [form of] labor all the days of our life. But the text does not simply command [us] to work six days. For in fact, under the law there were other solemn occasions whose purpose was not rest; there were feasts that could come in the middle of the week. But because their number was small, four days out of the year, they are not mentioned here; He simply speaks of rest.

And when He says, *You shall work six days,* our Lord shows us that we must not begrudge giving and dedicating one specific day to Him, seeing He has given us six for one. It is as if He were saying: "Is it asking too much of you to choose one day that can be fully reserved for my service in order that you might do nothing else in it but read and practice my law, or at least hear the doctrine that will be preached to you, or come to the temple in order that you might be confirmed there by the sacrifices which are offered in it, or call upon my name and confess that you belong to the company of my people? Is it not fitting that you should do that, seeing that you have six entire free days for taking care of your needs and business affairs? Therefore, when I act with such humanity toward you, asking not for seven but only one day, does it not amount to unacceptable ingratitude when you complain about that time as if it were badly employed, or behave parsimoniously toward me over the seventh part of time? I give you all your life; the sun never shines on you but that you ought to be able to recognize my goodness and that I am a generous father toward you. For I cause my sun to shine in order to give you light for your path, in order for each of you to pursue your needs. Therefore why should I not have one day out of seven [in which] each person withdraws from his affairs in order that you might not be enveloped by such worldly solicitude so as to be unable to think of me?" Thus we now see that this statement about working six days was not given as a commandment, but it is rather a permission God gives in order to reproach people for their ingratitude, unless, as He has indicated, they observe the Sabbath day and keep it holy.

Now from this we need to glean a good and useful admonition, that when we are slow to obey God, it is helpful to remember His gracious favors. For what could better stimulate our zeal for following what God commands than the thought that He does not treat us harshly or excessively crowd us? For God could use a stern check if He pleased. He could restrain us by things so difficult that it would be impossible for us to break free of them. But He prefers to guide us as a father does his children. Seeing then that He so upholds us, should not we be that much more motivated to do what He commands us? Therefore whenever the commandments of God are difficult for us, or seem to be so, let us realize that if He pressed us as much as He could, they would be exceedingly more [difficult]. For if our Lord wanted to exercise His authority to the fullest, we would be harassed far more. Therefore let us understand that He upholds us and utilizes an infinitely paternal goodness [toward us].

In truth the law of God is impossible for us [to fulfill], let alone keep with perfection, but when a person relying on his own strength wants to acquit himself before God, he cannot lift a finger or have one single good idea as to how it should be done. In fact, we are so far from being ready to obey God and to do what His law contains that all our thoughts and affections are at enmity with God. If people were able on their own strength to fulfill the law, He would have said to them: "Work!" But on the contrary He said: "Rest in order that God might work." Thus from our perspective the law may well be impossible to do, but it is possible for God to engrave it upon our hearts and to govern us by His Holy Spirit, indeed, so much so that it will seem like a gentle and light burden to us, involving no hardship that we cannot bear. Thus once people have carefully considered it, they will be convinced that God upholds them like a father who is merciful toward his children. Still, let us learn to be not ungrateful but to be exceedingly more motivated to worship our God, [especially] in view of the fact that He does not command us [to do] things that might seem too galling to us, or too painful, but He remembers our frame. That is what we need to note in this passage where our Lord reveals that He permits people [to enjoy] their comfort.

It is true, as was touched on yesterday, that we ought to be so spiritual as to gather every day to call upon the name of God and aim at a celestial life, forgetting all [our] earthly concerns. But what actually happens? God sees that we are surrounded by our flesh, that we creep upon the earth, that our weaknesses so dominate us that we are unable to lead an angelic life. Thus God, seeing such ignorance and debility in us, [and] having mercy because we cannot fully carry out what we ought to do, releases us and does not at all display His utmost rigor. He even says that He will be satisfied if we will dedicate one day to Him; especially will He be content if this day helps us throughout the rest of the week. And why? For (as I have said) He has not gone to the extremity, for He knew that we were too weak. Therefore seeing that He upholds us in this way and that He permits us to enjoy our comforts, so much the more are we cowardly, and shameless, and inexcusable, if we are not inspired to surrender ourselves to Him.

Now at the same time it is said, that *neither shall [your] manservant, nor chambermaid, nor cattle, nor ass, nor beasts work on the Sabbath day, nor the stranger who is within your gates* (5:14). As for the beasts, we might find it strange that God included them under the commandment to rest, seeing that it is a high and holy mystery as was discussed yesterday. But does it apply to cattle and

253

donkeys? God says: "I gave you the Sabbath day as a sign that I sanctify you, [and] that I am your God who reigns in your midst; that is something which is not common to all mortals." For God does not extend that grace and privilege to pagans and unbelievers; He does not sanctify them. He speaks only to the people whom He has chosen as a heritage and whom He has adopted. Therefore insofar as the Sabbath day is a sign that God has separated the faithful of His church from all the rest of the world, why is that extended to [cover] cattle and donkeys? Now let us note that this [action] was not taken for the sake of dumb animals, but in order that people might have a reminder before their eyes in order to be that much more moved. Therefore this sacrament was not addressed to beasts, which possess neither intelligence nor reason, but it is addressed to people who must keep it for their [own] benefit. We see that the sacrifices were made of dumb beasts; we know that they engaged in elaborate preparations; that they possessed vessels of gold and silver and similar things. And when all of that was sanctified, are we to suppose that God had put His Spirit into corruptible metals, into materials that had no feeling? No! But all of that existed for people, as all creatures are made for our usage and benefit. [For] God not only uses them [to aid us] in this present and transient life, but in these things He provides us with the marks of His grace in order that they might be that many more means and aids for drawing us up to heaven. Thus when God willed for cattle and donkeys to be rested on the seventh day, it was not because He had made them participants in that spiritual rest that I have discussed earlier, but it was in order that the Jews, seeing their stables closed, might understand.

And what were they to understand? [That] God sets in our midst before our eyes even dumb animals as a sign and visible sacrament. And their purpose is that, for our part, we might be that much more retained for God's service, knowing that we would be violating the entire law if we did not think of that which forms the principal point of all our life, which is, that we learn to denounce ourselves and no longer follow our [own] appetites, or reason, or wisdom. For our God should govern us. And we should become like dead creatures in order that He might live in us and we no longer pursue our own course, which is so utterly corrupt. Accordingly, that is how God meant for the Jews to regard dumb brutes: as a visible sign He had given them to the end that they might be that much more restrained and thereby admonished to keep the Sabbath day in complete reverence. We also see how God has always treated people according to their hardness and has provided them with remedies that were appropriate to them, seeing that they are not very inclined to come to Him, before whom they might be so attracted. And that is [true] not only of the Jews, but equally of us. Therefore let us perceive the goodness of our God when we see that He neither forgets nor neglects anything at all that can heal our vices. And at the same time let us also understand the perversity that dominates us in order that we [might] neither flatter nor ease up on the reins of our affections, seeing that we need to be constrained and that God gives us so many coaxing nudges, as to stubborn horses. Therefore seeing that God goads us in this way, let us understand that it is not without cause that He does, but it is due to the fact that we are perverse and still rebellious. Therefore let us be displeased with all our affections and learn to become enslaved by nothing that might impede our following the course that God commands us. And furthermore, lest our nature resist this, let us be so captivated [by what God commands] that we may press on without ceasing until we are fully subdued by our God. That is what we must emphasize in this passage beyond what will soon be said next with regard to slaves and servants.

Now concerning the latter, God reminds the Jews *that they had been slaves in the land of Egypt* (5:15) and that now they must humanely treat those who are under their powers. He says: *Your servant and your maidservant shall rest* (5:14). And for what reason? Because you were once in bondage. Certainly you would have liked for them to have given you some rest and relief; therefore it is imperative that now you show such a humanity toward those who are in your hand.

Now it certainly appears here that God may have ordered the Sabbath day as [a form of] civil order, [and] not as a spiritual one, as we earlier discussed, it being done for [the sake of] charity. For He says: "If you were in bondage, would you not want someone to give you some reprieve? Would you want to be harried all the time? Certainly not! Therefore it is crucial for you to be considerate of others." [Now that would mean that] this command is not given for the service of God but rather serves as a common charity that [we] ought to exercise toward our neighbors, no matter to what degree they might be inferior to us. But [on the contrary] insofar as this commandment is contained in the first table of the law, certainly this argument is only accessory.

I say the first table. For it is not without reason that God divided His law in this way, that is, that He wrote it on two stones. Had He willed, could He not have simply written it on one stone? Why then did He do it in two parts? It was not without reason. For there are two principal articles in the law of God: the one concerns what we owe Him; the other what we owe our neighbors with whom we live. Everything that concerns our life is grounded here. In the first place, knowing that we have a God to whom we belong, we ought to walk in His obedience. Then [knowing] that we owe our life to Him, we ought to do homage to Him; [and] insofar as He has created us to a better hope and adopted us as His children, we ought to glorify Him for such a goodness. Seeing [then] that He has purchased us through the blood of His Son that we might be totally His and has taken the trouble to retrieve us from the pollutions of the world in order that we might be His true sacrifices, let us call upon His name and put our refuge in Him alone. Let us praise Him for all His benefits. That is the first point of our life, that is the honor we must render to our God. And second, seeing that He wishes to test our obedience, there is also [the fact] that, when we live with others in complete integrity, we should not abandon ourselves to our own particular interests, but we should undertake to help each other. Indeed, there should be a mutual honesty [between us], not simply for the purpose of abstaining from fraud, violence, and cruelty, but in order that our life might be sober and modest, and that we might not become profligate, shameless, and brutal. That is the second point of our life.

Now insofar as this is the case, that the commandment concerning the Sabbath day is contained in the first table, it follows that it belongs to the spiritual service of God and that it is pointedly not a question about the charity that we owe our neighbors. Why then is it mentioned here? It is as much as if our Lord were saying: "This superabundant day of rest will serve you in order that your servants and maidservants may have respite with you." Not that this was the goal toward which God was tending, [for] it was not His principal aim for there to be one day a week in which people ceased to work in order to catch their breath and be spared total exhaustion. This was not the reason why God was motivated to ordain the Sabbath day. It was in order that the faithful might understand that it is truly necessary to live in a holy way, that they must rest from all their affections and desires, and that God must entirely work in them. Besides, as the saying goes, there is something here of an unexpected nature. "Listen" (our Lord says), "remember that when you have this testimony in your midst, I am at work sanctifying you, and [when] you are trying to surrender yourself to Me, consider that there is still one thing that will benefit you and that exists for your profit: that your family will not have to exhaust itself forever, for it is appropriate that your servants and maidservants and your beasts enjoy some respite. Therefore you shall have that as [a kind of] superabundance."

Now we see why it is purposely mentioned here that the Jews were slaves in Egypt and that it is incumbent upon them to have respect for those who were held as captives under their hand. For Moses, [when] speaking of servants and chambermaids, does not mean the same as is meant among us today. For, lo, servants were slaves whom one worked like cattle and donkeys; there existed such a harsh and inhumane condition that it was pitiful. Thus God shows that the Jewish people, [by] observing the Sabbath day, will even gain profit and comfort for their family. "So far from" (He says) "being grieved over the fact that I have reserved one day out of every seven for myself, if you are not too cruel, and if you do not exercise tyranny against those who are in your power, that day" (He says) "is still to your benefit. If you should have no other consideration than this order, that is, that on the Sabbath day your servants enjoy rest, the commandment would serve you well.

"But always be aware that I have not simply ordered the commandment for your family, but in order that you might be advised concerning what I have shown you, that, when you are separated from unbelievers, you might be a royal sacrifice to Me, asking for nothing but to serve Me with full integrity and pure conscience. When you hold that view, then you understand that this day can still provide you with some earthly gain; nevertheless, that is not what you ought to seek." In sum, our Lord shows us here what Jesus Christ also proclaimed: if we seek the kingdom of God, the rest will be added to us (Matt 6:33). For it appears to us that if we aspire to a heavenly life, we shall die of hunger, that such will deprive us of all our pleasures; in brief, when it comes to serving God, the devil always surfaces to solicit our disgust under the shadow and ruse that if we want to engage ourselves in God's service, we shall surely die of hunger, it will be a pity for us, [and] we shall have to take leave of the whole world.

Now it is true that we cannot serve God, if we are not emptied of our affections and if we do not cast aside those earthly cares that press on us from every side; but nevertheless it is still necessary for us to lean on this benediction we are promised, that is, that when we seek the kingdom of God, we shall be blessed in transient things, that our Lord will have mercy on us and will give us all that He knows we need for this present life; only let us look to Him for those things we cannot acquire by our [own] industry. Thus you see what we are shown in this passage.

Now this counsel must always serve us as a goad to induce us to follow what God commands us. For the primary thing that prevents us from regulating and submitting our life in obedience to God is the conviction that being slaves to ourselves is more to our advantage. Plus we always want to provide for our own comforts, no matter what, and [enjoy] whatever belongs to the world. That is why people cannot follow God, but rather wander farther from Him and pull in the opposite direction of His law, because it seems to them that in serving God they will not be able to do so to their advantage.

Now this is such a wretched, ungrateful response that it [only] aggravates their rebellion a hundred times more. What then must be done? Let us carefully note that we shall never be able to serve God with a free and easy heart, for we do not have that [kind of] resolve [that believes] that God will provide for our entire life and never forget us, as is said in the person of Joshua (Josh 1:5). For the apostle in the Letter to the Hebrews applies this doctrine to all the faithful, especially to spare them too much anxiety. He says: "Your God will never abandon you; He will never forget you" (Heb 13:5). Now if we could only be persuaded just once that God watches over us and that He will provide for all our necessities, certainly we would not be so mired in our earthly concerns, we would not be led astray from serving Him, we would not be prevented from meditating on the spiritual life, so much that we would pass through this world and make use of created things as if not using them at all, because we will know that it is always necessary to await more than this. Therefore, in brief, you see what we have to retain in this doctrine our Lord points out. [For] although what He has commanded with respect to keeping the Sabbath day is spiritual, nevertheless people will not fail to be conscious of their benefit, knowing that God will bless them when they rightly remember Him and do not look everywhere for what they know serves their earthly comfort.

Now nevertheless we are admonished that if there are some who rule over others, they must not scorn their neighbors, no matter how inferior they may be to them. And this [provision] extends even further. For we must not only take into account servants and chambermaids, but [also] the poor, and all who are not in authority or esteemed, all subjects who are not deemed worthy in the eyes of the world to be compared to us. For we know how proud people are, for although we may have no occasion to be swelled, we are each covetous for some preeminence. Seeing, then, that such arrogance indwells us, that we each want to be elevated over our neighbors—in spite of any basis for it—what happens when we are elevated? Look at those who are in the seat of justice. It almost appears to them that the world was created for them, except for the fact that God restrains them by His Holy Spirit and shows them that they must walk in all forbearance and must not oppress those who are under their charge. Rather, they must fulfill a fatherly function on their behalf, regarding their neighbors as their children, and still further, seeing that God honors them, they must walk in the greatest humility. [As for] those who proclaim the word of God and have charge of leading others, how unfortunate they are if they think that they ought to be exempt from the common ranks and [may] despise others. For it would be better if they broke their necks while mounting the pulpit than to be unwilling to be the first to walk after God and to live peaceably with their neighbors, demonstrating that they are the sheep of our Lord Jesus Christ's flock.

Now, nonetheless, it is true that the rich can certainly help the poor. When someone has servants and chambermaids working for him, he does not set his servant above himself at table, nor does he permit him to sleep in his bed. But in spite of any [right of] superiority that might exist, it is essential that we always arrive at this point: that we are united together in one flesh and we are all made in the image of God. If we believe that those who are descended of Adam's race are our flesh and our bone, ought that not make us subject to humanity, though we behave like savage beasts toward each other? When the prophet Isaiah wants to persuade people of their inhumanity, he says: "You shall not despise your flesh" (Isa 58:7). That is how I must behold myself, as in a mirror, that is, in as many human beings as there are in the world. That is one point.

But there is still more; that is, that the image of God is engraved in all people. Therefore not only do I despise my [own] flesh whenever I oppress anyone, but to my fullest capacity I violate the image of God. Therefore let us carefully note that God willed in this passage to point out to those who are in authority and who receive esteem, who are richer than others and who enjoy some degree of honor, that they must not abuse those who are under their hand; they must not torment them beyond measure. They must always reflect on the fact that we are all descended from Adam's race, that we possess a common nature, and even that the image of God is engraved on us. That is what we have to note. And especially now that our Lord Jesus Christ has descended to earth for the purpose of being entirely destroyed, in order to condemn all pride and to show that there is no other means of serving God except in humility. That being the case, He has made us all members of His body, including slaves and those who are masters and superiors, without any distinction.

When we come to our Lord Jesus Christ and behold Him, it is essential that we follow [His example]. Seeing that both the great and the small are members of His body and that He is our master, that is reason enough for each [of us] to be conformed to his neighbors. And in addition, seeing that God has declared Himself our father in more familiar terms than He did to those who lived under the law, may that inspire us to maintain fraternity among us. That again is what we have to glean from this text. Now there is still one point with regard to what God institutes [as] a reminder to the Jews: *that they were like poor slaves in the land of Egypt* (5:15). Now we know that they were badly treated there with cruelty. But insofar as they sighed and groaned to God, and were heard, and behold! wanted someone to help them, God declares that indeed they must also do the same [for others]. Now this contains a good lesson, which is that when we think of ourselves, we will always be caught up in the need to perform our duty. And on the contrary, when we are cruel toward our neighbors, it is as much as if we are intoxicated with our comforts and do not think about our poverty and miseries. Whoever has been hungry and thirsty, [and] especially wanted someone to relieve his need, and sees a poor man, and thinks: "Now I have been in that condition and certainly wanted to be helped; indeed it seemed to me that people ought to have pitied me in order to help me." Whoever (I say) entertains thoughts like that upon seeing a poor person in need, must he not have a soft heart? But what [is the usual case]? When we are comfortable, it is not a matter of our remembering our human poverty; rather, we imagine that we are exempt from that and that we are no longer part of the common class. And that is the reason why we forget and no longer have any compassion for our neighbors, or for all that they endure. Therefore, seeing that we are blindly in love with ourselves, and are content to be plunged in our [own] delights, and hardly think of those who are suffering and in want, so much the more do we need to hear this passage that our Lord may point out: "And who are you? Have you not been in need yourself?" And even if you should happen to get angry with them, does it ever occur to you that they are creatures made in the image of God? And if we insult them, why should God have mercy on us?

Therefore let us practice this doctrine all our life. And as often as we see people racked with misery, may this [thought] come to mind: "Lo, have I not been in need as well as they?" And if right now we were to be in such a state, would we not want to be helped? Therefore, insofar as this is true, is it right for us to be exempt from such a condition? The least we can do is to do unto others as we would have them do unto us (Matt 7:12). Our [own] nature teaches us that. We do not have to go to school to learn that. Thus we need no other trial to condemn us than what our Lord already teaches us by experience. When we are guided by that thought, certainly we will be touched by humanity to aid those who are indigent and in need. We will be moved to compassion, seeing them suffer, so much so that if we have the means and capacity to help and assist them, we will use it. Therefore you see what we have to note in this passage when it is said that you were strangers in the land of Egypt, therefore it is now proper for you to consider how to alleviate those who are in your hand, for when you were a slave, you certainly wanted someone to help you.

Now we come to those who were not [members] of the Jewish people but solely did business among them. Indeed, God also wills for them to keep the Sabbath day, even if God has not sanctified them and even though this sign could not belong to them, as we have already said. Thus it seems that God profanes the sacrament when He makes it apply to unbelievers and to those who were not circumcised as a sign of the covenant, to those who possessed neither the law nor the promises. But we have to observe that what God says here about strangers always applies to the people whom He chose and adopted. For we know that if we permit conditions [to exist] that are contrary to the service of God, even though some might say that "these people are not [members] of our group," we may [still] be misled by their bad examples. [For] if one had permitted foreigners to work among the Jewish people, what would it have led to? The Jews would have traded with them and would have been profaned; there would have been no discretion on that day. For when opportunity presents itself, we are easily led toward evil. And though it may not be a great occasion, our nature is so inclined toward evil that we are immediately led astray. Therefore what [good] does it serve if everything is corrupted? Thus if one had given foreigners the liberty to work in the midst of the Jewish people, they might have been induced to corruption; each would have exempted himself and given himself license to violate the Sabbath day and not keep it. Therefore, in the same way that God willed for animals to rest, He ordered the same for foreigners in order that such an evil occasion might be avoided and this day be kept with the greatest reverence.

Now this [commandment] must serve us today. For its purpose is to show us that vices must not be permitted in a people who make a Christian confession, so much so that they have to be punished even among those who are only passing through. Why is that? When blasphemies are condemned among ourselves, if we were to hear a passer-by blaspheme, or make fun of God, and such should be endured and kept secret, would it not be a kind of profanation that would infect everything else if such blasphemies were upheld, or considered in vogue, and nothing were done to repress them? Yet it exists. [For] the truth is that blasphemies are far from being punished as they should be in those who are not of our religion, as in those who mix with us and make the Christian confession; [indeed] we see how they are tolerated much to our own confusion.

But in any event, if we permit papists and others just anything (for today the world is crammed full of those who despise God), if we permit them (I say) to slander the doctrine of the gospel and to blaspheme the name of God, it creates a corruption that lives on in such a way that it becomes increasingly difficult to cure. If we allow the debauched and ruffians to influence us with their corrupt ways and bring into our midst more evil than we have, if we permit the profligate and corrupt to come here to practice their lewdness, will we not of necessity become debauched and totally corrupt with them?

Therefore let us carefully note that our Lord wills to train His people in complete purity to the extent that those who profess to be Christian may not only abstain from evil, but insofar as possible, may equally refuse to tolerate it at all. For we must understand that the earth is profaned when the worship of God is contaminated here and His holy name is dishonored. The ground on which He wants us to live is polluted and cursed and nothing will make Him come to us. In any event, when God gave this privilege to His children in order that they might remove idolatry from the country in which they [were to] live, it is certain that if they failed they would provoke His anger and vengeance against themselves. [In the same way] today if we were to ask for the abominations of the papacy to be combined here with the pure worship of God and out of privilege were to grant a Mass to the obstinate papists who would like to live here, thus providing them some corner in which they could perform their idolatries and superstitions, it would be like inviting God's anger against us and lighting the very fire of His vengeance. And why? Because since God has given those who hold the sword of justice in hand, who control the government in this life, the power to root out idolatries and these papal infections, then certainly if they were to maintain them, it would be like running God out in order to end His presence and reign in their midst.

Therefore let us carefully note that it is not without cause that our Lord willed for the foreigners who were living in the midst of the people—though they were of a different faith and religion—to be forced to keep the seventh day. He willed it not on their behalf or for their instruction—for they were incapable of that—but in order to curtail any scandal that might corrupt the people and violate the worship of God, that the land He had given his servant Abraham as a heritage might be totally dedicated to Him.

Now hereby we are not only admonished to be sanctified by the word of God, but not to tolerate in our midst any commission of scandals and corruptions. For all of that must be put away from us. Besides, when our Lord wills for us to have such a zeal for maintaining His service that even those who have not professed to belong to His church are constrained to affiliate with and conform themselves to us when they are living in our company, I beg of you, what excuse will we have if on our part we are not totally yielded to Him and are not like mirrors for drawing and winning poor unbelievers to our God? For if we hope to recover them when they have fallen and nevertheless they perceive in us similar and even worse vices, will they not be justified in mocking all our remonstrances? Therefore seeing that foreigners have been prohibited from doing anything that is contrary to the worship of God, let us understand that we have been doubly commanded to walk in all solicitude and in such humility and sobriety that foreigners may be convinced that it is in good conscience and without hypocrisy that we want God to be honored and that we cannot allow anyone to bring opprobrium to His majesty and glory.

Consequently that is what we have to emphasize in this text if today we want to keep what was commanded to the Jews, as by right in truth and substance it belongs to us. Thus in the same way that our Lord of old delivered His people from Egypt, so today He has delivered us from the pit of hell and reclaimed us from eternal death and the abyss of flames into which we have plunged in order to gather us into His heavenly kingdom, as it has been purchased for us through the blood of His beloved Son, our Lord Jesus Christ.

We bow ourselves before the majesty of our good God in acknowledgment of our offenses, asking that He may make us feel them more than we have done, so that we may make an effort to reform ourselves more and more to His righteousness, daily fighting against the lusts of our flesh; and that we may continue in this struggle until He may have entirely delivered us and reformed us to His image, in which we were fully created. May He grant this grace not only to us but also to all peoples and nations on earth....

JOHN CALVIN

The Pattern of the Law for Piety

BOOK 2: THE KNOWLEDGE OF GOD THE REDEEMER IN CHRIST, FIRST DISCLOSED TO THE FATHERS UNDER THE LAW AND THEN TO US IN THE GOSPEL

Chapter 7: The Law was Given, Not to Restrain the Folk of the Old Covenant Under Itself, but to Foster Hope of Salvation in Christ Until His Coming

12. The third and principal use, which pertains more closely to the proper purpose of the law, finds its place among believers in whose hearts the Spirit of God already lives and reigns. For even though they have the law written and engraved upon their hearts by the finger of God, that is, have been so moved and quickened through the directing of the Spirit that they long to obey God, they still profit by the law in two ways.

Here is the best instrument for them to learn more thoroughly each day the nature of the Lord's will to which they aspire, and to confirm them in the understanding of it. It is as if some servant, already prepared with all earnestness of heart to commend himself to his master, must search out and observe his master's ways more carefully in order to conform and accommodate himself to them. And not one of us may escape from this necessity. For no person has heretofore attained to such wisdom as to be unable, from the daily instruction of the law, to make fresh progress toward a purer knowledge of the divine will.

Again, because we need not only teaching but also exhortation, the servant of God will also avail himself of this benefit of the law: by frequent meditation upon it to be aroused to obedience, be strengthened in it, and be drawn back from the slippery path of transgression....

Chapter 8: Explanation of the Moral Law (The Ten Commandments)

Sixth Commandment "You shall not kill."

39. The purpose of this commandment is: the Lord has bound the human race together by a certain unity; hence each person ought to concern himself with the safety of all. To sum

up, then, all violence, injury, and any harmful thing at all that may injure our neighbor's body are forbidden to us. We are accordingly commanded, if we find anything of use to us in saving our neighbors' lives, faithfully to employ it; if there is anything that makes for their peace, to see to it; if anything harmful, to ward it off; if they are in any danger, to lend a helping hand. If you recall that God is so speaking as Lawgiver, ponder at the same time that by this rule He wills to guide your soul. For it would be ridiculous that He who looks upon the thoughts of the heart and dwells especially upon them, should instruct only the body in true righteousness. Therefore this law also forbids murder of the heart, and enjoins the inner intent to save a brother's life. The hand, indeed, gives birth to murder, but the mind when infected with anger and hatred conceives it. See whether you can be angry against your brother without burning with desire to hurt him. If you cannot be angry with him, then you cannot hate him, for hatred is nothing but sustained anger. Although you dissimulate, and try to escape by vain shifts—where there is either anger or hatred, there is the intent to do harm. If you keep trying to evade the issue, the Spirit has already declared that "he who hates a brother in his heart is a murderer" (1 John 3:15); the Lord Christ has declared that "whoever is angry with his brother is liable to judgment; whoever says 'Rata' is liable to the council: whoever says 'You fool!' is liable to the hell of fire" (Matt 5:22).

40. Scripture notes that this commandment rests upon a twofold basis: each person is both the image of God, and our flesh. Now, if we do not wish to violate the image of God, we ought to hold our neighbor sacred. And if we do not wish to renounce all humanity, we ought to cherish his as our own flesh. We shall elsewhere discuss how this exhortation is to be derived from the redemption and grace of Christ. The Lord has willed that we consider those two things which are naturally in each person, and might lead us to seek his preservation: to reverence His image imprinted in each person, and to embrace our own flesh in him. He who has merely refrained from shedding blood has not therefore avoided the crime of murder. If you perpetrate anything by deed, if you plot anything by attempt, if you wish or

267

plan anything contrary to the safety of a neighbor, you are considered guilty of murder. Again, unless you endeavor to look out for his safety according to your ability and opportunity, you are violating the law with a like heinousness. But if there is so much concern for the safety of his body, from this we may infer how much zeal and effort we owe the safety of the soul, which far excels the body in the Lord's sight.

Eighth Commandment "You shall not steal."

45. The purpose of this commandment is: since injustice is an abomination to God, we should render to each person what belongs to him. To sum up: we are forbidden to pant after the possessions of others, and consequently are commanded to strive faithfully to help every person to keep his own possessions. We must consider that what each one possesses has not come to him by mere chance but by the distribution of the supreme Lord of all things. For this reason, we cannot by evil devices deprive anyone of his possessions without fraudulently setting aside God's dispensation. Now there are many kinds of thefts. One consists in violence, when another's goods are stolen by force and unrestrained brigandage. A second kind consists in malicious deceit, when they are carried off through fraud. Another lies in a more concealed craftiness, when a person's goods are snatched from him by seemingly legal means. Still another lies in flatteries, when one is cheated of his goods under the pretense of a gift.

Let us not stop too long to recount the kinds of theft. Let us remember that all those arts whereby we acquire the possessions and money of our neighbors—when such devices depart from sincere affection, to a desire to cheat or in some manner to harm—are to be considered as thefts. Although such possessions may be acquired in a court action, yet God does not judge otherwise. For He sees the intricate deceptions with which a crafty person sets out to snare one of simpler mind, until he at last draws him into his nets. He sees the hard and inhuman laws with which the more powerful oppresses and crushes the weaker person. He sees the lures with which the wilier person baits, so to speak, his hooks to catch the unwary. All these things elude human judgment and are not recognized. And such injustice occurs not only in matters of money or in merchandise or land, but in the right of each one; for we defraud our neighbors of their property if we repudiate the duties by which we are obligated to them. If a shiftless steward or overseer devours his master's substance, and fails to attend to household business; if he either unjustly spends or wantonly wastes the properties entrusted to him; if the servant mocks his master; if he divulges his secrets; if in any way he betrays his life or goods; if the master, on the other hand, savagely harasses his household—all these are deemed theft in God's sight. For he who does not carry out what he owes to others according to the responsibility of his own calling both withholds and appropriates what is another's.

46. We will duly obey this commandment, then, if, content with our lot, we are zealous to make only honest and lawful gain; if we do not seek to become wealthy through injustice, nor attempt to deprive our neighbor of his goods to increase our own; if we do not strive to heap up riches cruelly wrung from the blood of others: if we do not madly scrape together from everywhere, by fair means or foul, whatever will feed our avarice or satisfy our prodigality. On the other hand, let this be our constant aim: faithfully to help all people by our counsel and aid to keep what is theirs, insofar as we can; but if we have to deal with faithless and deceitful people, let us be prepared to give up something of our own rather than to contend with them. And not this alone: but let us share the necessity of those whom we see pressed by the difficulty of affairs, assisting them in their need with our abundance. Finally, let each one see to what extent he is in duty bound to others, and let him pay his debt faithfully....

Ninth Commandment
"You shall not be a false witness against your neighbor."

47. The purpose of this commandment is: since God (who is truth) abhors a lie, we must practice truth without deceit toward one another. To sum up, then: let us not malign anyone with slanders or false charges, nor harm his substance by falsehood, in short, injure him by unbridled evil speaking and impudence.

To this prohibition the command is linked that we should faithfully help everyone as much as we can in affirming the truth, in order to protect the integrity of his name and possessions.... Hence this commandment is lawfully observed when our tongue, in declaring the truth, serves both the good repute and the advantage of our neighbors. The equity of this is quite evident. For if a good name is no less precious than all riches, we harm a person more by despoiling him of the integrity of his name than by taking away his possessions. In plundering his substance, however, we sometimes do as much by false testimony as by snatching with our hands.

48. And yet it is wonderful with what thoughtless unconcern we sin in this respect time and again. Those who do not markedly suffer from this disease are rare indeed. We delight in a certain poisoned sweetness experienced in ferreting out and in disclosing the evils of others. And let us not think it an adequate excuse if in many instances we are not lying. For He who does not allow a brother's name to be sullied by falsehood also wishes it to be kept unblemished as far as truth permits. Indeed, although He may guard it against lying only, He yet implies by this that it is entrusted to His care. That God is concerned about it should be enough to prompt us to keep safe our neighbor's good name. Hence, evil speaking is without a doubt universally condemned. Now, we understand by "evil speaking" not reproof made with intent to chastise; not accusation or judicial denunciation to remedy evil. Nor does evil speaking mean public correction, calculated to strike other sinners with terror; nor disclosure before those who need to be forewarned lest they be endangered through ignorance. By "evil speaking" we mean hateful accusation arising from evil intent and wanton desire to defame.

Indeed, this precept even extends to forbidding us to affect a fawning politeness barbed with bitter taunts under the guise of joking. Some do this who crave praise for their witticisms, to others' shame and grief, because they sometimes grievously wound their brothers with this sort of impudence. Now if we turn our eyes to the Lawgiver, who must in His own right rule our ears and heart no less than our tongue, we shall surely see that eagerness to hear detractions, and unbecoming readiness to make unfavorable judgments, are alike forbidden. For it is absurd to think that God hates the disease of evil speaking in the tongue, but does not disapprove of evil intent in the heart. Therefore, if there is any true fear and love of God in us, let us take care, as far as is possible and expedient and as love requires, not to yield our tongue or our ears to evil speaking and caustic wit, and not to give our minds without cause to sly suspicion. But as fair interpreters of the words and deeds of all, let us sincerely keep their honor safe in our judgment, our ears, and our tongue.

The Golden Book of the Christian Life

BOOK 3: THE WAY IN WHICH WE RECEIVE THE GRACE OF CHRIST: WHAT BENEFITS COME TO US FROM IT, AND WHAT EFFECTS FOLLOW
Chapter 6: The Life of the Christian: and First, by What Arguments Scripture Urges Us to It

2. Now this scriptural instruction of which we speak has two main aspects. The first is that the love of righteousness, to which we are otherwise not at all inclined by nature, may be instilled and established in our hearts; the second, that a rule be set forth for us that does not let us wander about in our zeal for righteousness....

3. And to wake us more effectively, scripture shows that God the Father, as He has reconciled us to Himself in His Christ, has in Him stamped for us the likeness to which He would have us conform (Rom 6:18)....

4....For [the doctrine of the gospel] is a doctrine not of the tongue but of life. It is not apprehended by the understanding and memory alone, as other disciplines are, but it is received only when it possesses the whole soul, and finds a seat and resting place in the inmost affection of the heart....We have given the first place to the doctrine in which our religion is contained, since our salvation begins with it. But it must enter our heart and pass into our daily living, and so transform us into itself that it may not be unfruitful for us....

5....I do not so strictly demand evangelical perfection that I would not acknowledge as a Christian one who has not yet attained it. For thus all would be excluded from the church, since no one is found who is not far removed from it, while many have advanced a little toward it whom it would nevertheless be unjust to cast away. What then? Let that target be set before our eyes at which we are earnestly to aim....Let each one of us, then, proceed according to the measure of his puny capacity and set out upon the journey we have begun. No one shall set out so inauspiciously as not daily to make some headway, though it be slight. Therefore, let us not cease so to act that we may unceasingly make some progress in the way of the Lord. And let us not despair at the slightness of our success; for even though attainment may not correspond to desire, when today outstrips yesterday the effort is not lost....

Chapter 7: The Sum of the Christian Life: The Denial of Ourselves

1. Even though the law of the Lord provides the finest and best-disposed method of ordering a person's life, it seemed good to the heavenly Teacher to shape His people by an even more explicit plan to that rule which He had set forth in the law. Here, then, is the beginning of this plan: the duty of believers is "to present their bodies to God as a living sacrifice, holy and acceptable to Him" (Rom 12:1), and in this consists the lawful worship of Him. From this is derived the basis of the exhortation that "they be not conformed to the fashion of this world, but be transformed by the renewal of their minds, so that they may prove what is the will of God." Now the great thing is this: we are consecrated and dedicated to God in order that we may thereafter think, speak, meditate, and do nothing except to His glory. For a sacred thing may not be applied to profane uses without marked injury to Him....

We are not our own: let not our reason nor our will, therefore, sway our plans and deeds. We are not our own: let us therefore not set it as our goal to seek what is expedient for us according to the flesh. We are not our own: insofar as we can, let us therefore forget ourselves and all that is ours.

Conversely, we are God's: let us therefore live for Him and die for Him. We are God's: let His wisdom and will therefore rule all our actions. We are God's: let all the parts of our life accordingly strive toward Him as our only lawful goal (Rom 14:8).

Oh, how much has that person profited who, having been taught that he is not his own, has taken away dominion and rule from his own reason that he may yield it to God! For, as consulting our self-interest is the pestilence that most effectively leads to our destruction, so the sole haven of salvation is to be wise in nothing and to will nothing through ourselves but to follow the leading of the Lord alone. Let this therefore be the first step, that a person depart from himself in order that he may apply the whole force of his ability in the service of the Lord. I call "service" not only what lies in obedience to God's word but what turns the mind of person, empty of its own carnal sense, wholly to the bidding of God's Spirit....But the Christian philosophy bids reason give way to, submit and subject itself to, the Holy Spirit, so that the person may no longer live to himself but have Christ living and reigning within him (Gal 2:20).

2. From this also follows this second point: that we seek not the things that are ours but those which are of the Lord's will and will serve to advance His glory. This is also evidence of great progress: that, almost forgetful of ourselves, surely subordinating our self-concern, we try faithfully to devote our zeal to God and His commandments. For when scripture bids us leave off self-concern, it not only erases from our minds the yearning to possess, the desire for power and human favor, but it also uproots ambition and all craving for human glory and other more secret plagues. Accordingly, the Christian must surely be so disposed and minded that he feels within himself it is with God he has to deal throughout his life. In this way, as he will refer all he has to God's decision and judgment, so will he refer his whole intention of mind scrupulously to Him. For he who has learned to look to God in all things that he must do, at the same time avoids all vain thoughts. This, then, is that denial of

self which Christ enjoins with such great earnestness upon His disciples at the outset of their service....

3....For, after He proffered the grace of God to hearten us, in order to pave the way for us to worship God truly He removed the two obstacles that chiefly hinder us: namely, ungodliness, to which by nature we are too much inclined; and second, worldly desires, which extend more widely....Thus, with reference to both tables of the law, He commands us to put off our own nature and to deny whatever our reason and will dictate. Now He limits all actions of life to three parts: soberness, righteousness, and piety. Of these, soberness doubtless denotes chastity and temperance as well as a pure and frugal use of temporal goods, and patience in poverty. Now righteousness embraces all the duties of equity in order that to each one may be rendered what is his own. There follows piety, which joins us in true holiness with God when we are separated from the iniquities of the world. When these things are joined together by an inseparable bond, they bring about complete perfection. But, nothing is more difficult than, having bidden farewell to the reason of the flesh and having bridled our desires—nay, having put them away—to devote ourselves to God and our brethren, and to meditate, amid earth's filth, upon the life of the angels....

4. Now in these words we perceive that denial of self has regard partly to people, partly, and chiefly, to God. For when scripture bids us act toward others so as to esteem them above ourselves (Rom 12:10, Phil 2:3), and in good faith to apply ourselves wholly to doing them good, it gives us commandments of which our mind is quite incapable unless our mind be previously emptied of its natural feeling....There is no other remedy than to tear out from our inward parts this most deadly pestilence of love of strife and love of self, even as it is plucked out by scriptural teaching. For thus we are instructed—to remember that those talents which God has bestowed upon us are not our own goods but the free gifts of God; and any persons who become proud of them show their ungratefulness....Let us, then, unremittingly examining our faults, call ourselves back to humility. Thus nothing will remain in us to puff us up; but there will be much occasion to be cast down. On

the other hand, we are bidden so to esteem and regard whatever gifts of God we see in others that we may honor those people in whom they reside. For it would be great depravity on our part to deprive them of that honor which the Lord has bestowed upon them. But we are taught to overlook their faults, certainly not flatteringly to cherish them; but not on account of such faults to revile people whom we ought to cherish with good will and honor. Thus it will come about that, whatever person we deal with, we shall treat him not only moderately and modestly but also cordially and as a friend. You will never attain true gentleness except by one path: a heart imbued with lowliness and with reverence for others.

5. Now, in seeking to benefit one's neighbor, how difficult it is to do one's duty! Unless you give up all thought of self and, so to speak, get out of yourself, you will accomplish nothing here. For how can you perform those works that Paul teaches to be the works of love, unless you renounce yourself, and give yourself wholly to others?...

But scripture, to lead us by the hand to this, warns that whatever benefits we obtain from the Lord have been entrusted to us on this condition: that they be applied to the common good of the church. And therefore the lawful use of all benefits consists in a liberal and kindly sharing of them with others. No surer rule and no more valid exhortation to keep it could be devised than when we are taught that all the gifts we possess have been bestowed by God and entrusted to us on condition that they be distributed for our neighbors' benefit....So, too, whatever a godly man can do, he ought to be able to do for his brothers, providing for himself in no way other than to have his mind intent upon the common upbuilding of the church. Let this, therefore, be our rule for generosity and beneficence: We are the stewards of everything God has conferred on us by which we are able to help our neighbor, and are required to render account of our stewardship. Moreover, the only right stewardship is that which is tested by the rule of love. Thus it will come about that we shall not only join zeal for another's benefit with care for our own advantage, but shall subordinate the latter to the former....

6....Scripture helps in the best way when it teaches that we are not to consider what people merit of themselves but to look upon the image of God in everyone, [the image] to which we owe all honor and love. However, it is among members of the household of faith that this same image is more carefully to be noted (Gal 6:10), insofar as it has been renewed and restored through the Spirit of Christ. Therefore, whatever person you meet who needs your aid, you have no reason to refuse to help him. Say, "he is a stranger": but the Lord has given him a mark that ought to be familiar to you, by virtue of the fact that He forbids you to despise your own flesh. Say, "he is contemptible and worthless"; but the Lord shows him to be one to whom He has deigned to give the beauty of His image. Say that you owe nothing for any service of his; but God, as it were, has put him in His own place in order that you may recognize toward him the many and great benefits with which God has bound you to Himself. Say that he does not deserve even your least effort for his sake; but the image of God, which recommends him to you, is worthy of your giving yourself and all your possessions. Now if he has not only deserved no good at your hand, but has also provoked you by unjust acts and curses, not even this is just reason why you should cease to embrace him in love and to perform the duties of love on his behalf (Matt 6:14, 18:35, Luke 17:3). You will say, "he has deserved something far different of me." Yet what has the Lord deserved? While He bids you forgive this person for all sins he has committed against you, He would truly have them charged against Himself....[W]e remember not to consider people's evil intention but to look upon the image of God in them, which cancels and effaces their transgressions, and with its beauty and dignity allures us to love and embrace them.

7....Now he who merely performs all the duties of love does not fulfill them, even though he overlooks none; but he, rather, fulfills them who does this from a sincere feeling of love....[O]f Christians something even more is required than to show a cheerful countenance and to render their duties pleasing with friendly words. First, they must put themselves in the place of him whom they see in need of their assistance, and pity his ill fortune as if they themselves experienced and bore it, so that they may be impelled by a feeling of mercy and humaneness to go to his aid just as to their own. The one who, thus disposed, proceeds to give help to his brethren will not corrupt his own duties by either arrogance or upbraiding. Furthermore, in giving benefits he will not despise his needy brother or enslave him as one indebted to himself. This would no more be reasonable than that we should either chide a sick member that the rest of the body labors to revive, or consider it especially obligated to the remaining members because it has drawn more help to itself than it can repay. Now the sharing of tasks among members is believed to have nothing gratuitous about it but, rather, to be a payment of that which, due by the law of nature, it would be monstrous to refuse....Rather, each person will so consider with himself that in all his greatness he is a debtor to his neighbors, and that he ought in exercising kindness toward them to set no other limit than the end of his resources; these, as widely as they are extended, ought to have their limits set according to the rule of love.

8. Let us reiterate in fuller form the chief part of self-denial, which, as we have said, looks to God....To begin with, then, in seeking either the convenience or the tranquility of the present life, scripture calls us to resign ourselves and all our possessions to the Lord's will, and to yield to Him the desires of our hearts to be tamed and subjugated....First of all, let them neither desire nor hope for, nor contemplate, any other way of prospering than by the Lord's blessing. Upon this, then, let them safely and confidently throw themselves and rest....

9....To sum up, he who rests solely upon the blessing of God, as it has been here expressed, will neither strive with evil arts after those things which people customarily madly seek after, which he realizes will not profit him, nor will he, if things go well, give credit to himself or even to his diligence, or industry, or fortune. Rather, he will give God the credit as its Author. But if, while other people's affairs flourish, he makes but slight advancement, or even slips back, he will still bear his low estate with greater equanimity and moderation of mind than some profane person would bear a moderate success which merely does not correspond with his wish. For he indeed possesses a solace in which he may repose more peacefully than in the highest degree of wealth or power. Since this leads to his salvation, he considers that his affairs are ordained by the Lord....

10. And for devout minds the peace and forbearance we have spoken of ought not to rest solely in this point; but it must also be extended to every occurrence to which the present life is subject. Therefore, he alone has duly denied himself who has so totally resigned himself to the Lord that he permits every part of his life to be governed by God's will. He who will be thus composed in mind, whatever happens, will not consider himself miserable nor complain of his lot with ill will toward God. How necessary this disposition is will appear if you weigh the many chance happenings to which we are subject. Various diseases repeatedly trouble us: now plague rages; now we are cruelly beset by the calamities of war; now ice and hail, consuming the year's expectation, lead to barrenness, which reduces us to poverty; wife, parents, children, neighbors, are snatched away by death; our house is burned by fire. It is on account of these occurrences that people curse their life, loathe the day of their birth, abominate heaven and the light of day, rail against God, and as they are eloquent in blasphemy, accuse Him of injustice and cruelty. But in these matters the believer must also look to God's kindness and truly fatherly indulgence....[T]he rule of piety is that God's hand alone is the judge and governor of fortune, good or bad, and that it does not rush about with heedless force, but with most orderly justice deals out good as well as ill to us.

Chapter 8: Bearing the Cross, a Part of Self-Denial

1. But it behooves the devout mind to climb still higher, to the height to which Christ calls His disciples: that each must bear his own cross. For those whom the Lord has adopted and deemed worthy of His fellowship ought to prepare for a hard, toilsome, and unquiet life, crammed with very many and various kinds of evil. It is the heavenly Father's will thus to exercise them

so as to put His own children to a definite test. Beginning with Christ, His firstborn, He follows this plan with all His children. For even though that Son was beloved above the rest, and in Him the Father's mind was well pleased, yet we see that far from being treated indulgently or softly, to speak the truth, while He dwelt on earth He was not only tried by a perpetual cross but His whole life was nothing but a sort of perpetual cross....Why should we exempt ourselves, therefore, from the condition to which Christ our head had to submit, especially since He submitted to it for our sake to show us an example of patience in Himself? Therefore, the apostle teaches that God has destined all His children to the end that they be conformed to Christ (Rom 8:29). Hence also in harsh and difficult conditions, regarded as adverse and evil, a great comfort comes to us: we share Christ's sufferings in order that as He has passed from a labyrinth of all evils into heavenly glory, we may in like manner be led through various tribulations to the same glory....

2. Besides this, our Lord had no need to undertake the bearing of the cross except to attest and prove His obedience to the Father. But as for us, there are many reasons why we must pass our lives under a continual cross....He can best restrain this arrogance when He proves to us by experience not only the great incapacity but also the frailty under which we labor. Therefore, He afflicts us either with disgrace or poverty or bereavement or death or other calamities. Utterly unequal to bearing these, insofar as they touch us, we soon succumb to them. Thus humbled, we learn to call upon His power, which alone makes us stand fast under the weight of afflictions....Believers, warned, I say, by such proofs of their diseases, advance toward humility and so, sloughing off perverse confidence in the flesh, betake themselves to God's grace. Now when they have betaken themselves there they experience the presence of a divine power in which they have protection enough and to spare.

3....(Rom 5:3) That God has promised to be with believers in tribulation they experience to be true, while, supported by His hand, they patiently endure—an endurance quite unattainable by their own effort. The saints, therefore, through forbearance experience the fact that God, when there is need, provides the assistance that He has promised. Thence, also, is their hope strengthened, inasmuch as it would be the height of ingratitude not to expect that in time to come God's truthfulness will be as constant and firm as they have already experienced it to be....

4. The Lord also has another purpose for afflicting His people: to test their patience and to instruct them to obedience. Not that they can manifest any other obedience to Him save what He has given them. But it so pleases Him by unmistakable proofs to make manifest and clear the graces which He has conferred upon the saints, that these may not lie idle, hidden within. Therefore, by bringing into the open the power and constancy to forbear, with which He has endowed His servants, He is said to test their patience....But if God Himself does right in providing occasion to stir up those virtues which He has conferred upon His believers in order that they may not be hidden in obscurity—nay, lie useless and pass away—the afflictions of the saints, without which they would have no forbearance, are amply justified. They are also, I assert, instructed by the cross to obey, because thus they are taught to live not according to their own whim but according to God's will....

5. Still we do not see how necessary this obedience is to us unless we consider at the same time how great is the wanton impulse of our flesh to shake off God's yoke if we even for a moment treat that impulse softly and indulgently....For not all of us suffer in equal degree from the same diseases or, on that account, need the same harsh cure. From this it is to be seen that some are tried by one kind of cross, others by another. But since the heavenly physician treats some more gently but cleanses others by harsher remedies, while He wills to provide for the health of all, He yet leaves no one free and untouched, because He knows that all, to a person, are diseased.

6. Besides this, it is needful that our most merciful Father should not only anticipate our weakness but also often correct past transgressions so that He may keep us in lawful obedience to Himself....Therefore, also, in the very harshness of tribulations we must recognize the kindness and generosity of our Father toward

us, since He does not even then cease to promote our salvation. For He afflicts us not to ruin or destroy us but, rather, to free us from the condemnation of the world....Scripture teaches that this is the difference between unbelievers and believers: the former, like slaves of inveterate and double-dyed wickedness, with chastisement become only worse and more obstinate. But the latter, like freeborn sons, attain repentance. Now you must choose in which group you would prefer to be numbered....

7. Now, to suffer persecution for righteousness' sake is a singular comfort. For it ought to occur to us how much honor God bestows upon us in thus furnishing us with the special badge of His soldiery. I say that not only they who labor for the defense of the gospel but they who in any way maintain the cause of righteousness suffer persecution for righteousness. Therefore, whether in declaring God's truth against Satan's falsehoods or in taking up the protection of the good and the innocent against the wrongs of the wicked, we must undergo the offenses and hatred of the world, which may imperil either our life, our fortunes, or our honor. Let us not grieve or be troubled in thus far devoting our efforts to God, or count ourselves miserable in those matters in which He has with His own lips declared us blessed (Matt 5:10). Even poverty, if it be judged in itself, is misery; likewise exile, contempt, prison, disgrace; finally, death itself is the ultimate of all calamities. But when the favor of our God breathes upon us, every one of these things turns into happiness for us. We ought accordingly to be content with the testimony of Christ rather than with the false estimation of the flesh. So it will come about that we shall rejoice after the apostles' example, "whenever He will count us worthy to suffer dishonor for His name" (Acts 5:41). What then? If, being innocent and of good conscience, we are stripped of our possessions by the wickedness of impious folk, we are indeed reduced to penury among people. But in God's presence in heaven our true riches are thus increased. If we are cast out of our own house, then we will be the more intimately received into God's family. If we are vexed and despised, we but take all the firmer root in Christ. If we are branded with disgrace and ignominy, we but have a fuller

place in the kingdom of God. If we are slain, entrance into the blessed life will thus be open to us. Let us be ashamed to esteem less than the shadowy and fleeting allurements of the present life, those things on which the Lord has set so great a value.

8....[W]e are too ungrateful if we do not willingly and cheerfully undergo these things at the Lord's hand; especially since this sort of cross most properly belongs to believers....Yet such a cheerfulness is not required of us as to remove all feeling of bitterness and pain. Otherwise, in the cross there would be no forbearance of the saints, unless they were tormented by pain and anguished by trouble. If there were no harshness in poverty, no torment in diseases, no sting in disgrace, no dread in death—what fortitude or moderation would there be in bearing them with indifference? But since each of these, with an inborn bitterness, by its very nature bites the hearts of us all, the fortitude of the believing person is brought to light if—tried by the feeling of such bitterness—however grievously he is troubled with it, yet valiantly resisting, he surmounts it....

9....You see that patiently to bear the cross is not to be utterly stupefied and to be deprived of all feeling of pain....Yet we have nothing to do with this iron philosophy which our Lord and Master has condemned not only by His word, but also by His example. For He groaned and wept both over His own and others' misfortunes. And He taught His disciples in the same way: "The world," He says, "will rejoice; but you will be sorrowful and will weep" (John 16:20) And that no one might turn it into a vice, He openly proclaimed, "Blessed are those who mourn" (Matt 5:4). No wonder! For if all weeping is condemned, what shall we judge concerning the Lord Himself, from whose body tears of blood trickled down? (Luke 22:44). If all fear is branded as unbelief, how shall we account for that dread with which, we read, He was heavily stricken? If all sadness displeases us, how will it please us that He confessed His soul "sorrowful even to death" (Matt 26:37)?

10. I decided to say this in order to recall godly minds from despair, lest, because they cannot cast off the natural feeling of sorrow, they forthwith renounce the pursuit of patience. This must

necessarily happen to those who make patience into insensibility, and a valiant and constant person into a stock. For scripture praises the saints for their forbearance when, so afflicted with harsh misfortune, they do not break or fall; so stabbed with bitterness, they are at the same time flooded with spiritual joy; so pressed by apprehension, they recover their breath, revived by God's consolation. In the meantime, their hearts still harbor a contradiction between their natural sense, which flees and dreads what it feels adverse to itself, and their disposition to piety, which even through these difficulties presses toward obedience to the divine will....But the conclusion will always be: the Lord so willed, therefore let us follow His will. Indeed, amid the very pricks of pain, amid groaning and tears, this thought must intervene: to incline our heart to bear cheerfully those things which have so moved it.

11. Now, since we have taken the prime reason for bearing the cross from the contemplation of the divine will, we must define in a few words the difference between philosophic and Christian patience....For if we obey God only because it is necessary, if we should be allowed to escape, we will cease to obey Him. But scripture bids us contemplate in the will of God something far different: namely, first righteousness and equity, then concern for our own salvation....Therefore, in patiently suffering these tribulations, we do not yield to necessity but we consent for our own good. These thoughts, I say, bring it to pass that, however much in bearing the cross our minds are constrained by the natural feeling of bitterness, they are as much diffused with spiritual joy. From this, thanksgiving also follows, which cannot exist without joy; but if the praise of the Lord and thanksgiving can come forth only from a cheerful and happy heart—and there is nothing that ought to interrupt this in us—it thus is clear how necessary it is that the bitterness of the cross be tempered with spiritual joy.

Chapter 9: Meditation on the Future Life

1. Whatever kind of tribulation presses upon us, we must ever look to this end: to accustom ourselves to contempt for the

present life and to be aroused thereby to meditate upon the future life....Then only do we rightly advance by the discipline of the cross, when we learn that this life, judged in itself, is troubled, turbulent, unhappy in countless ways, and in no respect clearly happy; that all those things which are judged to be its goods are uncertain, fleeting, vain, and vitiated by many intermingled evils. From this, at the same time, we conclude that in this life we are to seek and hope for nothing but struggle; when we think of our crown, we are to raise our eyes to heaven. For this we must believe: that the mind is never seriously aroused to desire and ponder the life to come unless it be previously imbued with contempt for the present life.

3. But let believers accustom themselves to a contempt of the present life that engenders no hatred of it or ingratitude against God. Indeed, this life, however crammed with infinite miseries it may be, is still rightly to be counted among those blessings of God which are not to be spurned. Therefore, if we recognize in it no divine benefit, we are already guilty of grave ingratitude toward God Himself. For believers especially, this ought to be a testimony of divine benevolence, wholly destined, as it is, to promote their salvation. For before He shows us openly the inheritance of eternal glory, God wills by lesser proofs to show Himself to be our Father. These are the benefits that are daily conferred on us by Him. Since, therefore, this life serves us in understanding God's goodness, should we despise it as if it had no grain of good in itself? We must, then, become so disposed and minded that we count it among those gifts of divine generosity which are not at all to be rejected....

And this is a much greater reason if in it we reflect that we are in preparation, so to speak, for the glory of the heavenly kingdom. For the Lord has ordained that those who are one day to be crowned in heaven should first undergo struggles on earth in order that they may not triumph until they have overcome the difficulties of war, and attained victory. Then there is another reason: we begin in the present life, through various benefits, to taste the sweetness of the divine generosity in order to whet our hope and desire to seek after the full revelation of this. When we are certain that the earthly life we live is a gift of God's kindness, as we are beholden to Him for it we ought to remember it and be thankful. Then we shall come in good time to consider its most unhappy condition in order that we may, indeed, be freed from too much desire of it, to which, as has been said, we are of ourselves inclined by nature.

4....For, if heaven is our homeland, what else is the earth but our place of exile? If departure from the world is entry into life, what else is the world but a sepulcher? And what else is it for us to remain in life but to be immersed in death? If to be freed from the body is to be released into perfect freedom, what else is the body but a prison? If to enjoy the presence of God is the summit of happiness, is not to be without this, misery? But until we leave the world "we are away from the Lord" (2 Cor 5:6). Therefore, if the earthly life be compared with the heavenly, it is doubtless to be at once despised and trampled underfoot. Of course it is never to be hated except insofar as it holds us subject to sin; although not even hatred of that condition may ever properly be turned against life itself. In any case, it is still fitting for us to be so affected either by weariness or hatred of it that, desiring its end, we may also be prepared to abide in it at the Lord's pleasure, so that our weariness may be far from all murmuring and impatience. For it is like a sentry post at which the Lord has posted us, which we must hold until He recalls us....But in comparison with the immortality to come, let us despise this life and long to renounce it, on account of the bondage of sin, whenever it shall please the Lord.

5. But monstrous it is that many who boast themselves Christians are gripped by such a great fear of death, rather than a desire for it, that they tremble at the least mention of it, as of something utterly dire and disastrous. Surely, it is no wonder if the natural awareness in us bristles with dread at the mention of our dissolution. But it is wholly unbearable that there is not in Christian hearts any light of piety to overcome and suppress that fear, whatever it is, by a greater consolation....If we should think that through death we are recalled from exile to dwell in the fatherland, in the heavenly fatherland, would we get no comfort

from this fact?...Let us, however, consider this settled: that no
one has made progress in the school of Christ who does not joy-
fully await the day of death and final resurrection....Let us, then,
take hold of a sounder view, and even though the blind and stupid desire of the flesh resists, let us not hesitate to await the
Lord's coming, not only with longing, but also with groaning
and sighs, as the happiest thing of all. He will come to us as
Redeemer, and rescuing us from this boundless abyss of all evils
and miseries, He will lead us into that blessed inheritance of His
life and glory.

6. This is obvious: the entire company of believers, so long
as they dwell on earth, must be "as sheep destined for the slaugh-
ter" to be conformed to Christ their head (Rom 8:36). They
would therefore have been desperately unhappy unless, with
mind intent upon heaven, they had surmounted whatever is
in this world, and passed beyond the present aspect of affairs
(1 Cor 15:19)....For before their eyes will be that day when the
Lord will receive His faithful people into the peace of His kingdom, "will wipe away every tear from their eyes," will clothe them
with "a robe of glory...and rejoicing" (Isa 25:8, Rev 7:17), will
feed them with the unspeakable sweetness of His delights, will
elevate them to His sublime fellowship—in fine, will deign to
make them sharers in His happiness....To conclude in a word: if
believers' eyes are turned to the power of the resurrection, in
their hearts the cross of Christ will at last triumph over the devil,
flesh, sin, and the wicked.

Chapter 10: How We Must Use the Present Life and Its Helps

1. By such elementary instruction, scripture at the same time
duly informs us what is the right use of earthly benefits—a matter
not to be neglected in the ordering of our life. For if we are to live,
we have also to use those helps necessary for living. And we also
cannot avoid those things which seem to serve delight more than
necessity. Therefore we must hold to a measure so as to use them
with a clear conscience, whether for necessity or for delight. By

His word the Lord lays down this measure when He teaches that the present life is for His people as a pilgrimage on which they are hastening toward the heavenly kingdom. If we must simply pass through this world, there is no doubt we ought to use its good things insofar as they help rather than hinder our course....

2. Let this be our principle: that the use of God's gifts is not wrongly directed when it is referred to that end to which the Author Himself created and destined them for us, since He created them for our good, not for our ruin. Accordingly, no one will hold to a straighter path than he who diligently looks to this end. Now if we ponder to what end God created food, we shall find that He meant not only to provide for necessity, but also for delight and good cheer. Thus the purpose of clothing, apart from necessity was comeliness and decency. In grasses, trees, and fruits, apart from their various uses, there is beauty of appearance and pleasantness of odor. For if this were not true, the prophet would not have reckoned them among the benefits of God, "that wine gladdens a person's heart, that oil makes his face shine" (Ps 104:15). Scripture would not have reminded us repeatedly, in commending His kindness, that He gave all such things to people. And the natural qualities themselves of things demonstrate sufficiently to what end and extent we may enjoy them. Has the Lord clothed the flowers with the great beauty that greets our eyes, the sweetness of smell that is wafted upon our nostrils, and yet will it be unlawful for our eyes to be affected by that beauty, or our sense of smell by the sweetness of that odor? What? Did He not so distinguish colors as to make some more lovely than others? What? Did He not endow gold and silver, ivory and marble, with a loveliness that renders them more precious than other metals or stones? Did He not, in short, render many things attractive to us, apart from their necessary use?

3. Away, then, with that inhuman philosophy which, while conceding only a necessary use of creatures, not only malignantly deprives us of the lawful fruit of God's beneficence but cannot be practiced unless it robs a person of all his senses and degrades him to a block. But no less diligently, on the other hand, we must resist the lust of the flesh, which, unless it is kept

in order, overflows without measure....First, one bridle is put upon it if it be determined that all things were created for us that we might recognize the Author and give thanks for His kindness toward us. Where is your thanksgiving if you so gorge yourself with banqueting or wine that you either become stupid or are rendered useless for the duties of piety and of your calling? Where is your recognition of God if your flesh boiling over with excessive abundance into vile lust infects the mind with its impurity so that you cannot discern anything that is right and honorable? Where is our gratefulness toward God for our clothing if in the sumptuousness of our apparel we both admire ourselves and despise others, if with its elegance and glitter we prepare ourselves for shameless conduct? Where is our recognition of God if our minds be fixed upon the splendor of our apparel? For many so enslave all their senses to delights that the mind lies overwhelmed....Therefore, clearly, leave to abuse God's gift must be somewhat curbed, and Paul's rule is confirmed: that we should "make no provision for the flesh, to gratify its desires" (Rom 13:14), for if we yield too much to these, they boil up without measure or control.

4....Therefore, even though the freedom of believers in external matters is not to be restricted to a fixed formula, yet it is surely subject to this law: to indulge oneself as little as possible; but, on the contrary, with unflagging effort of mind to insist upon cutting off all show of superfluous wealth, not to mention licentiousness, and diligently to guard against turning helps into hindrances.

5. The second rule will be: they who have narrow and slender resources should know how to go without things patiently, lest they be troubled by an immoderate desire for them. If they keep this rule of moderation, they will make considerable progress in the Lord's school....To this end, then, let all those for whom the pursuit of piety is not a pretense strive to learn, by the apostle's example, how to be filled and to hunger, to abound and to suffer want (Phil 4:12).

Besides, scripture has a third rule with which to regulate the use of earthly things. Of it we said something when we discussed the precepts of love. It decrees that all those things were so given to us by the kindness of God, and so destined for our benefit, that they are, as it were, entrusted to us, and we must one day render account of them. Thus, therefore, we must so arrange it that this saying may continually resound in our ears: "Render account of your stewardship" (Luke 16:2). At the same time let us remember by whom such reckoning is required: namely, Him who has greatly commended abstinence, sobriety, frugality, and moderation, and has also abominated excess, pride, ostentation, and vanity; who approves no other distribution of good things than one joined with love; who has already condemned with His own lips all delights that draw a person's spirit away from chastity and purity, or befog his mind.

6. Finally, this point is to be noted: the Lord bids each one of us in all life's actions to look to his calling...lest through our stupidity and rashness everything be turned topsy-turvy, He has appointed duties for every person in his particular way of life. And that no one may thoughtlessly transgress his limits, He has named these various kinds of living "callings." Therefore each individual has his own kind of living assigned to him by the Lord as a sort of sentry post so that he may not heedlessly wander about throughout life....

It is enough if we know that the Lord's calling is in everything the beginning and foundation of well-doing. And if there is anyone who will not direct himself to it, he will never hold to the straight path in his duties. Perhaps, sometimes, he could contrive something laudable in appearance: but whatever it may be in the eyes of people, it will be rejected before God's throne. Besides, there will be no harmony among the several parts of his life. Accordingly, your life will then be best ordered when it is directed to this goal. For no one, impelled by his own rashness, will attempt more than his calling will permit, because he will know that it is not lawful to exceed its bounds. A person of obscure station will lead a private life ungrudgingly so as not to leave the rank in which he has been placed by God. Again, it will be no slight relief from cares, labors, troubles, and other burdens for a person to know that God is his guide in all these things.

JOHN CALVIN

The magistrate will discharge his functions more willingly; the head of the household will confine himself to his duty; each person will bear and swallow the discomforts, vexations, weariness, and anxieties in his way of life, when he has been persuaded that the burden was laid upon him by God. From this will arise also a singular consolation: that no task will be so sordid and base, provided you obey your calling in it, that it will not shine and be reckoned very precious in God's sight.

SECTION II:
PASTORS AND PEOPLE IN THE CRISES OF LIFE

As Calvin was always ready to state frankly, faith and piety do not protect believers from the afflictions of life. The saving word of God, ministered by human beings to human beings, comes amid the crises and trials of life, transforming the understanding of these afflictions and enabling those who suffer them to see God's providence and love in their sickness, imprisonment, and death, their persecution and perplexity. That same word stirs up believers to act for each other, to intercede and seek justice for the oppressed, even to the point of sharing their mistreatment, "suffering for righteousness' sake" (3.8.7).

The first division of this section gives a glimpse of Calvin's understanding of pastoral care for the sick, the dying, and the bereaved. The next letters express the counsel that could be offered to people facing distress in their personal lives and faith. The last part examines briefly various facets of the work for justice and the challenge of martyrdom. A number of these letters are addressed to women, not because Calvin had more female correspondents than male, but partly to illustrate a range of personal and ecclesiastical issues, partly to give attention to an often neglected dimension of his pastoral work.

Visiting the Sick and Dying

Both Calvin's liturgy, *La forme des prières,* and the Genevan church order, the *Ecclesiastical Ordinances,* provide brief statements about how pastors and those close to the sick should minister to them. Calvin himself undoubtedly spent more of his life attending the sick and dying than is usually remembered; some of these occasions are reflected in his letters to the bereaved. The original texts are found in OS 2, pp. 56–58, 355–56, the translations are by E. A. McKee.

291

JOHN CALVIN

Instructions

"The visiting of the sick" *La forme des prières*

The office of a true and faithful minister is not only publicly to teach the people for whom he is ordained pastor, but also, as much as he is able, to admonish, exhort, reprove, and console each one individually. The greatest need anyone ever has of the spiritual teaching of our Lord is when he is visited with affliction by God's hand: whether of illness, or other troubles. This is especially so at the hour of death, because it is then that he feels more strongly than any other time in his life the suffering in his conscience, as much of God's judgment before which he will soon be called, as of the attacks of the devil, who then exercises all his efforts to beat down the poor person and cast him down and destroy him in disorder. And therefore it is the duty of a minister to visit the sick and comfort them with the word of the Lord, exhorting them that all which they suffer and endure comes from the hand of God and His good providence, that God who never sends anything to His faithful people except for their good and salvation. The minister will offer the appropriate testimonies from the scriptures.

And if he sees that the illness is serious, the minister will give the sick consolations that go beyond this; and that according to how he sees them moved in their feelings. That is, if he recognizes that they are terrified by the horror of death, he may exhort them that there is no cause for the faithful, who have Jesus Christ as their guide and protector, to be desolated by death, by which He will lead them to the life into which He has entered. And by such exhortations he may relieve them of the fear and terror they have of the judgment of God. If he does not see them sufficiently cast down and afflicted with the feeling of their sins, the minister tells them about the justice of God before which they cannot stand except by His mercy, clinging to Jesus Christ for their salvation. On the contrary, if he sees them suffering in their consciences and troubled by their offenses, he will show and vividly present Jesus Christ to them, and tell them how all poor sinners who distrust themselves may repose on Christ's goodness, and find comfort and refuge. Thus a good and faithful minister must consider what means are good to use to console the patient and the afflicted, according to the feelings he sees in them; and all this is done by the word of our Lord.

And if the minister has anything by which he can aid or console the poor afflicted ones physically, let him not spare these means but show to all a good example of love.

"Concerning visiting the sick" *Ecclesiastical Ordinances* 1541

Since many neglect to seek consolation in God by His word when they are sick, it happens that some die without any admonition or teaching, which is more salutary then than ever. Therefore we have decided and ordained that no one shall remain sick in bed for three whole days without making this known to the minister; and let each one take care to call the ministers when he wants them, but at an appropriate time in order not to distract them from their duty by which they serve the whole church in common. And to eliminate all excuse we have decided this. Especially let there be commanded that the relatives, friends, and guardians not wait until someone is about to die [to call a minister], since for the most part in that extremity consolations serve scarcely any purpose.

Consolation

Bonnet LXIV.—To Monsieur de RICHEBOURG, #295 in OC 11:188–94

Ratisbon, [April 1541] *[revised translation–A French student boarding in Calvin's home to study at Strasbourg's Academy, and his tutor Claude Féray, died during a severe visitation of the plague while Calvin was at the colloquy at Ratisbon.]*

When I first received the intelligence of the death of Master Claude [Féray] and of your son Louis, I was so utterly overpowered that for many days I was fit for nothing but to weep. And although I was somehow comforted and upheld before the Lord by those aids wherewith He sustains our souls in affliction, with regard to human society, however, I felt as if I were not at all

293

myself. So far at least as regards my discharge of duty, I appeared to myself quite as unfit for it as if I had been half dead.

On the one hand, I was sadly grieved to have lost—at a time when we most needed him—such an excellent and faithful friend [as Féray], a friend with whom I was so familiar that none could be more closely united than we were. On the other hand, there arose another cause of grief, when I saw a youth of most excellent promise as your son was, taken away from us in the very flower of his age. He was one whom I loved as my own son because on his part he showed such respectful affection toward me as he would to another father. To this grievous sorrow was still added the heavy and distressing anxiety we experienced about those whom the Lord had spared to us. I heard that our whole household was scattered here and there. The danger of Malherbe caused me very great misery, in part for his sake, in part it warned me also as to the rest. I considered that it could not be otherwise but that my wife must be very much dismayed and weighed down with great affliction.

But especially your [other son] Charles was continually recurring to my thoughts. For in proportion as he was endowed with that goodness of disposition and had always had for his brother as well as his preceptor not only a natural love but also a fitting attitude and reverence, it never occurred to me to doubt but that the poor child would be steeped in sorrow and soaked in tears. One single consideration somewhat relieved me, that he had my brother along with him, who I hoped would prove no small comfort in this calamity. Even that, however, I could not reckon upon, when at the same time I recollected that neither of them was yet beyond the reach of danger. Thus until other letters arrived which informed me that Malherbe was sick but no longer in danger, and that Charles, my brother, my wife, and the others were well, I would have been all but utterly cast down, except that (as I have already mentioned), so that I might not succumb completely, my heart was refreshed in the presence of our Lord by prayers and holy meditations which He provides for us by His word.

These circumstances I mention on this account, lest those exhortations by which I now desire to console you may seem to you of less value, because you may consider it an easy matter for me to be constant and valiant in contending against another person's grief. I do not, however, boast here of firmness or fortitude in dealing with another's sorrow, but since it has been granted me by the special goodness of God to be in some degree either delivered from the affliction and sorrow which I have in common with you in almost the same degree, or to have it lightened, I desire to communicate to you insofar as that is possible in a short letter, the remedies I took advantage of and which were of greatest benefit to me in the midst of such a sorrow. Though in this place I know I must consider carefully the sadness you feel in such a situation, yet at the same time, I shall remember that I am writing to a person of a very serious mind, mature in prudence, of very constant character. For I am aware how well you are furnished with all those good resolutions and helps appropriate to bearing affliction patiently and always to keeping to a fitting moderation. Neither shall I remind you of those common topics of consolation which are customary among people of knowledge and consequence in the world: such as that you should not weep for the death of one whom you know was born subject to mortality, that you should show forth in this sorrowful occurrence that virtuous courage and nobility required by your excellent nature and disposition, expanded as it is by the most elegant accomplishments, as indeed is fitting to your mature age, your varied experience, in sum, to your reputation. In your case I set aside all exhortations of this kind, and others of the same description.

For there is one sure and certain source of consolation, in which you and those like you ought to acquiesce completely, which flows from that inward feeling of the true knowledge of God that I know to abound in you. Therefore, see in a single word what you must do, that is to call to mind those thoughts which our good Master sings to us and repeats so often in the school of His true religion. It is not necessary at present that I should state these truths, which are all as familiar to you as to myself. Yet, notwithstanding, because of your true fear of God and that love which in your grace you express toward me, you will be very glad and take in good part to see again in my letters thoughts which have spontaneously occurred to your own mind at some other time.

The Lord has taken back to Himself the son whom He had given you and as if entrusted into your hands. There is no ground, therefore, for those silly and wicked complaints of foolish people: "O blind death! O horrid fate! O inflexible disaster, inescapable and intractable! O cruel fortune!" The Lord who had lodged him here for a season, at this stage of his career has called him back. When we hear that it is something the Lord has done, let us at the same time consider that it has not been done rashly, nor by chance, neither from having been impelled from without; but by that counsel whereby He does not ordain or do anything except what He foresees to be just and upright in itself, and also good for us and our salvation. Where there is what is right, just, and fair, there it is not permitted to remonstrate or contradict. When, however, our own advantage is bound up with that goodness, how great would be the degree of ingratitude not to receive with a calm and well-ordered temper of mind whatever is the wish of our Father! Nevertheless, the providence of God alone of itself supplies the faithful abundantly and fully sufficient comfort and alleviation of their sorrows, whatsoever may happen. For there is nothing which is more dispiriting to us than while we vex and annoy ourselves with this sort of questions and complaints: "Why is it this way? Why is it not otherwise with us? Why has it so happened that we came to this place?" These questions would be well and suitably put, if there were something in ourselves that needed reproof and if we had failed in our duty. But where there is no fault on our part, there is no room for this sort of complaint. It is God therefore who has taken back from us the son whom He had committed to us to be educated, on the condition that he might always be His own. And therefore He took him away, because it was of advantage both to him to leave this world, and to you by this bereavement to humble you or to give you occasion to practice patience. If you do not now understand the good and advantage of this, first of all, ask of God that He may show you. Should it be His will to afflict and exercise you still further by concealing it from you, you must do Him this honor, to believe that He is more wise than the smallness of our understanding.

In what regards your son, if you bethink yourself how difficult it is in this most deplorable age to maintain an upright course through life, you will judge him to be blessed, who, before encountering so many coming dangers which already were hovering over him and which are to be encountered at the age he was entering upon, was so early delivered from them. For it is like one who has set sail upon a stormy and tempestuous sea, and before he has been carried out into the deeps he is suddenly drawn back in safety to the secure haven. Nor, indeed, is long life to be reckoned so great a benefit of God that we can lose anything when, after the space of only a few years, we are withdrawn and transported to a better life. Now certainly because the Lord Himself, who is the Father of us all, had willed that Louis should be your son, He bestowed this benefit upon you, out of the multitude of His mercies, that you might see the excellent fruit of your careful education before his death. He gave you this grace, I say, that you might know that you have a part in His blessing, which is: "I will be your God, and the God of your seed" (Gen 17:7).

From his earliest boyhood, so far as his years allowed, [Louis] was grounded in the best studies, and had already made such good progress that we entertained great hope of him for the future. His manners and behavior met with the approval of all good people. If at any time he fell into error, he not only patiently suffered the word of admonition but also that of reproof, and proved himself teachable and obedient and willing to hearken to advice. At times, indeed, he was rather unruly, but never so far as to be obstinate or sulky. Those sallies, therefore, wherein he exceeded due bounds were repressed with little trouble. That however which we rate most highly in him was that he had drunk so largely of true piety from first acquaintance, that he had a correct and true understanding of religion, and had imprinted on his heart a real fear of God. This exceedingly great kindness of God toward our offspring ought with good reason to prevail more effectually with us in soothing the bitterness of death, than death itself has power to inflict grief upon us.

297

With reference to my own feelings, if your children had never come hither at all, I should not now be feeling grief on account of the death of Master Claude and Louis. However, this most crushing sorrow, which I suffer on account of both, should never cause me to regret that day on which they were brought hither to us, by the hand of God rather than led by any settled purpose of their own; when that friendship commenced which has not only continued to the end, but which from day to day was rather increased and confirmed. Therefore, given the character they had, I rejoice that they lived under the same roof with me. And since it was appointed them to die, I rejoice also that they died under my roof, where they rendered back their souls into the hands of God more composedly, and in greater circumstances of quiet, than if they had happened to die in those places where they would have experienced greater annoyance from the importunity of those by whom they ought to have been assisted, than from death itself. On the contrary, it was in the midst of pious exhortations, and while firmly calling upon the name of the Lord, that these faithful spirits left this world below, gladly in Christ's company. Nor would I desire now to be free from all this sorrow at the cost of never having known them. I hope to hold their memory ever sacred to me, and even sweet and comforting, to the end of my days.

But what advantage, you will say, is it to me to have had a son of so much promise, since he has been torn away from me in the first flower of his youth? As if, forsooth, Christ had not merited by His death the supreme dominion over the living and the dead. And if we belong to Him (as we ought), why may He not exercise over us the power of life and of death? However brief, therefore, either in your opinion or in mine, the life of your son may have been, it ought to satisfy us that he has finished the course which the Lord had marked out for him. Moreover, we may not reckon him to have perished in the flower of his age, who had grown ripe in the sight of the Lord. For I consider all to have arrived at maturity who are summoned away by death; unless perhaps we would contend with Him, as if He can snatch away anyone before his time. This, indeed, holds true of everyone; but in regard to Louis, it is yet more certain on another and more peculiar ground. For he had arrived at that age when by true evidences he could prove himself a member of the body of Christ: having put forth this fruit, he was taken from us and transplanted. Yes, instead of this transient and vanishing shadow of life, he has gained the real immortality. Nor can you consider yourself to have lost him, whom you will recover in the blessed resurrection in the kingdom of God. For they had both so lived and so died, that I cannot doubt but they are now with the Lord; let us, therefore, press forward toward this goal which they have reached. There can be no doubt but that Christ will bind together both them and us in the same inseparable society, in that incomparable participation in His own glory. Beware, therefore, that you do not lament your son as lost, whom you acknowledge to be preserved by the Lord, that he may remain yours forever, who, at the pleasure of His own will, lent him to you only for a season.

Nor will you derive small consolation from this consideration, if you only weigh carefully what is left to you. Charles survives to you, of whom we all entertain this sentiment, that there is not one of us who does not desire that he might have such a son. Do not suppose that these expressions are only intended for your hearing, or that there is exaggeration here, in order to bespeak your favor. This is no more my habit than it is my disposition. I therefore express what are my real sentiments, and what I would say among strangers, that the young man excels in the first place in singular piety and in the true fear of God, which is the highest sum [beginning and end] of our wisdom; then in the kindliness of his disposition, in gentleness of manner, and in rare modesty and continence. Nor do I assign these virtues to him upon mere rumor or hearsay; for I have always been anxious upon this head, and kept close observation of his particular disposition.

During the lifetime of both the brothers, I have remarked this distinction between them: Louis excelled in quickness of apprehension, but Charles in solid judgment and intelligence was much in advance of his brother. The deceased brother was more ready in bringing into play what he had read or heard; the other is slower, but also surer. The one was more ready and quick in mastering the various arts as well as in all the active business of life; the other more considerate and more steady: his constitution of body, also, indicated as much. Louis, however, as he was of a more sanguine temperament, was also more lively and cheerful. Charles, who has somewhat of melancholy in his disposition, is not so easily drawn out of himself. He was always the more modest and courteous of the two, which distinguished him to such a degree that he could subdue his brother's impetuosity by the forbearance which he exercised. In moderation, in gravity like that of manhood, and in a certain equability of demeanor, in these points he was far the superior. You will, therefore, yourself be judge how far the possessing such a son ought to avail for taking off the pain of the bereavement wherewith the Lord has now afflicted you, and you will then conclude, that even on this account you must not be ungrateful to God.

It is difficult, notwithstanding, you will say, so to shake off or suppress the love of a father, as not to experience grief on occasion of the loss of a son. Neither do I insist upon your laying aside all grief. Nor, in the school of Christ, do we learn any such philosophy as requires us to put off that common humanity with which God has endowed us, that, being human, we should be turned into stones. These considerations reach only so far as this, that you set bounds and, as it were, temper even your most reasonable sadness; that, having shed those tears which were due to nature and to fatherly piety, you by no means give way to senseless wailing. Nor do I by any means interfere because I am distrustful of your prudence, firmness, or high-mindedness; but only lest I might here be wanting and come short in my duty to you. Although, however, this letter shall be superfluous (which I can suppose), you will nevertheless take in good part, because of your distinguished and kindly courtesy, this my perhaps over-anxious importunity—pardonable, however, notwithstanding, because it proceeds from my unbounded affection toward you. Moreover, I have requested Melanchthon and Bucer [with me at the colloquy in Ratisbon] that they would also add their letters to mine, because I entertained the hope that it would not be unacceptable that they too should afford some evidence of their goodwill toward you.

Adieu, most distinguished sir, whom I much respect in the Lord. May Christ the Lord keep you and your family, and direct you all with His own Spirit, until you may arrive where Louis and Claude have gone before.

Bonnet CCXL.—To Madame de CANY, #1179 in OC 13:244–48
  Geneva, 29 April 1549. *[Laurent de Normandie and Anne de la Vacquerie de Normandie, French nobility of some importance, had moved to Geneva in 1549; she was already ill at the time. Shortly after his own wife died, Calvin ministered to Mme de Normandie in her last hours. To convey the news to her father, Calvin wrote to her friend Mme de Cany, signing the letter with one of the pseudonyms he used in correspondence where his own name might cause difficulty for the recipient.]*

Madame, Although the news which I communicate is sad and must also sadden the person to whom I beg you to impart it, nevertheless I hope that my letter will not be unwelcome to you. It has pleased my God to withdraw from this world the wife of my kind brother, M. de Normandie. Our consolation is that He has gathered her unto Himself; for He has guided her even to the last sigh, as if visibly He had held out a hand to her.

Now, since her father must needs be informed, we have thought there was no way more suitable than to request that you would please take the trouble to ask him to call on you, that the painful intelligence may be broken to him by your communication of it. What was written to us by the gentleman who recently presented our letter to you has emboldened us to take this step, which is, that you had introduced the good man in question [Mme de Normandie's father] to the right way of salvation, and that you had given him understanding of the pure and sound doctrine which we must maintain. We do not doubt, therefore, that you are willing to continue your good offices, and that even in this present need. For you cannot employ yourself better than in carrying this message in the name of God, to comfort him to whom you have already done so much good, that he may not be beyond measure disconsolate. Therefore, Madame, I leave you to set before him the arguments and reasons which you know to be

301

suitable for exhorting to patience. Only I shall shortly relate to you the history, which will furnish you with ample matter for showing him that he has reason to be thankful. And, according to the grace and wisdom that God has given you, you will draw thence for his comfort as opportunity shall require.

Having heard of the illness of the good woman, we were amazed how she could have been able to bear so well the fatigue of the journey, for she arrived quite fresh, and without showing any sign of weariness. Indeed she acknowledged that God had singularly supported her during that time. Weak as she was, she kept well enough until a little before Christmas. The eager desire which she had to hear the word of God upheld her until the month of January. She then began to take to bed, not because the complaint was as yet thought to be mortal, but to prevent the danger which might arise. Although expecting a favorable termination and hoping to recover her health, she nevertheless prepared for death, saying often that if this were not the finishing blow, it could not be long delayed. As for remedies, all was done that could be. And if her bodily comfort was provided for, that which she prized most highly was nowise wanting, to wit, pious admonitions to confirm her in the fear of God, in the faith of Jesus Christ, in patience, in the hope of salvation. On her part she always gave clear evidence that the labor was not in vain, for in her discourse you could see that she had the whole deeply imprinted upon her heart. In short, throughout the course of her sickness, she proved herself to be a true sheep of our Lord Jesus, letting herself be quietly led by the Great Shepherd.

Two or three days before death, as her heart was more raised to God, she also spoke with more earnest affection than ever. Even the day before, while she was exhorting her people, she said to her attendant that he must take good heed never to return thither where he had polluted himself with idolatry; and that since God had led him to a Christian Church, he should be careful to live therein a holy life. The night following she was oppressed with great and continual pain. Yet never did one hear any other cry from her except the prayer to God that He would have pity upon her, and that He would deliver her out of the world, vouchsafing grace to persevere always in the faith which He had bestowed. Toward five o'clock in the morning I went to her. After she had listened very patiently to the doctrine which I set before her, such as the occasion called for, she said: "The hour draws near, I must needs depart from the world; this flesh asks only to go away into corruption; but I feel certain that my God is withdrawing my soul into His kingdom. I know what a poor sinful woman I am, but my confidence is in His goodness and in the death and passion of His Son. Therefore I do not doubt of my salvation, since He has assured me of it. I go to Him as to my Father."

While she was thus discoursing, a considerable number of persons came in. I threw in from time to time some words, such as seemed suitable, and we also made supplication to God as the exigency of her need required. After once more declaring the sense she had of her sins, to ask the pardon of them from God, and the certainty which she entertained of her salvation, putting her sole confidence in Jesus and having her whole trust in Him, without being invited by anyone to do so she began to pronounce the *Miserere* as we sing it in church, and continued with a loud and strong voice, not without great difficulty, but she entreated that we would allow her to continue. Whereupon I made her a short recapitulation of the whole argument of the psalm, seeing the pleasure she took in it. Afterward, taking me by the hand, she said to me, "How happy I am, and how am I beholden to God, for having brought me here to die. Had I been in that wretched prison, I could not have ventured to open my mouth to make confession of my Christianity. Here I have not only liberty to glorify God, but I have so many sound arguments to confirm me in my salvation." Sometimes, indeed, she said, "I am not able for more." When I answered her, "God is able to help you; He has, indeed, shown you how He is a present aid to His own," she said immediately, "I do believe so, and He makes me feel His help." Her husband was there, striving to keep up in such sort that we were all sorry for him, while he made us wonder in amazement at his fortitude. For while possessed with such grief as I know it to have been, and weighed down by extremity

303

of sorrow, he had so far gained the mastery over self as to exhort his better part as freely as if they were going to make a most joyful journey together.

The conversation I have related took place in the midst of the great torment she endured from pains in her stomach. Toward nine or ten o'clock they abated. Availing herself of this relaxation, she never ceased to glorify God, humbly seeking her salvation and all her well-being in Jesus Christ. When speech failed her, her countenance told how intently she was interested in the prayers as well as in the exhortations which were made. Otherwise she was so motionless, that sight alone gave indication of life. Toward the end, considering that she was gone, I said, "Now let us pray God that He would give us grace to follow her." As I rose, she turned her eyes upon us, as if charging us to persevere in prayer and in consoling her; after that, we perceived no motion, and she passed away so gracefully that it was as if she had fallen asleep.

I pray you, Madame, to excuse me if I have been too tedious. But I thought that the father would be well pleased to be fully informed of the whole, as if he himself had been upon the spot. And I hope that in so good a work you will find nothing troublesome. St. Paul, in treating of charity, does not forget that we ought to weep with those who weep (Rom 12:15); that is to say, that if we are Christians, we ought to have such compassion and sorrow for our neighbors that we should willingly take part in their tears and thus comfort them. It cannot otherwise be but the good man must at the first be wrung with grief. However, he must already have been long prepared to receive the news, considering that his daughter's sickness had increased so much that her recovery was despaired of. But the great consolation is the example which she has afforded to him and to all of us, of bowing to the will of God. And thus, seeing that she has presented herself so peaceably to death, let us herein follow her, willingly complying with the disposal of God; and if her father loved her, let him show his love in conforming himself to the desire which she exhibited of submitting herself to God. And seeing that her dismissal has been so happy, let him rejoice in the grace of God vouchsafed to her, which far surpasses all the comforts we can possess in this world.

In conclusion, Madame, having humbly commended me to your kind favor, I beseech our good Lord to be always your protector, to increase you with all spiritual blessing, and to cause you to glorify His name even to the end. Your humble servitor and brother, Charles D'ESPEVILLE.

Counsel and Mutual Encouragement

Pastoral counsel for the troubled might take various forms. Calvin wrote to those who suffered in their domestic lives for standing against their families' confession; he offered sympathy but also a strong exhortation to witness for their faith. He could also express gratitude to those who encouraged him and others by their support for the gospel.

Bonnet CCCXIX.—To Madame de CANY, #1751 in OC 14:556–58
Geneva, 7 June 1553 *[This lady, converted by M. and Mme de Normandie, suffered abuse from her husband for her faith until eventually he also became a Protestant. Again Calvin signs a pseudonym.]*
Madame, Although I am not so devoid of compassion as not to feel my heart pained in hearing of the more than ever strict captivity in which you are now held, yet I shall not cease to exhort you to furnish yourself with courage and constancy, according as you feel the trial to be vexatious and hard to bear; for it is just when pressed by Satan and the enemies of the faith to the uttermost that we ought to make the most of the grace of God. St. Paul glories in this, that although he was chained in prison, nevertheless the doctrine which he preached was not bound but following its course and thriving powerfully (2 Tim 2:9). And indeed, seeing that it is the truth of God which reaches far beyond this world and upward above the heavens, it is not likely that it should restrict itself according to the human fancy or tyranny. Consequently, the more the devil contrives to torture us by distress, the more let us strive to enlarge our hearts by faith so as to meet all assaults. Moreover, our Savior has formerly afforded you examples of the kind, and gives us all similar things daily in various places; so that we ought to take great

shame to ourselves if we are not strengthened by them. For were we to grow faint under the strokes of the rod, when others are not at all dismayed by death, what excuse should we have for our cowardice?

You had not counted on the possibility of meeting with such rude conflicts at home. But you know how the Son of God forewarns us so that nothing should trouble us, seeing that we have been prepared for it beforehand (John 14:1, 15:18ff.). Think rather that this is not the end, but that God is trying you very gently, supporting your weakness, until you have more strength to sustain blows. But be this as it may, beware of letting yourself be cast down by indifference or despair. Many are overcome because they allow their zeal to grow cold and run off in self-flattery. Others, on the contrary, become so alarmed when they do not find in themselves the strength they wish, that they get confused and give up the struggle altogether. What then is to be done? Arouse yourself to meditate, as much upon the promises of God which ought to serve as ladders to raise us up to heaven and make us despise this transitory and fading life, as upon threatenings which may well induce us to fear His judgments. When you do not feel your heart moved as it ought to be, have recourse (as to a special remedy) to diligently seeking the aid of Him without whom we can do nothing. In the meantime, strive to your utmost, blaming coldness and weakness, until you can perceive that there is some amendment. And in regard to this, great caution is required so as to hold a middle course, namely, to groan unceasingly and even to woo yourself to sadness and dissatisfaction with your condition, and to such a sense of misery as that you may have no rest; without at the same time having any doubt that God in due time will strengthen you according to your need, although this may not appear at once. It can be nothing strange to you to see the poor church of God so miserably afflicted, to see the pride of enemies increase more and more with cruelty. If your mind is in too great perplexity, it is this that you should find strange, as a proof of your having forgotten what we ought to have rooted in the depths of our heart: the duty of conformity to the image of the Son of God, patiently bearing the shame of His cross until the day of our triumph come. Nevertheless, let this not hinder but rather induce you to follow on in the way, for we must yet be sifted even more thoroughly.

Had I heard that, being deprived of the little liberty you had, you did not cease to have your heart set aright and to persevere in the service of Him who merits well that His honor be preferred to all beside, I should have reason to rejoice more fully. However, I do rejoice, whatever be the result, in the good hope I have of this: therefore, do not wrong me by disappointment. However, you must consider most of all what you owe to our gracious God, and to the Lord Jesus Christ who has shown how dear we were to Him since He has not spared Himself for us; therefore see to it that Satan and his underlings, who have thought to trample your faith beneath their feet, be confounded. But as so great a victory requires greater strength than your own, take refuge in this kind Lord Jesus, who has been made the strength of God His Father for us so that in Him we might do all things. And for my part I shall beseech Him that He would pour out upon you such a help of His Spirit, so that you may know by experience what it is to be upheld by Him, and that He may be glorified thereby, praying also that He would take you into His holy protection against the fury of wolves and the wiles of foxes.

Whereupon, Madame, after having humbly commended me to your kind favor, likewise to your prayers, I shall now make an end.

Your humble brother and servant, J. de BONNEVILLE

Bonnet DCLXIV.—To the Duchess of FERRARA, #4074 in OC 20:244–49

Geneva, 24 January 1564. *[Princess Renée of France, Duchess of Ferrara, had suffered many restraints from her Catholic husband during his life but still kept a Protestant minister and court as well as possible, a stance which became easier when the widowed duchess retired to France. This letter from her long correspondence with Calvin illustrates a different angle of the religio-political conflict from that seen in the letter to Mme de Cany. The duchess's Calvinist minister had declared that her recently deceased son-in-law, the Duc of Guise, one of the leading persecutors of Protestants in France, was among the reprobate, and the duchess protested about this to Calvin.]*

Madame: When I learned from your last letter that you had intimated to Messire Francisco that it would be expedient that I should exhort to charity those who make a profession of being Christians, I understood that to refer to some ministers that you have found not to be very charitable according to your judgment. In the meantime, I can gather that you alluded to the too great asperity with which they have condemned the late Duke of Guise. Now, Madame, before I proceed to examine more closely that question, I pray you in God's name to reflect seriously that on your part also it is requisite to observe moderation. For it is only one void of reflection who will fancy that we can ever have too much of it. And without taking into account the report of others, I have perceived in your letter that affection makes you forget what otherwise you should have sufficiently known.

Respecting what I had alleged to you that David teaches us by his example to hate the enemies of God, you reply that it was only during those times when people lived under the rigor of the law that it was permitted to hate enemies. Now, Madame, this gloss would lead to the overthrowing of the whole scriptures, and for that reason we should shun it as we would a deadly plague. For we see that David surpassed in kindness of character the best of those that would be found in our days. Thus when he protests that he has wept and in secret shed tears for those who were plotting his death, that his hatred consisted in mourning for their death, that he rendered back good for evil (Ps 6:8, 1 Sam 24:17), we see that he was as meek spirited as could possibly be desired. But when he says he holds the reprobate in mortal aversion, it cannot be doubted that he glories in an upright, pure, and well-regulated zeal, for which three things are requisite: first, that we should have no regard for ourselves or our private interests; next, that we should possess prudence and discretion not to judge at random; and finally that we observe moderation not to exceed the bounds of our calling. All this you will see, Madame, more in detail in several passages of my commentaries on the psalms, when you shall be pleased to take the trouble to look into them.

So that indeed the Holy Spirit has given us David as a model, that in this respect we might follow his example. And in fact we are told that in this ardor he was the type of our Lord Jesus Christ, and if we pretend to surpass in meekness and humanity Him who is the fountain of pity and compassion, woe to us.

But to cut short all disputes, let it satisfy us that St. Paul applies to all believers this passage: "The zeal of thy house hath eaten me up" (Ps 69:9). Wherefore our Lord Jesus, reproving His disciples because they desired that He should cause fire to come down from heaven as Elijah had done, and consume those who rejected Him, does not allege that we are no longer under a law of rigor, but simply shows them that they are not led by the same spirit as the prophet (Luke 9:54–55). Nay, St. John, of whom you have retained nothing but the word love, clearly shows that we ought not (under show of an affection for people) to become indifferent to the duty we owe to the honor of God and the preservation of His church. It is when he forbids us even to salute those, who, as much as in them lies, turn us aside from the pure doctrine (2 John 9–11). On that subject, I pray you, to pardon me if I tell you frankly, that in my opinion you have taken the comparison of the bow, which we bend in an opposite direction when it has been too much bent on one side, in a different [wrong] sense from the way it was meant by the one who used it. For he doubtless only meant to say that, in seeing you carried to excess, he had been constrained to be more vehement, not that he might falsify the scriptures or disguise the truth.

I come now to the fact which, not to annoy you by my prolixity, I shall only briefly touch upon. You have not been the only one to suffer much anguish and bitterness during these horrible troubles that have fallen out. True it is, the evil might sting you more keenly, on seeing the throne with which you are connected by your royal descent subject to such disorder. But certainly the sorrow was common to all the children of God, and though we might all have said "Woe to him by whom this scandal is come," nevertheless there was special reason for groaning and lamenting, seeing that a good cause had been very ill-conducted. Now if the evil distressed all good people, the Duke of Guise who had kindled the conflagration could not be spared. For my own part, though I have often prayed God to show him mercy, yet it is certain I have often desired that God should lay His hand on him in order to deliver out of his hands the poor church, unless it pleased God to convert him. So that I may protest that before the war, I had but to give my consent to have had him exterminated by those men of prompt and ready execution, who were bent on that object and who were restrained only by my exhortation. To pronounce that he is damned, however, is to go too far, unless one had some certain and infallible mark of his reprobation. For that we must guard against presumption and temerity, for [there is no one who can know that] but one Judge before whose tribunal we have all to render an account.

The second point seems to me still more exorbitant, that of pronouncing the King of Navarre in paradise and the Duke of Guise in hell. For if we institute a comparison between them, we find that the former was an apostate, the latter always an avowed enemy of the truth of the gospel. What I should wish then in this matter would be more moderation and sobriety. In the meantime I have also to pray you, Madame, not to show so much displeasure at the expression "not to pray for anyone" without having made a due distinction between the form and the reality of the subject in question. For though I pray for the salvation of someone, that does not imply that in all respects and everywhere I recommend him as if he were a member of the church. We demand of God that He would bring back into the right path those who are on the way to perdition. But this will not be in placing them in the rank of our brethren in order to desire for them all kinds of prosperity.

On this subject, I will relate to you an anecdote of the Queen of Navarre, very applicable to the matter in question. When the king her husband had fallen off from us, the minister at her court ceased to make mention of him in the public prayers. Irritated, she remonstrated with him that he ought not to make this omission, if for no other reason at least from consideration for his subjects. [The minister], excusing himself, declared that if he had altogether abstained from [mentioning him], it was to conceal the dishonor of the king her husband, inasmuch as [the minister] could not pray to God for [the king] in reality, unless he made supplication for [the king's] conversion, which was only uncovering his fall. If he asked God to maintain [the king] in prosperity, it would be a mockery and a profanation of prayer. Having heard this answer she said not a word till she had demanded advice of others and, finding that they all agreed, she mildly acquiesced. As I know, Madame, that this virtuous princess [a relative of Renée] would be disposed to take a lesson from you as a thing due to your age and your virtues, in like manner I entreat you not to be ashamed to conform your conduct to hers in this matter. Her husband was a closer connection to her than your son-in-law to you; nevertheless she mastered her affections in order not to be the cause of having God's name profaned, which it would assuredly be if our prayers were feigned or militated against the repose of the church. And to have done with this pretext of charity, judge, I beseech you, Madame, if it is reasonable that at the capricious desire of a single man we are to make no account of a hundred thousand, that charity should be so confined to one who had endeavored to throw everything into confusion, that the children of God should be kept completely in the background. Now the remedy for all that is to hate evil, without taking persons into the account, but leaving every one to his Judge. If God granted me the favor of speaking with you, I trust I should speedily satisfy you. In the meantime I entreat you to weigh well what I have handled briefly, that you may not disquiet and irritate your mind for a little idle talk, which you could afford to treat with the most thorough contempt.

You are solicited to permit the shops of the papists to be robbed and pillaged. I take good care not to approve of such a step, whoever may have taken it. I commend on the contrary your virtue and greatness of mind, in having been unwilling to acquiesce in so unjust a demand. I say the same thing of the other excesses which you mention. Touching the quarrel which has arisen in your household between the two persons whom you name, I know not what reason there is for speaking against the woman. I have no doubt of what you tell me, Madame; but I know not whether there have been any bad symptoms that have forced

M. de Colonges [a minister sent from Geneva] to give such an admonition as a kind of preventive remedy, or whether he has gone too for and there has been want of due reflection on his part. One thing is certain; that the husband gave loose to too much violence when they offered to satisfy him, and the answer and refusal of M. de Colonges also savors more of his ambition and of worldly vanity than of the modesty of a man of his calling, at which I am very sorry, for he must have forgotten himself too far. If the parties agree to lay before us an account of their affair, I will do all in my power to remedy the evil on whichever side it may be found.

On this point, Madame, I confess, that it is much to be feared that God will not leave us long to enjoy the blessings He has granted us; since everyone is so taken up with his self-interest that we do not know how to support our neighbor in a spirit of meekness and humility. And so far are we from loving our enemies, striving to overcome evil with good, that there is no gentleness among us to keep up brotherly love between those who boast that they are Christians. Nevertheless, I pray you again, Madame, not to dwell any longer on that distinction which deceives you, while you imagine that it was permitted under the law to avenge oneself because it is there said, "an eye for an eye" (Exod 21:24). For vengeance was as much forbidden then as it is under the gospel, seeing that we are commanded to do good even to the beast of our enemy (Exod 23:4–5). But each individual applied to himself what was addressed to the judges. There remains the abuse of the precept which our Lord Jesus Christ corrects. Be that as it will, we are all agreed that in order to be recognized as children of God it behooves us to conform ourselves to His example, striving to do good to those who are unworthy of it, just as He causes His sun to shine on the evil and the good (Matt 5:38ff.). Thus hatred and Christianity are things incompatible. I mean hatred toward persons—in opposition to the love we owe them. On the contrary we are to wish and even procure their good; and to labor as much as in us lies to maintain peace and concord with everyone.

Now if those who are commissioned to dissipate all enmity and rancor, to reconcile enemies, to exhort to patience, and repress all lust of vengeance, be themselves brands of discord—so much the worse, and so much the less are they to be excused. At any rate, Madame, the faults which displease you ought not to cool your zeal or prevent you from continuing as you have so well begun. And I know that God has fortified you with such courage that it is unnecessary to solicit you yet more. Wherefore I am confident that you will set an example of charity to those who do not know what it is, and by your integrity and plain dealing cover with confusion those who practice toward you hypocrisy and dissimulation. On the other hand I bless God for having made known to you the real character of the Admiral [Coligny], to inspire you with a taste for his probity. When it will please Him He will do the rest....

Bonnet DCXI.—To the Comtesse de ROYE, #3532 in OC 18:736–37

Geneva, 24 September, 1561. *[This noble woman and members of her family were strong supporters of Protestants in France; like others, they looked to Geneva to supply trained ministers, but there were never enough. Calvin's apology concludes with appreciation for the countess's work for the gospel.]*

Madame: If I have delayed so long in answering your letters, it is partly because I did not know whither to address mine; and partly from shame, inasmuch as I was unable to satisfy your holy desire, for you asked me for three men capable of being employed in the service of God and of His church, designating the places where you intended to send them, in order that I might be the more incited to make all diligence. The same message had been already conveyed to me orally by a man of Noyon, who said he had been charged with such a commission.

Now I assure you, Madame, that we are at the present moment so unprovided with ministers that I preferred, not having found suitable persons, to delay the execution of my commission rather than send persons that might not have given you satisfaction. I wish indeed that I had had a less valid excuse. But when M. Beza shall have confirmed it, I hope you will accept it. For the rest, Madame, I have much reason to glorify God for

JOHN CALVIN

the great courage with which He has inspired you for advancing the reign of our Lord Jesus Christ, and, for causing you to make a frank and pure declaration of following the truth of the gospel in life and in death: since all our happiness stands in being disciples of this great Master, and subjects of this sovereign King, who has been sent to us from heaven to withdraw us from perdition to the hope of eternal salvation, which He has purchased for us.

Wherefore without this heritage, woe to all the riches, delights, and honors of the world. And yet as we see how this inestimable treasure is despised by most people and held in no esteem, so much the more reason have you for rejoicing that God has made you a partaker of the privilege of renouncing all the vanities of this world which dazzle our eyes and cause us to float in continual anxiety, in order to find a true rest and abide therein. You have also another blessing in addition to those which have been already bestowed on you, in seeing your daughters, the princess as well as her sister, keeping you company in tending toward the chief end of our existence, giving themselves up with one accord and dedicating their lives to the obedience of the pure truth. Now, Madame, though I have heard with what zeal you desire to serve God, nevertheless I pray you to take more and more courage, striving to overcome all the obstacles that might retard you, as you may be sure you shall always have many. And indeed these are the exercises of our faith, to fight against all the temptations which Satan devises and employs to turn us aside from the straight path. Aim then, Madame, at this perseverance, not doubting but the heavenly Father will conduct you even to the end, as He has a more than singular care about your salvation, and that Jesus Christ, that good Shepherd who has undertaken the charge of you, will keep and protect you.

Madame, having humbly commended myself to your indulgent favor, I will supplicate our heavenly Father to govern you by His Holy Spirit, and increase you in all good and prosperity.

314

PASTORS AND PEOPLE IN THE CRISES OF LIFE

Advocacy for Justice and Pastoral Care for the Afflicted

Calvin's understanding of pastoral care included the obligation to seek to help those who were suffering for the faith. This could take a number of different forms, including not only letters of counsel and material aid but also interceding with political powers for those who were imprisoned and encouraging others who served as their advocates. Several cases give a glimpse of Calvin's efforts in these areas.

In 1544–45 the people of Provence, France, were being severely persecuted by the royal authorities, and Calvin worked to arouse Protestant powers to intercede for these afflicted brothers and sisters. When those who escaped from the persecution sought refuge in Geneva in 1545, he also was instrumental in encouraging the Genevan government to offer them a place and employment and means of subsistence.

In the 1550s there began to be a growing number of instances of French Protestants being executed for their faith. In 1552 five young men returning from their theological studies in Lausanne to be pastors in France were apprehended and imprisoned in Lyons. Over the following months Calvin and others corresponded with the prisoners and worked with people of good will, like the merchant John Liner, to try to free them. Although their faith was sustained, efforts to liberate the men failed, and in the spring of 1553 the five were burned at the stake. Soon several others who were also imprisoned, including Mathieu Dimonet and Denis Peloquin, followed their brothers to martyrdom. (Here only a few of the letters are included, to indicate both the comfort Calvin offered and the respect he had for the witness of these men who faced martyrdom.) Men were not the only prisoners who suffered death for their faith. In 1557 Calvin was writing to women incarcerated in Paris before they too were put to death.

Advocacy for the People of Provence

Bonnet CXXII. To BULLINGER, #586 in OC 11:773 (772–75) (Excerpt of letter) Geneva, 24 Nov. 1544. *[Calvin informs Heinrich Bullinger, minister of the powerful Church of Zürich, of the persecution of the people of Provence.]*

There is another affair, besides, in which I wish very specially to implore your aid. There are brethren in Provence, for whom you are aware that we have always taken much pains. Nor were they any way undeserving that we should do so; for they are a people so harmless, and withal so piously disposed, that their peace and safety ought to be the peculiar care of all good people. It is now

315

three years bypast, since they were so far advanced as to have presented to the Parliament of Aix a confession of faith, pure and simple as we could have set it forth ourselves. And besides, so that you may not suppose that such a step was taken from some sudden impulse, which might immediately have evaporated, whenever they have been called to account concerning it they have constantly stood firm to their profession.

In the meantime, however, they were cruelly harassed. After they had been exposed for some time to the savage tyranny of their enemies, they obtained at length of the king [Francis I] that he would appoint a commission, who might hear evidence and report truly upon the whole case. The king commissioned two persons, whose duty was to make inquiry; he wished to take the entire cognizance of the cause to himself, and so to pronounce an award. The tenor of the commission was that the persons who were to be sent were to inquire particularly and to take special knowledge concerning their doctrine and morals, both in public and private. This the brethren have no dread or anxiety about. For they have so conducted themselves toward all around them as to have an unexceptionable testimony to their sterling worth, even from their adversaries. As for their doctrine, they are about to present their confession of faith, clear and sincere, to the king as he has required, which document comprises, and that distinctly, far more points than can be alleged against them.

At this present time, both the bishops, the royal officers, and even the parliament itself, are striving with all their might to set aside the royal commission; if it be quashed, they [the Protestants of Provence] will then be exposed to the fury of lions and wolves, that they may spend their rage upon them. Indeed, their adversaries are mainly desirous that they may have full license to discharge all their fury upon these wretched people. If the commission be received and acted upon, even in that event they will not have escaped the danger. For in three small towns and in very many of the villages they profess the pure doctrine of the Evangel. In one little town they have thoroughly cleansed the parish church from all its defilements, and there they celebrate the supper and baptism in the same manner as we do. The more immediately the danger is impending over them on either side, they are all the more on that account to be succored by us; especially in this their wonderful steadfastness, to which, should we be found wanting, we would be chargeable with the basest cowardice. You must also take into account that it is not their cause alone which is here concerned; but either a way will be opened by their destruction to the cruel persecution of the godly throughout the whole kingdom, or, according to this method, he will assault and break up the Evangel. What can we do, therefore, but strain every nerve that these godly brethren may not, through our shortcoming in duty, become the victims of such cruelty, and that the door may not for a long time be shut against Christ?

I have desired beforehand to warn you of the likelihood of this coming to pass, that if sooner or later they fly to you, you may have inclined the hearts of all your friends to render them all the help they can. One or the other of these two things will have to be done: either the king must be besought, that he may allow them to enjoy the benefit which has been already granted, or his anger must be appeased if it shall have begun to wax hot against them.

Bonnet CXXXI.—To FAREL, #639 in OC 12:75–76
Geneva, 4 May 1545. *[Consulting Farel about how to help the people of Provence.]*
After those two brothers about whom I had written, on my suggestion returned to their friends, the one of them has returned to us with the melancholy intelligence that several villages have been consumed by fire, that most of the old men had been burned to death, that some had been put to the sword, others having been carried off to abide their doom; and that such was the savage cruelty of these persecutors, that neither young girls, nor pregnant women, nor infants, were spared. So great is the atrocious cruelty of this proceeding, that I grow bewildered when I reflect upon it. How, then, shall I express it in words? On hearing of this dreadful tragedy, and considering what ought to be done, it seemed advisable to the brethren [ministers in Geneva] in the first place, that we

should send a man to you with my letter which commends the cause of all the churches to the ministers; and in the next place we asked the advice of the [Genevan city] Council, because we were not so clear among ourselves what measures ought to be taken. It was the opinion of the Council that I should go in person to the Swiss Churches [as an ambassador for the people of Provence].

I shall therefore set out tomorrow on the journey. I can scarcely be able to reach Bern before Thursday. As soon as I can, I shall urge the Senate to grant me an audience with the Council. If you approve, you had better come to Bern on Friday. From thence we shall go together; but if otherwise, I can proceed alone. Because Bucer in his last letter has almost entirely cut off all hope [of help from the government of Strasbourg], I almost fear that I may lose my pains by going to Strasbourg. Should the brethren at Basel advise it, I shall make the attempt for all that. It will at any rate be most refreshing to me to have a sight of you at Bern. Adieu, my dear brother; salute all. I write, worn out with sadness, and not without tears, which so burst forth that every now and then they interrupt my words.

—Yours, John CALVIN.

Bonnet CXXXVII.—To BULLINGER, #664 in OC 12:110–12
Geneva, 24 July 1545. *[Calvin's journey in Switzerland led to a gathering at Aarau at which some of the Swiss Protestant cantons agreed to send messages to the French king in support of the people of Provence. When this embassy was delayed, Calvin urged Bullinger to assist this work to go forward.]*
So far as I understand from the correspondence of friends, the object which I had obtained through your kind endeavor and that of all good men (I mean that of sending a deputation to France), will stagnate after all, unless the business is pressed a second time on their attention. The king's pensioners have so far attained their object by falsehood [as to make it] that we, forsooth, must not judge worthy even of compassion those whom we behold cruelly slain for the same cause which they maintain in common with ourselves. It was quite apparent to

me, while I was at Aarau, that there were certain of them not so very favorable to us, or at least they were not so warm and friendly as not to be affected by underhand reports. A most false accusation had been forged in order to overwhelm our unfortunate brethren. They are said to have been treated with such savage rigor because they refused to pay tithe, although it is quite certain that this has never been charged against them, even by their enemies. Yea, and more than that, it is quite well known that they had voluntarily promised that they would give as much to the priests for doing nothing, as the [latter] were accustomed to exact when they discharged their functions; for they [the people of Provence] have always had modest and prudent men among them, by whose sound advice they suffered themselves to be guided. You can therefore assert on my authority, that this has by no means been the cause of the persecution which has been set on foot against them. And not even Grignan, who is now the king's ambassador at Worms, has attempted to put forward this pretext for lessening the odium of this atrocious business. And must he not have known best of all the facts of the case, when it was by his own perfidy that the whole of this fire of persecution has been lighted up? For when he was summoned by the king himself from Provence, where he was governor, he promised to our brethren that he would faithfully plead their cause at Court; and yet, to flatter Cardinal Tournon, under whose patronage he hoped for an embassy, he stirred up the king to a height of fury hitherto unheard of.

Now, it is of great importance to know correctly what may be the state of matters and how it fares with our godly brethren. The king (that he might give some satisfaction to the Germans) wrote thither lately that he had sent a commissioner to make inquiry concerning the massacre which had been perpetrated. But what good can be expected to come of that? There is no one hitherto who has even dared to mutter a word in favor of succoring and defending the unhappy sufferers; their cause therefore lies prostrate beneath oppression. There are even at this present more than four hundred bound in iron;

for even the lower hold of the ships are also full of prisoners in chains. They make daily incursions from the Comtât d'Avignon upon those who yet remain; although it is done without the express command of the king, it is nevertheless quite certain that this takes place by his permission. For he would not thus connive if he did not approve; and the legate would not take so much upon him, if he did not clearly perceive that it was according to the king's desire.

Wherefore, now is the time for rendering them all the assistance we can, whatever we may have been able to do before. There are very many besides who have been scattered hither and thither in their flight; others lie concealed with worthy men, who have not hesitated to place their own lives in jeopardy by harboring them so as to snatch them away from death. Others are held captive. What the king promises secures no remedy, nor even a mitigation of the evil, but as it were a sort of cavern in which darkness the misfortunes of our brethren may be entombed. And shall we thus only look on and be quiet while innocent blood is shed? Shall the savage fury of the ungodly trample down our brethren with impunity? Shall Christ then be held up to ridicule and mockery? All this will happen, unless you bestir yourself anew along with others who care about what concerns the kingdom of Christ. I hear indeed that at Bern and Basel they have grown cold, unless indeed they now begin again to become more earnest in the cause. We shall not cease to strive with all our might. Do you also, with your colleagues, do your utmost that your friends may seriously take up the case.

Adieu, most accomplished sir, fellow laborer in the ministry, and my very much respected friend. Salute reverently in my name the learned Masters Pellican, Megander, Theodore, Gualther, Collin, and others. May God preserve you all the day long in safety, and govern you perpetually by His own Spirit. Amen.

Yours, John CALVIN.

Correspondence with Prisoners and Their Advocates

Bonnet CCXCVI. To the five Prisoners of Lyons, Martial ELBA, Peter ESCRIVAIN, Charles FAVRE, Peter NAVIHERES, Bernard SEQUIN #1631 in OC 14:331–34.

Geneva, 10 June 1552.

My very dear Brethren, Hitherto I have put off writing to you, fearing that if the letter fell into bad hands it might give fresh occasion to the enemy to afflict you. And besides I had been informed how God wrought so powerfully in you by His grace that you stood in no great need of my letters. However, we have not forgotten you, neither I nor all the brethren hereabouts, as to whatever we have been able to do for you. As soon as you were taken we heard of it and knew how it had come to pass. We took care that help might be sent you with all speed and are now awaiting the result. Those who have influence with the prince in whose power God has put your lives are faithfully exerting themselves on your behalf, but we do not yet know how far they have succeeded in their suit. Meanwhile all the children of God pray for you as they are bound to do, not only on account of the mutual compassion which ought to exist between members of the same body, but because they know well that you labor for them in maintaining the cause of their salvation. We hope, come what may, that God of His goodness will give a happy issue to your captivity, so that we shall have reason to rejoice.

You see to what He has called you; doubt not therefore that according as He employs you, He will give you strength to fulfill His work, for He has promised this and we know by experience that He has never failed those who allow themselves to be governed by Him. Even now you have proof of this in yourselves, for He has shown His power by giving you so much constancy in withstanding the first assaults. Be confident, therefore, that He will not leave the work of His hand imperfect. You know what scripture sets before us to encourage us to fight for the cause of the Son of God; meditate upon what you have both heard and seen formerly on this head, so as to put it in practice. For all that I could say would be of little service to you, were it not drawn from this fountain. And truly we have need of a much more firm support than humans give, to make us victorious over such strong enemies as the devil, death, and the world; but the firmness which is in Christ Jesus is sufficient for this and all else that might shake us were we not established in Him. Knowing then in whom ye have believed, manifest what authority He deserves to have over you.

As I hope to write to you again, I shall not at present lengthen my letter. I shall only reply briefly to the point which brother Bernard has asked me to solve....[Here the discussion of a number of theological issues is omitted.]...I do not heap up quotations because these will be quite enough for your purpose. In conclusion, I beseech our good Lord that He would be pleased to make you feel in every way the worth of His protection of His own, to fill you with His Holy Spirit who gives you prudence and virtue, and brings you peace, joy, and contentment; and may the name of our Lord Jesus be glorified by you to the edification of His church!

Bonnet CCXCIX.—To John LINER, #1642 in OC 14:347–48
Geneva, 10 August 1552. *[Liner was a Protestant merchant who was working to try to free the prisoners.]*

Very dear Sir and Brother, we are all bound to give thanks to God for having made choice of you to assist our poor brethren who are detained in prison by the enemies of the faith, and for having so strengthened you by the power of His Spirit that you spare no pains in so doing. I say that we are bound to give thanks to Him; for we must recognize this work as His, and that it is He alone who has disposed and directed you thereto. You have also reason to rejoice at the honor He has done you, in employing you in so worthy and honorable a service and giving you grace to perform it. For however people despise and reject the poor believers who are persecuted for the sake of the gospel, yet we know that God esteems them very pearls; that there is nothing more agreeable to Him than our striving to comfort and help them as much as in us lies. The Lord Jesus declares that whatsoever shall have been done to one of the least of His people will be acknowledged by Him as done to Himself (Matt 25:40). How then if we have furthered those who fight His battles? For such are as it were His agents, whom He appoints and ordains for the defense of His gospel. Yea, He declares that a cup of water given to them shall not be lost (Matt 10:42). If then you have hitherto had the courage to present so goodly a sacrifice to God, strive to persevere. I know well that the devil will not fail to whisper in your ear on many sides to divert you from it, but let God prove the strongest, as it is fitting He should. It is said that they who comfort the children of God in their persecutions which they endure for the gospel are fellow laborers for the truth (Phlm 1; 3 John 8). Be content with this testimony, for it is no light matter that God should uphold and approve us as His martyrs even though we do not personally suffer, merely because His martyrs are helped and comforted by us.

And therefore, although many tell you the contrary, do not leave off so good a work or show yourself weary halfway. I feel assured that you did not look to human approval at the first; follow on then as the servant of Him to whom we must cleave to the end. Reflect, moreover, how many worthy brethren there are who glorify God for what you are doing, who would be scandalized if you altered your course. As for the dangers which they set before you, I have no fear of their coming to pass, for the good brethren for whom you have done so much feel themselves so indebted to you that, were they at liberty, far from being cowardly enough to betray you, they would expose themselves to death for your sake. You must also consider, that by the support which they receive from you they are the more confirmed, for they have no doubt whatever that God has directed you to them, as indeed He has. And they have reason to lean still more firmly upon Him, seeing the paternal care He shows them. Be of good courage therefore in this holy work, in which you serve not only God and His martyrs but also the whole church.

Whereupon, my very dear sir and brother, after having heartily commended myself to you, I pray our good Lord that would increase you more and more with the gifts and riches of

His Spirit, for the furtherance of His own honor; and meanwhile, that He would have you in His keeping.   John CALVIN.

Bonnet CCCXVIII.—To the Five Prisoners of LYONS, #1746 in CO 14:544–47.
   Geneva, 15 May 1553. *[Final comfort.]*
My very dear Brothers, we have at length heard why the herald of Bern did not return that way. It was because he had not such an answer as we much desired. For the king has peremptorily refused all the requests made by Messieurs of Bern, as you will see by the copies of the letters, so that nothing further is to be looked for from that quarter. Nay, wherever we look here below God has stopped the way. There is this good, however, that we cannot be frustrated of the hope which we have in Him and in His holy promises. You have always been settled on that sure foundation, even when it seemed as though you might have human help, and that we too thought so; but whatever prospect of escape you may have had by human means, yet your eyes have never been dazzled so as to divert your heart and trust, either on this side or that.

   Now, at this present hour, necessity itself exhorts you more than ever to turn your whole mind heavenward. As yet, we know not what will be the outcome. But since it appears as though God would use your blood to sign His truth, there is nothing better than for you to prepare yourselves to that end, beseeching Him so to subdue you to His good pleasure that nothing may hinder you from following whithersoever He shall call. For you know, my brothers, that it behooves us to be thus mortified in order to be offered to Him in sacrifice. It cannot be but that you sustain hard conflicts, in order that what was declared to Peter may be accomplished in you, namely that they shall carry you whither you would not go (John 21:18). You know, however, in what strength you have to fight—a strength on which all those who trust shall never be daunted, much less confounded. Even so, my brothers, be confident that you shall be strengthened according to your need by the Spirit of our Lord Jesus, so that you shall not faint under the load of temptations, however heavy it be—any more than He did, who won so glorious a victory that in the midst of our miseries it is an unfailing pledge of our triumph.

Since it pleases Him to employ you to the death in maintaining His quarrel, He will strengthen your hands in the fight, and will not suffer a single drop of your blood to be spent in vain. And though the fruit may not all at once appear, yet in time it shall spring up more abundantly than we can express. But as He has granted you this privilege, that your bonds have been renowned and that the noise of them has been everywhere spread abroad, it must be (in despite of Satan) that your death should resound far more powerfully, so that the name of our good God be magnified thereby. For my part I have no doubt, if it please this kind Father to take you unto Himself, that He has preserved you hitherto, in order that your long-continued imprisonment might serve as a preparation for the better awakening of those whom He has determined to edify by your end. For let enemies do their utmost, they never shall be able to bury out of sight that light which God has made to shine in you, in order to be contemplated from afar.

I shall not console nor exhort you more at length, knowing that our heavenly Father makes you experience how precious His consolations are, and that you are sufficiently careful to meditate upon what He sets before you in His word. He has already so shown how His Spirit dwells in you that we are well assured that He will perfect you to the end. In leaving this world we do not go away at a venture [haphazardly], as you know not only from the certainty you have that there is a heavenly life, but also because from being assured of the gratuitous adoption of our God, you go thither as to your inheritance. That God should have appointed you as His Son's martyrs is a token to you of superabounding grace. There now remains the conflict, to which the Spirit of God not only exhorts us to go, but even to run (Heb 12:1). It is indeed a hard and grievous trial to see the pride of the enemies of truth so enormous, without its getting any check from on high; their rage so unbridled, without God's interfering for the relief of His people. But if we remember that, when it is said that our life is hid (Col 3:3) and that we must resemble the

325

dead, this is not a doctrine for any particular time but for all times, we shall not think it strange that afflictions should continue. While it pleases God to give His enemies the rein our duty is to be quiet, although the time of our redemption tarries. Moreover, if He has promised to be the judge of those who have brought His people under thraldom (Gen 15:14, Acts 7:7), we need not doubt that He has a horrible punishment prepared, for such as have despised His majesty with such enormous pride and have cruelly persecuted those who call purely upon His name.

Put into practice then, my brethren, that precept of David's, that you have not forgotten the law of God (Ps 119:61), although your life may be in your hands to be parted with at any hour. And seeing that He employs your life in so worthy a cause as is the witness of the gospel, doubt not that it must be precious to Him. The time draws nigh when the earth shall disclose the Blood which has been hid, and we, after having been disencumbered of these fading bodies, shall be completely restored. However, let the name of the Son of God be glorified by our shame, and let us be content with this sure testimony, that we are persecuted and blamed only because we trust in the living God. In this we have wherewith to despise the whole world with its pride, till we shall be gathered into that everlasting kingdom, where we shall fully enjoy those blessings, which we now only possess in hope.

My brethren, after having humbly besought your remembrance of me in your prayers, I pray our good God to have you in His holy protection, to strengthen you more and more by His power, to make you feel what care He takes of your salvation, to increase in you the gifts of His Spirit, to make them subserve His glory unto the end.

Your humble brother, John CALVIN.

I do not make my special remembrances to each of our brethren because I believe that this letter will be common to them all. Hitherto I have deferred writing on account of the uncertainty of your state, fearing lest I might disquiet you to no purpose. I pray anew our good Lord to stretch out His arm for your confirmation.

Bonnet CCCXX.—To [Two Other] Prisoners of Lyons (Mathieu DIMONET & Denis PELOQUIN), #1754 in CO 14:561–64
  Geneva, [June–July 1553]

My Brethren, I believe you have been informed that I was absent from town when the tidings from your prison arrived, and did not return for eight days after. I need not therefore excuse myself for having so long delayed writing to you. Now, although these tidings have proved sorrowful to the flesh, even in consequence of the love we justly bear you in God as we are bound to do, yet must we submit ourselves to the will of this kind Father and sovereign Lord; and not only consider His way of disposing of us just and reasonable, but also accept it with a gentle and loving heart as altogether right and profitable for our salvation, patiently waiting until He palpably show it to be so. Besides, we have whereof to rejoice even in the midst of our sorrow in that He has so powerfully aided you, for need was that you should be strengthened by His Spirit so that the confession of His sacred truth should be more precious to you than your own lives. We all know too well how difficult it is for people to forget themselves.

Therefore our gracious God must put forth His strong arm; then, for the sake of glorifying Him we do not fear torments, nor shame, nor death itself. Now since He has girded you with His power so as to sustain the first assault, it remains to entreat Him to strengthen you more and more according to your further conflict. And seeing that He has promised us victory in the end, do not doubt, that as He has imparted a measure of His strength, so you will have more ample evidence in the future that He does not make a beginning only to leave His work unfinished, as it is said in the Psalm. Especially when He puts such honor upon His people as to employ them in maintaining His truth, and leads them (as it were by the hand) to martyrdom, He never leaves them unprovided with the needful weapons. Yet meanwhile remember to lift up your eyes to that everlasting kingdom of Jesus Christ, and to think of whose cause it is in which you fight; for that glance will not only make you overcome all temptations which may spring from the infirmity of your flesh, but will also render you invincible against all the wiles of Satan, whatever he may devise to darken God's truth. For I am well assured, that it is by His grace you are so settled and grounded, that you do not walk at a venture, but that you can say with that valiant champion of Jesus Christ, I know on whom I have believed (2 Tim 1:12).

This is why I have not sent you such a confession of faith as our good brother Peloquin asked me for, for God will render that which He will enable you to make, according to the willingness of mind which He has allotted you, far more profitable than any that might be suggested to you by others. Indeed, having been requested by some of our brethren who have lately shed their blood for the glory of God, to revise and correct the confession they had prepared, I have felt very glad to have a sight of it for my own edification, but I would neither add nor take away a single word; believing that any change would but lessen the authority and efficacy, which the wisdom and constancy we clearly see to have proceeded from the Spirit of God deserved. Be then assured, that God who manifests Himself in time of need, and perfects His strength in our weakness, will not leave you unprovided with that which will powerfully magnify His name. Only proceed therein with soberness and reverence, knowing that God will no less accept the sacrifice which you offer Him according to the measure of ability which you have received from Him, than if you comprehended all the revelations of angels, and that He will make effectual what He puts into your mouth [to say], as well to confirm His own as to confound the adversaries. And as you know that we must steadfastly withstand the abominations of the papacy unless we would renounce the Son of God, who has purchased us to Himself at so dear a rate; meditate, likewise, on that celestial glory and immortality to which we are invited, and are certain of reaching through the Cross—through ignominy and death.

It is strange indeed to human reason that the children of God should be so surfeited with afflictions, while the wicked disport themselves in delights; but even more so that the slaves of Satan should tread us underfoot, as they say, and triumph over us. However, we have wherewith to comfort ourselves in all our miseries, looking for that happy issue which is promised to us, that He will not only deliver us by His angels, but will Himself wipe away the tears from our eyes (Rev 7:17). And thus we have good right to despise the pride of these poor blinded people, who to their own ruin lift up their rage against heaven; and although we are not at present in your condition, yet we do not on that account leave off fighting together with you by prayer, by anxiety and tender compassion, as fellow members, seeing that it has pleased our heavenly Father of His infinite goodness to unite us into one body under His Son, our head. Whereupon I shall beseech Him that He would vouchsafe you this grace, that being stayed upon Him, you may in nowise waver, but rather grow in strength; that He would keep you under His protection, and give you such assurance of it that you may be able to despise all that is of the world. My brethren greet you very affectionately, and so do many others.

Your brother, John CALVIN

As this letter will, I hope, be in common to you both, I shall merely add, that there is no need whatever for a long exhortation from me; it is enough that I pray God that it may please Him to impress still better and better upon your heart, what I see by your letter that you already enjoy. However grievous it may be to pine so long, if you got no other benefit by it than God's showing you that He has not reserved you until now without cause, you have good reason not to grow faint nor wearied out thereby. And as for the sickness, it is well for you to consider that God in this way wishes to prepare you better for a greater conflict, so that the flesh being entirely subdued may be more able to resign itself. Thus we ought to turn to profitable improvement everything that the heavenly Father sends us. If you can communicate with the other brethren, I pray you to salute them also from me. May God uphold you all by His strong hand, preserve and guide you, and make His own glory to shine forth in you more and more.

Bonnet CCCCLXXVI.—To the Women Detained in Prison at PARIS, #2716 in OC 16:632–34

Geneva, 16 Sept. 1557 *[Mme Phillippe de Luns, a noble widow, was burned at the stake in Paris on 27 Sept. 1557, along with two men. She had been imprisoned with some other women, both four*

noble ladies and a number of women of lesser rank, who were seized
along with some men when they were discovered worshiping together
in Protestant fashion.]

I do not wonder, dearly beloved sisters, if you are astounded by
these hard assaults, and feel the natural repugnance of the flesh
which strives so much the more as God wills to work in you by
His Holy Spirit. If men are frail and easily troubled, the frailty of
your sex is yet greater by reason indeed of your natural constitution. But God, who works in frail vessels, knows well how to display His strength in the infirmity of His followers.

Wherefore it is to Him it behooves you to have recourse,
invoking Him continually, and praying that the incorruptible
seed, which He has sown in you and by which He has adopted
you to be in the number of His children, may bring forth its
fruits in time of need, and that thereby you may be strengthened
to bear up against all anguish and affliction. You know the saying of St. Paul: God has chosen the foolish things of this world to
confound the wise, and the weak things to cast down the strong;
and those things which are despised and of no account to destroy
the proud and the lofty (1 Cor 1:27–28). This it is which should
give you great encouragement in order that the consideration of
your sex cause you not to fail, though it is often lightly esteemed
of men. For however haughty and proud they may be, and however out of contempt and disdain they may make a mock of God
and those who serve Him, yet are they constrained to hold in
admiration His power and His glory wherever they see them
shine forth. And so much the more, when they see that the vessel
by which God works is frail, shall they be forced to acknowledge
and be invincibly convinced in their own hearts of the power of
God which they cannot gainsay.

You see that the truth of God, wherever it is found, is the
object of their hatred; and it is not less detested by them in men
than in women, in the learned than in the ignorant, in the rich
than in the poor, in the great than in the little. If they avail themselves of sex or external condition to fall more furiously upon us
(as we see in what derision they hold women and poor artisans,
as if these had no right to speak of God and know the way of

their salvation!)—know that such conduct is a testimony against them and to their utter confusion. But since it has pleased God to call you as well as men, for He has no respect either of male or female, it is needful that you do your duty to give Him glory, according to the measure of grace He has dealt out to you, as well as to the greatest personages whom He has endowed with knowledge and courage. Since Jesus Christ has died for you, and through Him you hope for salvation, having been baptized in His name, you must not shrink from rendering Him the honor that belongs to Him. Since we have a common salvation in Him, it is necessary that all with one accord, men as well as women, should maintain His cause. When He calls us to do battle and puts us to proof before the enemy, it serves us nothing to allege our weakness as an excuse for abandoning or denying Him, except to expose ourselves to be condemned for disloyalty. For He who marshals us to battle, arms and shields us at the same time with the necessary weapons and gives us dexterity in wielding them. Our sole task then is to accept them and allow ourselves to be governed by Him. He has promised to give us a mouth and wisdom which our enemies will not be able to gainsay. He has promised to give firmness and constancy to those who put their trust in Him. He has shed His Spirit on all flesh, and caused to prophesy sons and daughters, as He had foretold by His prophet Joel; which is evidently a sign that He communicates in like manner His other necessary graces, and leaves neither sons nor daughters, men nor women, destitute of the gifts proper for maintaining His glory. We must not be indolent then in asking Him for them, nor faint-hearted in receiving and making use of them at need when He shall have distributed them to us.

Consider what was the courage and constancy of women at the death of our Lord Jesus Christ: when the apostles had forsaken him, how they continued by Him with marvelous constancy and how a woman was the messenger to announce to the apostles His resurrection, which the latter could neither believe nor comprehend (Matt 27:55–56, 28:1ff.; Luke 23:55–24:10; John 19:25, 20:1–19). If He then so honored women and endowed them with so much courage, do you think He has less power now or that His purposes are changed? How many thousands of women have there been who have spared neither their blood nor their lives to maintain the name of Jesus Christ and announce His reign! Has not God caused their martyrdom to fructify? Has their faith not obtained the victory over the world as well as that of martyrs? And without going further, have we not still before our eyes examples of how God works daily by their testimony, and confounds His enemies in such a manner that there is no preaching of such efficacy as the fortitude and perseverance which they possess in confessing the name of Christ? Do you not see how deeply rooted in their hearts is this saying of our Lord: he who denies Me before others, him will I deny before God my Father; and he who confesses Me, him also will I confess, and avow before God my Father? (Matt 10:32–33; Luke 12:8–9). They have not feared to quit this perishable life to obtain a better one, full of glory and everlasting.

Set before you then these noble exemplars, both ancient and recent, to strengthen your weakness and to teach you to repose on Him who has performed such great things by weak vessels; and recognize the honor which He has done you, in order that you may suffer yourselves to be led to Him, being confident that He is powerful to preserve your life if He wishes yet to make use of it, or if it is His will to exchange it for a better, you are most blessed in employing this perishable existence for His glory at so high a price and with the assured hope of living eternally with Him. For to that end have we been sent into this world, and illuminated by the grace of God, to glorify Him, both in our life and in our death, and be finally fully united to Him. May the Lord grant you the grace to meditate attentively on these things, and impress them on your hearts in order that you may conform yourselves wholly to His holy will. Amen.

NOTES

1. Bernard McGinn, "Introduction," *Christian Spirituality: Origins to the Twelfth Century*, ed. B. McGinn, J. Meyendorff, with J. Leclerq (New York: Crossroad, 1992), xv–xvi.

2. After some consideration I have decided not to include a survey of the literature about Calvin and spirituality in this place. However, the bibliography provides an annotated introduction to some of the better known (primarily) English-language publications on Calvin's spirituality. A fuller picture will be presented in *The Pastoral Ministry in Calvin's Geneva*, the book-length study in process on which many of the notes in this volume are based.

3. McGinn, "Introduction," xvi, xxii.

4. See Bernard McGinn, "The Letter and the Spirit: Spirituality as an Academic Discipline,"*Bulletin of the Society for the Study of Christian Spirituality*, no. 2 (1993), 1–10. On pages 1–4 McGinn gives a brief survey of the history of the word *spirituality* and the ways it has been understood; in the present context it is the biblical and medieval definitions that are important (p. 3). The idea of the spiritual *(pneumatikos)* in the New Testament is related to rebirth and the establishment of the community through the Spirit, while the conflict between flesh and spirit [which is often now identified with spirituality] "originally had nothing to do with a dualistic anthropology contrasting body and soul, but rather addressed the concrete human choices between life lived according to egotistic satisfaction and that conducted according to God's purpose." This interpretation was retained, but over time others were

added. In the Middle Ages, a new meaning of *spiritualitas* came to be "what pertains to the soul as contrasted to the body," while the word was also used to refer to ecclesiastical offices and goods. Calvin readily employs the adjective form *spiritualis* (*Inst.*, 3.19.16, provides a key discussion of the term), but instead of the substantive *spiritualitas* he chooses the classical word *pietas*, to which he gives a biblically influenced interpretation. See various articles or treatments of his use of this term in the selected bibliography.

Quotations from the *Institutes* are usually cited by book, chapter, and paragraph; the reference above, then, means Book Three, chapter 19, paragraph 16.

5. Calvin's piety is essentially trinitarian in foundation. Traditionally the greatest emphasis has been placed on the glory of God as the basis not only of Calvin's theology but also of his piety. Modern interpreters have realized afresh the centrality of the engrafting into Christ ("mystical union"—Hageman); some have reemphasized the vital role of the Holy Spirit (Hesselink); and others offer a reminder that Calvin understands this service of God as the source of real human happiness (Oberman). On the other hand, Calvin's piety encompasses both liturgical-sacramental and ethical-activist traits. Traditionally, focus on the preaching of the word has greatly outweighed attention to the sacraments, but now sometimes the reverse is true. Where liturgies and sacraments are presented it has been customary to skip the sermon, and the two (liturgy and sermon) are never printed together. Sometimes studies of Calvin's understanding of sanctification have given more space to personal morality than to the broader implications of social and communal structures, or works on his doctrine of prayer have failed to relate this closely to ethics and vice versa. To grasp the full contours of Calvin's teaching on and practice of piety, it is most important that these emphases not be split apart, with any one made to explain all the others or dominate the picture to the point of unbalancing the whole.

6. See E. A. McKee, *John Calvin on the Diaconate and Liturgical Almsgiving* (Geneva: Droz, 1984), 258ff.

7. Calvin's expulsion from Geneva and the respective roles of church autonomy/discipline, and Genevan internal politics and relationships to the Swiss Confederacy and France, have been much argued. The traditional view focuses on the importance of church order, while a contemporary revisionist picture most forcibly expressed by William Naphy emphasizes politics and the objection of many

NOTES

Genevans to the French ministers based on their foreignness, particularly after a large group of French refugees became a factor in Genevan life (cf. *Calvin and the Consolidation of the Genevan Reformation* [Manchester: University Press, 1994]). Naphy's argument adds richly to the picture and corrects the imbalance of seeing things only through Calvin's eyes. However, he effectively does not distinguish Zwinglian and Calvinist ideas of church government. For example, he states that some of Calvin's colleagues in 1541 urged the city council to beware of giving the ministers some powers Calvin was claiming for the pastors and Consistory; he concludes, "Thus, they presented socio-political arguments against Calvin's system, not religious or moral ones" (56). This misses the point that for Calvin autonomous church government was a religious issue, a theological matter, not merely a political question. For further discussion, see McKee, *The Pastoral Ministry in Calvin's Geneva*, chap. 1.

8. Some of Calvin's translations of the psalms for this psalter, and the foreword he wrote in 1542–43 for the expanded version, which explains the value and use of the psalms in public and personal devotion, are included, see pages 86–97.

9. See his letter to an unnamed correspondent in January 1542, describing how he took up again his work in Geneva, OC 11:366.

10. For Calvin's thought on these offices and their relationship to the pastoral ministry, and something about Genevan practice of the diaconate, see E. A. McKee, *John Calvin on the Diaconate and Liturgical Almsgiving* (Geneva: Droz, 1984) and *Elders and the Plural Ministry* (Geneva: Droz, 1988).

11. The phrase is that of Robert M. Kingdon, the foremost authority on Geneva's Consistory records and practice, in "Calvin and the Family: The Work of the Consistory in Geneva," in *Calvin's Work in Geneva*, ed. R. C. Gamble (New York: Garland, 1992), 96. See also other writings by Kingdon and his associates, who are editing the Consistory records for Calvin's lifetime. An English translation of the first volume of the critical edition has just been published: *Registers of the Consistory of Geneva in the Time of Calvin* ed. R. M. Kingdon, *Volume 1:1542–54*, ed. T. A. Lambert and I. M. Watt, trans. M. W. McDonald (Grand Rapids, Mich.: Wm. B. Eerdmans, 2000).

12. For a fuller examination of this issue, see McKee, *The Pastoral Ministry in Calvin's Geneva*, chaps. 3, 5.

13. For a contrasting of this life and the future one: *Inst,*. 3.9–10 and sermon on Genesis in weekday service (see pp. 283–90, 141). For

enjoyment of beauty and stewardship of material things: *Inst.,* 3.10.2–3; the body as prison: 2.7.13; 3.9.4; 4.1.1; for pastoral visitation instructions: OS 2, pp. 56–58, 255–56 (see pp. 292–93).

14. The account of Calvin's last days and death comes from Theodore Beza's biography, OC 21:40–45. In English, *Tracts Relating to the Reformation*, ed. Calvin Translation Society, 3 vols. (Edinburgh: Calvin Translation Society, 1844) 1:xix–c (quotation lxxxiv). See "belong to God," *Inst.* 3.7.1 (pp. 272–73) and Genesis sermon (p. 150).

15. Sermon 43 on Ephesians 6:1–4 (*Sermons sur Ephesiens*, p. 832 = OC 51:783).

16. For a fuller discussion of this service, and the practice of marriage in Geneva, see McKee, *The Pastoral Ministry in Calvin's Geneva*, chaps. 3, 5.

17. See James F. White, *Protestant Worship: Traditions in Transition* (Louisville, Ky.: Westminster/John Knox, 1989), 67.

18. Some examples: Christ's death and passion are prominent in the daily prayer with which Calvin closed his regular weekday sermons (see p. 151); the theme is also found in the sermon on nativity (Luke 2) and sermon 10 on Ephesians. Resurrection-heavenly glory/life: sermon 1 and sermon 15 on Job, sermon 65 on Isaiah, sermon 2 on Acts, lecture 3 on Micah, lecture 8 on Zephaniah, lecture 14 on Zechariah, lecture 10 on Malachi. Union with Christ: sermon 8 on Isaiah, lecture 10 on Jeremiah, lecture 23 on Ezekiel, lecture 29 on Hosea.

19. Perhaps the best expression of these ideas is found in the two sermons on the Sabbath commandment; see Benjamin Farley, *John Calvin's Sermons on the Ten Commandments* (Grand Rapids, Mich.: Baker Books, 1980), 97–132; the second is presented on pages 250–65. The McNeill-Battles translation of the *Institutes* discussion of this commandment (2.8.34) is somewhat confusing, and can in fact incorrectly suggest that Calvin believed the Sabbath commandment was binding on Christians, so those who are interested in the subject may find reading the sermon more helpful.

20. For the development of the schedule of preaching in Geneva, see McKee, *The Pastoral Ministry in Calvin's Geneva*, chap. 2; for baptismal practices, see chaps. 3, 5.

21. A full picture will be found in McKee, *The Pastoral Ministry in Calvin's Geneva*, chap. 3.

22. The phrase is John Knox's famous praise of Geneva "the most perfect school of Christ that ever was in the earth since the days of the apostles," in a letter to Mrs. Anne Locke, November 19, 1556 (in

NOTES

The Works of John Knox, ed. David Laing (Edinburgh, 1855), vol. 4, pp. 239–41 (quotation on p. 240, spelling modernized).

23. A slightly modified form of the tables is found in Pierre Pidoux, *Le Psautier Huguenot du XVIe siècle: Mélodies et documents, vol. 2, Documents et bibliographie* (Bâle: Editon Baerenreiter, 1962), 44, 62, 135. The tables themselves indicated how much of a psalm would be used by the words "up to _____" and a quotation from the next verse, but Pidoux has instead given the number of metrical strophes.

24. Here Battles seems to have misread the French "Qui pour sa maison luy a pleu," evidently interpreting *pleu* as the past participle for *pleuvoir* instead of *plaire*. It would seem that something like "And for His house been pleased to take" would be more accurate. It may also be noted that Battles translates Psalm 46 "every man"/Psalm 91 "wicked man"/Psalm 113 "lowly man" where the French is neutral: *tous/l'inique/le pauvr'.*

25. For the dawn service, see McKee, *The Pastoral Ministry in Calvin's Geneva,* chap. 3.

26. For a fuller discussion, see McKee, *The Pastoral Ministry in Calvin's Geneva,* chap. 3.

27. The editors of OC indicate the earliest date of publication as 1553; however, Rodolphe Peter demonstrates that the shorter version appeared in a small primer in 1551. See Rodolphe Peter, "L'abécédaire genevois ou catéchisme élémentaire de Calvin," in *Regards Contemporains sur Jean Calvin* (Paris: Presses Universitaires, 1965), 171–205. For fuller discussion of the catechetical service, see McKee, *The Pastoral Ministry in Calvin's Geneva,* chap. 3.

28. See discussion, McKee, *The Pastoral Ministry in Calvin's Geneva,* chap. 5.

29. In Geneva this prayer was left to the minister's free choice, but in Calvin's Strasbourg service a prayer is provided, of which the 1545 edition is presented here (cf. OS 2, pp. 19–20), and the slightly different 1542 version is used in the Day of Prayer liturgy (variants at OS 2, p. 19, lines 31–32, p. 20, lines 5–8).

30. "and share His Holy Supper" added on the days the supper was celebrated.

31. Here begins the paraphrase of the Lord's Prayer, which continues for the next two paragraphs.

32. The rest of the service, up to the final benediction, was specifically added on the days the supper was celebrated.

33. There are no explicit rubrics to indicate that the Decalogue followed the Apostles' Creed when it was moved to this location in 1561/62; discussion of the evidence and an argument for this order will be provided in McKee, *The Pastoral Piety of John Calvin*, chap. 3.

34. For explanation of the practice of the supper, see McKee, *The Pastoral Ministry in Calvin's Geneva*, chap. 3.

35. See E. A. McKee, *John Calvin on the Diaconate and Liturgical Almsgiving* (Geneva: Droz, 1984), 50–63.

36. For a fuller picture of baptism, see McKee, *The Pastoral Ministry in Calvin's Geneva*, chaps. 3, 5.

37. For the gesture and form, see McKee, *The Pastoral Ministry in Calvin's Geneva*, chap. 3.

38. For a full picture of the Day of Prayer, see McKee, *The Pastoral Ministry in Calvin's Geneva*, chap. 3.

39. This version of the prayer comes from Strasbourg 1542 (cf. OS 2, pp. 19–20); the ending used in Strasbourg 1545 is given above in the Sunday service.

40. Later, in some versions, the following is substituted for this last sentence: "Please, also, O Lord God, illumine us by Your Holy Spirit in the true understanding of Your holy will. And grant that we may give You the love and fear that faithful servants owe their masters, and children their fathers, because You have given us this grace to receive us among Your servants and children."

41. See McKee, *John Calvin on the Diaconate and Liturgical Almsgiving*, 258ff.

BIBLIOGRAPHIES

BIBLIOGRAPHIES *(IN CHRONOLOGICAL ORDER)*

Parker, T. H. L. "A Bibliography and Survey of the British Study of Calvin, 1900–1940." In *Evangelical Quarterly* (April 1946): 121–31.

McNeill, J. T. "Thirty Years of Calvin Study." In *Church History* 17 (1948): 207–40. Also appears as part of an updated "Fifty Years of Calvin Study," in the reprint of Williston Walker, *John Calvin* (Schocken, 1969), xvii–lxxvii.

Dowey, E. A. "Continental Reformation: Works of General Interest, Studies in Calvin and Calvinism Since 1948." In *Church History* 24 (1955): 360–67, and 29 (1960): 127–204.

Niesel, W. *Calvin-Bibliographie 1901–1959*. München: C. Kaiser, 1961. Also corrections and additions in P. Fraenkel, "Petit supplement aux bibliographies Calviniennes," *Bibliothèque d'Humanisme et Renaissance* 23 (1971): 385–413.

"Calvin Bibliography 1960–1970," *Calvin Theological Journal* 5 (Nov. 1971): 156–95, and annual supplements thereafter. This bibliography aims to be exhaustive, not critical; it provides the fullest coverage for Calvin and matters related.

Church History and *Archiv für Reformationsgeschichte* keep lists up to date with periodic bibliographic articles and book reviews. More critical assessment than the *Calvin Theological Journal* but less complete.

Peter, Rodolphe, and Jean-François Gilmont. *Bibliotheca Calvini-ana: Les oeuvres de Jean Calvin publiées au XVIe siècle*. Vol. 1. *Ecrits théologiques, littéraires et juridiques*, 1532–1554. Vol. 2. 1555–1564. Vol. 3. 1565–1600. Geneva: Droz, 1991, 1994, 2000. This is a defini-tive listing of all of Calvin's works printed during the sixteenth cen-tury, complete with photocopies of title pages, descriptions, information about writing and publication, locations of copies, mod-ern editions, etc.

PRIMARY SOURCES

Major Printed Collections of Calvin's Writings

OC = *Ioannis Calvini opera quae supersunt omnia*, edited by G. Baum, E. Cunitz, and E. Reuss. 59 vols. Brunsvigae: C. A. Schwetschke, 1863–1900. (= *Corpus Reformatorum*, vols. 29–87). The main col-lection of Calvin's original works, reissued in the twentieth cen-tury. The editors included only texts published in the sixteenth century, and tended to neglect matters of piety; for example, they dropped out the prayers at the ends of the sermons.

OS = *Ioannis Calvini opera selecta*, edited by P. Barth, W. Niesel, et al. 5 vols. München: Christian Kaiser. 1926–62. Critical editions of certain of Calvin's works, including the 1536 and 1559 (Latin) *Institutes*, plus a variety of shorter works.

SC = *Supplementa Calviniana*, edited by H. Rückert, E. Mülhaupt, G. Barrois, et al. Neukirchener-Vluyn: Neukirchener Verlag, 1936– . Modern publication of Calvin's sermons, which remained in man-uscript form until the twentieth century.

Sources Used in This Volume

Opera Omnia. 9 vols. Amsterdam: J. J. Schipper, 1667–71.

Opera Quae Supersunt Omnia = OC.

Plusieurs sermons touchant la divinité, humanité et nativité de nostre Seigneur Iésus Christ. Genève: Michel Blanchier, 1563.

Predigten über das 2. Buch Samuelis, edited by Hanns Rückert. Vol. 1 of SC. Neukirchen Kreis Moers: Neukirchener Verlag, 1936–61.

Sermons de Iean Calvin sur l'Epistre de S. Paul Apostre aux Ephesiens. Genève: Iean Baptiste Pinereul, 1562.

BIBLIOGRAPHIES

Sermons de M. Iean Calvin sur le livre de Iob. Genève: Iean de Laon, 1563.

Sermons on the Acts of the Apostles, edited by Willem Balke and Wilhelmus H. T. Moehn. Vol. 8 of SC. Neukirchen Kreis Moers: Neukirchener Verlag, 1994.

Sermons sur la Genèse, Chapitres 11,5–20,7, edited by Max Engammare. Vol. 11/2 of SC. Neukirchen Kreis Moers: Neukirchener Verlag, 2000.

Sermons sur la première Epitre aux Corinthiens 1–9, edited by E. A. McKee. ms. in preparation for SC.

Sermons sur le Livre de Michée, edited by Jean-Daniel Benoît. Vol. 5 of SC. Neukirchen Kreis Moers: Neukirchener Verlag, 1964.

Sermons sur le Livre d'Esaïe, chapitres 13–29, edited by Georges A. Barrois. Vol. 2 of SC. Neukirchen Kreis Moers: Neukirchener Verlag, 1961.

Sermons sur le Livre d'Esaïe, chapitres 30–41, edited by Francis M. Higman, T. H. L. Parker, and L. Thorpe. Vol. 3 of SC. Neukirchen Kreis Moers: Neukirchener Verlag, 1995.

Sermons sur les dix commandemens. Genève: Conrad Badius, 1557.

Sermons sur les Livres de Jérémie et des Lamentations, edited by Rodolphe Peter. Vol. 6 of SC. Neukirchen Kreis Moers: Neukirchener Verlag, 1971.

Vingtdeux sermons de M. Iean Calvin ausquels est expose le Pseaume cent dixneufieme. Genève, François Estienne, 1562. Reprint of 1554.

Translations

The Institutes of the Christian Religion has been published in numerous translations. Two nineteenth-century ones by William Allen and Henry Beveridge are dated in language but good in their understanding of the theology. The major twentieth-century translation by Ford Lewis Battles, edited by John T. McNeill, was published in the Library of Christian Classics series (Philadelphia, 1960). The notes for this edition are excellent and the biblical indices are the fullest to be found anywhere (more even than in the critical editions of the OS or SC).

All of the commentaries were published by the Calvin Translation Society in the nineteenth century, along with three volumes of *Tracts and Treatises,* and four volumes of Jules Bonnet's collection of *Calvin's*

JOHN CALVIN

Letters. These were reissued in the twentieth century, primarily by Wm. B. Eerdmans.

Various one-volume collections of Calvin's writings provide anthologies of different kinds. Also, a number of volumes of sermons have been published, some being facsimiles or reprints of sixteenth-century English texts, others being fresh translations. These are of varied quality.

Specific translations used in this volume are acknowledged at the front of the book, in the list of permissions.

AN ANNOTATED LIST OF SUGGESTED READINGS ON CALVIN'S PIETY

The subject of Calvin's spirituality has been defined in different ways and approached from many varied angles. This note makes no claim to be comprehensive or even representative; it intends primarily to offer some suggestions for further reading on different aspects of Calvin's piety for the English-language student of the Reformation. Occasionally, where some of the best treatments of a topic are found in another language, those items are mentioned as well. Articles and books provide brief discussions on a number of issues, grouped according to topic.

Anthologies

Battles, Ford Lewis, ed. *The Piety of John Calvin*. c.1969. Grand Rapids, Mich.: Baker Books, 1978.

Leith, John H., ed. *John Calvin: The Christian Life*. San Francisco: Harper & Row, 1984.

Definitions or Descriptions of Calvin's Spirituality or Piety

More General

Bouwsma, William. "The Spirituality of John Calvin." In *Christian Spirituality: High Middle Ages and Reformation*, edited by J. Raitt, 318–33.

New York: Crossroad, 1987. Lively, impressionistic, emphasizing Calvin's humanism, experiential and practical orientation.

Hageman, Howard G. "Reformed Spirituality." In *Protestant Spiritual Traditions*, edited by F. C. Senn, 55–79. Mahwah, N.J.: Paulist Press, 1986. Perhaps the most precise definition of Calvin's piety, beginning with the union with Christ and giving particular weight to the liturgical-sacramental aspects, without neglecting the word.

Lambert, Thomas A. *Preaching, Praying, and Policing the Reform in Sixteenth Century Geneva*. Ph.D. dissertation, University of Wisconsin-Madison, 1998. Lambert sets the Protestant reform of Genevan piety in the context of late medieval piety, focusing primarily on the social experience of religion, providing a lively, down-to-earth picture of Genevan practice.

Old, H. O. "What Is Reformed Spirituality? Played Over Again Lightly." In *Calvin Studies VII*, edited by J. H. Leith, 61–68. Davidson, N.C., 1994; an earlier version of this article appeared in *Perspectives* 9 (Jan. 1994): 8–10. A broad sketch, from a theological-practical orientation, giving more attention to prayer and lived piety.

Richard, Lucien. *The Spirituality of John Calvin*. Atlanta, Ga.: John Knox, 1974. The one well-known book-length English study of Calvin's spirituality (labeled as such), which examines the Reformer's concept of spirituality in the context of the late medieval Modern Devotion. Unfortunately, although his work provides some interesting and helpful contributions, Richard misunderstands the corporate context of Calvin's piety, seeing it instead as extremely individualistic in the context of a Lockean view of the church.

Tamburello, Dennis. *Union with Christ: John Calvin and the Mysticism of St. Bernard*. Louisville, Ky.: Westminster/John Knox, 1994. Describes one intriguing but very elusive aspect of Calvin's spirituality in an appealingly ecumenical fashion. The comparative approach contributes to a somewhat inadequate understanding of the meaning and role of the *unio mystica* element in Calvin's full theology.

Specific Studies of "Pietas" Language

Battles, Ford Lewis. "True Piety According to Calvin." In *Interpreting John Calvin*, edited by R. Benedetto, 289–306. Grand Rapids, Mich.: Baker, 1996. Originally published in the anthology listed above, pp. 13–26. Explores the various ways that Calvin uses *pietas*, with particular attention to the classical nuances and Calvin's own life and practice.

Jones, Serene. *Calvin and the Rhetoric of Piety*. Louisville, Ky.: Westminster/John Knox, 1995. Presents a discussion of Calvin's language about piety in the first three chapters of the *Institutes*, viewing his work as an artistic creation (rhetoric). The discussion does not integrate this linguistic study into a wider examination of Calvin's teaching or practice of piety itself.

Lee, Sou-Young. "Calvin's Understanding of *Pietas*." In *Calvinus Sincerioris Religionis Vindex*, edited by W. H. Neuser and B. G. Armstrong, 225–39. Kirksville, Mo.: Sixteenth Century Studies, 1997. Also discusses *pietas*, an overview based on the *Institutes,* and some commentaries.

McKee, Elsie Anne. *John Calvin on the Diaconate and Liturgical Almsgiving*. Geneva: Droz, 1984. Chapter 10 discusses Calvin's use of *pietas* through his commentaries, particularly the ways he relates it to *fides* and *caritas*.

Worship, Preaching, the Sacraments, Prayer, and the Psalter (and the Question of Images)

Garside, Charles. *The Origins of Calvin's Theology of Music: 1536–1543*. Philadelphia: American Philosophical Soc., 1979. A full examination of the theological development of Calvin's understanding of music.

Gerrish, B. A. "Calvin's Eucharistic Piety." In *Calvin Studies Society Papers, 1995, 1997*, edited by D. Foxgrover, 52–65. Grand Rapids, Mich.: CRC, 1998. For a much fuller treatment of this subject, see Gerrish, *Grace and Gratitude: The Eucharistic Theology of John Calvin*. Minneapolis, Minn.: Fortress, 1993. An exposition of Calvin's supper doctrine in the context of a wider discussion of his theology, including baptism, which emphasizes the importance of this teaching-practice for his piety.

Harman, Allan. "The Psalms and Reformed Spirituality." In *The Reformed Theological Review* [Australia] 53: 2 (1994): 53–62. Very brief definition of Reformed spirituality, with discussion of the role of the psalms.

Kingdon, Robert M. "The Genevan Revolution in Public Worship," In the *Princeton Seminary Bulletin* 20: 3 (1999): 264–80. A foretaste of the larger forthcoming work exploring the social dimensions and practice of worship from the perspective of the new information gained from the Genevan Consistory records.

McKee, Elsie Anne. "Contexts, Contours, Contents: Towards a Description of Calvin's Understanding of Worship." In *Calvin Studies Society Papers, 1995, 1997,* edited by D. Foxgrover, 66–92. Grand Rapids, Mich.: CRC, 1998. Overview of Calvin's doctrine of worship in the context of his wider theology.

Old, H. O. *The Shaping of the Reformed Baptismal Rite in the Sixteenth Century.* Grand Rapids, Mich.: Wm. B. Eerdmans, 1992. A full picture of the ritual and theological developments, including Calvin's part in them, particularly his views on relating catechesis and admission to communion.

Parker, T. H. L. *Calvin's Preaching.* Louisville, Ky.: Westminster/ John Knox, 1992. The standard work, and good on the theology of the sermons; also repeats some older inaccuracies about Calvin's liturgical practice, for example, schedules of preaching and patterns of administering baptism and celebrating marriages.

Partee, Charles. "Prayer as the Practice of Predestination." In *Calvinus Servus Christi*, edited by W. H. Neuser, 241–56. Budapest: Pressabteilung des Raday-Kollegiums, 1988. An interesting juxtaposition of two key doctrines that may well cast a more friendly light on predestination.

Pidoux, Pierre. "Au XVIe siècle: La Genève de Calvin et le chant des psaumes." In *Revue musicale de Suisse romande* 44: 3 (1991): 139–59. A brief summary of the development of the French psalter by the scholar who has mastered the sources.

Pitkin, Barbara. "Imitation of David: David as a Paradigm for Faith in Calvin's Exegesis of the Psalms." In *The Sixteenth Century Journal* 24: 4 (1993): 843–63. An exploration of Calvin's understanding of the faith-piety of the biblical model with whom he most closely identified, based on the author's full work, *What Pure Eyes Could See: Calvin's Doctrine of Faith in Its Exegetical Context.* Oxford: Oxford University Press, 1999.

Scholl, Hans. *Der Dienst des Gebetes Nach Johannes Calvin.* Zürich: Zwingli Verlag, 1968. The fullest recent study of Calvin's teaching about prayer, ranging over all aspects and drawing on many different sources.

Tripp, Diane Karay. "Daily Prayer in the Reformed Tradition: An Initial Survey." In *Studia Liturgica* 21 (1991): 76–107, 190–219. Wide-ranging preliminary survey. This should be used with caution for comments on Calvin; it is based essentially on secondary sources and confuses ordinary weekday and Day of Prayer liturgies, sermons, and academic lectures.

VanderWil, Jeffrey T. "John Calvin's Theology of Liturgical Song." In *Christian Scholar's Review* 25 (1996): 63–82. Good notes, generally useful overview, though some minor confusion about changes in liturgical singing between Strasbourg and Geneva.

Willis-Watkins, David. *The Second Commandment and Church Reform: The Colloquy of St. Germain-en-Laye, 1562.* Princeton, N.J.: Princeton Theological Seminary, 1994. A study of Catholic-Protestant debate over reform, focused on the use or rejection of images, including Calvin's teaching as the basis of the Reformed argument.

Witvliet, John. "The Spirituality of the Psalter: Metrical Psalms in Liturgy and Life in Calvin's Geneva." In *Calvin Studies Society Papers, 1995, 1997*, edited by D. Foxgrover, 93–117. Grand Rapids, Mich.: CRC, 1998. Wide-ranging, with the aim of setting the psalter in a larger sociocultural context than is usually done.

The Holy Spirit, the Christian Life, and Pastoral Care

Armstrong, Brian. "The Role of the Holy Spirit in Calvin's Teaching on the Ministry." In *Calvin and the Holy Spirit*, edited by P. De Klerk, 99–111. Grand Rapids, Mich.: Calvin Studies Society, 1989. Emphasizes the inward working of the Spirit, alongside the better known outward ecclesiastical call to ministry.

Benoît, Jean-Daniel. "The Pastoral Care of the Prophet." In *John Calvin: Contemporary Prophet*, edited by J. T. Hoogstra, 51–67. Grand Rapids, Mich.: Baker, 1959. A very brief summary of Benoit's longer and very useful work, *Calvin: directeur d'âmes* (Strasbourg: Oberlin, 1947), which examines in depth Calvin's correspondence and what it reveals about his pastoral practice and spiritual direction.

Hesselink, I. John. "Governed and Guided by the Spirit: A Key Issue in Calvin's Doctrine of the Holy Spirit." In *Das Reformierte Erbe: Festschrift für Gottfried W. Locher*, edited by H. A. Oberman et al., Part 2: 161–71. Zürich: TVZ, 1992. Also in *Calvin Studies V*, edited by J. H. Leith, 29–40. Davidson, N.C., 1990. Points to the working of the Spirit in the Christian's life, in accord with but not restricted to the precise details of scripture.

Kolfhaus, Wolfgang. *Die Seelsorge Johannes Calvins.* Neukirchen Kreis Moers: Buchhandlung des Erziehungsvereins, 1941. A fine examination of Calvin's pastoral thought and practice drawn from throughout his writings.

———. *Christusgemeinschaft bei Johannes Calvin*. Neukirchen Kreis Moers, 1939.

———. *Vom christlichen Leben nach Johannes Calvin*. Neukirchen Kreis Moers, 1949. Older, but still one of the most thoughtful studies of Calvin's teaching on fellowship in Christ, including the mystical union and the fellowship with the neighbor in Christian life.

Krusche, Werner. *Das Wirken des Heiligen Geistes nach Calvin*. Göttingen: Vandenhoeck & Ruprecht, 1957. Old, but still one of the best studies of Calvin's teaching on the work of the Holy Spirit.

Leith, John. *John Calvin's Doctrine of the Christian Life*. Louisville, Ky.: Westminster/John Knox, 1989. A broad overview of the topic in the context of justification, history, church, and society.

McKee, Elsie Anne. *Diakonia in the Classical Reformed Tradition and Today*. Grand Rapids, Mich.: Wm. B. Eerdmans, 1989. Outlines the connection between worship and ethics in Calvin's piety, and the corporate-church ministry to the neighbor.

Oberman, Heiko A. "The Pursuit of Happiness: Calvin Between Humanism and Reformation." In *Humanity and Divinity in Renaissance and Reformation: Essays in Honor of Charles Edward Trinkhaus, Jr.*, edited by J. W. O'Malley, T. M. Izbicki, and G. Christianson, 251–83. Leiden: E. J. Brill, 1993. A provocative and lively picture of Calvin's anthropology, with implications for his concept of the earthly religious life of Christians.

Willis-Watkins, David. "Calvin's Theology of Pastoral Care." In *Calvin Studies VI*, edited by J. H. Leith, 37–46. Davidson, N.C., 1992. Perhaps the best recent English summary.

SUBJECT INDEX

Index to Biblical Citations

INDEX TO BIBLICAL CITATIONS

Jeremiah
2:36–3:4, 241
17:4–27, 221
31:33, 206
33:8, 206

Ezekiel
2:1, 69
8:15–9:4, 241
39:7 ff., 170
39:25 ff., 170

Daniel
1:17–2:2, 241
2:44–46, 242
12:2, 116
9:8, 170
9:20, 170
9:24, 116

Hosea
2:5, 171
10:14–11:5, 242

Joel
2:1–11, 243

Amos
3:15–4:6, 243

Micah
1:15–2:6, 243
2:1–3, 221
2:4–6, 221
4:3–4, 244
6:1–4/5, 222
6:6–8, 222

Zephaniah
3:6–9, 244

Zechariah
7:10–14, 244

Malachi
1:12, 166
3:4–8, 245

NEW TESTAMENT

Matthew
5:4, 282
5:10, 281
5:22, 267
5:38 ff., 312
6:14, 276
6:33, 258
7:12, 262
7:15, 45, 128
7:15, 45
10:32–33, 332
10:33, 118
10:42, 323
11:28 ff., 190
15:14, 49
18:19–20, 127
18:35, 276
19:13–15, 155
22:37–40, 156
23:9, 198
24:35, 45
25:40, 323
26:26–29, 93
26:26, 93
26:36–39, 234
26:37, 282
27:45–54, 234
27:45–53, 179
27:46, 182
27:49, 185

JOHN CALVIN

12:15, 304
13:14, 288
14:8, 273
15:2, 91

1 Corinthians
1:1–5, 237
1:22–25, 238
1:27–28, 330
7:14, 155
10:13, 208
10:31, 203
11:23–29, 131
11:28, 110, 132
14:15–17, 92
14:16, 92
14:26, 91
15:4, 113
15:6, 121
15:19, 286
15:20ff, 189
15:33, 96

2 Corinthians
2:15–16, 119
3:7–16, 186
3:18, 121
4:6, 81
4:9, 184
5:6ff., 141
5:6, 285
10:4ff., 129

Galatians
2:20, 273
6:10, 199, 276

Ephesians
1:5f., 162
1:20, 123

1:23, 1999
2:3–6, 238
3:20—4:2, 239
4:11, 79
4:29, 91–92
5:19, 96

Philippians
2;3, 274
3:1, 95
3:12ff., 126
3:20, 141
4:4, 95
4:12, 288

Colossians
2:14, 179
2:17, 187
3:1ff., 123, 125
3:1, 116
3:3, 183, 325
3:16, 96

2 Thessalonians
2:8, 202

1 Timothy
2:1–2, 127
2:2, 127
2:8, 199
2:19, 81
4:8, 204
6:15, 127

2 Timothy
1:12, 328
2:9, 305

Hebrews
2:11, 117

356

INDEX TO BIBLICAL CITATIONS

Proper Name Index

Abraham, 69, 136, 137–51, 264
Augustine, St., 93, 94, 96

Battles, F. L., 35–36
Beza, Theodore, 85
Bourgeois, Louis, 85
Bucer, Martin, 1, 8, 12, 15, 27, 51, 62
Bullinger, Heinrich: letters from Calvin, 315–17, 318–20
Bure, Idelette de. *See* Calvin, Idelette (de Bure)

Calvin, Gérard, 6–7, 59
Calvin, Idelette de Bure, 12; death, 18, 52–54
Calvin, John, 1, 39; biographical sketch, 6–19; break with Roman Church, 7, 45, 46–50, 59; Genevan ministry, 9–12, 13–18; letter to Anne de la Vacquerie, 301–5; letter to Comtesse de Roye, 313–14; letter

about wife's death, 52–54; letter to Heinrich Bullinger, 315–17, 318–20; letter to John Liner, 322–24; letter to Madame de Cany, 301–7; letter to Monsieur de Richebourg, 293–301; letter to Renée, Duchess of Ferrara, 307–13; letter to Viret, 53–54; letters to Farel, 13–14, 50–53, 317–18; letters to prisoners of Lyons, 321–22, 324–29; marriage, 12; in Strasbourg, 12–13; *see also* specific headings in subject index, e.g.: *Institutes of the Christian Religion, The* (Calvin); Piety
Cany, Mme de: letter from Calvin, 301–7
Capito, Wolfgang, 51
Chrysostom, 96

PROPER NAME INDEX

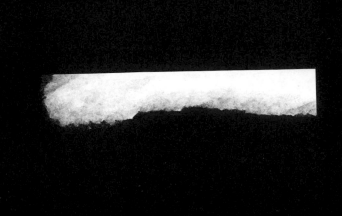